MONET

a biography by

Charles Merrill <u>*Mount*</u>

Simon and Schuster · *New York*

TO SALLY
AFFECTIONATELY
AND
IN GRATITUDE FOR MY SON

Contents

CONTENTS

Preface

IN 1926 CLAUDE MONET at last went where his furious indignation no longer could lacerate his heart. He was eighty-six years old; for thirty years had been a revered master.

At the pinnacle of his success Monet exercised a privilege granted few people; like Caesar, he took history into his own hands to rewrite his life. Monet was made to suffer after his death for his eminence when alive. That no serious biography of him has appeared in English is an index to his neglect, even in French the one small posthumous effort conveys a pale image. A by-product of that neglect has been that Monet's own rendering of his life has stood without challenge: no scholar examined his omissions, nor turned a suspicious glance to his distortions.

The events of Monet's long life naturally left behind a mass of documentation to astonish posterity. But locating these documents, unknown when I began this work, has been the greatest part of my labors. To the John Simon Guggenheim Memorial Foundation I am grateful for the grant on which my searches were begun in 1956, when the Foundation and its director, Henry Allen Moe, graciously waived their age requirement to make me the youngest scholar so honored. Laborious and costly burrowings continued for a decade, sustained by my own professional labors as a portrait painter.

They accomplished something undreamed of by me when I began—the re-creation of Camille, Monet's first wife, as a three-dimensional human being. In 1955 no more existed of her than one Christian name fortuitously attached to a few pictures. Over these ten years information has grown vast, and Camille Léonie Doncieux (January 15, 1847–September 4, 1879) has reassumed human form.

The leavening of these pages is the inspiring sight of her passionate love, noble but doomed. For if in this volume no effort is made to prove that Claude Monet was more sinned against than sinning, it is undeniable that he was more loved against than loving. Camille is the undisputed heroine of this book.

New documentation has produced at least nine essential points strongly bearing on interpretation: (1) the irregular parentage, adoption, and unusual marriage of Monet's father created an unstable family background responsible for the artist's neurotic youth; (2) his army career was shorter and less happily borne than Monet pretended; (3) he remained Gleyre's pupil for seventeen months, and never quit the studio nor led anyone out of it; (4) his seduction of Camille Léonie Doncieux in 1865 was an expression of youthful lust; (5) Camille was a well-born Parisian whose bourgeois family possessed two separate fortunes, from both of which she ultimately was disinherited; (6) at the time their first child was born in 1867 Monet refused to marry Camille, despite his father's suggestion that he do so; (7) the dowry promised Camille by her family was the sole reason Monet finally married her, June 28, 1870; (8) Camille died from the aftereffects of a clumsy abortion; (9) the dowry of another woman Monet seduced, the wife of his patron Ernest Hoschedé, permitted him to achieve his final enormous position in French art.

Compared to my previous subjects—Sargent, the wholesome, wholly dedicated human being, and Gilbert Stuart, the brilliant privileged lunatic—Claude Monet emerges as a sacred monster. The methods by which such a man can be presented adopt an urgency all their own, for it is quite possible Monet is among the really heroic figures in the history of painting, one of those who wrestled with his times and imposed his personality on them. That he made history, not simply manipulated events, is undeniable, and such a man cannot be presented by a bland approach. It was of that sort of book, so common during his lifetime, that Sigmund Freud wrote:

> . . . biographers are fixated on their heroes in a quite special way. In many cases they have chosen their hero as the subject of their studies because—for reasons of their personal emotional life—they have felt a special affection for him from the very first. They then devote their energies to a task of idealization, aimed at enrolling the

great man among the class of their infantile models—at reviving in him, perhaps, the child's idea of his father. To gratify this wish they obliterate the individual features of their subject's physiognomy; they smooth over the traces of his life's struggles with internal and external resistances, and they tolerate in him no vestige of human weakness or imperfection. They thus present us with what is in fact a cold, strange, ideal figure, instead of a human being to whom we might feel ourselves distantly related. That they should do this is regrettable, for they thereby sacrifice truth to an illusion, and for the sake of their infantile phantasies abandon the opportunity of penetrating the most fascinating secrets of human nature.

Unraveling these secrets to which Freud referred is precisely the purpose of this book. It neither defends nor indicts, attempts neither to gild nor to destroy an image.

On one level this volume presents the history of a man's life in purely biographic terms. On a second, parallel, plane it is an equally intense study of his art—for the great scope of biographic reference has enabled me to project a continuous study of Monet's creative work at all periods, something never before attempted. Apart from biographic discoveries, the most important component of this book is the definition it sets forth to explain the nature of that much abused art, impressionism. In doing so I register fundamental disagreement with the fictional premise that the impressionists were a band of innovators whose sufferings were the normal attribute of their daring and genius. Presented here, biographically and in technical analysis, is a more accurate view.

CHARLES M. MOUNT
Dublin, 1966

Prologue

THE GREEKS WERE INCLINED *to view both personal destinies and large-scale history with certain comforting doctrines of inevitability. Among these was that those whom the gods wish to destroy they first make mad. Questions of individual responsibility, which our own era is likely to weigh so gravely, they also lightened and gave more imaginative scope by interpreting history as a succession of titanic struggles high on Olympus, in which the gods sought advantage by making earthly habitants the pawns of their heavenly clashes.*

If ever an individual was cast in this mold of haphazard heroism it was Claude Monet. A simple young man from Le Havre, possessed of no more than a lyric gift for landscape painting, he was made the gods' instrument in mighty battles. By no will of his own he was thrown brutally against the high and upreared walls of a system epitomized by the Salon, each time struggling back tattered and bewildered. The extent of the violence and the indignities visited upon him and a young girl who loved him is the burden of these pages. And in the end, by a miracle, he triumphed so mightily and with such sense of grandeur and theatricality that the very Salon against which he had bloodied himself not only fell but faded away in a fog of calumny and vituperation.

The Salon

EVEN TO A GENERATION inured by runaway materialism the bright and splashy style of the Alexander III bridge maintains a certain fierce splendor. Surging across the river Seine in the heart of Paris, it transforms mere roadway into fantastic embellishments of winged and prancing horses led by trumpeting attendants. Cupids entwined with laurel wreaths dance about bronze-encrusted lampposts, allegorical figures occupy colossal thrones, and a bevy of dedicatory inscriptions are guarded in triumphant pedantry by benignly motivated lions and half-draped river gods. A few of these Olympian inhabitants of a notoriously mortal city are seen to have suffered from time and weather and to have been patched with sheet metal. Significantly, a typical French practicality has approved such rough repairs, fastened by workmanlike rivets that offer no apology for irreverence.

Once the proud symbol of an age, this sumptuously ornate bridge is a conspicuous irrelevance in ours, when the great Salon beside which it stood, to facilitate the passage of great crowds, has vanished as completely as the spirit inspiring its own exuberant embellishments.

Even when erected, this bridge was symbolic of a system that had been struck its mortal blow. Not even the huge Palais de l'Industrie now stands in its once splendid position between the Champs-Élysées and the Seine. Once it sprawled beside the Alexander III bridge, rising from spacious gardens that straddled sites occupied since by those lesser progeny, the Grand Palais and Petit Palais. When dedicated in 1855, it was considered the largest and most lavish modern structure in Paris, and that was only proper, for the Palais de l'Industrie was dedicated to an embodiment of the new spirit of imperial France.

Shaped like an enormous figure eight, two courtyards were engulfed within the Palace's outstretched members. Its front on the Champs-Élysées was flanked by fountains, and beneath the inscription on its façade a giant sculptured relief represented Agriculture, Industry, and the Arts, each offering an homage of thunderous banality to the Emperor Napoleon III. Yet such obeisance was deserved as much as desired, for it was entirely true that both the building itself and its function owed their birth to the Emperor. Here were to be housed exhibitions of French produce and commerce on which Napoleon planned to base the prosperity of his nation, among which the spectacular semiannual exhibition of paintings and sculpture took a high place.

Though they had in fact another, more formal, title, these exhibitions held in the grandiose rooms of the Palace were simply the Salon. No person who lived at that time harbored doubt that within its precincts was found all that was worthy in contemporary painting and sculpture. For in the arts France held an unchallenged preeminence: in France it was to the Salon that the great living masters sent their works, and it was to the Salon that art lovers and collectors flocked from around the world. From the established reputations of its leading exhibitors, and the governmental nature of its sponsorship, the Salon took its huge prestige. To its younger members it gave in turn that stamp of recognition so important in the rude business of keeping alive by exercise of pencil, brush, or chisel.

This was no happy accident, for in the officialdom of government the Salon held a definite place. Behind it stood the Académie des Beaux-Arts, a division of the Institut de France, whose influence exercised a virtual control over all branches of French culture. In painting the control of the Academy was very real, for from members of the Academy were chosen those who taught at the École des Beaux-Arts as well as the directors of the French Academy in Rome. The approved avenues by which the young could learn their craft thus were held firmly in official hands. And the Academy, through its members, also controlled the juries of admission and of awards at the Salon. However despotic these restraints appear, and were, they had another function now largely overlooked. The very knowledge that such an authoritarian control existed was an assurance to the picture-buying public that works shown at the Salon had met an established standard of excellence. It is a paradoxical reflection that the public felt it saw only great works, and it made purchases with an engaging optimism.

The importance of the Salon was enhanced by the strictness of its disciplines, which effectively transferred its enormous prestige to those finding a place under its roof. By means of its influence with the Director of Fine Arts, the Academy had the power to grant still greater rewards. The possibility always existed of a well-paid mural commission to decorate one of the public buildings rising as a part of the Emperor's ambitious program, or the purchase for the Emperor's private collection of a painting exhibited at the Salon.

By all these means the Academy naturally favored those by whom its standards and ideals were upheld. But it is also true that the Academy had factions within itself and more than one sort of art was found at the Salon. Advocates of smoothly brushed mythology and rudely painted contemporary life each had their day, and their place on the walls, while the true believers in line, and the ideologically suspect followers of color, held angry discussions in the courtyard and had their allotted membership on the jury of selection. This arrangement was exquisitely calculated to increase discord, yet before the public each element appeared no more than a foil to the others, creating a deceptive solidarity. The greatest contribution of the Academy—and the Salon, therefore—was the quiet confidence they gave patrons that no matter to what school they inclined, the appearance of a work at the Salon was an assurance that it was a work of merit. So long as such conditions prevailed, pure charlatanism was impossible; nor could the amateur impose himself upon a gullible public.

The young man who wished to become established as an artist had before him the single prospect of doing so at the Salon. Were he able to flutter the critical dovecotes, his praises spread through the press by critics would attract to his studio a stream of patrons. He expected that these patrons would buy his works, not only as articles of beauty but for their sound commercial value. And he had a definite expectation that once he had reached this position of eminence he would live by the money brought him from sales.

So great was its influence, and so firmly established its right to importance, that the Salon was the legitimate goal of all aspiring artists. Whatever their ideals, their theories, or their concepts of art, to be represented on the walls of the Salon meant the difference between achievement and failure. More than that, the Salon gave to art an importance and a substance such as it never before had enjoyed—and which, without the Salon, it since has lost. Patrons bought with confidence, frequently at high prices, and to be an artist was to practice an honorable profession that might lead up a respectable path to honors, awards, and in many instances to wealth. Everywhere, one saw important artists who lived on a grand scale, whose work had the admiration of an insatiable public, and who were respected as masters.

At the opposite pole it was equally true that for the outcasts, and those who, despite an artistic temperament, had not mastered the rudiments of their craft, the severity of the system imposed a harsh restriction. They could not exhibit. They could not receive official sanction. They were for the most part incapable of finding dealers to handle their works. They were, in fact, restricted to the dire hand-to-mouth existence that provincial sales and menial employment might bring. For them there was no promise except poverty, no future except more of the same, and no hope.

For nearly two years every person in France with enough conceit to think himself an artist gave time, thought, and labor to the work he planned for the next Salon. To students acceptance would mark a coming of age. For young artists it might mean the notice for which they had waited, and upon which their hopes were pinned. For the better-established it represented the challenge of competition with one's confreres, and the production of a work to bring a higher price, attract more attention, or achieve a more imposing position among the four thousand paintings and two thousand sculptures. To the masters it meant retaining the old standard, and suppressing the taunt that they were less strong than at the last Salon.

For a week in the privacy of the Palais de l'Industrie a committee, or jury, labored secretly to make a selection from among the multitudes of works submitted. To be a member of that committee was no light task. Envied and castigated on every side, they were subjected to a strenuous routine. The work was prepared each day by attendants, who arranged an endless display against the walls and on the floor of the Palace's second-floor galleries. At one o'clock each afternoon, led by their chairman carrying his little bell with which to call them to order, the forty members of the committee started their round. Two men, with a length of rope, interposed themselves between committee members and the pictures. Verdicts were pronounced on the spot, as briefly as possible, casting out obviously bad pictures without a vote. Occasionally the progress was held up by a discussion. Then a paunch might stretch the rope and ten minutes of acid denunciations ensue, at the end of which the work might be put aside for the evening's revision.

Behind the committee itself marched an army of seventy white-coated attendants, working under the orders of a foreman. As the jury progressed through the rooms, these attendants sorted out the rejected pictures, to be laid aside like corpses after the battle. To do a round of the galleries consumed at least two hours, without opportunity to rest or sit. It was a wearisome ramble through a suite of cold drafty rooms, and made the most vigorous wrap themselves in bulky fur coats.

At three o'clock came the day's rest. An hour was passed at a buffet where claret and chocolate and sandwiches were served, and where the bargaining for mutual concessions was done. Most of the committee were so heavily bombarded with recommendations that they carried little notebooks, to be certain they were forgetting none of their obligations, and which, when voting for a colleague's protégé, they freely consulted to verify whether the assistance was returned. Others, either by principle or through indifference, remained aloof from intrigue, and stood by smoking. Quarrels were not infrequent, and were quickly patched up, though beneath the neat surfaces remained much outraged vanity.

After this rest the task was resumed, now in a more leisurely manner. Together the members of the committee entered a room provided with chairs and tables that were prepared with pens, ink, and paper. Here all the pictures measuring less than one and a half meters were judged "on the easel," lined up ten or twelve at a time along an improvised platform covered by green baize. Many of the committee sat happily ignoring the proceedings. Others settled down to write their letters, forcing the chairman to assert himself at frequent intervals to insure a correct majority. Occasionally there was a wave of enthusiasm, and the vote, by a show of hands, meant a violent agitation of hats and sticks above the seething mass of heads.

After meeting for three days the committee granted itself two days of rest, to enable attendants to put the pictures in order. Then came the final revision, a wearisome task. Once more they were obliged to examine the rejected works, to choose a number sufficient to bring up the total accepted to the regulation figure. In one six-hour session the committee tore through the maze, now once again spread on the floors and against the Palace walls. For a time they were able to keep fatigue at bay, but from four o'clock onward they were a disorganized rabble. Stragglers were left breathless in the rear, and individuals marooned in the little pathways between frames helplessly tried to find their way out.

At the very end, with only forty minutes to go, it was the custom that each member of the committee should have a "charity"—the right to pick any canvas, however bad, which then was accepted by the others without question. Usually this was reserved as a kind gesture toward artists known to be poor, and the forty pictures thus chosen at the last moment were not unlike starving beggars allowed in to pick up the crumbs of a banquet.

When, finally, the work of the committee was done, and the gigantic clerical task of notifying the received and rejected got underway, the pictures themselves were hung according to a numbered list. Panels were taken down from the walls, and on the floor the pictures were attached, before they were hung. In principle no one was given preference; though in reality this was a polite fiction shrouding vast opportunism.

As the influence and importance of the Salon came to full flowering, even Varnishing Day, originally intended for artists to make final adjustments to their canvases on the walls, became established as an acknowledged event for which Paris turned out in force. For a week before, artists monopolized both press and public. They fascinated Paris, and Paris focused all its interest on them, their pictures, and their sayings, in one of those sudden irrepressible crazes to which it is subject.

On the appointed day vast throngs entered the Palace through its great entrance hall. Behind an old ragged curtain, at the far end the more acute might spy a row of statues, rejects from the sculpture section, which some of the poorer artists did not trouble to fetch away. The room itself, built of steel girders supported by heavy metal pillars, gave an impression of being under a railway bridge. From above came a perpetual icy blast, which contributed to a damp and soggy sensation underfoot. More alarming was the ceaseless din overhead, made by the masses of people tramping through galleries. At times it was deafening, and it went on as though endless trains were rattling over the network of girders above.

At the head of the stairs, young men with a thirst for distinction busily roped influential visitors. The wealthy celebrity, a smile of triumph on his lips, held a reception against a background of his works. The rivals who hated each other exchanged loud compliments. Shy artists, who not for the world would have gone into the room where their pictures hung, stood apart, their eyes filled with self-commiseration. Others made jokes to hide their disappointment. Earnest visitors became absorbed in methodically making the rounds of all the galleries, forecasting which would be the prizewinners. Artists' families were represented too, from the charming young mother to the sour-faced ultra-respectable matron. And models were everywhere, deplorable clothing distorting their fine bodies as they dragged each other through the rooms to look at pictures of themselves in the nude.

At noon the better-established artists, to whom elegance was of importance, led the way to taverns outside the Palace, like Ledoyens, a few steps up the Champs-Élysées. For the rest a buffet was served, in another gloomy ground-floor room resembling a cavern, of brown serge hung between girders that supported the floor above. Half hidden by darkness, tables were set out with symmetrically arranged plates of fruit, while at right and left were sharp-eyed ladies presiding over delicacies. Behind the draperies was a constant clatter of pots, pans, and crockery, from a kitchen improvised on sand, like open-air kitchens at a fair, and from this hidden quarter waiters issued with a steady stream of sodden trout and overcooked beef.

The buffet afforded a view out into the garden, where a central group of tall palms stood surrounded by a wide circle of statues against a background of brown draperies. Immediately one saw the vigor and amplitude of the shapely hind quarters of a female fawn, the dainty profile of a young girl and the tip of her firm little breast.

Beside her was the awkwardly emphatic bulk of a warrior in bronze, the milk-white body of a woman suspended by her wrists, and beyond, statues and still more statues, no longer identifiable in the jumble, but presenting rows of shoulders stretching in one direction, a receding perspective of legs and arms the other way, the ravishing sight of a row of bosoms, or an extraordinary series of noses. Then, at the very stroke of six o'clock, attendants ushered out the last remnants of the crowds, and Varnishing Day was over.

A week later, at the start of May when the weather was propitious for a display of finery, the Salon made its official opening. Coaches and carriages, joined by hired fiacres, now lined the Champs-Élysées, whose chestnut trees were in sparkling bloom. To go, to see, and to be seen, to be among those who had the joy and surprise of witnessing the emergence of a new immortal, was a necessary part of Parisian life, and a social occasion of the first importance.

The boulevards of Paris suddenly led only to the Salon. Bridges carried a traffic of hurrying vehicles, and gardens surrounding the imposing Palais de l'Industrie early were filled with carefully turned-out gentlemen and ladies carrying parasols. The richness of attire made an overwhelming impression, for all the elegance of Paris was present. The women had come to show off their clothes, and the clothes had been chosen with an eye to the following day's newspapers. Less vividly clad, the masculine element moved around in a succession of starts and stops, congregating at the base of a marble caryatid in the garden, or dispersing from the front of a bronze Hercules. And though a sprinkling of nonentities always was present, the crowd was largely made up of men with some claim to Parisian fame, whose appearance brought their names to every lip.

Come to attract attention and be part of a spectacle, the crowd never forgot that the day's chief interest was the exhibition. With deft touches of Parisian raillery the merits of the year's masterpieces were discussed. The exclusion of a man previously thought headed for Parnassus made elegant conversation, and all speculated whether some master would condescend to paint a replica of the work he already had sold. Lost in the crowd were the anxious eyes of an unknown who hoped the appointed gods would lead someone from these well-garbed ranks to his painting, high on a forgotten wall. The man suddenly enjoying success was surrounded by friends, all of whom turned respectful eyes to the arrogant figure of a *Membre de l'Institut,* who by ancient right had preempted for himself the center of a wall and filled it with a scene of medieval pageantry.

However spectacular the social flavor of its opening, without doubt the Salon occupied the very center of the art world. Eyes peered at it from every nation and every continent. Its jury was final arbiter in a global sense, with powers of life and death over aspirations, fame and fortune. The brilliance of its opening was only a means of displaying its strength.

No matter what his ideas, every artist, whether young or old, felt he belonged among the elite whose work appeared on these walls. From diverse backgrounds and schools, solemn student or rowdy boor, romantic, classic, or contemporary in his choice of subjects, whether polished or fiery in his execution, every artist knew his rightful path lay through the Salon. One young man who felt this way eventually would be responsible for toppling the mighty structure; in 1859 for the first time he traveled from Le Havre to see the great exhibition.

Part One

WHOM THE GODS WISH TO DESTROY

1. Like a Motherless Child

In May, 1859, a young man of eighteen, olive-skinned, broadly proportioned, and not overly tall, first viewed the Salon. A succession of cavernous damp rooms opened before him, each fantastically illumined by diffused daylight filtered through fresh white cloth suspended from glass ceilings. His eyes soon were accustomed to the unreal glow, and the walls, hung with gaudy, irregular, intricately carved and gilded frames, seemed feathered in iridescence. The massive quantity of four thousand paintings was so great, and their size frequently so large, hours could be consumed wandering complexes of galleries, refreshing oneself by gazing from balconies to an equal profusion of sculptures exhibited below in a glass-enclosed garden, then returning to the paintings galleries' lustering walls.

Everywhere he was most naturally drawn to landscapes, which he thought were a majority of the pictures exhibited. Even so his eye noted the breadth of a portrait by Pils, and dogs exhibited by the Belgian Joseph Stevens. He found Constant Troyon's huge canvases of animals, marked by the beauty of rich earth colors. At first glance they were admirable; then, making an effort to apply conscious knowledge, he wondered whether the shadows did not lack luminosity. Highly wrought landscapes by Théodore Rousseau also attracted him, but toward *Bertrand & Raton,* the elaborate composition of Charles Monginot, to whom he carried an introduction, he felt severe. Hamon, a public favorite, this year exhibiting a portrait and a still life with goat, he considered to have "no idea of nature." Even Delacroix, whose reputation he knew, the young man felt must have earned his renown by better things than those exhibited.

Unpretentious works by Daubigny moved him deeply. A view of Honfleur by this master of moody weather-conscious landscape suggested the word "sublime." But to Whistler's etchings he gave no attention, nor did three examples of Bouguereau's polished skill rouse appreciation, and this reticence was equaled when he passed in silence before youthful essays by Carolus-Duran and J. L. Gérôme. He noticed not at all an extraordinary series of sixty-four Members of the Institut, drawn by François-Joseph Heim, who long before had been commissioned to decorate ceilings in the Louvre. Even works by Millet and Puvis de Chavannes, soon to be so fashionable, he passed without comment.

Troyon, Daubigny, and Corot, names redolent of a tranquil landscape, were those this young man plucked unself-consciously from the complex image of French art spread over the Salon's massive walls. At eighteen he found in them simple and compassionate observation and a magical effect of sustained rapture to which his inner self responded. In even the less-admired works by Amand Gautier it was a parallel effect of "calm in a gray tone of profound sadness" he remembered. Despite the more ingenious flutterings displayed everywhere, and the enormous historical scenes buttressed by quotations from assorted sages, it was to a somber incantatory melancholy that he gave his heart. Such nostalgia was immensely revealing of the delicacies and weaknesses of which he was formed, and the uneasy environment from which he had sprung.

Much attention is given to the imbalance so often arising in a child raised by one parent. Whether indulgent or strict, one parent alone cannot supply the varied emotional background against which a normal individual develops to maturity. From the time his mother died, twelve-year-old Oscar Claude Monet had found himself the spoiled and self-assertive youngest member of a large household. In later years he took pleasure proclaiming, "I am a Parisian from Paris." With deliberately misused literalness this was true, for he had been born in the Rue Laffitte, November 14, 1840, "under good King Louis Philippe," as he continued, "in a circle entirely given over to commerce, and where all professed a contemptuous disdain of the arts."

These words reflect with surprising lucidity the conflict that marked his earliest years. For though he was raised at Le Havre and frequently was thought to be of Norman stock, Monet's family was distinctly Parisian. His first recorded ancestor, Pascal Monet, though he may have been born elsewhere, lived in Paris, and it was in the bustling military capital of the First Consul Napoleon Bonaparte that Pascal Monet's son, father of the artist, was born on February 3, 1800, and given the name Claude Adolphe. Concerning Claude Adolphe's mother some mystery may be said to exist, and this attached not only to her origins but also to her civil status, and that she transmitted to her son. Variously recorded in documents Catherine Chaumea and Catherine Chaumerat, Claude Adolphe's mother may in fact have migrated to Paris together with Pascal Monet. But Paris records themselves are barren of any recorded marriage between them, and their son Claude Adolphe entertained doubts concerning the conditions of his birth. In one of the two documents he left behind referring to it, he significantly failed to claim that his mother was the *wife* of Pascal Monet.

Whatever their origins or the nature of their relationship, after producing the infant Claude Adolphe both Pascal Monet and his Catherine fade into shadows. The young boy went to live with Claude Eulalie Perroty and his wife, who reared him as their own son. One assumes these kind folk to have been in good circumstances, and possibly childless. Their deed was duly rewarded fourteen years later, when, at Toulon, March 27, 1814, Armande Caroline Catherine Motte, wife of Claude Eulalie Perroty, was delivered of a daughter. Christened Sophie Caroline Armande Perroty, this infant became Claude Adolphe's sister.

Claude Adolphe grew up ambitious, sturdy, and handsome. At thirty-five he was a *propriétaire,* presumably of a small shop, and lived in Paris at 7 Rue d'Enghien. Well-spoken and debonair, he became acquainted with the twenty-nine-year-old widow of Emmanuel Barthélemy François Despaux, who enjoyed material circumstances rather more elevated than his own. When he called on her at 2 Rue Tronchet, in the fashionable quarter behind the newly dedicated church of the Madeleine, the widow Despaux was not above finding Claude Adolphe attractive. Six years her senior, a sensible, level-headed, and fully mature man, he possessed the virile good looks that characterized his descendants. Marriage was proposed and agreed upon, and on May 20, 1835, Adolphe Monet solemnized this most advantageous match. In the record executed that day he boldly asserted that his father and mother were married, writing his mother's name as Chaumerat. Thus established in his new estate as a gentleman, he set about to cultivate the ultra-respectability of the French bourgeoisie in whose ranks he had confirmed his membership, adopting the strict and authoritarian social ethic which conceived of life as a task to be accomplished by responsible people.

His wife, Louise Justine Aubrée, previously the widow Despaux, herself had been born at Lyon, and, either from her early training or the easy years of her first marriage, she retained interests that were larger and more cultivated than the purely commercial instincts of her new husband. Probably from her first deceased spouse she brought Claude Adolphe the funds which she invested in his business. They moved to new quarters at 39 Rue Caumartin, where, on April 14, 1836, a first son was born and christened Léon Pascal. In the official report of birth both parents described themselves as *propriétaires,* demonstrating that with notable French caution the new Mme. Monet had taken a partnership in return for the funds invested in her husband's business.

A pedantic, prim, incorruptible man of commerce, Adolphe Monet was doubtless gratified the following year when his sister Sophie made a marriage advantageous as his own. On December 27, 1837, at the Mairie of the first arrondissement, twenty-three-year-old Sophie Perroty wed Adolphe Aimé Lecadre, a recent graduate from the Paris Faculty of Medicine. Sophie departed Paris for her husband's native city of Le Havre, where Dr. Lecadre began the practice of his profession. His choice of vocation perhaps demonstrated a modest strain of independence, for Adolphe Lecadre belonged to a dynasty of merchants with wide interests in that city, which so long had been France's principal port.

Soon after the marriage of his sister, Adolphe Monet and his wife moved to the Rue Laffitte, where in 1840 their second and famous son, Oscar Claude, was born. The little family of four remained in this abode, and prospered, until 1845, when Adolphe Aimé Lecadre invited his brother-in-law to Le Havre. With his wife and sons the Parisian man of affairs settled into that neat little port city, successfully managing a Lecadre family business that supplied edibles and other necessities to ships in port. This happy arrangement left Dr. Lecadre to follow his profession free of distractions, and put into

Adolphe Monet's capable hands more weighty matters than ever before.

The seven years that followed were a period of growing prosperity. Dr. Lecadre became distinguished in his profession, and was named to the Legion of Honor. Adolphe Monet found his delight in accumulating, nourishing, and managing his own little fortune. Then, after seventeen years of marriage, her role of forming the Monet family and elevating its fortunes accomplished, about 1852 Louise Justine Aubrée Monet died. Her husband was left in comfortable circumstances, well established at Le Havre, and with sons aged sixteen and twelve.

The older son, Léon Pascal, colorless and limited though he was, inherited his father's practical business sense and shrewdness, following in the somewhat dull but rewarding routines of provincial bourgeois life. He appears not to have been sympathetic toward the younger and more tempestuous Oscar Claude. Established at a pinnacle of bourgeois respectability from which he always was ready to deliver portentous sermons, Oscar Claude's father unfortunately provided nothing to approximate the affections of the more gentle mother who had encouraged him to draw, and whom he too soon had lost. Only his father's "sister," Oscar's aunt, Sophie Lecadre, softened the harshness of these formative years.

As time passed, Aunt Sophie played an increasingly vital role. Fortunately she was well able to care for her two nephews, in addition to a daughter of her own born in 1842. Adolphe Monet and his sons joined the Lecadres in their spacious, well-proportioned town house at 13 Rue Fontenelle, strengthening the business partnership by emotional ties of proximity. Each summer these three adults and three children shared another little property set between the cliffs and beaches of Ste.-Adresse, a suburb two miles from Le Havre. Here craggy sea-bronzed fishermen waddled precariously in their shoes of wood, small fishing boats pulled up on the heavy shingle, and rough shacks guarded odorous treasures of fishing gear and bait.

This uncouth, less cumbersome life made an especial appeal to young Oscar Claude, who even at Le Havre, where his family lived in the high and dry manner of provincial worthies, followed his taste for the sea and ships. Two short streets from the Rue Fontenelle was the fascinating Bassin de Commerce, where ships from every nation could be seen, foreign languages sounded on the breezes, and an energetic lad could find his way across decks into the knotted ropes of soaring ladders, or careen on the quayside among heavy bales of cotton.

This wild existence influenced Oscar deeply. He grew up a lad of unembarrassed daring, rebellious and self-willed, whose actions seemed unaccountable in that chaste well-mannered household, and whose transgressions never failed to be noticed by his father. "My youth was . . . essentially that of a vagabond," he remembered. "I was undisciplined by birth; never would I bend, even in my most tender youth, to a rule. It was at home I learned the little I knew. Schools always appeared to me like a prison, and never could I make up my mind to stay there, not even for four hours a day, when the sunshine was inviting, the sea smooth, and when it was a joy to run about the cliffs in the free air, or to paddle in the water."

The sea played a large part in emotions that during adolescence became increasingly disturbed: "I always wished to be near it, and when I died, to be interred in a buoy. Until I was fourteen or fifteen years old I led this irregular but thoroughly wholesome life, to the despair of my poor father. Betweentimes I picked up in a haphazard way the rudiments of arithmetic and a smattering of orthography. This was the limit of my studies. They were not overly tiresome for they were intermingled for me with distractions. I made wreaths on the margins of my books; I decorated the blue paper of my copybooks with ultra-fantastic ornaments; and represented thereon, in the most irreverent fashion, deforming them as much as I could, the face or profile of my masters."

A disinterested student, more at peace in idle pursuits found out of doors, at the Collège de la Rue de la Mailleraye, which he attended from the age of fourteen, Oscar's was the reputation of a ferocious and wandering street arab. Turbulent and critical as well as rebellious, he took a perverse delight in the annoyance of others. A notorious lack of discipline was especially apparent in drawing classes. Asked to draw from casts of Diana, Juno, or Agrippa, he took a malicious pleasure in parodying their features, making the mouth a bird, the chin a wooden shoe, the eye a one-horse chaise.

These erratic activities, to which Oscar so persistently turned himself, were eloquent of the extent to which his boyish imagination had run wild. His extremes of romantic devotion to the sea, extending to burial in a buoy—so original, unnatural, and imaginative in a grotesquely Gothic way—were the counterpart of his equally grotesque and Gothic habit of making distorted drawings. Nor were these limited to the casts he was asked to draw, but extended to the sacred persons of his masters, among them the drawing master, M. Ochard, whose local celebrity derived in part from his studies under Jacques Louis David. With every good attribute, warmhearted, distinguished in appearance and bearing, Ochard was bred in a severe classic tradition and divined the presence of no talent in his lively, rebellious pupil.

But the boy's gift was noted elsewhere, and in one of those fortuitous passages which history too rarely can boast, the port city provided a perfect therapy. "At fifteen I was well known all over Le Havre as a caricaturist. My reputation was so well established that I was sought after from all sides and asked for caricature portraits." Such eminence was extremely pleasing to a young man who suffered, perhaps more intensely than from any other cause, from feeling himself without any niche of his own. And even at this early age his skills had developed to a degree that enabled him to produce highly competent cartoons of his sitters, his natural abundance of comic invention adding force to the one characteristic of each person he selected for stress.

His first drawing teacher, the eminent M. Ochard, was shown peering through his corded and ringed monocle, a ridiculously sly head well poised on a diminished body. In charcoal and white chalk he skillfully rendered the flowing muttonchop whiskers and carefully tended hair of an attorney, whose diminished form became spidery against a wall covered by the notices associated with his profession. By an equally deft use of medium Oscar turned Jules Dubois into a human butterfly fluttering at the end of a leash—held, alas, by a female centaur.

Each of Oscar's essays into caricature demonstrated a flair for drawing and an actual control of his simple medium that was remarkable for a boy his age. None was yet the work of a mature caricaturist, who in the tradition of Daumier and Gavarni, then so strong, might have been more attentive to linear precision. But he enjoyed the practice of his skill, and exhibited much pride in showing the product of it—which, to a bourgeois family like his own, became even more disturbing. Such a family conceivably might look

33

with pride on the comic gift of its wayward and difficult son, or find its own private humor in the fact that people allowed him to make mock of them. Still, it was not a circle that encumbered its offspring with an excess of funds, and they were scandalized when young Oscar, who felt he was not given the allowance he required, was inspired with the bold resolve to take money for his little portraits.

With typical independence Oscar continued to do precisely as he wished, and soon another characteristic trait asserted itself. Coupled with his fierce self-will he too inherited some of the petty shrewdness of his family. Relying for his index on the appearance of clients, he quickly learned to gauge their capacity to pay between ten and twenty francs for a portrait. Oscar was in a transport of delight. Never, he felt, in the whole history of the world, had such an unquestionable and victorious stroke of villainy been so skillfully brought off.

Le Havre boasted only one frame maker, located in the Rue de Paris, four or five streets from the Rue Fontenelle. Oscar's caricatures soon were brought to him for frames, and thereafter were exhibited in his window, five or six in a row, covered by glass and surrounded in bright gold frames. Now so eminently displayed, Oscar took new conviction in his abilities. He claimed there were days when he executed seven or eight portraits, and immediately he decided to put his savings into safekeeping. It is interesting that for guardianship he chose neither a bank nor his father but the one person from whom he felt feminine sympathy, his aunt Sophie Lecadre, who herself painted amateurishly in an untidy studio in the Ste.-Adresse house.

The self-assurance Oscar brought to his daily life now bore an air that one might reasonably have confused with smugness, and this appearance was not contradicted by the erect, stiff-necked carriage he adopted. In striped waistcoat of bright tweed, worn with contrasting dark jacket and light trousers, he became a conspicuous figure. Well marked by a flowing cravat and large cape-shouldered overcoat, he was a provincial dandy, dapper and animated, whose full stature, never much exceeding five feet seven inches, was topped off by a bushy tuft of dark hair worn long and brushed back from a full round forehead. Like his figure, his face was broad rather than long, a fact at first less noticed because of the finely chiseled profile that contributed an air of distinction. Deep-set eyes, in whose brown recesses lurked a look of purpose and a hint of slyness, were balanced by a wide thin-lipped mouth, its mobility persisting even when the corners were drawn tight in the way habitual to those who speak French.

Vitally obsessed by its own characteristic antipathies, the pubescent imagination of a young man is prone to extraordinary fantasies. These Oscar already had demonstrated to a marked degree, and, as he matured, they became even more evident. At the bottom of all was an undefinable dissatisfaction. The imprisonment of school, which to him seemed never-ending, continued to hold him in measured tedium. Though to others he seemed engaged in a life of perpetual undergraduate antics, he himself considered that he followed a morose, taciturn, and gloomy existence.

Even when he went to stand among the loungers who admired his caricatures displayed in the Rue de Paris, he was disturbed by the paintings frequently hung above his own work. He never ceased to abuse the "idiot" Eugène Boudin, who had the complacency to sign them. Gentle self-effacing sketches from nature, each a miracle of relaxed lyricism in a predominantly cold and gray tonality, Oscar was certain these little pictures were not art at all.

This same Eugène Boudin, fourteen years earlier, had opened the stationery and framing shop in the window of which Oscar's caricatures and his own despised paintings were now hung. At the age of twenty, in 1844, Boudin had begun business by framing and occasionally hanging for display works by the many artists who passed their summers on the nearby shores. Among his seasonal clients were Couture, who taught at the École des Beaux-Arts, and Troyon; and when the following summer Jean François Millet arrived at Le Havre, still unknown, and obliged to earn his living by painting portraits for a meager thirty francs each, he too had bought his supplies from Boudin. One day the humble shopkeeper brought out his own sketches, which Millet corrected, and from that moment Boudin lost interest in everything but himself becoming an artist. Millet did not fail to stress the poverty and hardship which might be expected, but Boudin left his shop in the charge of an associate while he went off to study in Paris.

By 1850 Boudin had made such progress that two of his pictures were purchased by the Society of Art Friends of Le Havre. Sponsored by Troyon and Couture, both names of importance at the Salon, the following year Boudin was granted a three-year fellowship by the city of Le Havre. The modest nature of Boudin's further development disappointed those who had adopted him, for when he returned from Paris, in his baggage were not the expected visions of fierce, turbulent, and amorphous gods, but unassuming little pictures painted in the open air and without higher significance. At Le Havre, where Boudin continued to work in this disappointing manner, he found few patrons and was considered eccentric.

Even so, the keeper of the framing shop never stopped urging Oscar to meet him. "You should make the acquaintance of M. Boudin," he would say. "You will see. Whatever they may say of him, he knows his trade. He studied it in Paris, in the studios of the École des Beaux-Arts. He could give you some advice."

Oscar resisted these well-intentioned admonitions. Nonetheless, one day he found himself face to face with Boudin, who had been standing in the rear of the shop when he entered. The frame maker grasped the opportunity to make an introduction: "Just see, M. Boudin, this is the young man who has so much talent for caricature."

Boudin's undistinguished face was marked only by sharply incised planes at the wings of a nose which seemed to plunge from his mustache and square-cut beard. He looked like a disappointed naval officer, and his voice was gentle as his eyes when he spoke. "I always look at them with much pleasure, your sketches. They are amusing, clever, bright. You are gifted; one can see that at a glance. But I hope you are not going to stop at that. It is very well for a beginning, but soon you will have had enough of caricaturing."

The man had an attractive tone of sincerity, but he aroused suspicion too, for his words proffered a too obvious defense of his own pictures. "Study, learn to see and to paint, draw, make landscapes," he went on. "They are all so beautiful, the sea and the sky, the animals, the people and the trees, just as nature made them with their character, their real way of being, in the light, in the air, just as they are."

Exhortations from a man so suspect as Boudin could have little effect on Oscar, no matter how sincerely the painter spoke. At sixteen Oscar was puffed up with vanity and self-importance. A success in his little art, he felt himself in sharp contrast to Boudin's evi-

dent failure. And though Boudin offered to take his new acquaintance sketching in the fields, Oscar always found a pretext politely to decline. Then the summer of 1856 arrived, and with it a
cessation of school, which left him without valid excuses. Weary at
last of such earnest entreaties, he agreed to go.

To see Boudin before nature, working with quiet sincerity, was to
realize that his was the unpretentious approach of an artisan going
about a job. His canvas was fixed to the fore end of a long camp stool,
in the middle of which his paints and pallette were spread. On the
farther end the artist himself was perched. Paints, canvas, painter,
and stool, all were more or less shaded by a large umbrella, fore-
stalling the sun's direct rays from bleaching colors or hindering his
accurate notation of hues. Seated within reach of his small canvases,
squinting at the scene before him, Boudin copied what his eye
reported with a careful but hurried touch.

Examined individually, each of the little canvases that Boudin
painted so lovingly from nature has about it a quiet truth and feeling
of reality that is altogether winning. Their fundamental charm is
that of truth delicately perceived and recorded with consummate
beauty of tone and an easy supple style. Craftsmanship played no
small part, for the flat sable brushes employed by Boudin and all
landscape painters of this period had a different characteristic from
the bristles which replaced them later. Strokes laid on by this
dexterous intrument seem viscous, and have the tightly packed characteristic of a mass discharged under pressure. They build a surface
possessing attractive consistency, not unlike butter spread on bread.
Fresh strokes fell on this with subtle appeal to the senses, and
Boudin's delicacy and perfect control enhanced such charms.

Only when larger numbers of his sketches are examined is it seen
how great is the similarity among them, as if they were created by
a reshuffling of too few elements. Boudin's scope, like that of many
nineteenth-century specialists, was absurdly limited. One recognizes
his modest canvases from afar, by the subject as much as the style. Yet
within his own sphere not only was Boudin a master, but his works
had a bold originality unlike the art of his time. Founded on Corot,
his practice had become so broad, ingrown, and individual, it resembled that of no other painter. And his pictures were capable of
making so strong an impression that Boudin's is the only discern-

ible influence on Winslow Homer, who in 1867 crossed his path in France.

It was also true that Boudin had an uncommon ability to communicate fundamental truths in a way that indelibly impressed them on others. His gift was less the philosopher's theories than the poet's evocative vision. "Everything that is painted directly on the spot has always a strength, a power, a vividness of touch, that one does not find again in the studio" is an example of his simple straightforward doctrine, expressing an essential truth grown from his experienced craftsmanship.

An essential difference between outdoor works and the composed product of the studio landscapist is the unity of effect that is gained when a picture has been painted before the subject. To explain this phenomenon it is possible to fly into clouds of theory, which Boudin avoided. Instead he gave Oscar a key to sustain this unity: "It is not one part which should strike one in a picture, but the whole." Again, a disarmingly simple conclusion that, when fully developed, would produce a new art.

Under Boudin's guidance Oscar soon learned to enjoy sketching nature in pastel and oil, and how much his first efforts partook of the teacher's qualities was apparent that same year, 1856. To encourage his protégé Boudin included one of Oscar's first pictures, painted in a suburb overlooking Le Havre, when four of his own were exhibited at Rouen. A local critic immediately noted the similarity, and young Oscar's first press notice read, "A view of Rouelles by M. Monet has the same qualities as M. Boudin." The acid overtones doubtless escaped Oscar, who found desired encouragement, and assiduously studied nature. His gifted use of pencil easily filled a sketchbook with precisely recorded, tonally accurate drawings of ships waiting outside Le Havre's busy port, while in the countryside he became a specialist in tree trunks' most gnarled aspects.

Among his family, opinions of young Oscar's new enthusiasm were mixed. Boudin was hardly respectable, arousing disquietude over the company Oscar kept. Alternately, however, his aunt Sophie gave an appearance of encouraging him. Her attic studio at Ste.-Adresse was put at Oscar's disposal, so that he might have the advantage of a place to work and proximity to the beaches. Many nights he slept in that untidy sanctum where from under accumulations of debris a picture caught his eye. When rescued, this little canvas proved to be a twilight scene of grape pickers. In admiration Oscar cleared away the dust that obscured its surface, to discover the signature of Daubigny. The elation of that moment, and the renewed assurance it gave him in the value of his own judgment, he never forgot.

Except for a few silhouetted details and the constant recollection of his inarticulate unhappiness, little is preserved of Oscar's youth. Encouraged by his aunt, taught by Boudin, he painted in the little attic studio, in the fields, and on the shingle beaches. His years at school ended at last, his caricatures provided a modest source of funds, and for two uneasy years Oscar continued in this haphazard existence before announcing to his father that he had decided to become a painter and wished to study in Paris.

Adolphe Monet did not entirely oppose this suggestion, which his sister may have encouraged. His son possessed abilities and had proved money could be earned by their exercise. Possibly even pleased to have a definite proposal from a lad who always had drifted off into irresolution, Adolphe Monet nevertheless felt unwilling to give Oscar financial aid.

Three months before Oscar turned eighteen, on August 6, 1858, Adolphe Monet accepted the bold proposition that he request the Le Havre Municipal Council to extend his son the same aid once given to Boudin. That his application might succeed could not be ignored. The boy already had a certain renown in the city, where, despite his youth, his drawings were seen at the framer's shop in the Rue de Paris. "I have the honor to state to you," Adolphe Monet wrote to the Council, "that my son Oscar Monet, aged eighteen years, having worked with MM. Ochard and Vasseur, wishes to become a candidate for the title of Pensioner of Fine Arts for the City of Le Havre. His natural inclinations, and his taste, which he has definitely fixed on painting, obliges me not to turn him away from his vocation, but since I have not the necessary means to send him to Paris to attend courses of the important masters, I hereby beg you to be so kind as to accept favorably my son's candidacy. . . ." In support of this request a painting of still life was submitted to the Council.

However the Council viewed this plea of poverty from a member of the prosperous Monet-Lecadre partnership, haste was not among its vices. For seven months it neither responded to Adolphe

Monet's letter nor granted his petition. Filled with the boisterous challenge of the life before him, Oscar meanwhile grew incapable of further waiting. On March 21, 1859, therefore, Adolphe
Monet submitted to the Council an identical letter, this time permitting the name of Boudin to join those of Oscar's other teachers.
Despite the absence of eminent sponsors such as those who had
backed Boudin, Oscar felt certain that his candidacy must be accepted. In his certainty, he fretted that he might not see the Salon
soon to open at the Palais de l'Industrie. Another Salon would not
be held for two years, and if the Municipal Council dallied further
this would be a grave loss.

Daily it seemed more pressing that Oscar visit Paris. Since a career
in the arts was the path before him, even Adolphe Monet understood
his anxiety. From Boudin, and that artist's few patrons, Oscar collected letters of introduction to the more eminent landscape
painters. These he hoped might encourage him further, and suggest
a master in whose studio he would study. Then, his preparations
completed, this swaggering, self-centered, emotional, and contentious
young man set off for Paris.

2. *Paris by Plan*

A SENSE OF PURPOSE was strong in the otherwise undisciplined young
caricaturist who arrived at the Gare St.-Lazare early that May, 1859.
He gave himself less to the gay and giddy improvisations one might
reasonably have expected than to a well-calculated plan of assault.
His swashbuckling tone and manners immediately were overpowered by the externals of a noisy city: the carriages, taxis, buses,
crowds of pedestrians, and wagons of debris and building materials
that rumbled across his path. At the Place du Havre, outside the
station, a group of imposing hotels were drawn up in a semicircle;

boldly he walked into the Nouveau-Monde, 125 Rue St.-Lazare. The expense was not of primary importance to a young man with no time to lose before seeing the Salon.

Oscar's path to the Palais de l'Industrie lay across a metropolis that suffered from an extraordinary narcissistic sadism. For five years this great city had been laid waste by teams of architects and masons, whose demolitions and scaffolds were found everywhere the Emperor's whimsicality decreed. North from the Place du Châtelet Napoleon III had directed that a new boulevard be cut through sundered rows of houses. A fountain that the first Napoleon had erected to throw an air of triumph over his Egyptian campaign relinquished half its site to this new artery, in recompense gaining vast theaters to frame it on both sides.

Perpendicular across this devastation ran the wide gash of another. Between the Hôtel de Ville and the Palais Royal three hundred houses were being felled, their sites forming a continuation of the Rue de Rivoli. At the farther end of this giant saber cut the Tuileries gardens were extended to join the Louvre's outstretched wings. Nor was the Louvre itself spared. The Pavillon de Flore had been razed, only to rise again like a phoenix some few feet farther north, where one wall abutted the extended Rue de Rivoli. At the other end of this holocaust additions were in progress at the Hôtel de Ville, which received also an entirely new and separate annex, the Caserne Napoléon.

The new church of St.-Jean-Baptiste, first of a mighty trio of ecclesiastical adornments Napoleon bestowed on his capital, had been consecrated the previous year. A great cast-iron *flèche* was about to be eased into position above the Gothic cathedral of Notre-Dame. On the Left Bank an imposing new fountain took shape at the Place St.-Michel. In the Bois de Boulogne heavy plantings of trees were under way, to create the first of those giant parks it soon became the fashion to dedicate in all the world's great cities.

Everywhere Oscar turned his eyes, the hand of the Emperor was at work in an elaborate mime of majesty, reshaping, beautifying, and glorifying Paris. Intended to crown his efforts was an opera house, whose elaborate form rose slowly above the dust of construction. By its commanding position at the head of newly formed avenues, and its lavish adornment of gilded sculptures and confettilike enrichment of colored marble, basalt, and obsidian, this sumptuous structure was expected completely to alter the interior aspect of the city.

Oscar's first prolonged visit to the Salon made a profound impression. The second part of his plan then was put into action immediately, and he called on those eminent artists to whom he carried introductions. To each he showed two still-life paintings brought from Le Havre before asking advice concerning a master under whom to study when the Municipal Council had granted his father's petition.

Amand Gautier received him with much kindness, remembered an earlier acquaintance with Boudin, and seemed disposed to easy friendliness. Oscar left his studio with an intention to return. Next he called on the Le Havre painter Charles Lhullier, whom he found lodged in a studio borrowed from Mme. Becq de Fouquières. Lhullier's picture exhibited at the Salon had been sold for 600 francs. He was in a happy state and already had in progress a work for the next Salon, in addition to several of the small, fresh, brilliantly pigmented portraits he executed at the modest fee of 100 francs each.

Easily most distinguished among the artists to whom Oscar carried introductions was Constant Troyon, whom Boudin, during earlier years in Paris, had assisted to paint the speckled and windswept skies that were a notable feature of his landscapes. Though the Emperor Napoleon himself had no taste for Troyon's work—remarking, "It seems that I do not understand painting," when on his Minister's advice he signed a decree decorating Troyon—*cows à la Troyon* were a prodigious vogue in the drawing rooms of the Second Empire. The artist, who worked easily in his Paris studio from sketches, often completing his canvases in one day, was besieged by dealers.

Tall, large-shouldered, heavy, his strong nose curved back onto his face like an ancient battering ram decorated with human physiognomy, Troyon's was a forceful presence. His voice retained the rough accents of the country, and his manner, though it betrayed a certain civilized balance and restraint, at first seemed frighteningly direct.

"Well, my good fellow, you'll have color all right," Troyon remarked when the little canvases were shown him. "It's correct in the general effect, but you must do some serious studying, for this is very nice but you do it too easily. You'll never lose that.

"If you want to heed my advice and be serious about art, begin by entering a studio where they do nothing but the figure. Learn to draw. That's what you'll find almost everyone lacks today. Listen to me and you will see I am not wrong. But draw with all your might. One never knows too much about it. Don't neglect painting. From time to time go to the country to make sketches, carrying them through. Make some copies in the Louvre. Come and see me often. Show me what you do, and, with courage, you will succeed.

Even more exciting was Troyon's further suggestion that the boy grasp immediately the opportunity afforded by his presence in Paris to set about learning the rudiments of drawing. "In this way you will acquire abilities," Troyon said. "You will go back to Le Havre and you will be able to do some good sketches in the country. And in the winter you will come to settle in Paris definitely."

Nothing could have delighted Oscar more than to remain longer in this exciting city of Paris. Happily he communicated Troyon's ideas to his father, who, impressed by this advice from a fashionable and decorated artist, quietly agreed. Lodged still at the Hôtel du Nouveau-Monde, Oscar received word that his father would provide a small allowance until the Municipal Council acted. By May 19 this was agreed, and Oscar dispatched a long letter to Boudin, recounting his Parisian experiences in a light exuberant style. Bubbling with his happy news, he displayed a greater ease of expression than might have been expected from a youth who had studied so little as he claimed:

Monsieur Gautier has charged me to send you his kind regards, and to say that he hopes to see you in Paris soon. That is the advice of everyone. You must not stay in that cotton town and be discouraged. As for myself, . . . [M. Gautier] has received me with an impeccable courtesy. He has a number of fine pictures in progress and very shortly will be starting a large lithograph.

Before departing Le Havre I was given a letter of introduction to Troyon. I have visited him, and to tell you what beautiful things I have seen there would be impossible; admirable cows and dogs. He spoke to me about you a great deal and is much surprised that you do not come to the Capital. He asked me to tell you to send him a dozen of your most finished pictures, some gray marine scenes, some still lifes, and several landscapes. He believes he can find buyers for them if they are a little more finished than those you gave him in the past. He advises you to come here. . . .

Already a confidant of the great and famous, charged with messages, Oscar Claude Monet felt the wonderful world of Paris had opened to him even more quickly than anticipated.

Frantic activity filled the weeks that followed. In three days Oscar located a less costly lodging. To find a school where he could draw was another pressing necessity, and, betweentimes, he returned to the Salon, paying his one-franc entrance fee to feast himself on the proud French school of painting. "Work, and this overwhelming Paris, make me forget a little the duties of a friend," he wrote again to Boudin, June 3. Troyon he had now seen twice, and Amand Gautier several times more. From both artists he transmitted kind messages to Boudin. The bulk of a lengthy epistle Oscar now devoted to descriptions of the Salon's many pictures, his opinions on them, and exhortations that Boudin come to Paris before the Salon closed. "Marine paintings are entirely lacking," he concluded his recital, "and this is a path which should take you far."

To Boudin he recounted Troyon's forthright manner. "Do you want to hear my advice?" that master had said in his rustic way. "If I were to begin my career over again I would go to Couture's studio. I recommend it to you particularly. There are also Picot and Cogniet, but I have always detested the style of these men."

Significantly, all three masters named by Troyon were teachers at the École des Beaux-Arts. Whether one entered the École to join their regular classes, difficult because of competitive examinations, or took instruction in the more accessible quasi-official studios these men taught outside the École, the purpose was the same. Wise in the ways of Paris, Troyon, who himself had climbed to honor, knew that the lowest rungs of that ladder reached into the classes at the École des Beaux-Arts. To learn one's trade thoroughly and well was essential. To come to the attention of the École's influential instructors, who might see that a pupil's work was accepted by the Salon jury, was a consideration of even greater importance.

Oscar heard Troyon's advice with that deference and respect proper to an artist so important. But among the painters he recently had met in Paris it was Amand Gautier, whose somber gray tones he noted at the Salon, that he found most sympathetic. In some respects Gautier's temperament was not unlike Oscar's own. Thirty-four years old, and eight years in Paris, where he had come from his native Lille, for two years Gautier had studied under Léon Cogniet. His taste was for sensitive studies of still life, simplification of form into tonal areas, and a Velasquez-influenced portraiture that precursed Whistler. In Gautier's studio Oscar admired a large recent *Promenade des Soeurs,* and with this delicate and conscientious painter he passed evenings at the Brasserie des Martyrs, where Gustave Courbet, one of the most controversial artists of the time, gathered with his friends.

Oscar was precisely in the wrong place, for Courbet had already departed for a summer near Le Havre. At Honfleur, on the south bank of the Seine estuary, Courbet encountered Eugène Boudin, who conducted him to a favorable location for painting, the St.-Siméon farm. For both artists the meeting was highly significant. "Name of God!" cried Courbet, after examining Boudin's canvases. "You are a seraph—only you know how to paint a sky!"

Though he missed this opportunity to meet on intimate terms the leading *realist* painter, in Paris Oscar himself passed through a stirring experience. Quietly sipping wine on the periphery of a disputatious conclave of painters and writers at the Brasserie des Martyrs, he experienced the fantastic delight of entering a world of intellectual stimulation. The new life these few short weeks had opened to him, and the promise they held, flattered and enchanted the eighteen-year-old boy.

Through so much excitement he awaited with mixed anxiety and fear the answer of the Municipal Council, upon which depended the future of all he had begun. It seemed impossible he could be refused what Boudin already had been granted. His still life, submitted to the Council with his father's letter, was surely the equal of those so favorably viewed by the artists of Paris. Nonetheless, when late in May the Council's answer was delivered to Adolphe Monet, he found it a stunning refusal. Minutes of the Council meeting of May 18, at which this decision had been taken, are revealing:

> Monet, having worked in contact with Messieurs Ochard, Vasseur, and Boudin, presented with his request a painting of still life by

which one would judge poorly of his talent, were it not well revealed
by his witty sketches known to us all.

In the path he has taken until now (a remarkable natural talent
for caricature, if it is necessary to give its name), Oscar Monet has
already found popularity, which is so slow to come to serious works.

But has he not, in this precocious success in the direction given
his facile pencil until now, a danger, which would hold the young
painter outside the more serious but less rewarding studies which
alone deserve Municipal generosity.[?]

This is the nature of our response.

Adolphe Monet relayed this sad news from Le Havre, and Oscar
found himself in emotional eruption. Swept away were all his expanding visions of a gloriously successful stay at Paris. When the
Council's motives were made known to him, their unfairness underscored the terrible impact. His weeks in Paris surely had proved
how men of eminence were willing to accept him for a person
of talent, certain to find his place in their ranks. Mindful of the
encouragement he had received, Oscar asked his father to continue
his allowance so that he might study in Paris.

"You shall not have a penny" was his own astringent account of
the paternal response. His own riposte he gave as "I will get along
without it!"

That such an interview took place between a father and son so
many miles apart is doubtful. If nothing more, this imagined col-
loquy illustrates that irate father and willful son already were intransigent opponents, and in this harsh spirit the fateful decision was
taken. Had Adolphe Monet the ability to reason with his son, that
recourse remained unemployed. Adolphe Monet was adamant that
his fortune would not be spent to send his son into an unwanted profession while the call of commerce remained unheard. Thus, after
three or four weeks, to force Oscar back to Le Havre, his contribution ceased. But the son's will was made of the same iron as the
father's. Determined to remain in Paris to meet his obvious destiny,
Oscar wrote to his aunt Sophie Lecadre, asking that she forward his
own savings from two years of drawing caricatures. Caught between
her brother and an honorable duty to the nephew who was nearly
her son, Oscar's aunt complied.

While he faced this first great challenge with dexterity and
aplomb, Oscar found, still unposted, the letter he had written seven

days before to Boudin. To it he appended a few words: "Since I wrote to you everything has changed. I will explain in my next letter, which will be more prompt than this, just how I have settled here. I think you will approve. Hasten to Paris; no more than eight days to see the Salon. My present address is 35 Rue Rodier."

Behind the brave words and resolute looks in which Oscar cloaked this new episode of his life was the less beguiling fact that at last he was free to shed all restraint. Passionately preoccupied with himself and his own emotions, the young man so embellished and exalted this break with his father that he imagined it to be the climactic event of his life. In celebration he gave up the name "Oscar," by which his family always had called him, and which he now shed as he shed his own provincial boyhood. With a cozy feeling of conspiratorial superiority he signed his occasional caricatures "Claude Monet," savoring this elegant rhythmical sound, which to him signified the birth of a new star in the constellation of the arts.

Under this new name Oscar made official entry into his country's most frustrated and controversial profession, his entire baggage the slapdash arrogance of a fledgling who refused to learn the basic disciplines of his craft. For *refuse* to learn he did, and what so shortly before had begun as a journey into serious study now deteriorated into ironic social comedy. The enjoyment extracted from his presence in Paris took precedence over all else. His savings were sufficient to relieve him of want, and his only consideration was his own pleasure and to carry on what little work his caprice required. Troyon reminded him of earlier advice to join the studio of Couture, counsel in which Charles Monginot concurred. But Oscar Claude heeded nothing. "I admit that it even cooled me, temporarily at least, in my esteem and admiration for Troyon. I began to see less of him . . ." to escape an advice he no longer desired.

More influential in the new way of life he adopted was Amand Gautier's introduction to the Brasserie des Martyrs, located behind the church of Notre Dame de Lorette, near the Rue Laffitte and the Boulevard des Italiens. In the gloom of gathering evening this was a meeting place where a lad freshly nineteen might see men whose names were familiar from journals and bookstalls, and bandied among painters. Vehemence too often prevailed among them to the

47

utter annihilation of reason, and insults here found target on even the best earned renown. But above all he had tasted of Paris, this spicy world of ideas and personal contact among the famous and near famous delighted Claude Monet. Himself unknown, too lacking in words to make himself heard, too young to be accepted as a serious contributor, he contented himself by watching Gustave Courbet when in the autumn that revolutionary realist painter returned to Paris, mixing among the critic Castagnary, the author Alphonse Daudet, and a host of more ephemeral luminaries.

To attract attention and prove his gifts, he still drew caricatures. More rapid and less developed than those he had done at Le Havre, these alfresco sketches nonetheless brought him the desired notice. One subject to whom he devoted great care was the wealthy Montpellian, Alfred Bruyas, Courbet's greatest patron. The author Firmin Maillard saw a sketch very successfully done of "Benassit," and Monet gained the attention of the publisher Cajart, in whose short-lived weekly, *Diogène*, his sketch of the actor Laferrière appeared the following year. Claude's now banal but still gripping skill at caricature caught another eye in Jules Andrieu, an idealist seemingly untested by realities, who happily read Sophocles to the Brasserie's assembled multitudes. Andrieu's father, also a publisher, may have asked Monet to contribute regularly to his *Presse de la Jeunesse*, where the works of a nineteen-year-old cartoonist might have appeared with singular appropriateness. Perhaps annoyed at the nature of the compliment, Oscar Claude refused—his reason, in any event, remains distinctly obscure, if in fact the invitation was not another soaring flight of fancy.

So earnestly sought, his opportunity to study in Paris was being submerged in such bizarre pleasures as a ball held Saturday, October 1, in the studio of Gustave Courbet, which featured the performance of a five-act comedy in verse by Fernand Desnoyers, a work refused by the Théâtre de l'Odéon. Champfleury's contribution was a performance of a Haydn symphony on the unaccompanied bass drum. During the intervals Amand Gautier and a crowd of other notables took part in one-act plays. Monet's life in the French capital had become a featureless chaos, from which only at length does one extract the few constructive facts that he remained in contact with Troyon, however resentfully, and eventually began to work.

That he had come to Paris for the serious purpose of mastering the discipline of drawing had been forgotten in the splendid company at the Brasserie des Martyrs. Slowly, however, some sense of purpose returned, and Claude proceeded, though in a manner carefully calculated not to be tiresome. Disciplines of every sort he brushed aside by working in a studio kept by the Barbizon painter Charles Émile Jacque, a scraggy-haired, bearded man with an enormous wart on his nose. In the studio of Charles Monginot, who tried briefly to help him, he painted a still life, and was interrupted in his labors by the entrance of the laughing sandy-haired Édouard Manet, who made a cruel joke of him.

Irregularly he also attended the Académie Suisse, where a model posed each day and could be drawn without the burden of criticism from a master. Housed in a sordid old building where on another floor a well-known dentist had a large practice extracting teeth at one franc each, aside from its freedom from instruction the chief recommendation of the Académie Suisse was that Courbet, hero of the Brasserie des Martyrs, once had frequented it. With an engaging optimism that was utterly misplaced Claude had thus contrived to "study" in two places without receiving any instruction at all. Even at this early age he never could resist the temptation to play a sly game, and already this was working consistently to his own disadvantage.

If his father felt that delicacy had been outraged by Oscar Claude's proceedings in Paris, the boy maintained contact with his more sympathetic aunt, Sophie Lecadre. He appears even to have visited her at Le Havre, or Ste.-Adresse, and as an encouragement to his not overly persistent labors, she permitted him to take away Daubigny's little picture of grape pickers which he so extravagantly admired. A discussion of proprieties may have ensued, Adolphe Monet looking upon Oscar Claude's furtive visit coupled with the picture's sudden absence as a theft. To Boudin's question Oscar made a characteristically adamant reply: ". . . you know that the little Daubigny in question is entirely mine. It hangs in my room."

Whatever the merits of this dispute, the little Daubigny had joined him in Paris, at 28 Rue Pigalle, and soon Oscar Claude had shown it to Amand Gautier, who made an etching of it. Even at this juncture, however, inconvenient if intermittent ideals remained with Claude, whose days were punctuated by agitated desires to advance himself in painting. Among the new acquaintances made at Jacque's studio some acted as a useful foil to this ardor. Most prominent among these was Camille Pissarro, a twenty-nine-year-old native of the Virgin Islands, educated in France, whose vast seriousness had beneficial effect on the too easily dissolved purpose of Oscar Claude.

Stabilizing influence of another sort was found in any public display of paintings, which fanned the embers of ambition that continued to burn beneath an irresistible apathy. Organized privately, and without the influence of the Académie des Beaux-Arts, an exhibition of French painting seen on the Boulevard des Italiens in February, 1860, stirred him to strong reaction. Oscar Claude delighted in the eighteen examples by Delacroix, and noted too that Troyon, who at the Salon had appeared a painter of great beauty, suffered among stronger companions. Rosa Bonheur's bucolic rural scenes likewise seemed to receive a timely rebuttal, and Couture, to whose classes he had been so lately recommended by Troyon, Claude considered to be a man who had "totally abandoned painting"—a judgment no doubt colored by self-justifying malice.

Overcome by the new brilliance of color he found, Monet wrote to Boudin effusively, exclaiming with joy "that we are not so far gone in decadence as it is said"—the familiar cry of every student in every age. Other bits of youthful gaucherie must have perplexed Boudin, as when he read, ". . . the only good sea painter we have, Jongkind, is dead to art. He has lost his mind. The artists are taking up a subscription for his needs. There is a nice seat for you to take." (!)

The otherwise clean, brisk prose in which Oscar Claude reported to Boudin his own activities omitted much, and was not free from overemphasis. His world was distinctly egocentric: "I am surrounded by a little band of young landscape painters who would be happy to meet you. Besides, they are real painters. . . . I find myself very well fixed here. I am drawing figures very hard. That's a fine thing. And at the Academy [Suisse] there are none but landscapists. They begin to perceive that it is a good thing." One of those he had in mind was certainly Camille Pissarro, then "tranquilly working in Corot's style. The model was excellent. I followed his example, but during my whole stay in Paris . . . I was governed by the advice of Boudin." In fact, Courbet—and, through Pissarro, Corot—already exerted other influences on him. His loyalty to Boudin remained a characteristic part of his nature, however, and on April 21, 1860, before leaving Paris to sketch in the country, probably with Pissarro, he sent Boudin a much retarded reply, signing himself "Your pupil and friend":

> First of all I must tell you that the exhibition has not closed and will be open some time yet. I cannot give you an exact date. I can only tell you that you are missing a great deal, because they have already changed a great number of the canvases, and not the least important. Their intention is to prolong this exhibition by changing canvases every month. For the rest, there is always much to see, I assure you.
>
> Come! I will be very happy to see you and to get your advice on my work.
>
> The weather is already superb here. I can tell you that I am going to pass fifteen days or three weeks in a charming part of the country, at Champigny-sur-Marne. I shall make a few landscapes there, accompanied by two of my comrades.
>
> M. Gautier always looks forward to seeing you. He has just made an etching from my Daubigny.

Like his situation, the view of himself taken by Oscar Claude Monet was characteristic and almost pathetic. Still the juvenile, on his way out to some revelry with new-found Parisian comrades, he discovered himself out of funds. That deplorable moment had come at last. His friends searched their own pockets, whose condition, predictably, matched that of his own. Thus is human popularity gauged and friendship made fast; the little band of young landscape painters seemed near dissolution.

"There is always my Daubigny," he said. "It can be sold."

This brilliant expedient was greeted with renewed spirit. A few moments later all were on the street, the Daubigny under Monet's arm. Together they hailed a fiacre and set out to find an art dealer. But no dealer approached by this group of young men felt great confidence in the merchandise they presented. Each in turn examined the canvas, examined its back, turned up his nose, and politely put them back on the sidewalk. The cost of the fiacre meanwhile grew larger, until, at last, in the Rue de Bac, a dealer named Thomas offered 400 francs for it, on condition they furnish an attestation from Daubigny himself that the picture was authentic.

Discouragement sat heavily on Oscar Claude, who felt possessed of none of the strength necessary to face Daubigny in his studio at 13 Quai d'Anjou. One of the friends, with more audacity and less delicacy, confronted the master, who, fortunately, recognized the spirit of his own youth and signed a paper. A quarter of an hour later the picture was transferred to the ownership of M. Thomas, and Oscar Claude Monet had a new fortune to sustain his life of idle apprenticeship.

Powerless to prevent Oscar Claude from continuing his happy debauch, the older generation of the Monet-Lecadre family understandably found in it no joy. Life seemed a battle of wits that their willful younger son fought unarmed. His older brother, Léon Pascal, his education completed, had become established as a chemist. Of him Adolphe Monet could feel proud. But for Oscar Claude the portents of disaster were everywhere. So long as he had funds his family could do little to bridle him. Time was running out, however, for at the age of twenty, like all the youths of France, Oscar Claude would be obliged to take part in the military lottery from which conscripts were selected for the army.

Before those who drew an "unlucky" number lay the prospect of seven years' service. The system, however, provided the attractive alternative of buying a substitute, who, for an established price, would serve the conscript's term in the army. With an air of serene contentment Adolphe Monet realized that once again the stronger hand soon would be his. "My family . . . had not forgiven me my flight," Monet later recalled. "They had let me live as I chose . . . because they thought they would catch me when the time came for me to do military duty. They thought that once my wild oats were sown, I would tame down sufficiently to return home, readily enough, and bend at last to commerce." Of course nothing was further from his mind. After a summer and a winter living by his own inclinations, far from his father's indignation and disapproving eye, he felt a strong antipathy toward renouncing such liberty. And with an endearing whimsicality he also was willing to gamble with that infernally tedious triangle of Paris, his father, and the army. By choosing a "lucky" lottery number he might win, and remain free of obligation to serve. His reply to the ultimatum issued by Adolphe Monet was therefore "a gesture of superb indifference."

For one of his independent nature it seems unfortunate that Oscar

Claude never at any time possessed a gambler's luck. He returned to Le Havre for the formalities which made him a part of the military class of 1860. The lottery was duly held, and his number was "unlucky." Nor did his father relent. On April 29, 1861, Oscar Claude Monet formally was incorporated into the French army, exchanging the playful ease of life in Paris for the more grim existence of a military camp.

Though he was immaturity itself, it is to his credit that Oscar Claude never took a sulky view of his misfortune, nor softened his proud contempt. Instead he had the unexpected strength to put a happy face on disaster, and through his sense of adventure to acquire a distinct taste for military life. Embarked with other conscripts for Africa, on June 10, 1861, he arrived in Algeria, where he joined the First Regiment of Chasseurs d'Afrique, the famous Zouaves. His splashy uniform consisted of boots and spurs, wide pantaloons, a huge sash that rose halfway up his chest, a long coat dripping gold braid, and a jaunty little peaked garrison cap. Nothing could have been more delightful. It was, after all, just one more lark in a life without fixed purpose.

3. *A Complacent Apprentice*

THE HOST of new and different experiences Algeria presented were distinctly more Delacroix than Boudin, and unrelated to anything Oscar Claude had known in the harried culture of industrialized France. The army had adapted itself splendidly to a haphazard mixture of alien races and to the desert heat, doting on and detesting an oppressively hot, sandy waste, peopled by unsavory descendants of Barbary pirates, romantically draped Arabs, and Bedouins inclined like Moses to wander across horizons forty years with their flocks. Against this background, the Chasseurs lived less a restricted garrison life than one of actual danger, frequent gaiety and harsh surprising humor. Oscar's hair was cut short to the military standard, and for the first time his fuzzy cheeks knew the keenness of a razor. The added grace of afterthought clings to his own rakish account:

> Nothing attracted me so much as the endless cavalcades under the burning sun, the dramatic raids, the crackle of gunpowder, the saber thrusts, the nights in the desert under a tent. . . . In Algeria I spent two really charming years. I incessantly saw something new. In my moments of leisure I attempted to render what I saw. You cannot imagine to what extent I increased my knowledge, and how much my vision gained thereby. . . .
>
> I fell ill at the end of two years, and quite seriously. They sent me home to recuperate.

Only his time sequence betrays the extent to which he romanticized fact. For if Oscar Claude did suffer a severe illness, not recorded in his military dossier, then his return to Le Havre for recuperation took place no later than May, 1862, thirteen months after his incorporation into the service, and less than a year from his arrival in Africa. But the season at which he returned home suggests it was really the unbearable heat of another African summer he feared. The "illness" he recounted bristles with loopholes and probably was a delicate exercise in tact. He had found Algeria a dazzling land that induced second thoughts; the "gesture of superb indifference" was retracted.

Immediately on his return to Le Havre the practice of painting on the beaches and in the fields, alone or in the company of Boudin, was resumed. On a farm near the cliffs above his family's property at Ste.-Adresse one fine afternoon he began a pastel sketch of a grazing cow. The good beast proved capricious, every moment shifting its position. His easel in one hand, his stool in the other, Oscar followed, endeavoring repeatedly, and with repeated failure, to achieve the sort of sketch Boudin painted so easily. His evolutions were amusing to be seen, and suddenly, from behind him, he heard a burst of laughter.

"Wait a minute," called a burly, puffing Englishman. "I'll help you."

In huge strides he came up to the cow, and taking her by the horns, he attempted to make her pose. Unaccustomed to such protocol, the cow took it in bad humor. Now it was Monet's turn to laugh. Discomfited by his efforts, the Englishman came over to talk, and proved well posted on French painters.

"Do you know Jongkind?" he asked.

"No, but I have seen his work."

"What do you think of it?"

"It is very strong."

"Right you are. Do you know he is here?"

"You don't say!" Monet replied. His astonishment was genuine, for two years earlier, in his first letters to Boudin from Paris, he had declared this same Jongkind "dead to art." The subscription he had mentioned, taken up among the artist's friends, successfully had provided for Jongkind's needs during a fit of madness, and now he was sufficiently recovered once more to work.

"Would you like to meet him?" asked the Englishman.

"Decidedly yes," replied Oscar Claude, anxious as ever to establish contact with famous figures. "But then you are one of his friends?" he half inquired.

"I have never seen him" was the cool British reply. "But as soon as I learned of his presence I sent him my card. It is an opening wedge. I am going to invite him to lunch with you."

The strategy worked, and to Oscar Claude's surprise the following Sunday all three lunched together in the open garden of a country inn. Seated between two admirers whose sincerity he could not doubt, Jongkind was at his best. A simple man of forty-three, he laughed too eagerly, then meditated quietly as though savoring a rare pleasure. His heavy Dutch accent lent unintentional humor to painfully ungrammatical French, and such constant temptation to laughter was strengthened by the appearance of this tall, angular man who walked with the rolling gait of a sailor. But what riveted attention and created sympathy was Jongkind's taut and ravaged face, where all his sufferings, and the excesses of his Bohemian alcoholic life, were clearly registered.

Though painting again, Jongkind still was haunted by hallucinations and rarely at ease except in the concentration of his work. Pleased to make the acquaintance of an admiring and enthusiastic young friend, Jongkind politely asked to see Oscar's sketches, then invited the lad to work with him. At once Oscar Claude saw that Jongkind attacked canvases in a bolder, less placid way than Boudin,

with whom his style shared clarity of tone and the excitement of
quick notation. But their agitated and remarkably haunting character was the special product of their author's cerebral derangement,
and this, Monet, who quickly adopted Jongkind's broadness and
daring use of pigment, may not fully have realized. "From that time
on," he remembered, "Jongkind was my real master, and it was to
him that I owed the final education of my eye."

Anxious to cultivate Jongkind, an artist of limited but more general fame than Boudin, and one who exhibited at the Salon, Oscar
Claude made efforts to bring him to performances of dramatic works
by Dumas and Victor Hugo. "Oh! I do not want to see those things!"
Jongkind cried in horror. "Let me go to see the marionettes"; and he
went, laughing and applauding with the children. "Jongkind was a
child, sensitive, charming, but sometimes really terrible," Monet
realized, and in deference to the eminence of the older man he
guarded their contacts from friction, avoiding, not always successfully, Jongkind's sudden deplorable rages.

In this unusual association with madness was displayed a tact not
associated with the tempestuous clang and clatter of Monet's earliest youth. But the strain was unfortunately too great, for, intent
on displaying this strange idol who exhibited at the Salon, Oscar
Claude erred seriously by wishing to have Jongkind invited to dinner by his family. An invitation duly went forth from the Rue
Fontenelle, and Jongkind arrived in that austere dining room with
a short silver-haired, heavily mustached woman, whose fierce aspect suggested a butcher to the Imperial Guards. Claude's aunt,
Sophie Lecadre, passed the roast to her nephew, remarking, "Give
this plate to Mme. Jongkind."

Jongkind emitted a piercing laugh. "She is not my wife!" he
declared.

Complete silence followed this declaration, as each member of the
family turned to his plate, hardly daring to steal even the briefest and
most inquiet looks at his neighbor. At last, aware of the tension,
Jongkind made an even more cryptic utterance: "She is not my wife.
She is an angel!"

Embarrassment spread among the entire Monet-Lecadre family
forced him to explain. Jongkind's recital encompassed the story
of his life, plagued by alcoholism and madness until at length he

had encountered this devoted woman, who by her own strength of character had saved him. Her name was Mme. Fesser.

However heartwarming this tale of devotion, it left in no doubt the nature of Jongkind's relationship with Mme. Fesser. To a family of the Monets' and Lecadres' middle-class orientation, her presence was an abomination. The success of the dinner was therefore less than overwhelming, and new alarm spread after this discovery that Oscar, not content with his idle pursuits nor the mild Boudin's bad company, now was associating with a preposterous cackling paranoid. Not only was their son degraded but unimprovable whether by art or education; even the army had failed.

His freedom from the army, however, remained provisional. His father had him on parole, subject to good behavior, while the elders of the Monet-Lecadre family wondered what to do. That their troublesome younger son had thrown himself into painting with a redoubled energy was certain. Mme. Lecadre now wrote to Amand Gautier for his advice: "His sketches are always rough drafts," she complained, "like those you have seen. But when he wants to complete something, to produce a picture, they turn into appalling daubs before which he preens himself and finds idiots to congratulate him. He pays no attention to my remarks. I am not up to his level, so now I keep the most profound silence."

Whether or not Gautier understood the full problem, he responded without hesitation that Oscar should return to Paris. That subtle distillation of moral and aesthetic dilemma with which Oscar had faced his family at last bore fruit:

My father became convinced that no will could curb me, and that no ordeal could get the better of so determined a vocation. As much from lassitude as from fear of losing me, for the Doctor [Lecadre] had led him to expect this should I return to Africa, he decided towards the end of my furlough to buy me out.

The allowance that two years before had been denied Oscar now would be given him. "But it must be well understood," Adolphe Monet admonished, "that this time you are going to work in dead earnest. I wish to see you in a studio, working under the discipline of a well-known master. If you resume your independent attitude I will stop your allowance without more ado. . . ."

Such a tone was certain to create its own destructive resentment. Not content with this unfortunate mixture of rant and cant, Adolphe Monet attempted to build around his son further safeguards. Marie Lecadre, a daughter in the Nantes branch of that family, was a young pastelist of promise who recently had married Auguste Toulmouche, an artist who followed a successful career in Paris. To Toulmouche, with whom Adolphe Monet and his sister now claimed cousinship, was assigned the unrewarding task of watching over Oscar Claude. He was given complete charge of the allowance, paid each month, and asked to render regular reports.

Final formalities were observed on November 21, 1862, when Adolphe Monet paid the stipulated fee for a substitute, and Oscar Claude Monet was "exonerated from service." With this costly freedom came his certificate of good conduct, essential for a resumption of civil rights.

For a second time Oscar Claude's family sent him forth, now providing funds on which he might undertake the serious study of art. If he appeared to act with bad grace, Adolphe Monet's final agreement is strongly to his credit, for it must have seemed more than mere waywardness that made his younger son so consistently take the wrong path. His rebellious nature had been asserted as a child. Now he was twenty-two, an age at which many another young man had assumed the burdens of life. Obsessed with his own strange ambitions and incapacity to accomplish them, Oscar Claude seemed satisfied that his family continued to provide for him.

That he should enter the family business, eventually replacing a father already sixty-two, or find some trade or craft of his own, seemed a right and proper course. If instead he wished to become a painter, his family willingly accepted this choice of occupation, only provided he was a good painter, not one who produced the fearful daubs that even his aunt, Sophie Lecadre, who so long had championed him, found it impossible to accept.

Outflanked, infiltrated, overrun by enemies from within, from his own point of view, Oscar Claude Monet knew that he wanted to paint in the exciting and beautiful manner he had seen practiced by Boudin and Jongkind. What hampered his bull-like determination was a fearful lack of rudimentary training. Nor had his own eye the sophistication to see his shortcomings. To attribute the attitude of his family to narrowness and provincial ignorance, as he so tactlessly had done with his aunt, was easier than to understand it was the rowdy, pneumatic quality of his studies that was responsible for their utter revulsion. Ferociously unpredictable, self-dramatizing and attitudinizing, he could not understand that in his own rough hands the artistic fabric of Boudin and Jongkind had crumbled. Nor did he remember his own honest reactions when first he saw Boudin's more accomplished and wonderfully controlled works in the framing shop's windows.

Impatient of slowly acquired disciplines that lay beneath that apparent ease of Boudin's and even Jongkind's creations, Oscar Claude's ambitions to match these men was a thing of inflated dimensions and emotions that rendered it vulnerable. And his nimble alacrity was predicated on an utter ignorance of the slippery artistic realm into which he precipitated himself. The fate that had already reached out to wrap Boudin in pauperish obscurity and permitted Jongkind to languish in a state of fearful and spectral persecution, had no effect on his resolve. Everything he saw he accepted with a complete confidence in his own abilities, and the entire disregard that at once was the strength and weakness of his character.

With characteristic resource and not too much scruple, late in November, 1862, Oscar Claude Monet arrived again in Paris, prepared to outwit his father. His first principle was to be without principle; and, to demonstrate one minor independence of view at the start, he had come to Paris with no example of his work to show "Cousin" Toulmouche.

The army had created a definite alteration in his attitude toward women, and Claude, for such again became his name, at first was more inclined to admire Marie, his host's "delicious" wife. But Toulmouche soon put him to work repairing the omission of a sample of his skill. The larder provided simple models. Without arranging them in any but the most commonplace manner, tight in the center of his small canvas, Claude began to paint a still life composed from a lamb chop, a kidney, two eggs, and a dish of butter.

However flippantly he began his trite task, as Claude labored his own tension rose. Soon he worked with fervor. What in fact might have been a fantastic banality he made an ingeniously treated pantry mixture, colorful, pleasing, and realistically convincing. At once Toulmouche saw that his young relative was talented.

"It's good," Toulmouche affirmed. Reservations then followed quickly: "But it's tricky! You must go to Gleyre's studio. Gleyre is the master of us all. He will teach you to make a picture."

Clearly at his most disingenuous, Claude duly called at the studio of Charles Gleyre, Toulmouche's own teacher. Though Gleyre was a master at the École des Beaux-Arts, his private studio was connected only indirectly with the school. Whereas the Beaux-Arts offered its free tuition to all who could pass examinations, a vexing inconvenience was presented by the fact that its teachers, like those at the Royal Academy in London, rotated on an irregular schedule. Pupils thus could gain no systematic guidance from a single master, but remained at the mercy of absurdly partial whims as instructors took turns coaching them.

At the École it too often was expedient to subordinate the noble exactitude and harmonious proportion of French art to a hasty obeisance before the principles of whichever master currently instructed. To avoid this confusion teachers opened private studios where students, whether from the École or not, could work under their single guidance. The free tuition of the Beaux-Arts naturally could not be applied, though, like many another master with unhappy memories of his youth, Gleyre permitted his students to be charged no more than ten francs a month, entirely for the costs of the studio. He himself took no fee.

Even so, Claude found Gleyre's studio an uninspiring sight. Located at the end of a large courtyard, the principal impression it made was of large and grimy windows facing north, each lazily bringing light into a musty and crowded interior. Some thirty or forty students each morning gathered from eight until noon, then for two hours in the afternoon. Saturdays were devoted to the much needed, but hardly successful, sweepings and cleanings. The simple furnishings were a stove to provide heat for the nude model, the platform on which to pose, stools, boxes, some fifty strongly built low chairs with backs, several score of easels, and a sprinkling of drawing boards. To this bewildering, monochrome interior, a perverse grandeur was lent by endless caricatures in charcoal and white chalk adorning walls, already covered by excesses of paint scraped from decades of palettes: a filthy and destructive habit, this latter was genuinely expressive of the students' prankish natures and their low regard for the surroundings in which they passed their days. But through a brazen effrontery to all decorative conventions it produced a multicolored decoration that was not unpleasant, and an atmosphere of wonderful decadence.

The human element present was also wildly incongruous. Some seemed able to handle the most complicated classical maneuvers with a reticent and unerring skill. Casual inspection found students of aristocratic mold, and others in whom a sense of futility was pronounced. Gray-bearded old apprentices were present, wrapped in their aura of self-aware nostalgia. To them this daily ritual had become a perennially unhappy battle before facetious commentary from the mixture of gay and irresponsible boys, all laughter, chaff, and mischief, who provided the mass of Gleyre's students. These latter were not without minor lords of misrule, wits, butts, and bullies. They divided also into further categories, as idle and industrious apprentices, or simply the clean and the dirty, the second somewhat in preponderance.

One of the more earnest students who had newly joined this class, Frédéric Bazille, almost immediately was forced to acknowledge he could not send home his sketches to Montpellier:

> My studies are generally very little presentable at the end of the week because they are very dirty and covered with caricatures made by my neighbors.
>
> M. Gleyre comes twice a week and sees each pupil, for whom he corrects a drawing or painting. From time to time he also gives out little subjects for compositions, which each of us do as well as we can.

As a prospective student, Claude Monet was introduced to Gleyre himself, a shy little man in spectacles, who on these occasions maintained an embarrassed silence and examined the student more than the proffered examples of his work. Were he approved by the master, the student might begin work immediately, though official entry only took place the Monday following. Then fees were paid: thirty francs for the entrance, to which were added three months' tuition in advance, or another thirty francs. Fifteen francs were demanded for a welcoming party at which a macabre pantomime of hospitality was performed. A song while balanced on one foot was requested of the neophyte, followed by progressively less dignified sport.

Still ambivalent in attitude, after observing these customary amenities Claude Monet took his place to begin painting the nude model posed before Gleyre's class. Under Boudin's influence he had become a passionate rhapsodist of nature, and he found this new occupation unsympathetic. Soon again, however, the use of pigments roused him, and he found himself working with as much application as spirit. He was pleased by lively and free felicities that tripped from his brush, and began to view with pride this first effort in a difficult genre.

On his next visit to the studio, Gleyre, himself a man of unhappy youth and sorrowful experience, who had lived mysteriously at Khartoum, reaffirmed that he was fundamentally quiet and modest, given to melancholy, without pedantic spirit, and disinclined to lecture his pupils. Slowly passing among them, he followed the common practice of making some alteration to the work of each, otherwise contenting himself by advising them to draw a great deal, and to prepare in advance the tones they would use, so that even while painting they remained free to devote themselves to linear beauty. If Gleyre showed any idiosyncrasy it was an anxiety that "devilish color" might go to the heads of his students. And if he ever betrayed irritation it was before the sketches of those whose preoccupation with color lessened their interest in line.

In his kindly, unostentatious way, when he came to Monet Gleyre desired to initiate this beginner into his methods. He sat down in the chair Claude had used. Firmly rooted to the spot from which his new pupil had worked, he carefully examined the study.

"Not bad," he said, holding his head on one side, and with a satisfied air. Aware of the agreeable diversity of this newest pupil's technical equipment, Gleyre immediately felt uneasy that an elusive but essential element was missing, for clearly Monet's painterly skill was superior to his intellectual penetration. No effort had been made to interpret what he saw, or to create a graceful figure from the nude model.

"Not bad at all, that thing there," Gleyre repeated. "But it is too much in the character of the model. You have before you a short thickset man; you paint him short and thickset. He has enormous feet; you render them as they are. All that is very ugly. I want you to remember, young man, that when one executes a figure one should always think of the antique. Nature, my friend, is all right as an element of study, but it offers no interest [artistically]. *Style, you see, is everything.*"

A pungent and disarming lesson from a noted instructor and highly prized painter who was attempting to be indulgent toward a new pupil, to Claude Monet the words of Gleyre were a grave shock. They conjured up the direst visions of a visual anarchy in which the faithful recording of observations, which he had learned from Boudin and Jongkind, was negated. Monet lacked entirely the intellectual development necessary to evaluate Gleyre's words as an artistic concept as valid as that other concept taught him by Boudin. He knew only that these words were a denial of everything he sought.

Limited by the shallowness of his knowledge and powers of reasoning, unaware of the art of Raphael, predisposed to dislike this studio into which his father's authoritarian manner had forced him, Claude Monet immediately felt that Gleyre's kind and gentle words had erected a barrier between them. "I saw it all. Truth, life, nature, all that which moved me, all that which in my eyes constituted the very essence of art and its only *raison d'être,* did not exist for this man. I no longer wished to remain under him."

Dangerously immature, still no more than a sensitive adolescent despite his twenty-two years, Monet's sudden flash of resentment was sufficient cause for him to depart Gleyre's studio. But though childish and arrogant, Claude had no desire to be anyone's fool. Departure from the studio would mean an end to the allowance that was his sole hope of living again in Paris. Gleyre therefore became no more than the suitable pretext for retaining his allowance. By his own account, after this first encounter with the master, Monet remained in the studio each week only long enough to execute a rough sketch from the model, and then, after inspection, to leave. At all costs determined to outwit his father, once again he had been unable to resist playing a sly game, and this inclination still worked consistently to his own disadvantage.

Even for one whose principle it was to be without principle, attendance at Gleyre's studio was a tiresome obligation. With that unique grasp of all that was most harmful to him, Claude Monet chafed at even this perfunctory obeisance to his father's will. One mitigating factor was found in the genial acquaintance he made, for even when dressed in these borrowed robes of tutelage, the gay superficiality of his outlook was both amusing and attractive. So, filled with disinterest and contempt, his devil-may-care attitude sounded precisely the correct note and gathered people to him by a curious magic.

Speaking one day with the tall, hipless Frédéric Bazille, Monet discovered that they had a mutual acquaintance at Le Havre. Further proximity to this haughty, languid, well-born and deceptively mild young man flattered Monet's vanity. Through Bazille, Monet made the acquaintance of another member of Gleyre's class, Ludovic Napoléon, Viscount Lepic, young son of the Emperor's aide-de-camp. Lepic followed all the arts with equal intensity, and after previous study with Verlet and Baron de Wappers, he showed rapid progress in painting, sculpture, watercolor painting, and engraving. Another luminary in that class, Louis Émile Villa, a former pupil of Gustave Courbet, like Bazille was a native of Montpellier, and with this fellow student at Gleyre's studio Bazille shared an apartment. Bazille, Villa, and Monet became inseparable companions, the latter two characterized by Bazille as "charming boys." "Monet has already invited me to pass a few days with his family at Le Havre next spring," Bazille reported to his own parents.

But though differences of taste were not infrequent between Gleyre and his students, no one viewed attendance with the same vexation as Monet. Most of the students, and this included those with whom Monet became most intimate, showed a genuine respect for the master. Surely this was the case with an emaciated, undersized, nervously gay tailor's son from Limoges. Auguste Renoir held the opinion that if Gleyre was of little real use to his students, at least he had the negative virtue of "leaving them pretty much to their own devices."

Renoir's existence was the familiar recital of grinding poverty, and his finances so precarious he was seen to pick up paint tubes discarded by other students, squeezing them to the last drop. He was attending Gleyre's studio in addition to regular courses at the École des Beaux-Arts, demonstrating a remarkable devotion to work. But because he had succumbed to the vice of color, in Gleyre's eyes Renoir was an outcast. The master had only glanced at his work the first week, remarking dryly, "No doubt it is to amuse yourself that you dabble in painting?"

"Why, of course," Renoir replied, more in naïve honesty than tact. "And if it did not amuse me I beg you to believe that I would not do it."

This rebuff from Gleyre had been the second that Renoir suffered. Signol, an instructor at the École des Beaux-Arts, was even more severe. Shocked by a startling red, he warned the young Renoir not to become another Delacroix.

The other members of Gleyre's studio shouted, broke windows, martyrized the model, and disturbed even the master's efforts at teaching. Renoir remained quietly and intensely at work in his corner—and they called him the revolutionary.

Given less to nervous gaiety than Renoir, and separate from Bazille's aristocratic little circle, Alfred Sisley was another student at Gleyre's studio with whom Monet found sympathetic acquaintance. Sisley was the only member of this studio whose primary interest, like that of Monet, was landscape. But also, Sisley's parents were of English origin, and belonged to the same commercial classes as the Monets and Lecadres.

Of these six students found in Gleyre's studio that winter of 1862–1863, only Monet and Sisley were occupied solely by that class. Renoir attended his regular courses at the École, and Bazille, though characterized by languor and moods of sullenness which contributed to his hauteur, was even more heavily engaged. It was principally to devote himself to the study of medicine that this lanky young brown-beard had come to Paris from Montpellier. Sisley was the person most free to rove outside the studio and sketch with Monet. Between them a special companionship of interests was established. In time, as the impressions of young men thrown together by chance became sorted out, Villa and Lepic remained more definitely the friends of Bazille, while Renoir and Sisley, drawn from the commercial classes, surrounded Monet. By a wayward piece of amusing malice, Monet, the only bridge between these two elements, became their leader.

Urged by their masters, all students streamed to the Louvre, not only to examine and study the old masters so impressively enshrined, but to make painstaking copies. The museum's rooms and corridors were a forest of easels from behind which aspiring artists of both sexes groped their way toward the glories of their profession. Tourists were forced to examine masterpieces from over these massed shoulders, taking care not to smudge wet paint on palettes, nor topple precariously perched bottles of oil and turpentine.

To make copies was not only valuable instruction, but a useful kind of industry, for they could be sold to the many and bothersome tourists. Fantin-Latour, another student, earned his meager living by precisely this tactic. Soon after his entry into Gleyre's studio, Frédéric Bazille undertook to copy a Rubens; urged by Fantin-Latour, Renoir too was introduced to this special labor at the Louvre, where he came to study the masters with pleasure. From all of this Monet stood aside. He did not need the money to be gained by painting copies, and he rejected it as an instructive exercise. To his dismay, Renoir found he had almost to force Monet to accompany him to the museum, and so contrary was Monet that once inside he would look only at landscapes, expressing active annoyance at all other pictures.

Fortunately the Louvre no longer was a unique avenue for viewing works of art. In March, 1863, not long after they became fast friends, Monet and Frédéric Bazille traveled across Paris to the Boulevard des Italiens, where at the Galerie Martinet they found a much abused exhibition of works by the little-known Édouard Manet. "You cannot know how much I learned by looking at these pictures!" Bazille exclaimed in a letter to his parents. "One session like this is worth a month of work."

Bazille's view was highly remarkable at that time when the press was universally unkind to Manet. In the *Gazette des Beaux-Arts*, Paul Mantz complained of "pictures whose patchwork of red, blue, yellow, and black was not color at all, but merely a caricature of color"—a valid objection in the contemporary context. Contrary to the methods of that time, and unlike the classic works of Titian and Rubens, whose richness of color was achieved by sonorous orchestration of many related hues, Manet was employing a system that, if not new in the annals of art, was drawn from models less close at hand. Deliberately, Manet composed his pictures of few tones, each carefully selected to offset the others. In the French capital of the Emperor Napoleon III, this was an approach highly singular, even eccentric, and the young students found it intensely exciting.

Like his presence in Paris, Claude Monet's attendance in Gleyre's studio remained a mean and shabby deception. If nothing more, it was expressive of his resolve to remain far from dour Adolphe Monet while eating his bread. Rebellious and discontented, as always, by the start of 1864 he found it was twelve months he attended in this useless and desultory fashion. But now there were demoralizing whispers in the corridors: "M. Gleyre is quite sick," Frédéric Bazille wrote to his parents. "It seems that the poor man is menaced by the loss of his sight. All his pupils are much distressed, because he is well liked. . . ."

Uncertain of continued instruction from Gleyre, despite the loyalty they demonstrated to their master, pupils streamed to other studios. Curiously, Monet remained to the last, surrounded still by Bazille, Sisley, and Renoir. The enrollment critically reduced, funds with which to pay the rent and models became short. The health of the studio thus was entwined with that of the master, as Bazille noted with acrid humor: "M. Gleyre is better; the studio is still sick." The downward slide toward insolvency could not be halted: "The studio is going to close, because of [the shortage of] money to pay models" was Bazille's final word.

Chagrined by this turn of events, Renoir sought advice from Gleyre personally, and may in fact have asked for private instruction. But that benevolent man felt unable to do more than advise Renoir and Monet to continue their work and make serious efforts apart from his supervision. In the early spring of 1864, after seventeen months of Gleyre's instruction, Claude Monet thus found himself relieved of the supervision he so much had disliked. Naturally he accepted this with a certain pervasive complacency bound to compromise any tragic view.

4. *The New Freedom*

FREEDOM had come again to Claude Monet, and it was unlike him not to celebrate. Other pupils of the defunct Gleyre studio faced their master's loss with an emotional response contrary to Monet's impulse. As always, he was more inclined to slip the traces entirely, to dash into the brilliant Easter countryside. An alluring ally was found in clear bright skies. "The admirable weather there has been for the last days, and the Easter holiday [from Medical School], have made me form a little project of which I hope you will not disapprove," Bazille explained to his family. Gay and noisy as he was in Paris, he adopted in letters a tone of exaggerated gravity that worked quiet miracles. "I am going to pass next week in the Forest of Fontainebleau with two or three comrades from the studio; I will endeavor to make a few studies of trees."

Among these comrades were Sisley and Renoir, and their goal was the little village of Chailly-en-Bière, two miles from the artists' colony at Barbizon. To paint in the open so long had been the special province of a messianic subculture—and of a few men like Corot, Boudin, and Jongkind, known to Renoir, Sisley, and Bazille principally through Monet—that the latter's ebullient influence is seen by the fact they joined this expedition. It was their first contact with nature, and believing in the good, lucid, mannerly craft taught by Gleyre, the unaccustomed brilliance of daylight caught them up in fearful struggles.

Bazille particularly felt obliged to Monet for assistance. When he returned to Paris at the end of his holiday from Medical School, Bazille reported to his parents that he had "spent eight days in the little village of Chailly, near the Forest of Fontainebleau. I was with my friend Monet, who is pretty good at landscape. He gave me some advice that helped me a good deal. I did a lot of work. . . . Two or three are not finished. I will go to Chailly a few Sundays in order to get them completed." A circumstance facilitating Bazille's jaunts was that Monet, entranced to find himself painting in a brilliant spring-time, had persuaded Renoir and Sisley to remain behind with him.

Monet's forceful figure and genial face, its contours now blurred by an undeterred growth of soft boyish beard, protected him from interference in the forest, where he worked with a new compulsion. If in the past his laziness was too apparent, after a winter beneath Paris's grim and dripping skies he found this work at which he excelled an extreme pleasure. By contrast the equally intense, nervous little figure of Renoir had about it an inherent ridiculousness. In his extreme poverty Renoir had preserved even the blue smock he wore when previously serving his apprenticeship in a porcelain-painting shop. No one strolling the forest could pass him, working furiously amid odd nervous mannerisms, without some humorous observation. Those less subtle bullied the frail little figure. One day Renoir was heavily beset, until his tormentors were driven off by a fierce man walking on a leg of wood.

"It's not badly drawn," his savior commented on seeing Renoir's effort. "But why the devil do you paint so black?"

This unexpected acquaintance was Virgile Narcisse Diaz de la Peña, known as Diaz, one of the Barbizon painters, who possibly had been attracted by Renoir's blue blouse because long before he too had begun as a painter on porcelain. Diaz took sympathetic interest in the obviously undernourished young artist, placing at his disposal a color merchant's account, so that Renoir lacked neither paints nor canvas. Diaz was equally free with instruction, urging strongly that "no self-respecting painter ever should touch a brush if he has no model under his eyes." On Diaz' advice, Renoir, already considered a revolutionary, shortly made use of brighter colors, much to the amazement of Sisley.

Aware that the principal Barbizon painters, Rousseau and Millet, had quarreled with his friend Charles Jacque, Monet appears never to have walked across those two miles of flat fields between the villages. Barbizon, however, lacked a church and belonged to the parish of Chailly-en-Bière, whose ancient timber-porched edifice stood on a bluff just behind the principal inn. Each Sunday Chailly was host to those of Barbizon's inhabitants who wished to attend Mass. But though Millet's best-known subjects were the humble devotions of peasants, there is no record that he ever attended Mass himself, nor passed under Monet's scrutiny to do so.

Toward evening each day, smoke from Barbizon's chimneys could be seen curling over the surrounding fields. Still, Millet, Rousseau, and Barye, those other members of the Barbizon group, remained a spectral presence even when known to be painting in the forest. Only the visiting Corot was glimpsed, and Renoir found that master was "always surrounded by a circle of idiots and I did not want to find myself a part of them. I liked him from a distance."

Despite enthusiasm for meeting persons of eminence, Monet seemed not to enjoy seeking acquaintance on unequal terms. Caught in a sudden downpour while attending an open-air ball in the Paris suburbs, he took refuge in a large tent, where to his surprise Jean François Millet was pointed out to him. "I admire him so much I must speak to him" was Monet's frank response. But a friend restrained him. "Don't go. Millet is a terrible man, very proud and haughty. He will insult you."

To Monet the air of the forest sweetly recommended itself. Enchanted to find himself continuously exposed to sunshine, he worked on with an ever-greater ardor. The laziness, disinterest, and emotional blight that had marked him so long passed away entirely, permitting his concentrated talents to come to bear for the first time.

April became May, and unaware of the experience their son was undergoing, at Le Havre the Monet-Lecadre family felt renewed anxieties over Claude's flight from Paris. Surely he would find a new master in whose studio he would enroll? In behalf of the family, Toulmouche wrote to his errant cousin: "It is a grave error to have so soon abandoned the studio." Mindful of the allowance which came to him through this mentor, on May 23, 1864, Monet penned a reply somewhat inclined to take a partial view of the truth: "I have not abandoned it at all. I found here a thousand charming things I was not able to resist."

At Paris, Frédéric Bazille, too, was facing an anxious moment of truth. His natural inclination had run more to noisy parties and wine-soaked dinners than to medical textbooks. After his week at Chailly, where he felt the urgency of Monet's compulsive effort, Bazille found himself with an increased affinity for painting, and none at all for medicine. Among his June examinations was one in dissection, which he faced with loathing as well as fear. His unhappy humors thus coincided with Monet's own, for since Gleyre's studio had closed, Claude retained no valid excuse for remaining in Paris. To find another master was not at all his intention, and what faced him, when finally he departed Chailly, was a return to Le Havre and his father's overfamiliar pieties.

Smooth as an eel, Monet appropriated Bazille's future to serve his own. Once again he proffered the previous year's invitation to visit with his family. One emendation to the protocols was that they would stay not at Le Havre itself but in the more retired and defensively secure bastion of Honfleur. "My voyage to Honfleur will not at all inconvenience me. I will only take the time to do two landscapes," ran Bazille's own exercise in tact, written to his family in Montpellier. Monet, meanwhile, prepared to leave Chailly, assured that in this aristocratic presence the storm of his homecoming could be evaded.

For two tired and melancholy young men the river steamer to Le Havre provided a pleasantly sylvan interlude. Despite original low spirits, they soon derived a renewed pleasure from the scenic delights of their native land. Occasionally the eye was caught by a church tower rising lazily off enclosing hills, or the dotting of high poplars, like so many exclamation points accentuating the horizon. Everywhere they passed through the varied green of fertile France, until, at Rouen, where the riverboat stopped to take on fuel and recharge boilers, they disembarked to investigate Gothic marvels. First they came on the cathedral, replete with its new cast-iron *flèche* intended to compete with Notre-Dame's own. A few streets away they discovered a Delacroix hung in the city museum.

Late that afternoon the refueled steamboat continued to Le Havre. Monet and Bazille disembarked, before crossing the Seine's broad estuary to a smaller, more ancient port. "As soon as we arrived in Honfleur, we looked for landscape motifs," wrote Bazille. "They were easy to find, because the countryside is a paradise. One could not find richer or more beautiful trees; everywhere cows and horses wander freely. The sea, or rather the Seine, broadening out, gives a delightful horizon to these masses of green."

Accommodation was of secondary importance. Invited to august chambers in the Rue Fontenelle, Bazille found that Monet proposed instead to rent two rooms from a baker. "We eat at the farm of St.-Siméon, situated on the cliff a little above Honfleur; it is there that we are working and where we pass our days," noted Bazille. They awoke at five in the morning, working well into dusk. "I make progress, and that's all," Bazille commented after a few days of this rigorous routine. "One asks no more. I hope to be more content after three or four years of painting."

Together they visited with "Wanner," the mutual friend whose name had brought them together in the Gleyre studio. They also lunched with the Monet-Lecadre family, who, as expected, were tactful before this alien presence, and impressed Bazille by their cultivation.

Pleased by Bazille's impeccable dress and manners, and delighted to find their son with a friend who was not an outcast, Monet's family urged Frédéric to return in August. Bazille actually felt some em-

71

barrassment refusing the urgent sincerity of this invitation. But though favorably inclined toward the Monet-Lecadre family, he could not overlook their restrained hostility toward Claude, or their uneasiness over the course he followed. Bazille even felt called on to warn his friend that a rupture seemed possible. To Montpellier, however, he reported in his *bon enfant* style the brighter side of his visit: "They possess at Ste.-Adresse, near Le Havre, a charming property, which seems very much like [our home at] Méric. . . ."

Aware of the calm with which his family received him, Claude now prolonged the stay at Ste.-Adresse. Together the young men passed their days in the sun, painting on the flintstone beach wrapped around the Pointe de la Hève. Monet sketched a composition of oppositions, employing the mass of rugged bluffs to hold firm a canvas given over to the trembling of glistening afternoon sea. Also looking into the sun before his easel, Bazille essayed the same subject, doubling the size and horizontal proportion of his friend's canvas, but demonstrating timidity by softening tonal contrasts.

His vigorous little work completed sooner than Bazille's, Monet added to it the small boat Jongkind inserted into views of that harbor. This done, he posed for a figure in Bazille's effort. And if perhaps neither painter achieved a mesmeric piece of stylization, both demonstrated boldness and an impressively uncompromising knowledge of the sterner schools of painting coming forward in France.

Now, at last, at Honfleur and Ste.-Adresse the summer of 1864, Claude Monet's life and art joined forces consistently. Each further step is revealed by his canvases, and in the freshness of this dawn a young artist of considerable and even surprising skill stands revealed. The still life of lamb chop and kidney, painted for Toulmouche, now assumes more significance, for though Monet's direct training and influences had come from Boudin, Jongkind, and Gleyre, a realization impossible to ignore is that he long had turned his face in another direction.

Those fleeting glimpses of Gustave Courbet at the Brasserie des Martyrs had not been merely a yearning after false and wasting glamour. Those earliest months passed alone in Paris, had seen Monet transform himself into the most abject of followers, imbibing

as much the generic mid-nineteenth-century socialism that characterized Courbet's subjects as that master's abrasive handling of pigment.
And as is the case with so many young artists caught in the toils of
another personality, Monet's final token of surrender to Courbet was
his signature, carefully patterned on the evenly spaced back-scrawl of
Courbet.

Gustave Courbet's art had been formed in the debris of an earlier
period, when France was slowly recovering from the fantastic and
melancholy dream of another Napoleon's supremacy. In the hostility
and civil tumult that followed defeat, all French arts had developed the strange, feverish romanticism seen in the melancholy
of de Musset, Chopin, and Delacroix's penumbral illustrations to
Dante, Byron, and Shakespeare. Napoleon had been to Moscow and
come back without his army; the aftermath was apathy, discontent,
and frustrating failure, a strange twilight world of Gothic romance
and abnormal imagery, from which emerged the men of 1830. The
ghastly reigns of all the false messiahs, each by personal intuition
destined to lead France to a new "realism," had begun. And though
himself of a later generation, it was among this garrulous band that
Gustave Courbet held rank as a very senior *enfant terrible*.

Possessed of wide contacts in the French social system, Bazille
already had made the acquaintance of Courbet. At Montpellier the
previous autumn he was given a letter of introduction, armed with
which he called at the famous studio in the Rue Hautefeuille. Significantly, Bazille made no effort to extend this acquaintance to
Monet. Just as he had done the following January, 1864, when at
a dinner at the Mamignards' he met Édouard Manet: Bazille prized
the association for himself.

If nothing more, the enthusiasms of these two young men were
shared, and much in Monet's first effort at the shore reflected Gustave Courbet. The arbitrarily darkened sky, so out of keeping with
carefully observed middle distances, was as much Courbet-inspired as
the backward-sloping copperplate form of his signature.

The departure for Paris of Frédéric Bazille left behind a deceptive
air of good feeling. Still at Ste.-Adresse, after a shaky, overemphatic
start, Monet now handled the elusive idiom of his shore subjects
splendidly. He hacked out a second view of weather-beaten break-
waters beneath looming cliffs, seen with a neater fusion of abrasive-

ness and poetic attention to detail. Another small boat perched incongruously high on the sea, and was painted with values that indicated it to be a late addition. But again one is conscious of both a touching poetic melancholy and that the artist is experiencing an obsessive delight in his medium.

For a roughly trained lad of twenty-three, it must be admitted, despite reservations, Monet's success with these canvases was considerable. His dulcet tones worked unspectacular miracles. Faults were not due to any lack of invention but to the vividness of his dramatic imagination and an abundance of inspiration, which drove him away from his true strength in clarity of observation. As he worked, orderly techniques, and even Courbet's influence, gave way before instinctive procedures. Feeling their surge, he began to explore larger canvases. A preliminary oil study depicted the mouth of the Seine and the lighthouse at Honfleur—a subject Jongkind was painting at just that moment.

Again based on Honfleur, where he awaited Bazille's quick return, on July 15 Monet coyly reminded his friend of all he missed at the shore. By its wandering nature and boldness of expression the letter well characterizes his vigorous undisciplined mind, hinting at the qualities which already gave him an ascendancy over friends:

I wonder a little what you are able to do in Paris in such beautiful weather. Here, my friend, it is marvelous, and every day I discover something more beautiful; it is enough to drive one mad. I have such a desire to do everything that my head is bursting with it!

Decidedly it is horribly difficult to make a thing complete in all aspects; I know that there seems no other sort but the people who are content even to get close. Ah well! my good friend, I shall just struggle, scrape off, and start over, because one can do that which one sees and can understand, because it seems to me that when I see it as though it were already done and written out; all that must be done is to put it down on canvas when one is working at it! All that proves it is not necessary to think about it: it is by the strength of one's observation and reflections that one succeeds. Also by working and working away continually.

Do you make progress? Yes, I am sure of it! But what I am certain of is that you do not work enough, and not in the best way. It is not with gay blades like your [friend] Villa and the others that you can work. It would be better to be alone, and yet, all alone there are some things that one cannot fathom, because at bottom it is very difficult and a terrible job.

Have you done your big nude figure? I have plans for some stunning things when I go over to Ste.-Adresse, and to Paris in the winter. Do you ever go into the country? And above all, come see me, not later than August first.

While awaiting you, I shake your hand warmly.

Your good friend,
CLAUDE MONET

P.S. Saint-Siméon is admirable just now, and one often speaks of Monsieur Bazille.

Whatever Bazille's plans when he departed Honfleur, everything had changed when at Paris he discovered that for a second time he had failed his medical examinations. "It causes me much pain, above all because of you," he wrote immediately to his father. "For myself I only regret that I have lost so much time that I would have had great need to employ for my painting, in studies which will never render me service. I worked very hard, I assure you. It was my dissection that made me fail." Bazille returned to Montpellier, where he sought his parents' consent to a final abandonment of medicine. After long hesitation he received their agreement. The joyous news was communicated to Monet, who replied from Honfleur:

I hope that you are doing a lot of work; you must do exactly that, and seriously, now that your family permit you to abandon medicine. We are in great numbers at this moment in Honfleur. . . . Boudin and Jongkind are here; we are getting on marvelously. I regret very much that you are not here, because in such company there is a lot to be learned and nature begins to grow beautiful; everything turns yellow and grows more varied; altogether it's wonderful. I want to tell you that I am sending a flower piece to the Rouen exhibition; there are some most beautiful at this time of the year. Do one yourself, because this is, I think, an excellent thing to paint.

Awaiting Bazille at Honfleur, Monet battled the change of seasons, problems of craftsmanship, and the emergence of his own vision. But if his presence at Gleyre's studio had been deception, since the closing of that studio his position had been one of open vulnerability. For if he deceived his father still, he did so with a conspicuous lack of stealth, shuttling between Honfleur, Le Havre, and Ste.-Adresse, working without guidance from an important master, and beside the same "idiots" as before.

His family doubtless were aware of the cleverness shown by Claude's recent works, and his new-found ardor possibly they could even applaud. But to the Monet-Lecadre family all this remained irrelevant and embarrassing, like the impromptu performances of a clever child who does not know when to stop and refuses to be told. They did not wish to become accustomed to such performances, for Claude soon would be twenty-four. Despite their undoubted power, his strange views of the seashore were a kind of secular blasphemy before which his family gave no appearance of an unseemly rejoicing.

His allowance was in danger, as Bazille earlier had warned, and Claude himself felt unable to placate his family in any other way than to hope for a return of that lanky friend in whose presence all had been more peaceful. Exploring the dark recesses of his predicament, Monet realized his only hope lay in sales of his pictures. Caricatures once had brought him an independent income, and the gold had corroded in his pockets. He must begin again, on a more elevated level of taste, and this need lit within him a great irrational hope: he must force the doors of the Salon.

Toward this single goal he began to mobilize all his resources. His flower picture, sent to the Rouen exhibition, had been a first fund-raising move in this campaign. The second essential was Bazille's presence, to stave off Adolphe Monet's inevitable ultimatum. Until the Salon was opened to him he must retain his allowance:

DEAR BAZILLE,
   Really, are you dead? I hope not, but you are absolutely the most ignoble lazy bugger I have ever encountered. Every day I wait for you to arrive by the evening train, or the Havre steamer. Do me the pleasure to write to me by return of post. If I do not receive a reply I shall no longer know by what saints to curse. I cannot remain here eternally.

In the presence of Boudin, who in the evenings sometimes played dominoes with him at the St.-Siméon farm, and more especially beside Jongkind, Claude worked with fiery ardor on an enlarged version of his lighthouse picture. An uncontrolled clatter of fishing boats and sunshine falling on distant water and sails enlivened it, until one heard sharp winds and the cry of gulls. The final product was a flashy showpiece full of daring artifice and visual horseplay. Rounding the corner of flat detail were stunningly apt passages, created with enormous passion and personality. The important consideration, of course, was whether this passion might prove commercially exploitable.

The fury of his work is impressive, and again one wonders how deep this sincerity ran in a young man so given to play-acting. Despite brilliant and florid passage work in canvases tendentially derived from those of Jongkind and Courbet, Monet had in fact become a voice in search of a song. His taste for elaborate, and latterly for sweeping, technical effects overlay a basic simplicity of vision. Though he painted with a mounting rhythmical excitement, the divisions of his pictures were simple, and a defective sense of three-dimensional form, stunted through his lack of assiduous studio training, gave to everything a curious one-sided flatness. Arriving from a different pole of creative activity, he was seen to be taking up a position not far from that already occupied by Édouard Manet, whose exhibition on the Boulevard des Italiens he had visited with Bazille the previous spring.

The vision of Manet's flat-toned canvases now floated back to Monet, and exhausting what he had taken from Boudin, Jongkind, and Courbet, again he helped himself to another's originality. Like any student confused between the style of an artist and his subjects, Monet was at pains to employ Manet's motifs, especially those found in *The Kearsarge and the Alabama,* illustrating an incident in the American Civil War that shortly before had taken place off the French coast. The extraordinary tone of the water in Manet's picture, and the appearance of a small fishing vessel at one side, were elements he found irresistible.

From doggedly honest visions of the seashore painted with an abrasiveness reminiscent of Gustave Courbet, and passionately brushed visions of the Seine estuary imitative of the wildly impasted compositions of Jongkind, Claude Monet switched his attention to solidly stroked flat tones in the manner of Édouard Manet. Ships were disposed with a nod at Japanese balances, and spray tossed under their bows was outlined in dense whites frequently touched over by the palette knife. On small canvases he formed fishing vessels

77

dipping far into a swell, their dark upturned hulls throwing water clean and white against the turquoise sea. Groups of these were depicted heading out in a mass, all observed from the same high angle that had characterized Manet's *Kearsarge and Alabama*. In what must have been a daze of drunken acquisitiveness, he finally appropriated the very fishing vessel that had appeared in Édouard Manet's picture for the most ambitious of his own!

Such wonderfully casual feats of magic intrigued Monet, until, in a curious inversion of tribute, at this moment when he all but abandoned the delicate tonalities learned from Boudin and Jongkind, he seized upon Jongkind himself for a little sketch portrait. Over a still life no longer worthy of preservation he brushed a rapid impression of Jongkind that was a crudely conceived pastiche of Manet. In his velvet-collared greatcoat, quietly smoking a long-stemmed Dutch pipe, the penumbral mood of that artist's melancholy reached canvas surprisingly well.

An essay into an unfamiliar genre, this casual portrait had obvious failings. Crudely applied strokes by which Monet wished to indicate Jongkind's hands failed in their purpose. The globs of pigment never assumed any of the roundness nor sense of weight and mass present in living hands. Lack of the studio work he had found so irrepressibly tiresome had left him with a defective eye, and the fault grew permanent. Jongkind's feet, too, are absurdly drawn, demonstrating a childish failure of proportion. And everywhere this small study's boldness of execution is overassertive. Brought to bear on any but the outdoor genre he adored, Monet's skills are seen in their true limitations.

Another work in a similar vein, a small-scale portrait of Dr. Leclenché, found him manipulating his tools with greater skill, though in his desire to concentrate more on his subject's facial characteristics, Claude soon made the head overlarge for a small body. This disparity once again his own eye was too untrained to see. Yet, despite failures attributable to his lack of rudimentary studio skills, this little canvas successfully conveyed an acute sense of personality, expressed in everything from the position of the hands to the characteristic upturned toe of one foot.

Whether this second portrait brought him any pecuniary advantage, in his own mind Monet made infinite progress by adopting Édouard Manet as a new model on which to pattern himself. He enjoyed what he did, and despite an uncertain future the new feeling for oppositions of color and tone blooming within himself brought a deceptive sense of security. Had he required confirmation, that too soon was found when Amand Gautier, who visited Le Havre, brought Monet to the attention of his own patron, the Le Havre shipowner Louis Gaudibert, who purchased two small studies.

Suddenly all seemed well in that autumn of 1864. He felt certain he was advancing, and he attributed this to the fact that he now worked alone. A letter to Boudin, painting at Trouville, showed his exuberant state:

> I am still at Honfleur. I am really having a great deal of trouble in leaving. Besides, it is so beautiful at present that I must take advantage of it. Also, I have wrought myself into a fury in order to make enormous progress before returning to Paris. I am alone at present, and, frankly, I work all the better for it. That good Jongkind left about three weeks ago.
>
> I should have been to see you before this if it had not been for my zeal for work. But on the first day that the weather forces me to stop, I shall go spend a day with you before leaving for Paris. I spent several days at Havre. I had two panels to do for M. Gaudibert. Gautier also did four or five for him, and M. Gaudibert asked me to beg of you to visit him when you go to Havre. He would be very glad, I believe, if you would do one or two panels for him.
>
> In my haste, my dear friend, I clasp your hand with all my heart.
>
> CLAUDE MONET
>
> My greetings to your wife. How the devil do you manage when there are no more little ladies on the beach?

The spectacle of their son working with such seriousness of purpose the Monet-Lecadre family found admirable morally perhaps, but realistically somewhat wearing. All this painting out of doors was a pleasant occupation, but the boy was approaching his twenty-fourth birthday. He had done abandoned and untutored work since he was eighteen, and little hope could be held out for it. The products of his labors were unsalable, the proof of which was that he had sold nothing but two small panels to Louis Gaudibert. However seriously Claude worked, he lived on the allowance given him each month by his father—an allowance which, as time passed, it became more irksome to give him. To the Monet-Lecadre family Claude's manner of living was highly injudicious, and ought to be discouraged. Convenient grounds were that he no longer worked under the direction of a master, as had been agreed. However much deception had been practiced in Paris, with some justice Claude could point out that for seventeen months he *had* worked under that estimable Swiss painter Charles Gleyre. Adolphe Monet's idea of an agreement, however, was of a less accommodating sort.

And even when Adolphe Monet indulged in what only intermittently was a polemic, attempting to demonstrate the folly of his son's wasted years, he met temporizing candor side by side with Machiavellian craft. For the truth was his son was not in search of organized human bliss, but only a shallow complacency sufficient to permit him to enjoy his allowance until the Salon's doors were forced open.

For the first time Claude Monet's existence took on a hectoring Old Testament quality. His object was only to exist until the Salon doors sprang ajar. But by October the situation that had smoldered all summer, since Claude's return from Chailly, grew more acute. Bazille remained at Montpellier, sheltering in the warm southern sun with his own more obliging family. *Bon enfant* always, his was the tact to do what Claude attempted disdainfully and from necessity. On the chance that Bazille might prove able to sell pictures to Courbet's famous patron, Alfred Bruyas, of whom Monet once had made a little caricature portrait, he shipped three canvases south:

> Among these three canvases there is a simple study that you saw me begin; it is entirely done from nature. You will find perhaps a certain relationship with Corot, but it is without any sort of imitation that this has come about. The subject and especially the calm and misty effect are the only reason for it. I have done it as conscientiously as possible, without thinking of any painter.
>
> I am deeply troubled by all the problems that I give you, and also your father, who does not know me and has been so good as to wish to assist. Also, you know very well, dear friend, that I will not forget your kindnesses. . . .

Measured cautious words that they were, Monet's letter to Bazille did not hide the anxieties that prompted his action. Nor, despite their evident good will, were the elder and younger Bazille able to interest Bruyas in his pictures. Increasingly aware of the precariousness of relations with his own family, troubled, and alone, Claude Monet continued to work into the autumn chill, until the smoldering fury of that summer burst into flame. In overblown petulance Adolphe Monet provoked a scene of dramatic significance: "Last night, at Ste.-Adresse," Monet wrote to Bazille, "I was told to go, and not to return too soon."

5. *A Nervous Winter*

THAT HECTORING Old Testament quality his existence assumed never left Monet. Cast out by his family, uncertain, still dependent on the allowance they sent him, in November, 1864, he brought back to Paris the fruits of his summer at the shore. Only by forcing the doors of the Salon could the raggedness of his prospects be repaired. But even before he could attempt this irrational act, for which a meager training left him unequipped, Monet was obliged to pass through the winter. Until April, when the jury met, he must concentrate on mere survival and employ the most careful hypocrisy before his family.

To Frédéric Bazille also this winter brought new difficulties. Before him lay the long task of remolding himself from dilettantish medical student to professional artist. Aware of Monet's plight, and filled with his own Protestant integrity, Bazille was too charmingly genuine to stand aside. Perhaps he also foresaw how heavily he would be forced to rely on his more experienced friend, for, unable to assist Monet materially, Bazille suggested they share a studio. Theoretically, each would halve his expenses; should any catastrophe descend in the months ahead, as Monet had every right to expect, they would be better able to meet it.

In November, 1864, Bazille gave notice at the quarters he shared with Villa in the Rue de Vaugirard. Familiar with the Left Bank surrounding the School of Medicine, he discovered a studio vacant in the little Rue de Furstenberg, near the École des Beaux-Arts. Whatever disadvantages lay in this area, so remote from Monet's interests, they were neutralized by the glamour of residing in the building associated with Eugène Delacroix. The abode they were about to rent was possibly the same from which, while students of Gleyre, they had watched Delacroix at work in his specially constructed garden studio. Visible, and fervently watched, had been the hand and brush of the master, rarely more.

Monet's interests had never resided on the Left Bank, so far from the Brasserie des Martyrs and the studios of Courbet and Amand Gautier, all located between the Bourse and Gare St.-Lazare. Only recently, seated on the terrace of a café in that region, Monet had heard a powerful voice thunder, "Waiter! A bock beer for the Master of Ornans!" He gave a startled swivel of the head. There was only one "Master of Ornans," Gustave Courbet, born in that Franche-Comté town. Courbet, in fact, was seated behind him, about to plunge his black beard into the beer's fresh foam. The two artists spoke, and, already possessed of so large a mutual acquaintanceship, they parted friends.

Despite the momentary exuberance of such an encounter, for Monet that winter of 1864 had grown singularly uneasy. Still a spoiled child, he felt bleakly adult. All his richly and imaginatively susceptible nature was willingly aroused by a tall dark girl, whose childish bloom gave her the entrancing appearance of a choirboy cheekily dressed as a fetching brunette. A feminine, enigmatical, and slightly mocking smile contributed to devastating charm. Nearly eighteen, her figure mature and well-formed, Camille Léonie Doncieux was innocently coltish and touchingly vulnerable.

Through the dark winter months of December and January this tousled cherub in grown-up dresses fascinated the depressed and unhappy Monet. Then, on January 15, 1865, Camille's eighteenth birthday, Claude Monet and Frédéric Bazille moved into their Rue de Furstenberg studio, and the last necessary element of drama fell neatly into place.

A studio, two bedrooms, and a toilet comprised this new abode. But it had charm in its design and the paneling of its walls, much light from large windows, and the contrast of bare chestnut trees in the garden visible from one side and the little Place de Furstenberg from the other. Here was a place where two young artists might be content. Yet from the moment they settled under the same roof it became obvious that Claude Monet and Frédéric Bazille lived on a different scale and in a different scope.

Frédéric had not been formed by the purely commercial world in which the rebellious Claude grew to manhood. Indeed, he seemed hardly aware of its existence. Nor did Bazille feel need to rebel against a society which had placed him in the singularly agreeable environment to which his temperament, talents, and social gifts were perfectly adapted. Disposed from birth toward a gentle intellectual life, he found his existence happy; and his superior education, so unlike the rude schooling which Monet had fled at Le Havre, made him conversant with everything current in Paris.

Like his height, the mild air of self-importance with which Frédéric moved set him apart in a crowd. Extravagance was a part of his nature. His voice could remain gentle in the face of frantic provocation, and anyone who had seen him at a party retained a stubborn faith in his madness. His patrician face sprouted a variety of experimental mustaches and beards, and his clothes were specially constructed to drape a narrow-chested form. Despite his "madness," and facial expressions that ranged from uncomprehending idiocy to a smiling self-satisfied ballerina impersonation, Frédéric retained a delicate air and spoke in careful circumlocutions. Against all of this Claude's earthy urbanisms, and frequently mournful and manic mien, made rude contrast.

All the force of that contrast was felt immediately, as Monet found himself immersed in the new music of Richard Wagner and theories plucked from every art. To visits from Frédéric's musical friends he set the balance of calls from Pissarro, who brought with him the strange figure of Paul Cézanne. Even Gustave Courbet visited the two in their Rue de Furstenberg studio, partaking of refreshment and encouraging them in their work.

Talk that filled the air that winter, and the matters touched on, though perhaps laborious stuff and with traces of youthful omnipotence, interested Monet less than formerly. These callow voices of intellect rang out with fervor and throbbed with ineffable rapture. But Monet was little equipped to follow them, or appreciate a weary echo of words. For Monet private problems loomed larger, inclining to blot out other considerations. His position, at the mercy of his father's threats, whims, and impeccable moral sentiments, remained one of constant insecurity. This was depressing enough while remittances arrived from Le Havre. And if they stopped? This life with Bazille had involved him in an extravagance that was surely unwise.

What feelings, or designs, toward Camille motivated him we cannot know, and indeed, as in most such cases, it is doubtful whether the persons themselves were aware of any direct course. This lovely child had been born at Lyon, the city of Claude's maternal ancestry. One wonders what unspoken impact this knowledge, and her trace of accent, exerted on the unstable and unloved youth. Camille lived with her parents and sister Geneviève, who, eleven years her junior, had been born after they came to Paris. A hardheaded former merchant, Charles Claude Doncieux supported his family entirely from the income of his investments. Indeed, the family had further expectations of wealth, for his wife, Léonie Françoise Manéchalle, had been named sole heir by Antoine Pritelly, a relative of enormous financial resources, who had been *receveur de finance*.

As the elder daughter of these fortunate people, Camille had received a careful and good upbringing, conformable to her station and their expectations. The attention she gave her coiffure, the jet-black lovelocks she combed onto her cheeks, and the number and variety of her frocks bespoke the easy frivolity of life for which she was intended. And though Monet too could feel he was not from the lowest orders of society, Camille was surely a person more on Bazille's level than his own, a realization that added subtly to the thrill he experienced.

He must have told this young girl he was an artist who had hopes of exhibiting at the Salon. In her engaging way she perhaps expressed some wish to see his paintings, all those canvases from the previous summer at Honfleur and St.-Adresse, stacked in the Rue de Furstenberg studio. Monet guided Camille to the Place Furstenberg, decorated by its solitary gas lamp. Together they walked past the outer door in the corner of the square, under the arcade that passed the inner court, then up a dark staircase to the studio.

When in time she came down, Camille Léonie Doncieux had learned something of art, of Claude Monet, and of the passions existing within him that could set her aflame. Her own will having dissolved before the urgency of his, Camille found herself desperately in love. However lightly Monet started on that little journey, it was the beginning of something new in his life.

Well hidden from old Adolphe Monet, whose allowance was required until the Salon opened, the affair sweetened the dark winter months of early 1865. An overtone of concentrated impudence, even sly mockery, cannot be dissociated from the fact that Claude now had contrived to make use of all the persons of his intimate acquaintance toward one end: the Salon. Adolphe Monet provided funds, and was delicately spared knowledge of infractions that he might employ for his own polemic purposes. Bazille helped to provide a roof, and was insurance against Adolphe Monet's less pleasant humors. Camille's affection, and physical warmth, added splendors to the miseries of that nervously exhausting winter. She contributed to it also those brief moments of courage and strength desperate people require to keep their spirits up even when their hearts are not filled with an unstained love. For, in truth, like Adolphe Monet and Bazille, Camille was being used to serve a purpose far from any she understood.

Whatever sort of emotional existence Monet had known before this winter, it is certain that never before had he found himself in the situation he did after his seduction of Camille. Sweet and sensitive, hers was a girlish vulnerability that involved her heart in every indiscretion. As he grew to know Camille better, Claude became aware how the expression of her face, for all its innocence, carried a suggestion of sadness. At times her childlike features, candid brow, and gentle eyes were less in evidence than the lower regions of her face—the strong jaw, brilliant red lips, and fine white teeth. Even then her long black lashes sharply accented clear dark eyes, which—closed in moments of passion, the lashes gleaming against soft sallow skin—gave an expression of exquisite tenderness.

Camille was lovely. But so deeply was Claude involved in his own dreams, perpetually oscillating between ambition and despair, he seemed unable to feel any permanence in their relationship. His disengaged attitude itself aroused in Camille a possessiveness. Whichever of them was truly in love, it is also true that, having been starved for feminine affection since earliest youth, Monet was aware of a deep response within himself. Camille attracted him and pleased him, and despite her eighteen years, hers were the arts by which a man's heart is softened. Enigmatically aware of the honesty of her emotions and the simple, selfless quality of the love she gave him, Monet felt responsible and perhaps a little guilty.

Long surrounded by a band of admiring friends, even the "idiots" to whom his aunt took exception, the unrestrained sympathy he derived from this young girl was a happy novelty, and one which he had never so much required. Camille was too young, and too unworldly, to know what situation faced him that winter, or how irrational was his single great hope of forcing the Salon's doors. In the sudden unreasoning rush of her feelings she believed in him. Her doubts were all reconciled in the flush of love she felt in his arms.

She had found a mate to whom she would cling. And once more though this made the problems of their relationship exclusively his, the existence of Camille, the affection she gave him, the grace of her person, and the pleasure and assurance of her company helped Claude Monet to forget the hectoring anxieties of that winter. This new and welcome experience more than made up for the fact that theirs was a startling misalliance between two unstable and emotional adolescents, each clinging to the other for support.

However fiendishly calculated his conduct was that winter, the single prospect that lay before Claude Monet remained the same that faced every young artist in France: the Salon. For those accepted by its jury that mighty institution opened the road to fame, prosperity, and all the rewards bestowable in a formidable bureaucratic maze. Collectors would purchase his works, dealers vie to exhibit them, journalists seek his opinions, students flock to him for counsel. Receiving day for the Salon of 1865 fell in April; and that exhibition would be the ultimate arbiter of his fortunes.

When first he journeyed to Paris six years before, Monet had noted at the Salon an absence of sea painters. In the years since, this condition had not altered. The moment had come for him to profit from his observation by sending before the jury seascapes painted at Honfleur. The decision long made, Monet awaited the passage of time with as good heart as was made possible by the encouragement of his friends, the confidence of Bazille, and the sweet persuasions of Camille.

Distractions were plentiful. Under his daily instruction Bazille was becoming a methodical workman, who ventured from the studio more rarely during precious winter daylight. "I have not been to the theater once in the last eight days," he wrote to Montpellier, obviously astonished by his own application. After dark Bazille felt more free, frequently dining with his kinsman Commandant Lejosne, aide-de-camp to Marshal Magnan, who soon invited Monet to a place at his table.

One of the exquisite sanctums of the Second Empire, artists, writers, and persons of note were always present in Lejosne's dining room. Met here, Edmond Maître soon became a close friend to Bazille, and others found at Lejosne's table include Aimé Millet, Victor Massé, Baudelaire, Barbey d'Aurevilly, Nadar the photographer, Henry Cazalis, and even Léon Gambetta, a future President of France. Here too Bazille and Monet again encountered the attractive, dandified, sandy-haired figure of Édouard Manet, who repaid their enthusiasm for his works by visiting the two artists in their Rue de Furstenberg studio.

With the example of Lejosne before them, Monet and Bazille held similar court at the Rue de Furstenberg. Maître, Courbet, Manet, Fantin-Latour, Renoir, Sisley, Pissarro, and, more rarely, Cézanne were among their guests, and Monet, pleased by this gilded existence, saw himself entering on the celebrity that would be his in fuller measure after his seascapes were exhibited at the Salon. Then, of course, further important works would be required to consolidate his fame at the next Salon. Even before submission day for the Salon of 1865, therefore, Monet's nimble brain turned over schemes for 1866. Some crisp invention was required that by sheer impressiveness would overwhelm alike public and critics: a profound and masterly work, entirely apt and beautiful, that by its imaginative scope would forever make his name renowned.

Immersed in this strange twilight world of imagined future, it perhaps was inevitable that real and unreal should suffer confusion. A compulsive competitor, Monet determined to stake everything on a wild scheme for which, by temperament and lack of substantial training, he was singularly unfitted. Impressed by Édouard Manet's large *Dejeuner sur l'herbe,* rejected at the Salon of 1863, and seen by a uniformly derisive public at the notorious Salon des Refusés, Claude Monet, his manner of painting now a frank imitation of Édouard Manet's, determined to do a similar composition on an even larger scale. He would give the studio-bound Manet a lesson in painting, for he planned to take longer flights and succeed where the older man failed.

Nothing could have been more dangerous. With almost no experience painting the human figure, Monet intended to surpass his model. Nor would he stoop to the employment of obviously unreal studio landscape, as Manet had done, nor make the mistake of combining his outdoor landscape with figures painted in flat studio light. Instead, so far as possible, he would execute his huge canvas out of doors, gaining thereby a consistency of vision sufficiently potent to flood the Salon's rooms with sunlight. Again, to escape the musty studio traditions that had been Manet's central error, he wished to avoid the juxtaposition of clothed and nude figures. Claude Monet intended to paint a realistic picnic luncheon of fashionably dressed Parisians.

At the end of March a return of good weather saw him depart for the familiar forest near Chailly. Left behind in the Rue de Furstenberg studio, Bazille's assigned task was to ship Monet's large seascapes to the Salon on the appropriate day, paying submission fees on his friend's behalf. A promise also was extracted that Frédéric would come to Chailly, to pose for male figures. For female figures provision already had been made. When her lover departed for Chailly, Camille accompanied him with a collection of lavish costumes, abandoning her parents to a state of outrage.

A handsome cheerful couple, preoccupied with themselves and the task before them, Claude Monet and Camille Doncieux arrived at the Cheval-Blanc, Chailly-en-Bière's principal inn, located at the village center where a country lane to Barbizon struck off the main Paris-Fontainebleau road. Inconspicuous as were these chosen headquarters, they were not hiding in any normal sense. Camille's break with her parents had been accomplished neatly and cleanly, and with finality. They did not pursue her.

Built as a relay station during the era when fast coaches charged to Paris from Fontainebleau's royal château, the two-storied, stone-fronted inn surrounded an elaborate cobblestoned yard where horses once had been rested, fed, and readied in harness. Now it was the quieter domain of the elderly père Paillard and his wife, and the dining room and lounge these hosts provided on street level afforded somewhat Spartan amenities. In a passage behind, the curved stair led creakingly to a succession of red-tiled, low-ceilinged chambers equipped with oversized beds. In these the scattering of neat white marble fireplaces hinted at theatrical contrivance, but actually survived from the inn's bustling and courtly past.

A different clientele now made merry at the Cheval-Blanc, which served as seasonal headquarters for artists overflowing the meager accommodations available at Barbizon. On rainy days they flourished in the dining room, an element at once gay, discordant, and unkempt, playfully sketching masterpieces across paneled walls. Fortunately that crowded season had not yet begun when Monet and Camille arrived, and by contrast, they were guests inclined to create an aloof well-dressed atmosphere. Mad young artist though his family considered him, at twenty-five Monet was not a scruffy hobgoblin, but a handsome, even graceful man, and Camille fluttered elegantly on his arm. One might have been forgiven for thinking them on honeymoon.

Unlike Barbizon, which directly abutted an arm of the forest, Chailly was two miles from the nearest point where deep woods swallowed the Paris-Fontainebleau road. The necessity of daily long walks, burdened by canvases and equipment, quickly became a tiresome tribulation. Yet as he entered the forest, tramping through russet and green undergrowth, Claude Monet always felt in his real element. The sense of assurance he experienced before nature permitted him to exploit brilliantly a section of forest interior on a canvas of large proportions. No mere sketch in an ordinary sense, this bold work studied an ancient spreading oak through whose extended branches splashed gaudy yellow foliage and brilliant blue sky. Easily his most successful forest study to date, its smartness and bounce of execution added a shrill harmony all its own.

He had captured the tone and magical flashing effect that he wished to preserve in his final great work. Unlike Manet's cold study of formalized figures, Monet's real subject was just such floods of light, filtering through trees. Figures were no more than a necessary medium of expression, the objects on which his dappling inundations might fall with explosive effect. On another canvas of larger proportions he began to consider their arrangement. Unlike Édouard Manet, he felt no need to derive a tightly knit group from a classic source. His people would be disposed naturally, in uneven balance around the central light mass contributed by a white cloth spread on the forest floor. A dozen figures would stand, sit by the cloth, spread themselves on the ground, or lean against the tree provided by his forest study. The Salon clearly in his mind, he hoped to emulate the faultless elegance, taste, and control of a well-known portrait group of the Empress Eugénie by Franz Xavier Winterhalter, considered Sir Thomas Lawrence's successor and an artist who practiced as court portraitist to most Continental royalty.

Eager to proceed, Monet and Camille impatiently awaited Bazille. But after he shipped Monet's two seascapes to the Salon jury, and had paid for the submission tickets, Bazille himself was short of funds: too short, in fact, for the necessary expenditure of a stay at Chailly. Not famous as a letter writer, he remained silent and unseen, leaving his plight painfully misunderstood at Chailly, where an obsessive venture waited on his appearance. Monet sent a string of letters scurrying to Paris. The first was dated April 9: "We are awaiting you. . . . My friend, it is admirable, the country here, come quickly. . . ."

Three weeks passed during which Bazille neither appeared at Chailly nor responded to the letter, a repetition of the previous summer when he was expected at Honfleur. The glowing spring passed, leaving dark green leaves to replace the gilded foliage that had excited Monet's ardor. Able to contain himself no longer, he wrote again April 28: "I have great need that you be here. I would like to have your advice on the choice of a landscape for the figures—at times I have a fear of making an error." Even this flattery from an individual so self-reliant as Monet brought no reply. May 4 he tried a third time: "I am going to write to you again, because you have not answered me whether my pictures were made ready in time to be shipped [to the Salon]. I would also like to know if my submission cards are paid. You gave me promises to help me with my picture. You ought to come pose for me for a few figures, and, if you do not, I shall have no picture. . . . I beg you, my friend, leave me no longer in this embarrassment. I cannot think of anything but my picture, and if I knew I should fail, I think I would go mad."

One suspects these words were just that bit too overpitched to quite convince Bazille. Yet, touching so strongly on the heart of the matter, the last outburst is a genuine cry from the heart, indicative of the extent to which the hopes and aspirations of Monet's young life had become entangled in this great effort. Artistically, in relation to his family, and personally with regard to Camille, all his eggs were in this one basket. As he struggled to get an enormous and complicated project under way, the strain on him was far too great for an emotionally unstable young man. Around the corner of failure were tragic penalties which utterly outweighed every hoped-for advantage.

Were Monet a consummate craftsman, with nerves of steel, he could perhaps have survived such pressures and succeeded. Instead, he was too obviously on the verge of a suicidal entanglement. Each stroke, each decision of place, position, or posture exerted an enervating anxiety lest the great masterpiece, for which he still did only preparatory work, should be less than he hoped. And when he grew despondent, he was oppressed by thoughts of his father, Adolphe Monet, living comfortably in Le Havre and awaiting his opportunity to pounce.

Camille, and his relationship with her, had become equally and inextricably entangled with this gigantic undertaking. As time passed, whatever the exigencies of their relationship, she pleased him more. He did not wish to lose her presence, nor did he wish to submit her to the pain and indignity of a return to outraged parental discipline. Possessed of her surprising and fresh innocence, young and slim, long of leg, narrow of waist, full-bosomed, passionately involved with and pathetically faithful to her lover, around whom she thought the world centered, Camille had made herself a necessity to Monet. By leaving the comforts of her parental home she had made a decision that was not easy, and one which could not be undone. For this Monet knew that he bore responsibility, and his responsibility thus extended to Camille altogether, as though she were some waif in a storm that had been cast on his doorstep.

In the midst of these many anxieties, and while he was still awaiting Bazille, other news came to Chailly. The Salon jury, rebounding from a much criticized harshness and the wholesale exclusions of 1863, had evidenced a decided inclination toward younger men. Not only was Édouard Manet's *Olympia* admitted, and two pictures each by Renoir and Pissarro, but both Monet's seascapes were accepted as well.

He had made it. At twenty-five, without regular academic training, and in his first attempt, by sheer force Claude Monet had pushed open the doors of the Salon!

Part Two

MADNESS

6. The Masterpiece

THE TURBULENCE of Monet's inner life gave way to that blend of heroic ardor and skittish elegance he could summon at will. In two hours the railway brought him from Fontainebleau to Paris, and he knew a period of wry and tentative hope. But on Varnishing Day from the moment he stepped into the Palais de l'Industrie with Bazille success burst upon him. Greetings and acclamation reached him from every side. Courbet seized his hand with enthusiasm, expressing interest in his further projects, and from the midst of the clamor he saw Édouard Manet stalk out in a passion.

"How goes it?" one of the crowd called to Manet.

"Ah, my boy, it is disgusting, I am furious!" Manet shot back. "I am being complimented only on a painting that is not by me. One would think it a mystification."

The cause of Manet's despair was that he too had been greeted with acclamation, handshakes, bravos, and felicitations. To his horror he discovered that because his pictures were hung in the same gallery with those of Monet, a natural confusion of names had resulted, and he was receiving congratulations on the two seascapes. That in the same gallery his own *Olympia* and *Ecce Homo* received only ridicule did nothing to improve his spirits. Manet studied the signatures on the seascapes, noted the similarity of names and obvious imitation of his style. Whether or not he realized the culprit was the same Claude Monet he had seen at Monginot's studio, dined with at Lejosne's, and visited in the Rue de Furstenberg, Édouard Manet left in a vile humor.

For Claude Monet that day was a complete triumph and the vindication of everything in his life most incorrigible. Despite his anxieties of the previous winter, and much suffering while chasing this fantasy, he had emerged barely bloodied, only slightly battered, and very triumphant. The cost had been unnecessary, but seemed not excessive now that champagne flowed in his honor. Compliments were extended by distinguished personages, felicitations generously proffered and modestly accepted. The editors of a popular souvenir album, *L'Autograph au Salon,* included him among the artists they invited to prepare hurried sketches of their exhibited works. The album appeared, Saturday, June 24, 1865, containing a woodcut after his wild scrawl of an ink sketch, and he had the pleasure to read:

> Monet [is] the author of a seascape the most original and supple, the most solidly and the most harmoniously painted, that has been exhibited in a long time. A tonality a little dull, as in the works of Courbet; but what richness and what simplicity of view! M. Monet, unknown yesterday, has at the very start made a reputation by this picture alone.

Nor was this verdict, that of his fellow artists, and the crowds, left unsupported by the more influential press. In the *Gazette des Beaux-Arts* Monet found another paragraph of fulsome praise, penned by the distinguished critic Paul Mantz. The vein was sufficient to assault even the complacencies of Adolphe Monet:

> The taste for harmonious schemes of color in the play of analogous tones, the feeling for values, the striking point of view of the whole, a bold manner of seeing things and of forcing the attention of the spectator, these are qualities which Monet already possesses in high degree. His *Mouth of the Seine* abruptly stopped us in passing and we shall not forget it. From now on we shall certainly be interested in following the future efforts of this sincere marine-painter.

Mantz had prefaced these praises with a line of caution and reservation: "He lacks here the finesse which one does not obtain but at the cost of long study. . . ." For it was by the sheer prodigality of his sight, an exact sensuous rendition so great it made other pictures look shoddy and mannered, that Monet had won this triumph.

These two paintings carried a truth of color, and a fresh feeling of the outdoors, that set them apart. Because they appeared so breathtakingly *authentic,* the elements of ineptitude also present were overlooked. The Salon, the critics, and the public were generous to the young man, and one can assume that he was approached by persons anxious to buy his pictures. Aware of Édouard Manet's heartwarming generosity as well as his sometimes contemptible petty egotism, Zacharie Astruc even suggested a new introduction to Monet, which Manet refused with a sweeping gesture.

"Monet has had a success very much greater than any he dared hope for," Frédéric Bazille reported to Montpellier. "Several talented painters with whom he is not acquainted have written him complimentary letters. He is at this moment at Fontainebleau, and I would much like to be there also."

His sudden and unexpected degree of success was an enormous moral stimulant to Monet, and not in every respect healthy. Impervious to disaster, and now with money in his pocket, he returned to his huge *Picnic* in a mood of triumphant and explosive abandon that was not without overtones of megalomania.

A brilliant June and July assisted his labors until he was ready to sketch the figures on a 51- by 73-inch canvas—and this merely a trial study for the final thrice-larger picture. Resplendent in a variety of costumes and postures, Camille's image charmed the eye everywhere. An attractive turmoil of bouffant skirts and petticoats in transparent summery muslin and crinoline, she was seen twice beside the picnic cloth. The most pleasing of these postures, at left, Monet had drawn from the foremost figure of Winterhalter's famous group, though the raw strength of his own creative force was injected into the pastiche.

Monet now became aware that Winterhalter also had devised miracles of ingenuity with light. His faces were treated with remarkable resourcefulness, delicately touched with half tone, lit by reflection, and immersed in soft shadow. The treatment was homogeneous and personal, but evocative of a forest interior. In his own daring way he determined to employ these alluring devices, confining them to the same left section of the canvas where Winterhalter used them to the best effect.

A more direct form of inspiration was one of the remarkable garden dresses of the period which Camille had brought to Chailly. A system of cords sewn into the seams permitted full skirts to be hoisted away from the ruin of damp grass, leaving modest ankles still clad in an abundance of white petticoats. In varied fawn tones, decorated in green, this elegant costume became the strongest note at the composition's left edge.

Garbed in soft whites or heavier street attire, no matter how hot the sun, Camille seemed resigned and patient. But her tall, rambling and beautifully knit form, so sensuous and acutely supple, reached the canvas with its obvious eroticism faded and replaced by a more listless air. Inexperience in rendering figures alone accounted for this lapse. At eighteen Monet's stunning mistress had become precociously mature. Yet from this fascinating creature Monet was creating a wholly artificial period piece that treated the human figure like so much stone, or draper's cloth.

To balance this female parade the need for male figures grew more acute. Bazille still was unseen, and Monet began a process of impressment on all those who out of curiosity, or benevolent interest, called at Chailly to see his progress. Among them was Lambron des Piltières, another pupil of Gleyre, who as a painter of genre subjects regularly exhibited at the Salon. Quickly Lambron was transferred to canvas, an enigmatic and slightly sinister figure, heavily shadowed and peering behind himself. Though he did not remain long enough to become useful elsewhere, Lambron's curiously circumspect image successfully introduced a meager human note to what had been a dance of marionettes.

Another visitor dragooned into Monet's service was Alfred Sisley, who, with Renoir, and Renoir's brother Edmond, also was at Fontainebleau, staying on the other side of the forest in the village of Marlotte. A head painted from Sisley was added behind the two seated figures of Camille: another effort to introduce the human contacts so lacking. Instinct rebelled against these haphazard methods by which Monet was being forced to proceed on an undertaking of such importance. His figures remained separate, no more than trite, or irrelevant, each of them an exercise. And while his few dragooned models were content to disappear on the morrow of their toil, he was unable to plan his moves with the efficiency and forethought of the great strategist he wished to be.

Awaited since April, Bazille still made no appearance. The final letter Monet penned to him August 16, by its firmness and assurance of tone, contrasts with those that had preceded:

> If you do not respond by return of post I will understand that you refuse to write to me or to be of service. I am in despair; I fear that you will make me ruin my picture, and that would be awful after

you promised me to come pose. Today is the sixteenth, and you cannot lack the money. If you are not coming immediately write to me without fail, because I have some money to send you.

Two days later Frédéric arrived on a midnight train, penniless, and hoping that five or six days of posing for Monet would suffice. From delicacy he stayed not at the overcrowded Cheval-Blanc, where Monet and Camille were established, but nearby at the Lion-d'Or. Almost immediately his assumption of a short stay was sent awry by rain, which came in violent floods permitting only two brief sessions of modeling.

The renewed appearance of sunshine brought with it furious activity. Bazille now posed again in the open sun. Beside him stood Camille, garbed in elaborately embroidered pale blue, worn with a Eugénie hat. Frédéric himself inclined to look swarthy in comic derby, white wing collar, gloves, and stick. To work rapidly before his model fled, Monet invented a visual slang: clarity of texture suffered first as he gave himself over to glittering passage work and abrupt attack, hoping only to fix the vision before him in the brief time allotted. Frédéric became a lanky figure seemingly devoid of specific gravity, held together by string and stuffed with sawdust. "Monet, who is working fast, will need me perhaps three or four days," Bazille reported to his parents August 23. "Thus I must again put back my departure, to my great regret. The moment he is finished I will leave."

Sometimes nearly achieved, the conclusion of Monet's labors remained always narrowly avoided, until one day, attempting to protect children from a runaway discus thrown by an English enthusiast, Monet was struck in his leg. The limb appeared not to be broken, but became painfully swollen and inflamed. Bazille sentenced Monet to prolonged rest in bed, where he ministered to him with a professional combination of severity, solicitude, and humor.

Immersion in cold running water was the treatment Bazille had been taught for swelling or infection, a feat difficult to organize. His ingenious improvisation was to suspend a bucket over Monet's bed, permitting the water to dribble down onto the bared leg. The water then ran off as best it could, presumably into buckets strategically placed on the chamber's tile floor. But nothing could prevent the bedclothes from receiving the same treatment as Monet, and it made his discomfort no less severe to pass the day gloomily in wet sheets.

Nor was emotional acquiescence possible for so compulsive an artist. While his huge project hung fire, he remained in markedly sullen humor, a comical sight lying in slit nightshirt against the pillows of a large bed provided for himself and Camille. As much to record his own ingenuity as to hold his patient quiet, Bazille brought an easel into the room to paint Monet impatiently smoking cigarettes in this damp and supine glory.

When recovered sufficiently to stand before his easel, Monet put himself back to work with renewed ardor, and completed the large preliminary compositional study. Technically unequipped for such complicated work, more by will than skill he succeeded brilliantly. Arbitrarily assembled into a composition which showed hardly more organic unity than a patchwork quilt were twelve magically modulated figures in a twinkling forest interior. The tone and effect alone gave his picture a remarkable unity, for Monet had worked this offhand miracle with a deceptive deftness, discovering new approaches and exploiting the old ones more ferociously than before. So recently hailed for Manet-like seascapes, he was ready to re-emerge as a forceful and original tone poet whose vocabulary was wider than had been generally supposed.

With this well-disposed, happy, and sparkling large sketch, itself the size of many of the Salon's bigger exhibits, his outdoor work ended. The scale of the Gargantuan Salon-bound canvas itself made it an impossible object to move to the forest each day. Prudence would have suggested the next stage was coped with the best in the Rue de Furstenberg studio, which, though empty of occupants, still consumed funds. Perhaps it was Camille who feared a return to Paris. Perhaps the sense of authenticity that had brought Monet to Chailly held him there. Whatever the cause, the huge canvas, approximately 15 by 19 feet, was brought to the inn, and put into position for work in the stables.

Bazille remained at Chailly, his attention riveted by what he saw in progress. To be close he set up his own easel on the cobblestones of the stable yard, painting a haphazard study of the inn's kitchen door. Otherwise confident and vigorous, a defective sense of proportion prevented him from succeeding fully. But in justice some blame must also be heaped on distractions, which now grew constant and varied.

A part of the noise doubtless was generated by Gustave Courbet, who worked in the forest nearby, painting the somber, brooding, woodland interiors for which he was renowned. Courbet had the personal force and strange audacity to dispose a few rocks and a stream bed across a canvas no smaller than that on which Monet had sketched his twelve figures. And his energies were sufficient for him to combine such labors with visits to the Cheval-Blanc, where he advised Monet on preparation of the large canvas. Monet also profited by watching the Ornans master at work: "Courbet always painted on a somber base, on canvas prepared with brown, a convenient procedure he endeavored to have me adopt."

"Upon it," Courbet explained to Monet, "you can dispose your lights, your colored masses. You immediately see your effect."

The older man's experience was an invaluable guide, and not aware that Courbet urged him toward an idiom from which the energy already was drained, Monet prepared his huge canvas with a too-generous brown undertone.

Frédéric posed again for Monet, now with Courbet present to watch, and he was equally delighted when, with Monet, he was introduced to the aged Corot, whom Courbet had discovered painting nearby in the forest.

September was well advanced when Bazille, his visit of a few days grown into as many weeks, at last took leave of Chailly. The summer's bright season of gaiety, work, and visits drew to a close. At the Cheval-Blanc the dining room mirror had a new harvest decoration painted by Charles Louis Vielcazal; but rowdy elements who had populated the inn drifted away as autumn inexorably approached. Because only the manual labor of completing the enlarged version of his picture remained, dull work executed in a stable, Monet called a brief halt, escorting Camille to Trouville.

That autumn of 1865 Gustave Courbet was on the eve of final overwhelming public acceptance, and already was enjoying enormous personal popularity among all orders of society. At Trouville he was surrounded by a court of apostle-admirers, to which were added Boudin, Daubigny, and a strange Francophile American, James McNeill Whistler. Courbet boasted his studio was invaded by *two thousand ladies*, a jest perhaps not too exaggerated, and among them he was attracted most to "the beauty of a superb red-headed girl whose portrait I have started"—Jo Heffernan, Whistler's Irish mistress.

Delacroix's death two years before, and the advanced age of Ingres, had left Courbet the last of those bizarre messiahs populating French nineteenth-century art. His rough realism now perhaps was diluted by a prevailing sweetness of tone and an obvious romanticism, but he dominated the artistic scene his older rivals had departed. Socially conscious themes and outspoken republican sympathies had made him a natural rallying point for dissident artistic and social elements. His apostles were not alone painters, but critics, authors, and social theorists, who, caught by a magical power of belief, proclaimed in unison his roughshod but undoubted divinity.

Arriving late at Trouville, Monet and Camille Doncieux took their little place in the pageant of triumph that surrounded Courbet. Camille's opulent wardrobe and flair for wearing plumed hats matched the smugly dandified air Monet himself affected. And though he dared not allow his family, so close by at Le Havre, to know of Camille or his relationship with her, at Trouville, where they formed a conspicuously stylish pair, she was accepted by his host of friends. In the wake of Courbet, who led in everything, Monet and Boudin painted on the beaches. Among the artists present Monet met Daubigny for the first time. But at night he took part with Camille in the dancing and games at the fashionable Casino, for all the pleasure of Trouville was not alone to stand in Courbet's shadow.

Courted by even that older nobility whose creation had preceded Bonaparte titles, Courbet himself was staying not at Trouville but at the villa of the Count de Choiseul at the contiguous resort of Deauville. Even there he could not think to leave Camille out of an invitation he extended his friends to share dinner on Choiseul's silver service:

My dear Boudin,

According to the wish of M. de Choiseul, I invite you and your lady to dine tomorrow, Wednesday, at six p.m. I have already invited M. Monet and his lady, who promised to come when I saw them last night at the Casino. I have no doubt that you will give us the pleasure of accepting.

Sincerely,

G. Courbet, Châlet Choiseul

Stop by for Monet on the way, and come without fail.

Notwithstanding loudly republican and socialist principles, Courbet was vastly impressed by the Count de Choiseul, whom he proclaimed to possess the "true distinguished grand manner of the most elevated period in French history." Added to such personal distinctions, in Choiseul's dining room it was undoubtedly true that the servants behind each chair wore black coats and white ties and shoes that were the same silver-buckled evening pumps Courbet previously had seen only on prefects in formal attire.

After dinner this curious little company filed into a salon hung with pearl-gray silk, its mantels piled to the ceiling with flowers. Seated on low divans, momentarily sharing the glory of a success he would never know, Boudin and his peasant wife perhaps thought of the contrast between such magnificence and their barefoot relatives in Brittany. And what may Camille have thought—she who by her bourgeois origin was the most likely to have viewed with vexation and with envy a manner of life she glimpsed, even so briefly, only by an unreasoning love?

About Monet's thoughts it is not necessary to guess. Once his enormous *Picnic* was exhibited at the Salon, he knew, the same success would be his.

An abrupt transition to confusion and crisis awaited him when early in October Monet returned to the Rue de Furstenberg. The previous August, Bazille had departed for Chailly crippled with debts. Doubt now existed whether he intended to retain his share in a studio which perhaps he thought Monet already had abandoned. And adding to this uncertainty was the fact that since reaching his family home at Montpellier Frédéric had transcended himself in ambiguity by writing to no one.

The extent of Monet's own slim resources is difficult to establish. Signs present suggest that his allowance was no longer forthcoming. In the happy and prosperous circumstances of the preceding summer that surely had seemed unimportant. Though conjectural, sales at the Salon had surely contributed to his high spirits, and perhaps in his own richly farcical way he had unloosed that cranky personal flair for alienating his family. He had every right to feel that his remarkable reception at the Salon had proved his worth. In spite of their spite, he felt capable of doing so again.

On reaching the Rue de Furstenberg, however, he began to find himself in difficulties. Debts left behind in Paris by Bazille were a further embarrassment over which Monet registered stern protest on October 14:

> On every side I see no one who does not complain of your silence. . . . You are going to find yourself seized [for debt], and quite rightly too, because this will not do. It is really quite enough already that you have just walked out. . . . Send me immediately the 125 francs for the quarterly rent payment; I can meet my part, but I have no more because I have had problems enough before leaving for Chailly. . . . I am going to dig away at my canvas. Everything is prepared.

Frédéric's credit thus in subdued and reduced condition, and his own resources nearing exhaustion, Monet arrived back at Chailly, prepared for the final laborious conclusion of his great work.

In the stable the huge canvas awaited him, and near it the vivaciously scintillating preliminary sketch, its tonal vocabulary variegated and immense. Unpretentious and workmanlike, Monet picked up again the long task of copying this brilliant picture onto the larger canvas. To establish the harmony, key areas of tone had been laid in over the dark undertone Courbet suggested. Figures and landscape elements next began their silent journey to the larger canvas. The transcription taking place was literal, his effort to match tones exacting. Each figure began slowly to rise in its place, and to be engulfed by the forest; sharp eye and meditative mind congratulated each other over how ingenious had been this stratagem of a large sketch. So much as possible he preserved its soft, big, bouncing rhythms by transposing actual strokes, appropriately enlarged, to perform their appointed functions and fill allotted places on the bigger canvas.

As he labored, struggling to attain the poetical summits this work demanded, Monet remained surrounded by a state of crisis. Shortness of funds had followed him from Paris. The rewards of success, he realized, were not monetary alone: they meant a cessation of these unnecessary tensions which prevented him from most effectively practicing his art. How difficult now to dispense tenuous melody and deliquescent harmony when the Rue de Furstenberg rent had gobbled his available cash, and this unfinished picture was a constant drain for space at the inn and the alarming quantities of paints, oils, and turpentine it consumed.

Fortunately, big, blustering, generous Gustave Courbet arrived again at Chailly, his interest in Monet's work now sufficient for him to assist the younger man through minor financial crises. Courbet's presence and interest were vastly encouraging, and, surveying Monet's progress, he even consented to take Lambron's place at the composition's center. Seated on the ground, his position painful for a man suffering from hemorrhoids, Courbet's huge burly form, complete with ferocious Assyrian beard and his red boutonnière of the Legion of Honor, became a crowning touch for Monet's masterpiece. No move could have been more shrewd. For an acknowledged and fashionable master of naturalism to be seen in this most ambitious essay of a younger artist meant sending to the Salon a picture that already bore an implicit mark of approval.

Throughout the approach of winter economic problems remained among Monet's sharper assailants. They were directly responsible for the condition of his large sable brushes, inch-wide brothers of those smaller instruments by which Boudin attained his most seductive surfaces. Abrasion by the canvas itself had worn them short, blunting the special combination of fiery nobility, elegant hauteur, and romantic dazzle Monet wished to impart. Shoddiness of texture abounded in sections he too often reworked, and an unpleasant, graceless roughness now characterized his strokes: a rather irritating problem added to those he faced already.

Worse than that, as his picture advanced, its difficulties multiplied rather than diminished. Skillfully as he enlarged the head on each figure, accurately copying the tone, and frequently following the original sketch stroke for stroke, when enlarged these ill-drawn areas of pigment carried less illusion of life. Lacking structure, flat and deficient in form, reflecting none of the lights surrounding them, and plainly brown in shadows, twelve such heads were a blot on his picture which no effort eradicated. Here was an intolerable affront, which, despite much maladroit maneuvering, he seemed unable to answer.

And sometimes, standing back in fatigue from the ladders he climbed before this enormous canvas, he worried over its increasing appearance of laboriousness and unevenness, and wondered where was the glow and resonance of the original sketch. For though by strenuous exertions the sketch was indeed reaching this larger canvas, all its twinkling allure remained behind. What came as an enormous shock to Monet was the sheer magnitude of the evil done by the dark undertone given this canvas on Courbet's advice. The small diminution of contrasts, the lack of absolute clarity and freshness, the constant loss of a slight accent or a delicate transparency of hue, effectively destroyed the original vibrancy. All that vivacious scintillation had disappeared. In its place Monet found himself examining a murky, scrubbed surface, clogged by excesses of pigment applied in unconscious and hopeless efforts to overpower the deadening tone beneath.

This new realization, at a time when his long labor already had exhausted much of his physical and emotional resilience, had the disenchanting effect of unleashing within Monet the personality of strange and wild turbulences always beneath his dapper exterior. Again Courbet visited Chailly, his presence bringing just enough reassurance to permit reflection. The dullness his picture stood wrapped in could not be erased. That dark undertone had done its dread work with permanence, every pigment lying over it feeling the restraining influence. As a partial solution Courbet therefore suggested that Monet introduce wider areas of strong pure color.

With an eagerness born of his despair, Monet slashed away at the pale blue figure of Camille on his composition's left edge. That lovely costume was roughly transformed into a second garden dress, the overskirt hoisted to allow scarlet petticoats to spread over a yard of his canvas. To ease the new and gaudy conspicuousness of this alteration Monet created a series of red tassels, and, adding further to the melancholy commotion, a red sash around the figure's waist.

However much they clashed with the good taste of Camille's normal dressing habits, such additions only compounded the original taunting error. And now, shoddiness and hectic fury written everywhere over that corner of the picture, Monet realized that however much he increased the color content in this arbitrary studio manner, by violating his original forest tonality he could gain none of the twinkling brilliance he sought. However much he adopted Courbet's studio color conventions, to that degree he sacrificed further what he most sought. For, in truth, Monet had lost his way.

His brilliant effort, so carefully prepared through the previous summer, and promising so well, had been reduced progressively to a middling and finally a mediocre travesty of the brilliant sketch. Be-for him was a vulgar, rough-edged, and sometimes hysterical daub. For Claude Monet, Chailly had become the chosen ground of desolation.

Sometime after December 20 Boudin wrote that Monet had "completed his enormous rigmarole, which has cost him the eyes out of his head." With that homely estimate of the fearful cost one need not contend. But Boudin's other information was incorrect. The vast project on which a year of thought and labor had been expended, and on which Monet's future and Camille's depended, was *not* completed. It was abandoned.

7. *First Flight*

THE DESTINY that had driven Monet so compulsively to one overwhelming victory now turned against him. Stripped of the picture necessary to consolidate his previous year's gains, without funds, in his agonized condition Monet was badgered unmercifully for arrears at the inn, and possibly as well for tradesmen's accounts in the village.

Information is tantalizingly short and incomplete: One is ignorant of how long these demands had been pressed, but it is not difficult to sympathize with the moments of lurking violence, smooth deceit, and false politeness through which the already demoralized young artist was made to pass. Of all the indignities heaped on him, the most revolting is that Monet's abandoned picture, his materials, clothing, and every possession brought to Chailly were seized, as security for his debts. Stung by this mean and shabby conclusion to so great an enterprise, bereft of every possession, he fled with Camille back to Paris and the Rue de Furstenberg, where, tired and distraught, they stumbled across the full rich flavor of another way of life. Frédéric, his own debts of the previous summer quietly paid by his mother, placidly had resumed work in the studio.

Hardly had they departed one area of indignity and disillusion than Monet and Camille found themselves in another. Their misfortunes at Chailly had the unavoidable consequence of introducing Camille into these Paris quarters shared by Monet and Bazille. Frédéric viewed her presence with a notable fastidiousness. Camille's domestic skills probably were useful; yet Bazille could not help feeling an uneasiness on finding himself housed under the same roof with this irregular union. At best it was awkward, at worst it embarrassed. Liaisons such as theirs were not listed among his approved happy endings, and the disapproval of Frédéric, with whom they lived on such close terms, became a new burden to the blighted couple.

Despite these strains, Monet now again fell to working mornings with Bazille in the studio, resuming his habit of the previous winter. But the fun of it had gone sour and panicky. Bereft of every hope on which his dreams had been founded, his pride shattered and his ambitions frustrated, Monet had been dealt a succession of shattering blows. He passed through a period of nightmarish apprehension, until, near Christmas, "by the greatest of good fortune his father came to Paris and gave him 150 francs"; as, in frank amazement, Bazille reported to Montpellier.

Better remembered for petty astuteness than any high principle or affection, Adolphe Monet probably had learned of his younger son's anxieties through Toulmouche or Amand Gautier. Unfortunately his generously inclined visit to Paris had the effect of arousing further questions in his mind about Claude's manner of living. Had he chanced on a petticoat forgetfully left in view, or one of Camille's many hats? Or was it only his years of widowerhood at Le Havre that made him sensitive to the touch of femininity in that Rue de Furstenberg studio?

His suspicions were the signal for other approaches. Adolphe Monet's sister, Sophie Lecadre, now again wrote to ask Amand Gautier to watch over the work and conduct of her nephew, at the same time expressing inquietude that he might have attached to himself some unworthy girl. Where it touched on Camille, the reply she received from Gautier was reassuring. And though Claude's family, those older Monets and Lecadres, now had specific information concerning Camille, they deceitfully pretended to know nothing.

The sum of 150 francs given Claude by his father was not sufficient to pay his debts or repossess the equipment, pictures, and clothing seized at Chailly. If Claude had considered setting the *Picnic* to rights in the greater convenience of the Rue de Furstenberg studio, his father had not provided the means. Adolphe Monet did not intend to extricate his son from misfortune, but only momentarily to alleviate its worst consequences and his own conscience. Claude's creditors still sought him, and the plague of that village calamity was allowed to prick and wound his mind. His father's degree of generosity was sufficient, however, for Claude to begin a new project, and this he appears to have done immediately. He also wisely sought relief from his distress, serving as joint host with Frédéric at a masked ball held in the studio. His Chasseur's uniform now stretched and pulled to cover Frédéric's elongated form, Monet himself was content with the beggarly disguise of an Honfleur fisherman. What Camille wore is unrecorded, and the only other detail preserved is that this party was so reckless a success that both hosts were given notice to quit the Rue de Furstenberg!

Misery piling on misery, Monet carefully nurtured his principal task. "[He] has been at work a long time; his picture is very advanced and I am sure it will be full of effect," Bazille noted soon after the New Year. This was of considerable gravity. Because of the abandonment and loss of his *Picnic* Monet had before him again the necessity of preparing for the Salon some work of importance. If he failed to do so, the alternative was to see himself unrepresented. He had no funds other than his father's gift, and his only hope of gaining any, as always, lay with the Salon. To make his mark in those stately galleries he required an imposing work. But now he was forced to think of a cheap instead of a sumptuous project.

The challenge was not one that a young man of Monet's temperament could accept with calm, casualness: immediately he made the plot thicker and the plausibility thinner by throwing it back in the teeth of fate. Sharing his hardships, hopes, miseries, and frequent bewilderment was Camille, who in calamity remained his only model. At this desperate moment he therefore reached deep into a genre he never before had attempted, to begin in wild haste a full-length portrait.

The area of his greatest experience and most obvious strength still was landscape. His shift away from it a second time, and under such appalling pressures, made it clear that this act was one of inclination as well as necessity. Faced by the grim necessity of consolidating a position gained by seascapes at the Salon, twice he had turned to life-sized figures. However unhappily it had concluded, the long struggle with the *Picnic* had left him with no sensation of inexperience or inadequacy. A battle for recognition waged by the painters of pure landscape, like his friends Boudin and Jongkind, now was no more to him than a melancholy commotion. And it is entirely remarkable, and revealing, that though his inexperience had made the enormous enterprise at Chailly only a gigantic bluff, Monet had emerged from that fiasco able to tackle the problems of a single figure with extraordinary confidence.

In his single-mindedness, all things, and other people's conveniences, once more were forced to conform to his requirements. Immediately he appropriated a gown of striped green satin Bazille had rented for his own use. Soon this stunning robe was seen on Camille, who took her place in a posture extracted from those used at Chailly. Monet's actual source probably was the small rapid sketch, all glittering passage work and abrupt attack, in which Camille appeared beside the bowler-hatted Frédéric: a picture which by its insignificance presumably had escaped seizure. The conspicuously easy posture of that essay, and its sweep of drapery and over-the-shoulder view of Camille's delicate and appealing profile, were attractive elements. When enlarged to the scale of life they were well calculated to astonish. A black fur-trimmed jacket and a small dark hat completed the ensemble. Camille raised one hand toward her chin, as though she were in the act of adjusting the trailing ribbons of her bonnet, and Monet set to work.

Strokes perilously flung and lacking in drawing quickly thumped Camille's enchanting head onto canvas. Caught in a difficult feat of foreshortening, which he would have been wiser in his state of ignorance to avoid, one of Camille's lovely dark eyes fell too low on her cheek. Her gently undulating nose was distorted in an equally alarming way. Even the sensitivity of Camille's mouth, its lips unwilling to close firmly over her prominent teeth, he confided to canvas with a harsh twist. The hand she employed to pull the netting of her bonnet, roughly impasted on the canvas, is crudeness itself, leaving one uncertain whether she wore a glove or had dark discolored flesh. Fairly quivering with nervous tension, such passages, each frequently resembling a one-act spasm of fury, betrayed that Monet still had learned no control over his great gifts.

By compensation there were skills other than purely technical ones upon which Monet could make call, and whatever he crudely dashed onto canvas had a miraculous illusion of life. In the dark green satin of the dress he rose to remarkable heights. A constant and unexplainable stylistic renewal alone enabled him to bring off convincingly such passages of pure pigment, for which he had neither technical equipment nor understanding. Unlearned in the restraints of studio techniques which he had contemptuously refused to learn, too impatient to hold back his brush, Monet was unable to work long on any canvas without piling up a labored surface. In that astonishing way he already had exhibited of converting his gravest weaknesses to strengths, these twin faults now worked together toward a portrait both fresh and unusual.

A more serious failing was that Monet's overwhelming delight in his medium, and obvious joy in the thump and swish of his brush, left him too easily content with effects cheaply bought. In every deeper requirement he failed. Beneath those infinite folds of lustrous green satin he gave no indication of a body, and this same obsessive delight in medium permitted him to allow such a secondary portion of the picture to take precedence over essential elements of portraiture. Camille's fascinating allure never reached the canvas at all. Without it the twisted woman he created resembled an amiable middle-aged field mouse. Inexperienced at placing a single figure within a picture plane, Monet also had misjudged entirely the ability of a figure to dominate surrounding space. The blank against which his distorted female was framed required far more ingenious treatment than the simple brown tones he flowed over it.

His errors were many and glaring. Added to incorrigible inaccuracies of draftsmanship, they combined to produce a picture again illustrating the sharp, distorted talent of its painter. For the work Claude Monet dashed out in those unhappy winter days too obviously was the product of an impetuous young man, gifted, but unaccustomed to his problems, too vain to take them seriously, and too arrogant to think he had not conquered them all. Courbet, who had resumed his visits to the Rue de Furstenberg, viewed this strange effort, and perhaps mindful of unfortunate advice given at Chailly, he complimented Monet without reserve. Yet compared to its multiple sins, the merits of this picture were slight. And on such a canvas Monet was depending for his place at the Salon.

By that January, 1866, a year had elapsed since Monet and Bazille together had moved into the Rue de Furstenberg studio. A practical arrangement at first, when Bazille had felt obliged to lean on his friend's greater experience, it had proved far too costly for both, and their tandem life now had grown fraught with complexities and embarrassments. For a month, since Monet's flight from Chailly, they had been *three* in the studio, and however much charm and grace Camille brought, the situation was indelicate.

After their overly enthusiastic masked ball, both tenants were under notice to leave the premises on expiration of their lease, January 15. Bazille considered it best to find new quarters for himself alone. On February 23, 1866, he moved to the Rue Godot-de-Mauroy. Not to explain Monet's affairs too explicitly, Bazille wrote to his brother Marc of this move in categoric statements: "I am not disturbed to live somewhat alone. There are a great many inconveniences in living two together, even when there is mutual understanding." The name of Camille thus escaped mention.

And still Monet was pursued. So shortly before at Trouville a confident, stylish, swaggering figure, the depth of the abyss into which he had fallen is astonishing. Did he in fact owe debts at Chailly alone, or was he being pursued for older and larger sums unpaid in Paris? No matter how uneasy, the six weeks passed shepherded by Bazille in the Rue de Furstenberg had been a respite, from which he profited by preparing his large work for the Salon. Two months more would pass before the April admission date, and another month before the Salon doors opened in May. Forced to quit the Rue de Furstenberg, Monet and Camille vanished without trace.

Where they lodged, what they ate, has escaped record. What short commentary has survived on their ignoble controversy with destiny is pathetic. Aware of the correspondence recently passed between his aunt Sophie Lecadre and Amand Gautier, an elemental instinct for survival urged Monet to employ this avenue for the help he could gain no other way. Again in frosty disfavor with his father, he directly implored Gautier to obtain assistance for him from his aunt: "Unquestionably certain people seek to ruin me in her eyes," he pleaded.

Gautier received an encouraging reply, and a trickle of money that reached Claude from his aunt could be applied to the daily problem of nutrition. With this pitiful handout came much advice, to which, in his dreadfully undermined state, he was obliged to reply meekly and respectfully. And though Sophie Lecadre deliberately treated him as a bright aunt might a dull nephew, the situation in which Claude found himself, so out of proportion to reason or the exigencies of merely completing his picture at Chailly, surely gives rise to wonder and a new look at the circumstances.

By April of the previous year, after only four months with Monet at the Rue de Furstenberg, Bazille had found himself without funds. That shortage had prevented him from joining his friend, as promised, to model for male figures at Chailly. How riotously had these two young men lived if between January and April Bazille had become crippled with debts? Of course the rent itself was preposterous, equal to the sum soon paid by the wealthy Doncieux family for large quarters in the newer Batignolles section. But in the Rue de Furstenberg Monet and Bazille had entertained a long list of distinguished guests, and done so in a style sufficient to make Bazille feel, by August, that he must abandon the costly joint ménage. Monet had treated that desertion briskly. He sternly reproved Bazille on October 14 for having "just walked out," and peremptorily demanded Bazille's share of the rent: 125 francs for the quarter. His tone quivered with outrage, and aware of his moral obligation, Frédéric had acceded. After his mother paid his debts, he resumed life in the studio.

If this had been Bazille's experience, while living on a regularly paid allowance previously sufficient to provide an excess for nightly attendance at the theater, how extraordinary that Monet, after March, had been able to afford duplicating these expenses at Chailly, and to keep a mistress! How preposterous of this young man thus to raise the confusion and inadequacy of his finances to a new pinnacle of absurdity. Already Courbet was assisting him financially, and his great, never-to-be-completed masterpiece surely added to his unfaltering self-confidence and an ecstatic view of the future. But his excesses had grown so imbecile that they amounted to sabotage.

Within seven months of his initial Salon triumph Monet's highly promising career had collapsed from reckless overexpansion and feckless management. The winter that followed was one of disgrace, and ignoble, ignominious flight. Like her brother, Mme. Lecadre had no intention to free her nephew from debts, as she made clear to Gautier:

> I thank you a thousand times for the interest you have shown in my behalf, especially because this poor boy is in such need at the moment. He is a sweet lamb, and he recognizes his wrongs. He is reforming according to my advice; God grant that this will last!
>
> At this moment he is terribly tormented. He is being searched for, and hunted down, by some creditors who have taken umbrage because he has got out of Paris to retire to Ville d'Avray. They threaten to seize even the exhibition pictures.

After an uneasy February and March spent hiding in Paris, that April Monet and Camille had indeed escaped the city, dragging onward to the suburbs the pageant of their disenchantments and resilience, tragicomic relations, and eager vulnerability to love and debt. On money provided by his aunt, Monet took a small house belonging to Bazille's acquaintance, Mme. Rolina, on the farther side of the Seine at Sèvres, near the Ville d'Avray railroad station. There living in almost painful intimacy and affection, still attempting to placate his aunt both directly and through Gautier; once more, and with much weariness of spirit, the coming of spring urged Monet to work.

The discovery of his whereabouts by those insistent creditors who hectored him, interrupting him, forced new approaches to his aunt. Retaining still his own truculent tone, expressing impatience, and demanding to know why Gautier wrote no faster to his aunt, in his beseechings there appears for the first time in Monet the note of mawkish self-pity, a reproachful plaintive wail that soon would become his anthem. Gautier passed on his pleas; but aware that the dribble of funds she sent her nephew was used for *two*, Mme. Lecadre discouraged talk of paying debts:

> I have already tried that. My intention is to furnish him only enough to live on each day. This month I have actually exceeded the usual sum. He hopes to escape from these troubles, the poor boy. If I were able, without question, I would not wait to be asked. But the impossible is not worth trying.

Already his family had taken the view that paying Claude's debts too much resembled plugging holes in a sieve. An ordeal of the most grievous kind, sadistically self-inflicted, thus dragged on.

Work was difficult in these conditions. The overmastering smugness and complacency of his family and the competing clamor and threats of his creditors created a deplorable distraction. But such things always strangely provoked in Monet irrational counterreactions. Under stresses nearly similar, if less violent, he first had decided to force his way into the Salon. Now he took note of the fact his little house at Sèvres had a garden, and there, with an amended strategy and more carefully considered tactics, in a situation of mounting indignity he began deliberately to refight the battle of the *Picnic.*

Aware that space along the Salon walls was grudgingly meted out, he made his canvas upright, preserving large dimensions while demanding considerably less from the admissions jury. The same practicality of approach motivated him as he plotted his composition. Camille was still his only model. Submissively devoted and romantically attainable, no fears need arise concerning her presence or willingness to pose, nor would she decamp before her stint was completed. His *Picnic* therefore would be slightly altered, to become *Women in a Garden.*

All that past experience with figures and outdoor effects was called into counsel. The large new canvas he acquired was given a useful undertone following on Courbet's prescription, this time kept pale and thin, not to interfere with the work done over it. Next he thought of those two seated female figures in the *Picnic,* which had reached canvas with an inimitable lyric quality worthy of recapture. Camille resumed her earlier pose, the crinoline skirts that had ruffled about her at Chailly exchanged now for heavier flat linen. Embroidery decorated it on the sleeves and short jacket, and formed a wide band down the front and around the hem of a flowing skirt. At Chailly the shadowed head, and dappled effects of light falling through the trees above, had been the special beauty of these figures. At Sèvres the light was reversed. The trees of Monet's garden were behind, and on another plane. To regain the required effect Camille raised overhead her own coy little parasol. Blue and mauve shadows fell from it, and suddenly flowing over Camille from shoulder to waist, they became a miracle of subtlety.

One figure well planned, again he drew on previous experience for others with which to surround it. Tight against the left side of the canvas he created two standing figures closely related to the principal group done earlier at Chailly. These two he grouped together as in a flirtatious conversation. Less diffuse and disorderly than the *Picnic,* his new effort was now a tight grouping of three figures arranged in uneven balance on the left of his canvas. For a necessary counterweight they would depend solely on elements of sparkling landscape, flowers, and foliage in sunlight, which Monet knew so well how to paint.

Determined that the heads, which had eluded him at Chailly, should give no trouble now, he moved cautiously. Each in turn was developed from the model, and all three were well advanced before he set in motion secondary parts of the composition. He had not forgotten the continuous tonal radiance Winterhalter had achieved by reflections into the half tones of shadowed heads. By a new discipline of technique he was able to hold the three heads of his own composition deliciously immersed in the transparent shadows, half tones, and reflections, intended to be his picture's chief beauty.

The foremost seated figure, her skirt catching a forceful blow of the sun, threw back all that brilliance into Camille's parasol-shaded face. Studying the exceptional dazzle of this light and bouncing color with an almost hypnotic absorption, Monet found his lovely mistress turned lavender. Enchanting gradations and accents were added by demurely downcast eyes and an enormous yellow fichu. Boldly, with the same brusque touch employed in Paris, he transmitted these surprising observations to the canvas.

So truthfully observed, this foremost head took on a bizarre appearance. Monet was alarmed, holding in greater restraint the two further studies of Camille's face higher up the canvas. A shadowed profile, directly inspired by one in Winterhalter's composition, evoked in its own charming way all the most youthful qualities of Camille. Radiant and pert and fresh, softly and affectionately painted, her hair piled high on her head, lovelocks pulled toward her fresh cheeks and braids tumbling down her back, despite the experiences of the past year she had contrived to retain her childlike innocence.

That profile, inserted in this garden picture, was Monet's finest substantial image of Camille, and a portrait of rare beauty. An aspect almost more impressive was its enormous technical advance over the uncouth image of this same model done in Paris so shortly before. Never impatient to learn tidy solutions to technical problems, Monet displayed an astonishing ability to grow with the work he undertook. His headstrong, impatient energy, and intensely sensitive response, permitted him to improvise the most difficult technical procedures. He did not do so without labors unnecessary to a better-trained artist, yet by sheer force and ingenuity he did arrive at the goal. And in the final full face of Camille he again excelled himself. Chin lowered, eyes raised, holding a colorful bouquet, once more Camille is a memorable vision of loveliness.

Soon he was ready to sketch landscape elements onto the canvas, its height creating new difficulties. Ladders and stools evidently had proved unsatisfactory assistants at Chailly. Because he now worked in a garden, summarily he had a trench dug, into which by a system of ropes and pulleys he easily lowered the picture. By raising it at will he could bring any portion to within his reach. His picture progressed, soft harmonies replacing the more stacatto style that had been his only resource at Chailly.

A more accustomed mood of jaunty confidence returned. He looked past his present difficulties and the fact that his family treated him like a conventional neurotic outcast. With that fierce kind of motor energy that always typified him, his activities were aimed beyond the Salon of 1866, to which he submitted the hasty Paris portrait of Camille and a landscape somehow rescued from Chailly. Again his eyes and his thoughts were centered on the *next* Salon (1867), where by the beauty and audacity of this new garden picture he surely would be proclaimed the great and original creator his talents deserved. Then, an object of veneration, his problems would solve themselves, and creditors and family fade into wholesale irrelevancies.

However confident he felt, his strengths and faults were equally due to his extraordinary temperament. His pictures to date had been a sequence of ecstatic utterances with no very coherent philosophy linking them. By contrast, an undertaking of the complicated sort he was engaged on at Sèvres presented so many difficulties it was inevitable that he would fall foul of some. He was engaged on producing a *Salon picture:* not merely an example of good and daring painting, but one of those specially designed and constructed vehicles that on the Salon's walls would shout down opposition. Still laboring under the awful necessity to make his name by this picture, as he had hoped to do with its predecessor, the *Picnic,* Monet was equally insistent that it be a picture closely representing his own concept of painting. The two goals were not necessarily compatible. The "Salon picture" element was being forced to struggle against realistic representation of outdoor sunshine effects, which, perhaps rightly, Monet believed that he alone could paint in a work of this scale.

A further element of confusion arose from the fact that Monet was enchanted still by the reserved coloration he admired in Édouard Manet's works. At Sèvres he tried to paint all the varied hues of nature in the heavy opaque facture and restricted flat tones Manet had employed for work done in the less brilliant, more uniform light of the studio. This contradiction Monet never understood.

Gustave Courbet did. After discovering again where Monet lived, Courbet journeyed out from Paris to watch progress of the new masterpiece. In a small way perhaps he again assisted Monet financially. To keep a little cash in hand was all that mattered: Monet's debts were impossible to pay, and would have to await some drastic alteration in fortunes, such as he firmly believed was just ahead. But Courbet, always sympathetic toward this astonishing young man he had befriended, felt reservations concerning the work he saw in progress. One day, finding Monet idle, he asked, "How is it, little one, that you are not working?"

"Can't you see there is no sun?" Monet retorted.

"That's nothing. You can always do the landscape," was Courbet's clearly ironic rejoinder.

Despite Courbet's heavy inflection, Monet chose to believe he had so far misunderstood this new art that he thought brilliant sunshine effects could be painted equally well when the sun was lacking. Yet, in fact, Courbet's gentle dart had been aimed at the curious lack of coordination in Monet's approach. From the theoretically sound premise that the only excuse for working out of doors was an attempt to catch true effects, Monet had been unable to proceed to a point where he realized how destructive to his logic was the use of Édouard Manet's arbitrarily restrained flat tones. Courbet implied that were Monet to work with flat tones, his figures could advance without sunshine, because their values already were established.

To that extent Boudin's doctrines and the nervous application of Jongkind had failed to coalesce with the style of Manet.

Touches of prickly quarrelsomeness, the complications of debt and contriving, the oppression of overwork, all were swept away when joyous news arrived that both works Monet had submitted were accepted by the Salon of 1866. Cautiously he had provided a false address, or left an earlier one, 1 Rue Pigalle, for the catalogue, lest creditors gain a further hint where to find him. Otherwise the old defiance still was evident. In place of the more appropriate and less specific "Portrait of a Lady" usually employed for Salon exhibitions, he had entitled his largest work *Camille:* tribute of an especial sort, but also a gesture that gave pause to the Doncieux family. Living in poverty, their daughter was being made notorious as well. Monet's humor was inflexible, and it is equally significant that, unlike most young men currying favor at the Salon, in the catalogue he failed to indicate a teacher. Clearly his months of poverty in no way had curtailed a natural inclination to wave his fist beneath every available nose.

At the Palais de l'Industrie Monet discovered that *Camille* deliberately had been poorly hung, high on the wall in a small dark corridor. Despite this official effort to show him in a bad light, his triumph was complete. The degree of his success was far greater than the year before, and he shone with enormous luster, like a new meteor on the Paris skyline. "Monet has had a mad success. His pictures and those of Courbet are the best in the exhibition," an overeager Bazille confided to his parents. In lowered voice he mentioned also that of his own entries only an insignificant still life was accepted.

Nor did any brusque encounter with Édouard Manet mar Claude's pleasure, for this time the jury had excluded Manet's works entirely. The obvious double relationship of style and name was too good to be forgotten, however, and in a satirical publication, *La Lune*, May 13, 1866, a caricature of *Camille* appeared from the pen of the cartoonist André Gill, with the legend: "Monet or Manet? Monet. But it is to Manet we owe Monet. Bravo, Monet! Thank you, Manet!"

Journals and critics picked up congratulating Monet where the public, artists, and patrons left off at the Salon. Ernest d'Hervilly wrote a poem to *Camille* which was printed in *L'Artiste,* and Bürger, the celebrated critic and author, heavily underscored Monet's achievements:

> Wait! here is another very young man, M. Claude Monet, more happy than his near namesake, Manet, of whom we will speak soon, because he has had the good fortune to have his *Camille* received, a large standing portrait of a woman seen from behind, trailing a magnificent robe of green silk, sparkling like the textures of Paul Veronese. I would much like to reveal to the jury that this opulent painting was done in four days. One is young, one gathered lilacs instead of remaining closed up in the studio. The hour of the Salon arrived. Camille was there, dreaming of gathering violets. . . .

Whether Bürger's own or whispered to him by Monet, such gay improvisation of facts surely made its impression on Claude's family and the parents of Camille. Fortunately this well-meant tribute also spread its stardust adjectives on the forest landscape Monet submitted as his second work: "an effect of evening, with the sun illuminating great trees. When one is truly a painter one can do anything one wishes."

Unquestionably *Camille* made an enormous impression, and as a picture was mentioned lengthily even by those who did not approve it, or who, like Paul Mantz the year before, were perceptive of the weaknesses of the artist. One of these was Edmond About:

> I admit that the woman with the robe, by M. Monet, has been badly hung. The reason is that a robe is no more a picture than a phrase written correctly is a book. One can ruffle silk with a certain effectiveness and even so have everything still to learn. How important is the costume if I am unable to find any trace of a body, not even the commonplace contour of the lay figure, if the head is not a head, if the hand is not even a paw.

To any who stopped to consider them, these strictures were accurate. But surely the most thundering words of all, and those that attracted far more attention, were the exalted praises of Émile Zola, in *L'Événement:*

> I admit that the canvas that stopped me the longest was the *Camille* of M. Monet. It is an energetic and vivid painting. After passing

through galleries so cold and empty, tired of finding no new talents, suddenly I caught sight of this young woman trailing her long robe and plunging into the wall as though there were an opening. You cannot believe how refreshing it is to admire a little, when one is tired of laughing and shrugging the shoulders.

I do not know M. Monet. I think that I have never looked attentively at one of his canvases; it seems, even so, that I am one of his old friends. And all that because his picture tells me the whole story of energy and truth.

Oh yes! Here is a temperament, here is a man in this crowd of eunuchs. Look at the neighboring canvases and see how piteously mean they are beside this window opened onto nature. Here, there is more than a realist: here is a powerful and delicate interpreter who can render every detail without falling into sweetness.

Examine the robe. It is soft and solid, it trails slackly, it lives, it cries out who this woman is. This is not the robe of a doll, one of those muslin chiffons in which one is dressed only in dreams; this is real silk. . . .

The stress Zola laid on Monet's powerful temperament was judiciously contrived to find his strongest point. Zola gained for Monet a great and wide new audience. The size of *Camille,* and the fact it so certainly was a portrait, militated against an immediate purchase. For once Monet's luck held, however. The dealer Cadart, in whose shop two years earlier Manet had exhibited his *Kearsarge and Alabama,* commissioned a small replica of *Camille* from Monet, who was able to extract payment in advance.

His frank enthusiasm is clear from the note Monet sent Gautier: "While you have been away I have earned eight hundred francs. I hope that when I am in relations with more dealers things will go better still." Equally enchanted was his aunt, who could feel now that her faith of the preceding years had been justified. She bubbled to see her difficult nephew's name spread so widely and with such glowing tributes in the journals. Zola's article from *L'Événement,* the important newspaper that later became *Le Figaro,* was almost more than she could bear: "She writes to tell me that she consents to make me an allowance," Monet penned to Gautier with new joy.

"My family at last gave me back their esteem," Monet later remembered. "With their esteem came also a resumption of my allowance. I floated in opulence."

8. Flight Again

THE OVERWHELMING degree of success he twice had found at the Salon impressed itself deeply on Monet. For him the administrative systems by which French art was governed worked unerringly well. Ardent interpretations he read of his own works were fully accepted, and against a background of ringing acclaim he moved again with his old swagger. His place at the Salon assured by this second wild reception, dealers interested in him, newspapers carrying his praises to the remoter parts of France, again to expect a regular allowance from his family, that charming, eager but slightly unlovable young man had redeemed himself handsomely.

Nor could he help feeling that the emotional and social effects of his regained celebrity were a satisfactory conclusion to the hardships preceding them. More unfortunately, he made the sadly mistaken assumption that such victories were inevitable. From his fresh funds he paid Mme. Rolina the second quarterly rent payment at Sèvres, falling due in June, and in the garden of that house work continued on his large picture. Despite the bitter suffering and bizarre folly of the past months Monet could feel certain he was not sustaining himself on illusions.

Thick daubs of color applied with an irresistible thumping momentum were giving his large canvas a fine melodic verve. Costumes received far greater attention than at Chailly, and a considerable delicacy was felt in the sunlit sheen on Camille's white linen frock. Simple chiffons worn by the profiled figure developed rhythmic gullies and sparkling touches of sun that created a striped splendor. To this Camille's girlishly abundant figure and awkward abominable stance added their own pleasing and coltish grace. No qualms of conscience were felt over the fact that he hid the hands whenever possible, nor did he muse over structural complications nor seek bizarre sonorities. However ingeniously brushed were its components, what he intended was a straightforward summation of his own special technical abilities: a dazzlingly simple and forthright picture able to compel attention.

Content with his progress, he felt assured. Now at last he would have a work able to support and augment his burgeoning reputation. Those he previously had exhibited were only the stray drops in a marvelous rain of invention, vividly painted, but conventional examples of a school of Courbet realism. Now he had a picture less fervent and flayed-looking than *Camille,* and entirely his own, able to inaugurate a stylistic trend and do so with eloquent orchestral swells.

His sense of self-importance was rife, and so was an endearing unconsciousness that to his many creditors this sense appeared less well founded. He neither paid his debts nor came to terms with creditors who followed him from Chailly to Paris. Dedicated as he was to all the benefits of a tangible material prosperity, painting in a manner obviously calculated to achieve it, he remained woefully inattentive to the smallest requirements of maintaining credit. Something irrational that lurked at the bottom of him cannot be overlooked. Payment already extracted from Cadart for the reduced version of *Camille,* when the original picture was returned from the Salon late that summer he began the replica in Bazille's Paris studio. Unfortunately he failed to complete it; and at Sèvres he failed to pay the autumn quarter of the rent, due in September.

After passing through the harrowing episodes the previous winter, once more he had precipitated himself to the brink of a seizure. His huge garden picture, essential for the next Salon, he spirited away. All his other possessions and pictures were held at Sèvres by his landlord. Sought after by creditors from Chailly, Paris, and now Sèvres, he fled with Camille to Honfleur, the only familiar location open to him. In four months all the grandeur of his regained career had evaporated.

Despite momentarily good, if fragile, relations with his family, he avoided returning to Le Havre and Ste.-Adresse. The lonely alliance with Camille instead was carried to the St.-Siméon farm, the same country inn where two years before Monet had stayed with Bazille. This wild strip of country not far above the sea was run in highly personal style by *Mère* Toutain, assisted by her husband, a worthless drunkard of a son, and one hard-working maid. Considerably less gentle than the Cheval-Blanc at Chailly, and without comparable history, from its guests the St.-Siméon farm had acquired much the same character.

Boudin's friend Alexandre Dubourg, who shared his studio, is credited with discovering St.-Siméon. Daubigny's patronage popularized it with Jongkind, and Boudin, who in 1859 brought Courbet there. An artist's ways and Parisian fame were not unwelcome; the tall and pretty Parisian girl, so clearly descended out of her own element to live with one, was no pretext for a display of smirks.

However much intelligence of Claude's newest defeats reached them, the carefully preserved view of the Monet-Lecadre family was that Claude had returned to Honfleur alone. Nor did relations remain at their previously amiable pitch. One suspects that the allowance promised Claude during the Salon's gay season had never been extracted altogether painlessly. Perhaps it had been repented of when his family learned the extent of their son's continued excesses and lack of judgment at Sèvres. A logical flaw again existed in his finances, and only if the allowance is subtracted from resources available to him do his maneuvers at Honfleur become understandable.

His first necessity was still to finish the large picture begun at Sèvres. Removed from that garden, working in a golden autumn too soon followed by December snow, attempting to complete indoors a picture conceived so boldly in the open, Monet was forced to think in arbitrary terms. In bewilderment he fell back on the system of flat tones derived from Édouard Manet, and beneath this renewed onslaught the finer qualities of his work took flight. The three figures completed at Sèvres existed in an almost classic harmony. These he left untouched. But whatever garden vista he had intended to paint around this compelling vignette no longer was available to him. In its place he elected to add a fourth figure.

Standing forward, balanced on her toes, and dressed in her polka-dotted frock, Camille resumed lengthy sessions of modeling. Monet gambled that this novel attitude could suggest movement strongly enough to effectively counterweight the three other figures. His previous choices of pose had been distinctive and some of them distinguished. But introduced against an unrelieved expanse of foliage, this new figure developed in a fashion so wooden it badly marred the others' truth. Accustomed to proceed by flaming outbursts of passionate painting, he was unequipped to evolve a pattern of beauty or elegance from masses of pigment already on canvas. Indeed, wherever the churned textures of his figures hit foliage, a harsh edge instantly identified his deficient craftsmanship.

Laboriously and destructively he then set about to remedy a fancied lack of tonal opposition. Areas near the figures, where contrast could be cheaply gained, were arbitrarily darkened. This procedure destroyed the original delicate harmony, leaving all four figures flat against an opaque background. In a winter of discontent he thus concluded the summery composition, transforming into a taut abstract ballet what by necessity he would send before the next Salon jury.

Earlier that autumn Claude had painted the road from Honfleur to the St.-Siméon farm. Roads always had interested him as an obvious device for leading the eye into distances. This taste, already demonstrated at Chailly, he had in common with Corot, Daubigny, and most painters of their generation. They in turn had adopted it from the Dutch, as a mode of reaction against the grandiose formulas of Claude Lorrain and Italian landscape masters, who had composed pictures in systematic horizontal planes. Monet's modest roadside study developed into an interesting research in the tonal oppositions created by trees and a bright broken sky, the former stark against and penetrated by the latter's darting lights. After snow fell, Monet felt again the impulse to work outdoors, and despite an already acute shortage of canvases he dashed once more into the breach with easel and paints, for convenience returning to that same place beside the road.

Snow lay deep on the road, and overhead the sky was leaden. Desperately and uneasily, aware that his few francs disappeared with no hope of replacement before the next Salon, six months away, Monet applied himself to two studies of barren white blight. By concentrating on vague silver and blue half tones, he added a soft nuance. The continued overcast he made pink and yellow steel, gaining a further delicate harmony. Commonplace methods for suggesting atmospheric quiet and expanse, they were cunningly blended to produce endless variations on a single color note, and became entirely fresh.

Away from the frigid atmosphere of the road portrayed, these two scenes then appeared too bland. An obvious method of improvement was to provide centers of interest. Honfleur itself doubtless had reminded him of Boudin's teaching, this aspect of which had been unused since first he went to Chailly and painted stark unpeopled scenes. Into one study he introduced a small wagon built of smudges and blobs. Matching tints crudely and dragging edges of white back against the wagon, he injured that silver study's perfect harmony. The structureless wagon itself indicated how uncertain a technician he remained, nor was he more inspired when populating the second sketch by faceless dwarfs trudging through its snow.

Yet, aware how great had been his initial success with these ventures, when at last the sun returned to the heavens and the snow threatened to melt, Monet chanced a larger undertaking in this same genre. Nothing more august than a gate and farmyard fence of woven twigs was selected for his foreground, but into this larger canvas he brought a bravura vision that established new immediacy and a sense of actual experience. With remarkable eloquence and sensitivity Monet then populated this proud work by a single magpie, seated on the gate and blithely unaware of the human tragedy he watched.

Planted everywhere in his life, and well tended by his excesses and startling obtusenesses, the seeds of tragedy had indeed begun to sprout. One sign was that the scene to which he added a wagon was painted over a previous landscape. Only thus, by devouring his older children so painfully brought into the world, could he proceed. He now remembered a large canvas left behind in Bazille's Paris studio—an unfinished full-length of Camille in white. Its size would be sufficient for a harbor scene he had wanted to begin the previous autumn, and which, the snow melting, soon again it would be possible to paint.

But more grim preoccupations had arrived to threaten him. Anxious for her lost rent at Sèvres, at the end of November Mme. Rolina sent a demand for immediate payment, which specified that the pictures and property she held would be sold at auction to make up any deficit. Under this lash he cringed. Unable to pay anything himself, nor expect assistance from his family, he wrote to Frédéric Bazille:

> 1st December 1866
> Saint-Siméon
>
> . . . You must send me my Salon picture, *Camille*, with the other canvas of the woman in white. I am going to paint over the latter an important sea picture. Send me the little reduction of Camille, that I was unable to finish at Paris, and which it is essential that I finish because I have been paid for it.

And would you do me one more service: I have just received a
payment order from Mme. Rolina. I beg of you, tell her not to make
a seizure. Even though I have not many things at Ville d'Avray
[Sèvres] it would be terrible for me if she sold them.

This incredible mixture of orders and requests, so blindingly
inept, if it did not antagonize Bazille entirely, made him less than
enthusiastic to comply. Throughout December Monet awaited word
that never came. New difficulties now surrounding him, on December 22 he wrote to Zacharie Astruc, asking his assistance. A letter
from Astruc to Bazille followed:

DEAR MONSIEUR,
I have just received a very unhappy and agonizing letter from
Monet. He is still waiting for his canvases. I copy out a few lines
which will give you the idea. Here is the fragment of his letter:
Has Bazille given you my canvases, and is there in the package
my Salon canvas, *Camille,* as well as the little reduction for
Cadart? I am very pressed for time because I have received a letter
from Luquet asking for it, and it is necessary that I have it finished
and delivered by the 26th of this month, so that he can send it
to America the following day. If not it cannot go, and I shall have
to reimburse him the money I have been paid. I have written to
Bazille about this, but I have had no response.
There it is, Monsieur, the very sad position of our friend. There is
nothing I need say to you in addition, knowing your lively affection
for him.

The canvases arrived in January, too late for the replica to be
shipped to America. Though he had lost his client, Cadart would
appear to have accepted the small *Camille,* which he kept in his
stock. But this, the only major economic gain to have flowed from
that mad success at the Salon, now seemed trivial, and had dwindled
to a tawdry anticlimax. Disappointment, pressures from his creditors,
the possibility that his works left at Sèvres would be sold for the
benefit of Mme. Rolina, and the uncertainty of relations with his
family—all brought to that cold snow-clad winter a damning, dispirit-
ing effect. Could anything have worsened the tragic circumstances in
which they lived, it was the fact that at Christmas Camille became
certain she was expecting a child.

Fortunately the infant would not come into the world until after the Salon of 1867. By then it was possible his new garden picture would have given Monet once more the light of stardust and the strut of triumph. A mounting crescendo of praises had followed his two previous exhibitions. This time, exhibiting what he believed to be a work finer than ever before, surely fortune would commit itself to him more irrevocably. Every hope therefore devolved on the next Salon: Through long and cold winter months this was the light toward which they groped their way. Ahead lay five months in which to avoid creditors' depredations, obtain new credit, and above all, to keep the bright hope burning.

Their poverty became not a single threat but a succession of minor hopes and disappointments, each sufficient to break the spirit and bring complete desolation. From these separate wounds, each so painfully inflicted, arose a larger realization of the contrast between the vision which had inspired and this present squalid reality. At the start of February, Dubourg, aware of everything that transpired in his native Honfleur, wrote to Boudin:

> Monet is still here, at work on enormous canvases which have remarkable qualities, but which I find inferior, or less convincing, than the famous *Robe* [*Camille*] which merited him a success that I understand and that is deserved. There is a canvas nearly three meters high with width in proportion: the figures are a little less than life size. These are women in elegant costume picking flowers in a garden, a canvas begun from nature and out of doors. There are qualities in it, but the effect seems to me a little dimmed, no doubt because of a lack of opposition, for the color is vigorous. He is also undertaking a large marine, but it is not yet sufficiently advanced to be able to judge. He has done some rather effective snow scenes too. The poor fellow is very anxious to know what is happening in the studios. Every day he asks me if I have news of you. . . .

New obstacles still grew everywhere in Monet's path. When he returned with Camille to Paris in March, to present his picture before the Salon jury, a possibility arose that creditors might seize this canvas before it was exhibited. The only protection possible was a change of ownership, to which, aware of his friend's increased plight, Bazille loaned himself. For the huge price of 2,500 francs he undertook to purchase the *Women in a Garden;* doubtless he agreed also that his rights would be waived were the picture to find another purchaser.

Unpossessed of the sum named in this Utopian transaction, Bazille considered paying for the picture by monthly installments of 100 francs, larger sums to be advanced when possible. Even this proved excessive for his budget. He promised Monet immediately 500 francs with which to make frames; but that sum shrank, and mooted payments of 100 francs each month were reduced to 50. On this Monet and the pregnant Camille were forced to live. Until the Salon neither could hope for improvement in a prospect that was uniformly bleak.

By framing pictures in hopeful anticipation, planning for the future, and by a massive exercise of faith, they existed, lulled and soothed to the inevitable and foreseeable climax. The *Women in a Garden* was sent to the Palais de l'Industrie for presentation before the jury of 1867, who, in solemnly pontifical conclave, rejected it.

Lavish praises heaped on Monet in the previous year's press, especially from the suspect pen of Émile Zola, bore particular responsibility for his rejection from the Salon. Emboldened by the absence of Corot and Daubigny, the jury had reacted to the excessive lenience of previous years, exacting a terrible retribution from those Zola gave his bombastic support. Zola himself was aware of this: "The jury, irritated by my *Salon* [articles], has shut the door on all those who take the new road," he wrote. Refused with Monet were Sisley, Renoir, Pissarro, and Bazille. Édouard Manet, all of whose works were rejected the previous year, had not troubled even to submit.

An additional factor was that Monet's *Women in a Garden* for the first time brought before the jury his own substantial vision. Those works previously accepted, during a period of unusual leniency, each had been a hasty effort of secondary importance. Sufficiently conventional in outlook, these minor moods had brought forth manifestations of disapprobation through the back door of unfavorable hanging. But the full force of Monet's own fresh personality and idiosyncratic craftsmanship the jury utterly rejected. Intent upon its fundamental mission of upholding standards and the dignity of French art, the Salon's staid jury were unconvinced that such violence as they saw in Monet's canvases meant vitality.

This should not have been unexpected. For a generation the constantly altering membership of that committee had yielded to encroachment only slowly. The Salon of 1867 had a different look entirely from that of 1830. But the change had been tactfully accomplished. More advanced painters had yearly insured their places by submitting specially created, less objectionable works. Corot had evolved his own curious genre of lilting nymph-infested landscape, far removed from the observant outdoor sketches for which he was ardently admired by Monet, Pissarro, Daubigny, and Boudin. Built on the horizontal organizing principles of Claude Lorrain, from whom his masses of trees frequently were borrowed, Corot's Salon works usually bore pseudoclassic titles denoting incidents from history and mythology. Even Daubigny and Courbet sent to the Salon their least revolutionary essays, and both rose into the personal favor of Napoleon III and the Empress Eugénie.

Whether Monet had contemptuously rejected this respectable path, suffered from ignorance of it, or was precluded from entering it by his insecure technical equipment, he had adopted no tactful evasion. That perennial ritual acted out at the Palais de l'Industrie saw only his determination to force an entrance by brute strength. Ill-conceived from the start, in 1867 this tactic had led him to a complete rebuff accompanied by the prurient sniggers of jury members. Anxious to learn what had transpired when his picture was before the jury, Monet found little consolation. To the question "Why are you refusing him when he is making progress?" Jules Breton replied, "It is exactly because he is making progress that I refuse him. Too many young men think of nothing but to march in this execrable path. The time has come to protect them and safeguard art."

Such massed rejections as were dealt out naturally brought reaction. Despite an obvious emotional involvement, Bazille's livelihood was not in danger, and he could write to his family on a philosophic note:

Do not let this news hurt you too much. It is no reason for discouragement. On the contrary, I have been joined in this rejection by all painters of quality in the Salon this year. A petition is being circulated for signatures to demand an exhibition of the refused works. This petition is being supported by all the artists of Paris who have any value. Even so it is likely to come to nothing. But whatever happens, this disagreeable experience will not be repeated, because I will never again send anything before the jury. It is far too ridiculous, when one knows one is not too bad, to be exposed to these administrative whims, especially when one cares nothing for their medals and distributions of awards.

What I say here a dozen young people of talent think along with me. We have therefore resolved each year to rent a big studio where we can exhibit our works in numbers as great as we wish. We shall invite painters we like to exhibit with us. Courbet, Corot, Diaz, Daubigny, and many others whom you perhaps do not know have promised to send us pictures and they support our idea. With people like these, and Monet, who is stronger than them all, we are certain to succeed.

In preparation for this group exhibition Bazille began a portrait of Monet, by exhibiting which he would firmly latch onto those ragged but powerful coattails.

Like Bazille, many of the younger men rejected that year were able to go their way, scathed certainly, but angrily defiant, and plotting against the officialdom that so grievously wronged them. Their calm and rational attitude was impossible to Monet. His need was immediate, already too prolonged, and as Camille's condition advanced, it became still more urgent. Avenues of communication with his family must have existed. Whether or not these subtle channels were in use, he gained no advantage from them. At Le Havre the Monet-Lecadre family did not understand rejection to be an administrative whim.

The absurdity and the affectation that were so deeply a part of Monet's nature now took complete control. Both arose from the certain irrepressible, essential innocence that ran deep into a character which had suffered arrested development during a stage of boyish willfulness. Because neither he nor Camille had advanced emotionally beyond adolescence, whatever struck at them both, as present circumstances did, found them wobbling in a doubled instability. Since the flight from Chailly, Claude had grown accustomed to gain sympathy for himself by an unpleasant means. Gautier and, through him, his aunt had been the first victims. But now to whoever would listen he revealed his hardships in an excessively dramatic tone of deep sincerity, making self-pity his reproachful, plaintive wail. This was an emotional technique, and a crude contrast with his stiff and truculent attitude of other moments, he employed it as circumstances required.

Faced by the conditions of absolute want in which Camille and he were about to accept parenthood, Monet utterly misjudged the mood of his father by revealing to him Camille's condition. More shocked than touched by this unexpected confidence, Adolphe Monet resolutely turned his back. To a man of his fastidious bourgeois ethics the condition of a mistress was morally irrelevant. If Claude wished to return home alone and be cared for, Adolphe Monet replied, he would attempt to have him received at Ste.-Adresse by his sister Sophie. But no other hope was held out.

Through early April Monet shuffled about, still seeking a means of support. One becomes oppressively aware of his tricks and twistings when confronted by this worst and most irrevocable of his mistakes. Nerves ragged, and with a frightened girl weighting him down, he continued doggedly to seek advantage in new strategies. Whether Bazille, his inevitable resource in every emergency, would have suggested the scheme he soon adopted is open to question. Monet's own low cunning rings through it, though Bazille, realizing Monet was caught between grim realities and impossible circumstances, surely agreed to the role of disingenuous friend he now played. On his visit to Le Havre and Ste.-Adresse three years before, Bazille had been favorably impressed by the Monet-Lecadre family. He had not forgotten their civilized air, nor that once when Claude was in need his father had arrived in Paris with 150 francs.

Aware that the Monet and Lecadre families had the means to help Claude, perhaps reservedly, but in the interests of his friend Bazille wrote to Adolphe Monet. His phrases were carefully considered: He attempted to put the Salon's rejection into proper perspective, to stress the rapid strides Claude had been making, and finally, to express the belief that Camille was worthy of regard. Adolphe Monet replied immediately:

MONSIEUR,
I have received your letter of yesterday and will begin by telling you that I have no need to excuse your friendly intervention in the affairs of my son. It is a proof of your friendship for him, and quite the contrary, I must thank you for it.

I understand perfectly his disappointment at being refused by the jury of the exhibition, but this vexatious circumstance, even though it affects me strongly because of him, who has so much need to advance, cannot at all influence our feelings toward him. Only his actions and his conduct can exert favorable or unfavorable influence in our eyes. It seems incomprehensible that he requires the advice of others to abandon a path that he has followed so long with ill-placed energy. However, when one realizes his errors it becomes easier to set forth on a line of conduct and of reform indispensable to arrive at a result that is honorable and advantageous in every sense.

If therefore he is honestly repentant and disposed to follow a good road to repair his disastrous past, which has been entirely of his own making, there is only one way to succeed, and that is resolutely to march down the path of hard work and methodical application.

Most remarkable is that in his own Philistine way Adolphe Monet had arrived at a curiously correct estimate of his son's errors. His reasoning was a gruesome travesty, yet he too deplored that so much talent was deployed in extravagantly antisocial behavior. He would assist in a small way, but he had no intention to be permissive:

And as I have said to him, I will try to have my sister receive him at Ste.-Adresse. He will be able to work there with calm and with whatever result he wishes; but, on the other hand, he will have to renounce all his extravagant ideas and conduct. My sister, at her age, must not be troubled in her inner peace as already has been the result several times. And, if I succeed in having her receive Oscar here, it will be for him a good place of refuge, but he must understand that he must do serious work while there and after, as much to advance in the route of progress as to produce pecuniary results, into which up to the present he has not penetrated very far despite knowing so well the importance and usefulness of money.

The terms are familiar. They reveal conversations that probably took place within the Monet-Lecadre family, for this is a restatement of what Mme. Lecadre had written a year before to Gautier: "My intention is to furnish him only enough to live on each day." The yoke would be tightened, for Claude was invited to work under surveillance in return for his food and a place to sleep. Of money Adolphe Monet offered none. His shock at Claude's degraded existence next becomes even more evident:

Now, there is the question of his mistress. I admit at the start that I have been much surprised by this confidence. These things normally remain in silence, and truthfully it is very naïve, but, as I have said to him, he alone is competent to know what must be done in his situation.

Clearly, Adolphe Monet is questioning why his son has not married Camille. His whole thought in the matter revolves about this simple unmentioned point. He expresses no lack of regard or approval for Camille, but questions whether she is free to marry:

> He pretends that this woman has certain rights because she will be a mother in three months. Evidently she cannot have the rights that he would wish to accord to her, and, in this regard, he must know better than me of what she is worthy and what she merits. Also, let me repeat, I have been extremely surprised by this very untimely disclosure.

In gentle evasions Adolphe Monet conveys that it is a foolish and naïve act, and an act of indelicacy, to inform one's father that a mistress was expecting a child. Propriety demanded one marry the mistress and inform the father of an event over which he could express happiness; otherwise it must be left in silence. Twice Adolphe Monet says only Claude is competent to know which he must do. For what reason had his son failed to marry this girl to whom he seemed so devoted? It was past his comprehension, unless some legal impediment to marriage existed. And were the union one forced always to remain illicit, he felt unable to encourage it. His conclusion on this aspect is precise:

> To sum up I need not say more than a word: it is that every day one sees people who are well and enduringly united by law separate. It is done even more frequently and easily in a case such as Oscar's, where he has no need to hide or to leave the country.
>
> I agree absolutely to all the ideas you have expressed concerning the future of my son. His progress has indeed been rapid, and this is one more reason he must trace a line of conduct which will gain and even reaffirm his success and obtain proper results. In this hope, I beg of you, Monsieur, to accept the expression of my best regards.
>
> A. MONET

Flight Again

That discreditable transaction that was Claude's relationship with Camille now had been brought into the open, and to what purpose? Though it had a slightly absurd ring, his father's letter, utterly characteristic in every line, had suggested he marry Camille or separate from her and return home. Overlooking the surprise that reasonably could arise from the disclosure that Adolphe Monet would accept Camille as his daughter-in-law, deep in his own quirks and failings Claude Monet had no desire to do either of the things suggested.

The shy fey creature he had carried off to Chailly had lived with him for three years. She had surrendered to her own feelings with complete and guileless abandon. Her whole life was freely offered; she partook of his successes and deprivations, suffered when he did, accepted the tawdry, shoddy role assigned to her. No history of passion, rage, or the lamentations of her father, mother, and sister follows her, for her own family ties were utterly gone and she had no one to whom she could appeal. Now she carried a child of calamity they could not afford to bring into the world. Admitting even that Claude was more loved against than loving, his obvious devotion in this critical hour implied a deep bond. Yet, as always, as during that first winter when she yielded herself, the truth was that Camille only served the necessities of his volatile nature. Overpowered by the force of his genuine passion, she had allowed herself to be made a young cynic's instrument of pleasure. Suddenly one catches sight of the sheer grubbiness of Monet's character, and slowly it alienates sympathy.

To himself Claude Monet doubtless admitted only a series of plausible half-truths. He hit upon a scheme more distasteful than the collusion it tried to conceal. To his family he would pretend that he had broken with the hapless Camille. With the little money he could gather, he would leave her in Paris, to face childbirth in poverty, illness, discouragement, and utter loneliness. Meanwhile he himself would take up residence with his aunt at Ste.-Adresse. In effect he would use his family as a cheap hotel, for their benefit maintaining a fiction that he had accepted their conditions.

It was only typical, and nothing more, that—as with every previous agreement made with his father—from the start he proposed to keep the letter with scant regard for the spirit.

9. *Child of Calamity*

BUT EVEN DUPLICITY WAS FORCED TO WAIT. A measure of Monet's chaotic emotional state is that the former decisiveness of his mind was no longer present. Poverty-stricken, unable to provide for Camille or himself, and probably sponging on Bazille's groceries, Monet remained in Paris to skulk about the edges of others' renown. Hungry but defiant, he made pathetic gestures of revenge against the administration of the Salon.

His career as a wild and wayward boy, an injudicious debtor, and an artistic fantasist already is a mine of bizarre incident. None exceeded this present incapacity to act on the appallingly squalid decisions he had taken, nor escape the attractive but illicit illusion that they could be coaxed away. Nor could Bazille remain impervious to the continued embarrassment thrust on him by the presence of his friend and the obviously pregnant Camille. After playing his role in that ignominious charade enacted between Claude and his father, Bazille had the delicacy to depart Paris for Montpellier. By this unusual springtime journey, made before he had seen the Salon, he provided Monet with a roof under which to keep Camille during these protracted days of parting.

It was essential that a place be found where Camille could be delivered of her child. For this purpose they had no funds. Yet daily Monet continued to sally forth to raid the Philistine or consort with allies, hoping to organize the private exhibition of which Bazille had written. This single obscure thread holds together all the improbable activities of the weeks passed in Paris.

Querulous smiles were aroused when it became known that Monet had weakened to the extent of painting at the Louvre. Of course the explanation was that he entirely ignored those varnish-brown masterpieces of older times, hung row on row and rising to the ceilings. For some, like Fantin-Latour, endless copying represented the production of a salable commodity on which to live. Deficient

in that department of his art gained only by such laborious application, suffering every possible torment because of that lack, again
it is not surprising, but only typical, that when finally he brought
paints and palette to the Louvre, Monet's purpose was to paint views
of Paris from a balcony!

Before his easel, placed at the eastern end in a bay of Louis XIV's
towering colonnade, Monet discovered a rarely glimpsed view of the
newly restored and regilded church of St.-Germaine l'Auxerrois.
With unexpected diligence he was soon at work on three views of the
city, seen in the sharply accentuated perspective natural to such
heights. Paris never before had been painted quite like this, and the
pictures on which he lavished his attention faithfully recorded altering hues of early springtime.

Joined by Renoir, whose nervous gaiety and good fellowship were
cheering, Monet progressed with care. Architecture, and the stony
complexities of a late Gothic church, presented a challenge to which
he found no facile approach. His strokes lost the separate identity
they normally retained, merging into a happier illusion of reality.
Present too was an agreeable sense of May sunshine falling on the
freshly scrubbed stone. And were that not sufficient, he further
marked the season of his labors by a careful dabbing of the chestnut
blossoms flickering before him.

Soon he began another canvas, concentrating on the river view
farther to his right. Trees along the quays sprouted leaves in a lacy
yellow fringe, a dancing embellishment too thin to block his view of
an equestrian Henry IV on the Pont-Neuf, or the red-roofed bathing
establishment which permitted Parisians so bold to plunge into
the Seine. Even muddy river water was seen, and beyond, as a
decoration and a springtime jest, the tightly packed little houses of
the Latin Quarter held aloft the Sorbonne and Panthéon domes and
juggled impiously with the jagged silhouette of St.-Étienne du Mont.

On his way to work, crossing the Tuileries, a heavy voice called
Monet's name. Turning, he found Courbet.

"Where are you headed, Monet?" that huge black-bearded figure
called.

"To the Louvre."

"Very well!" Courbet drawled in his Franche-Comté style. "We
can go together. We will visit little Fantin. He is quite at home in
the Louvre and can do us the honors of the house."

At the Salon Carré they indeed found Fantin, laboriously making probably the twentieth copy of Veronese's *Marriage at Cana*. Courbet's hearty manner much upset the studious atmosphere of that vast room, so thronged with copyists and easels. Nonetheless he marched about, staring fiercely at Italian masters of an earlier century. Suddenly he shot out, "Never mind! If my [portrait of] Mère Gregoire were here all this would look decadent."

Fantin-Latour next conducted him to Raphael's image of Baldassare Castiglione. Courbet leaned heavily on the railing before it; they heard no breath escape him. Then he whirled on Monet and Fantin: "The great Raphael had better watch out!" he shouted in defiance.

Courbet in his glory was a grave distraction to Monet, whose own labors perhaps were not consistent. How could it be otherwise as he experienced the pressures of that appalling May? Springtime's first yellow glory had passed when he turned his attention to a final canvas painted from the Louvre balcony. Placing it upright on his easel, across it he sketched the little *Garden of the Princess* inside the Louvre railings. The entirety of this work was seen in broader, flatter, more rudely attacked areas of pigment. His insensitivity to three-dimensional form became troublesome, and, as in the previous efforts at this same view, it was inevitable that his technique would make scores of tiny figures on the street mere dabs, while horses drawing carriages suggest the spastic convolutions of disarticulated insects.

Threatened by instant annihilation every moment he stayed in Paris, Monet yet made no move to leave. As May advanced, his lingerlonging developed its own peculiarly insalubrious atmosphere. His efforts to organize the group exhibition continued, though he possessed little of the stuff from which leaders are made. The prospect, nonetheless, was invigorating to a man in his social and psychological circumstances, and the active adherence of Courbet went far toward drawing together the disorganized ranks of the rejected into a coherent, organized relationship.

The general effect of Monet's activities is impressive but puzzling, for while he tagged after Courbet, his own purpose was lost. Just as he had done for the Fair of 1855, Gustave Courbet was in the process of building his own pavilion, on the far side of the Pont de l'Alma, to participate in an International Exhibition on the Champ de Mars. Disheartened by successive rejections at the Salon, Édouard Manet also had adopted this means of showing the public his works. To Courbet, already the hero of the hour, it was another bombastic gesture; to Édouard Manet, a plaintive effort to be seen.

Through Monet, Courbet learned that Bazille had returned to Montpellier. This became a convenient channel through which to send a message. Monet wrote:

> Courbet has charged me to ask a favor of you. It is to go see M. Bruyas and tell him that Courbet would like every picture of his in the collection, and that he must send them quickly and without fail. The pavilion is in an advanced state, and will certainly be open before Manet.

The fascination that Courbet exercised on everyone is not difficult to understand. Everything about him was larger and more robust than life. Anxious to see the Salon and these pavilions, Bazille paid a brief visit to Paris. To his disappointment he discovered that neither the Courbet nor the Manet pavilion was yet completed, and the Salon was "the most mediocre" he had seen. He also grasped the crucial fact that seemed to elude Monet, or to which perhaps Monet had kept his eyes shut. The private exhibition for which they had hoped, and toward which Monet worked, was impossible for lack of funds. Bazille wrote:

> Bleeding ourselves as much as possible, we were able to gather together the sum of 2,500 francs, which will not suffice. We are therefore forced to renounce what we wished to do. We must return to the bosom of the administration, from which we have not had much milk, and who now disown us.

The collapse of this plan hit Bazille deeply, and was a worse blow to Monet, who bore responsibility for the tone of truculence with which it had been prepared. Another illusion had collapsed into sordid reality.

And how very sordid that reality had become. For reality and creditors were the things Monet had become most adept at avoiding. He was unwilling to concede, like Bazille, that the group exhibition was not possible, and concentrating on this melancholy effort, he seems hardly to have known that pregnancy in such circumstances was making Camille ill. Unable to look into those dark haunted eyes, Bazille hurried away from Paris after he introduced Monet to a Gascon named Cabadi, who probably had been a fellow medical student. For a fee he agreed to take Camille into his home at 8 Impasse St.-Louis, in the seventeenth arrondissement, and to deliver her. Under the combined strains of illness, being penniless, pregnant, and now obliged to separate from Monet, toward the middle of May Camille moved to the Cabadi home, where straightway she took to bed.

Bazille wrote from Montpellier that the large garden picture had arrived and was much admired. "I have received your letter, which gives me the greatest pleasure," Monet replied. "The compliments you send me are very touching. . . . It is a painful thing to be the only one satisfied with what you have done. Try to show it to M. Bruyas, and if it pleases him do not forget me." The chance hope that Bruyas, who twice before had refused Monet's works, might purchase this picture from Bazille, paying over at once the entire sum, could not be neglected. But it was an illusion, and the elusive part of his character that harbored scores of such wild fancies comes closer into view when one realizes that despite his own singularly unillumined life, and Camille's need, Monet was at this same moment hypnotized by the spectacle of his two artistic idols opening private pavilions at the International Exhibition. To Bazille he wrote:

> Manet opens in two days and is in a state of frightful apprehension. Courbet himself opens today in de luxe style. Imagine that he has invited all the Paris artists for the first day; he is sending out three thousand invitations, and at the same time for each artist he attaches his catalogue.
>
> He intends to keep his pavilion, where he has already made a studio for himself on the first floor. Next year, or whenever it is wanted, he will rent the place to those who would make an exhibition. We must work hard, and we will accomplish this with works that are without reproach.

That last line apprises us that no illusion would be allowed to die. From this enthusiastic account he passes to his own affairs, the contrast suggesting mental and emotional interplay between personages not entirely real:

No other news just now. Renoir and I are still working on our views of Paris. I saw Camille yesterday. I do not know what to do. She is sick, in bed, and has not much, or really very little, money. Because I must leave [for Ste.-Adresse] the second or the third at latest, I am going to remind you of your promise to send me at least fifty francs for the first [of June].

Those larger public events he recounts reach us across time with only a vague muted impact; his private suffering and that of Camille, so ill-conveyed by distracted words, touch us with riveting attention.

His once brilliantly successful emotional and artistic liaison with Camille was being ground down under remorseless poverty. After the dash and sparkle they had exhibited at Trouville and dining with the Count de Choiseul, Monet was reduced to little more than a truculent neurotic, slightly haunted and of incredible endurance, but living out of touch with reality. Twelve months before, he had been a mad success. That was difficult to recall, but some in Paris recollected the fact, and entertained private and penetrating views concerning the jury's harshness.

One does not know how the influence of Courbet on Monet must be assessed at this juncture. To dealers, that pompous figure of fun was also an important artist with a large and growing following among patrons. Monet figured among Courbet's closest disciples, whom in some measure the excess of patronage concentrated on the master must find. Despite the bad passage of the *Camille* replica, Cadart now followed up by purchasing a small marine. It was a safe investment, reflecting the kind of picture that gained such renown at the Salon of 1865.

Dealers assumed their clients were too humbly endowed for anything more testing than works exhibited at the Salon, or others thematically or harmonically related. Latouche, however, demonstrated greater initiative by purchasing the *Garden of the Princess*. Placed in his window, this attracted a considerable attention from those passing. One evening, watching these crowds as had been his habit in Le Havre so long before, Monet saw three or four well-dressed men pass, among whom he recognized Édouard Manet. They stopped to look, and Manet, shrugging his shoulders, cried disdainfully: "Just look at this young man who attempts to paint out of doors. As if the ancients had ever thought of such a thing!"

Twice Monet's path recently had crossed that of this idol, whose work had become the stylistic basis of his own. Twice he had heard himself insulted. Such treatment deeply wounded the proud and needy young man, living largely by his conceit. Yet this single injury was not all Monet suffered, for Daumier, as he passed, was even more direct. Pushing open the door, he called, "Latouche, are you not going to take that horror out of the window?" Monet paled. Neither he nor Latouche made a reply.

Later they saw Renoir's champion, Diaz, come down the street on his noisy wooden leg. Diaz seemed to exude a recognizable air of approbation, and anxious for relief from the embarrassments experienced, Latouche went out to him.

"It is very fine, is it not, M. Diaz?" Latouche urged, hastily adding, "The artist is inside!"

Whatever pain was dealt Monet by these transactions, the significance of two such important sales cannot be underestimated. The sum realized hardly could have been less than 400 francs. Here was what Camille's care required, and because his own expenses at Ste.-Adresse would be negligible, he selflessly gave her the entire proceeds. Even now, however, he concentrated his attention more on the peerless idiocy of Courbet and Manet, engaged in battling each other and the artists hung in an official pavilion for attention at the International Exhibition. "God, but Courbet has brought out some awful things," he wrote Bazille; "it is a great mistake, because he has enough fine things not to be in need of these." He learned too that Manet's gate receipts were falling behind expectation; "and for him they would have done a lot of good. He shows some very fine things that I do not know. The *Woman in Pink* is very bad; he has painted better things than he does now. God, but it is vexatious to let oneself go, as he does, to flattery, because he needs to be at his best!"

Then, penniless except for his fare to Ste.-Adresse, with sorrow and hope and a deep sense of having been wronged, in the first days of June, 1867, Claude Monet departed Paris. The gravely ill mistress he had refused to marry was left with Cabadi to bear her child in disgrace, while Monet himself was fed and housed by his family on the strength of a promise he did not expect to keep.

At Ste.-Adresse the kettle drums were almost never silent. Received with some show of cordiality by his father and aunt, "Oscar" added to the irony of their unctuous pretenses by immediately painting a large and curiously inventive conversation piece of his family assembled on the flag-draped terrace of their house. Limited space forced him to work through a window, and once more, by necessity, he found himself adopting the downward perspective of the Paris scenes.

In the middle distance, wearing a sumptuous red-embroidered party dress, holding aloft her parasol and innocent of contention, was placed the figure of his aunt Sophie Lecadre's daughter. Stage center thus was granted a girl two years his junior, who had followed an unadventurous path that led to marriage within the family. Her husband, Paul Eugène Lecadre, found a place in the Monet-Lecadre partnership, and doubtless assumed increased burdens when Adolphe Monet retired. Against low garden railings this youthful Mme. Lecadre provided a vivacious figure as she spoke with her graciously disposed and silk-hatted father, Dr. Adolphe Lecadre. Shielded by her own parasol, Aunt Sophie Lecadre sat in the foreground, her back kept to her nephew as he worked. Beside her, but more fully visible, sat the dapper, gray-bearded, and Panama-hatted figure of her "brother," Adolphe Monet.

Claude's presence at Ste.-Adresse was an elaborate charade. But the conspiratorial air hovering over both sides is not suggested by Monet's picture. Lost are the moral subtleties, complex ironies and dissimulations of bourgeois life. Monet, in fact, reaches for no gift of satire; neither does he express his indignation; the poignant display of domestic infighting has been lost—or ignored. For whatever reason this bizarre record of the gathered clan was executed, all those present doubtless displayed the most agreeable side of their perverse natures, and carried away private impressions. By its very irrelevance to Camille, left impoverished in Paris, the gaudy illumination of this sun-drenched picture makes it a harrowing document.

Adolphe Monet had suggested to Bazille that Ste.-Adresse would be "a good place of refuge" where Claude might work "with calm." An important but impertinent fact is that this conversation piece, a brave undertaking painted with sustained care and carrying the Zoffany tradition to a new scope, seemed to prove that estimate correct. Removed from the anxieties he so recently had known, Claude surpassed himself rendering the effect of sunlight. Whether figures, flowers, sparkling greenery, or the distant speckling of ships that rode an expanse of sea, whatever it fell on is handled with unmistakable vigor and competence.

No shortage of ideas nor of resourcefulness in their treatment was to be expected of him. A second equally brilliant effort, and nearly as large, quickly followed. In the garden behind the same house he did a small study of roses, geraniums, and the corner of a neighboring house. Then he launched on a major composition of geraniums, standing roses, and flowering white rhododendrons, all strongly contrasted against dark foliage. His cousin again became a sparkling parasol-bearing figure in this radiant June garden.

Urged on by magnificent weather which continued unabated, he next turned his attention to the beach, where a dozen years before all his troubles commenced. His buried ferocity was forced into this channel of his work, and soon the studious application of the family picture and garden scenes failed him. Tension became more evident in the ragged facture of marine studies, some of which he transformed into regatta views of the harbor entrance obscured by little sails. When they ventured down onto the flintstone shore to see the distant proceedings, both Adolphe Monet and Sophie Lecadre became tiny personages to fill his foregrounds. Nor was the Salon neglected. With it specifically in mind he began a large study of a steamboat: "It is very strange," he wrote to Bazille.

After three weeks at Ste.-Adresse he unburdened himself further:

[June 25, 1867]

You know that before leaving Paris I was able to sell a little marine to Cadart, and one of my Paris views to Latouche. This did me a lot of good, and gave pleasure too, because I was able to come to the aid of that poor Camille! Ah, my friend, what a painful situation all the same.

She is a very sweet, a good child, and has become very sensible. By these good qualities she only saddens me the more. In this regard I am going to ask you to send me as much as you can, the more the better; send me the money for the first of the month, because here, even though I am getting on well with my family, they have expected that I would be able to stay longer than I wish, without it costing me a penny, as is only right. However, if I have need of money I must be able to find it. Please do not let me down.

On the 25 July Camille will be delivered. I am going to Paris, and will stay ten or fifteen days, and will need money for a lot of things. Try to send me a little more, perhaps 100 or 150 francs. Think about it, because otherwise I shall be in a beastly position.

The tenacity of such a strong if misguided young character battling against the loneliness of personal disaster is admirable, until
one recollects it was his refusal to marry Camille which created this
situation. Through the horrific framework an extraordinary picture
emerges; and at the end of this same letter his mind returns much
more perturbingly where directed by a stricken conscience:

> Before leaving Paris I saw that Gascon you knew, Cabadi, who will
> take care of and deliver Camille. Afterward I felt a little better. I do
> not know, Bazille, but it seems to me terribly wrong to take a baby
> from its mother; the idea of it makes me sick.

Only now, from this potpourri of indecision, does it emerge
that the real purpose of Cabadi's services was to dispose of Camille's
baby. At this eleventh hour, struggling amidst a kind of divine
folly, Monet's conscience raised violent objection. Could he, who
had been everything else, now become so atrociously callous? Was
this the subject on which he had persuaded Camille to "become
very sensible"? How much better when she had been that agreeably
unpitiable and firm little girl, a shade neurotic, who after seduction
had held onto her lover by pathetic arts. Everything had gone wrong.
After continual dreariness, failure, and defeat, with a mounting
sense of torment they were obliged even to give away this new little
part of themselves.

A developing Gothic horror sequence was spared no gruesome
detail. Cabadi wrote for more money at a moment when the force
of the sun in which he worked had affected Monet's eyes. His vision
was so critically disturbed he was forbidden to work in the open.
Bazille failed to send his monthly pittance, and in July Monet felt no
compunction about employing what for him were normal means to
inspire a greater pity and tenderness:

> July 3
>
> I had hoped to receive a letter from you about now, and still
> nothing has come. It is only that I am upset to see Camille without a
> penny. I have just received a letter from Cabadi, who tells me to
> send some to him—and I am without anything.
>
> Excuse me therefore, my friend, if I importune you in the same
> way—but that poor woman has need. Send me immediately what
> you can—I am heartbroken. Can you imagine that I am losing my

sight. I can hardly see at the end of half an hour's work. The doctor says I must give up painting in the open. What shall I do if this does not pass?

That once querulous and overcombative note had passed from the letters of the young artist, who now began to live in a monotonous state of near hysteria.

Antoine Guillemet, landscapist pupil of Corot, was painting nearby and strongly praised Monet's newest efforts. Sisley also had journeyed out from Paris with his family, to profit by the fine weather at Honfleur. Monet himself presumably continued to work in some inferior fashion that rested painful eyes.

But no external facts touched a young man whose drama now was internal. So monumentally self-centered as he had been, flouting convention and treating family, self, mistress, and even unborn child with transparent dishonesty, his classic piece of Machiavellian virtuosity had reversed itself to wound him deeply. He tugged crudely at the heartstrings, and in letters to Bazille grew mercilessly repetitious:

July 9

MY DEAR BAZILLE,

It is unkind of you not to write to me. I am in the greatest inquietude over Camille, who hasn't a damned penny. I have no more than she. I have a horror that she will be delivered from one day to the next. In what a position she would find herself, that poor unfortunate girl!

I beg of you, my dear friend, help me from where you are, because my state is visible to everyone. I must leave here in eight days at the latest. I am going to bring back with me some studies I have just finished. If you are not in funds for the moment, send me the smallest sum, just so that I can make a gesture of good will.

I would be terribly depressed were she delivered without the things she needs, without necessities, without even a blanket for the little one. And at all costs I must be there.

In response Bazille sent only the monthly remittance of 50 francs and some unpreserved words of advice concerning Camille and the child. Whereas Monet counted the full 2,500 francs agreed for the garden picture a debt owed him by Bazille, it became apparent that Bazille still recollected that his motives had been merciful. After exceeding the agreed sum of 50 francs in May, to provide Monet with funds for frames, Bazille was not in a humor to despoil himself again. Because argument with Monet was useless, his replies were few, and one suspects they inclined to exchange the dark incomprehensibility of his silence for emptiness of phrase at best and platitudes at worst.

On receipt of Bazille's 50 francs, Monet sent it off immediately to Camille in Paris. Then, seeing nothing outside the nightmare world he had constructed around himself, he recommenced the solemn din of his demands:

> July 16
>
> I received your letter yesterday. I hardly know what to think of your silence. You do not tell me whether you are sending me further money, as I have asked of you, at least so that I can leave for Paris. I have already sent the 50 francs to Camille. She lacks every sort of indispensable thing. She must take care of herself, and must buy necessary things for the little one to wear, and find a nurse for the mother. These 50 francs will not go far, and I have nothing with which to leave.

Bazille did not reply.

Haunted by suspicions, trapped still at Ste.-Adresse, where he was forced to dissimulate every emotion churning within him, Monet saw the time of Camille's expected delivery pass. He himself experienced a desperate spiritual struggle, then summoned the unexpected courage to send Cabadi word that the child must not be taken from Camille.

For a fortnight Camille continued in momentary expectation, until at six o'clock on the evening of August 8 Cabadi delivered her of a big and healthy son. In the father's absence two of Monet's friends, Zacharie Astruc and Alfred Hatté, undertook the delicate mission of going to the Mairie of the seventeenth arrondissement to report the birth. Under their instructions the parents' names were entered as Oscar Claude Monet and Camille Léonie Doncieux, without the addition of that significant word *married,* which normally completes the line in every French register.

Herself only twenty, Camille had brought a son into the world. Bereft of family, unattended by friends, a depressed underling in the house of a dubious medical practitioner, at least she was relieved to know she would keep the little babe nestling in her arms. This sad treasure exhibited his father's brow and massively broad forehead. The delicacy of Monet's small ears and pouting mouth also were clearly copied, and such constant reminder of that distant eminence kept Monet in her mind. For the rest, Camille awaited her lover.

If she were no longer innocent nor conventionally pure, Camille nevertheless surely displayed praiseworthy qualities that proceeded from an innocent and pure heart. Yet fate had dealt with her harshly and in a style highly idiosyncratic and undeserved. On May 28 Antoine Pritelly, to whom her mother was sole heir, had died in Rueil. Another worthy bourgeois, Pritelly had been aware of Camille's defection from the paths of virtue. Rigorous in the maintenance of his own standard of behavior, Pritelly too had judged Camille harshly. In his will, written December 14, 1866, Antoine Pritelly was at pains to eliminate any possibility that Camille might profit from his fortune. "I give and bequeath to Madame Doncieux, née Léonie Françoise Manéchalle, wife of Charles Claude Doncieux, the use during her life, and to her daughter Geneviève Françoise Doncieux . . . the property that I possess" were words he employed to disinherit Camille in favor of her younger sister.

Such vengeance was a patrician art, and it willfully combined with bitter paradox. Two days before Camille gave birth in conditions of misery, her mother appeared in the study of a notary on the Boulevard de Bonne-Nouvelle. August 6, 1867, Mme. Doncieux formally executed a *substitution*, the document by which she entered into her inheritance from Antoine Pritelly. Indeed memorable was that at one and the same moment virtue should have been so roundly rewarded and its absence so grievously punished.

Still at Ste.-Adresse, Monet meanwhile reacted to the news that he had a son with a special emotional intensity. It pleased him strangely. As a part of himself, the unseen child immediately was gathered up into the enormous self-love that was his foremost characteristic. Though Adolphe Monet and his sister surely noted obscure bouts of depression, Claude was unable to approach them for funds with which to reach Paris. His only hope was Bazille, whose silence grew more dense and inexplicable when even the monthly pittance for August did not arrive. Four days after the birth of his son, Monet wrote again. No hymn to human nobility was to be expected:

> August 12, 1867
>
> You have been very stubborn not to answer me. I have sent you letter after letter, and you have done nothing. Moreover, better than anyone else you know me and my position too. It is as though I were asking help of strangers to receive such affronts. Oh! I have begged you so much, I did not think that you would leave me like this. It is so awful. . . .
>
> One last time I am going to ask this service of you in my horrible torments. Camille has been delivered of a beautiful and large boy, who, despite everything, I do not know how, I seem to love. I am suffering from the thought that his mother has nothing to eat. Neither she nor I have a damned penny.
>
> Oh! how I beg of you, my poor friend. Repair your fault quickly. Answer me by telegraph—I am so terribly anxious. Come, Bazille, there are things one cannot leave for the next day. This is one of them and I am waiting.

That Bazille remained silent strains credulity, yet in this special extremity of circumstances his sympathy was withdrawn. His friend had received a total in excess of the 50 francs a month promised. Bazille did not feel he could give more. Despite the frantic appeal of such letters, he could not shoulder the full burden of Monet's existence. Again obvious is the fundamental deviation of view each party entertained concerning the 2,500 francs Bazille pledged for the garden picture. To Monet this sum was a debt sufficient to wipe out his own debts and remove him from these tragic circumstances. To Bazille it was a benevolent charity that had grown tiresome.

For eight days the situation remained at an impasse. Then Monet unleashed a further broadside of despair:

> August 20
>
> Naturally I can no longer attribute your silence to forgetfulness. I know your negligence, it is true; but after the requests and pleas I have sent you one after another and by so many means I would think that you would hasten to write to me. One is sensitive to the pain of his friends, if only from habit. Also, I no longer dare to believe in your friendship.

My need is greater than ever, you know the reasons, and I am
ill. If you do not answer me by return, all is finished. One last time,
I tell you that I have a terrible need.

And still no response from Bazille. Possessed of no other resources,
stranded at Ste.-Adresse, unable to go to Paris to see his son or its
mother, Monet grew wilder in his ideas. Frantic with anxiety, he
conceived the impossible scheme of writing to Bazille's father at
Montpellier. Based on the firmly held notion that Bazille owed him a
debt on which he had a right to expect payment, this ill-advised
tactic, so entirely at variance with Frédéric's own view of the matter,
only angered Bazille, whose reply was harsh.

10. Annals of the Poor

RENOIR AND BAZILLE, both of whom were living in Bazille's studio at
22 Rue Godot-de-Mauroy, were singularly astonished that September, 1867, when Monet arrived at the door surrounded by his large
canvases. What they did not immediately appreciate was that the
friend who demanded a place to sleep was in some respects an altered
man. That relentless intransigence which distinguished his art even
when its craftsmanship was shaky, or its style unformed, would never
alter. Now, however, he inclined to look ineffably lugubrious, despite a mild indulgence in gallows humor. Bazille reported to
Montpellier:

Since my last letter there is news. Monet has fallen on me from
the sky with a collection of magnificent canvases. He will sleep here
until the end of the month. With Renoir, that makes two needy
painters whom I shelter. It is like a barracks, and I am enchanted.
I have enough space, and they are both very gay.

Quickly Monet sold the smallest of his garden studies to Bazille's
exuberant friend Victor Frat, nor was this the only embarrass-

ment he brought Frédéric. Camille was not of her lover's irreligious sort. When the two met again after the holocaust through which they had passed separately, she asked her baby's father to arrange a christening. Here was a little-suspected detail, suggesting qualities of uplift, earnestness, and solemnity. In later years when Émile Zola, whom at this time Bazille often visited, looked back with ripe sagacity on his recollections of Claude Monet and Camille, he concluded that Frédéric Bazille was asked to be godfather because Camille wished to give her son "a firm support in life in the shape of a godfather whose steady reliability she had not been slow to discern." To note what impression Bazille made is more amusing than otherwise, in view of the fact Zola's information was entirely from him.

Had the author been acquainted with the more intimate details of that friendship, and especially of the discord preceding and accompanying this birth, he surely would have written otherwise. But if he had not the "steady reliability" that Zola attributed to him, Bazille surely was in possession of the only regularly paid allowance in Monet's intimate circle. To ask anyone else would have disgraced his ingenuity. Whether Bazille was pleased by the request, or to what extent he, a Protestant, obliged at a Catholic ritual out of duty, only he could answer. As godfather to Camille's irregularly born child he tacitly acknowledged his own disused prenom of Jean; the second name chosen, Armand, was probably drawn from among the names of Zacharie Armand Théodore Astruc. The third, Claude, was surely contributed by the reluctant and proud father.

The months following that christening were the most difficult period Monet was ever to know. Reunited with Camille, the needs of an infant also to be provided, his voice never sounded but that it was shrill and strident. Most hurtful is how little their torments were noted, for the record of this autumn and winter of 1867 is thin beyond belief. From the end of September all trace of Monet, Camille, and little Jean is lost.

In October Frédéric Bazille returned to Paris from a holiday at Montpellier and sold to his kinsman, the Commandant Lejosne, one of Monet's still lifes. Two hundred francs were realized; but with his pathetic little family Monet remains unseen. A friend and patron of Édouard Manet and Courbet, Lejosne was happy with his purchase, even eager to find others who would follow his adventurous lead. "M. Lejosne has given me an appointment for this morning, and we have shown some works by Monet to several persons who are buying them," Bazille recorded. But only the lack of acknowledgments for his monthly 50 francs from Bazille implies that Monet was near Paris. Bazille continued the grand life of the capital: He attended soirées at his relative Lejosne's, and painted the portrait of a dog belonging to Mme. Rolina, Monet's former landlady at Sèvres. By contrast, Claude Monet, Camille, and little Jean had settled into the short, simple, and unrecorded annals of the poor.

No season depressed Monet more than New Year, the traditional French period of gift-giving. Reduced to an appalling poverty that sad New Year's Eve of 1867–1868, Monet visited Bazille. The latter's record of somewhat loud loyalty made it difficult for a sensitive, impoverished man to speak of money, for truly Bazille had occupied himself in Monet's behalf. Yet it was equally true that Frédéric seemed always lost somewhere in the land of lobelia and tennis flannels, unable to manifest an observant eye on Monet's increasingly heavy burden of poverty. No word of this delicate subject passed between the two, and both seemed to hope the New Year would bring an appropriate gift from Le Havre.

They were deceived. Neither Adolphe Monet nor his sister Sophie Lecadre could forgive Claude's perfidy of the previous summer. Meanwhile Monet's supply of coal was exhausted, and Camille's baby suffered from a head cold. In response to this, unable himself to speak, Monet asked his coalman to demand from Frédéric the four francs for coal. Until three o'clock that festive afternoon, watching over an ill and fretful baby, they awaited his return. But when the coalman came back it was only to report Bazille was not at home.

In the past Monet had demonstrated no shortcomings as a groaner. On this occasion, as he took his pen in hand, neither passion nor rage nor lamentation was evident. No man who reverenced law or was sensible of shame could have withstood the gentle indictment he penned:

January 1, 1868

MY DEAR BAZILLE,

I have received nothing from my family. I am without a penny. I have passed the whole of today nearly without a fire, and the baby is ill with a cold. My position is very difficult; I have much to pay tomorrow and the day after.

It is urgent that you at last give me a sum of money. I never torment you about it, knowing full well that you do not always have a lot of money. But in the end you must admit that if you pay me by twenty pennies and ten pennies, we must continue until the end of the world. When you purchased my picture, you were to give me 100 francs each month. For last May you assured me 500 francs, and, at the moment of Camille's delivery, you said you would assist me. All of that is reduced to 50 francs each month, and such little sums that you give me help not at all.

I never dare to say anything to you because you seem to believe that you have taken my picture as a matter of charity, and when you give me money you have the air of lending it to me. Again the day before yesterday I wanted to talk with you about that because for several days we have lacked the necessities, and even for so short a time it is not good to be without a fire with a baby and a wife. I was unable to say anything to you, because you cut me short speaking of the 800 francs that you must pay, and gave me to understand that you can give me nothing.

The point is that if you have 1,000 francs or more to pay, you are always able to find it. For me it is more than ever impossible to find anything. See if you cannot get it for me. It seems to me that you could, and the position is critical enough to warrant an effort. It is very painful for me, you know well, to act like this with you, though you had no difficulty at all putting me in my place when I asked your father to make me a reply. Even so I cannot remain longer like this without recalling to you your first promise. I had always hoped that seeing me in such embarrassments you would come to my aid yourself. At least, I hope tomorrow you will be able to send me something until you find more.

Believe me, my dear friend, that only necessity obliges me to enter on these discussions, and you know the pain it costs me.

With all regards,

CLAUDE MONET

Despite the strain under which he wrote, his case was justly and correctly put. But a continuous confrontation with poverty, the constant failures of his gambles with fate, the mean and belittling attitude of his family, were a harmful and embittering experience. They so ruined his relations with those about him that even when he was right, as surely he was in this letter, an habitual response of anger and mistrust greeted him.

The preliminary draft of Bazille's reply has survived. His greater literacy contrasts with Monet's rude style, but its tone is unworthy of one who so easily could peer into the tortured soul and desperate fate of a friend:

> If I did not understand your misfortunes I would certainly not take the trouble to respond to the letter which has come to me this morning. You try to demonstrate that I do not keep my promises, but you have succeeded only in proving your ingratitude. I have never, that I know, had the air of giving you charity. To the contrary I know better than anyone the value of the picture that I have bought, and I regret very much not being rich enough to make you better conditions. In any event, and as bad as they are, I am the only one to have proposed them to you, and I beg you to take account of that.
>
> We would have, you say, until the end of the world if I give you twenty pennies at a time. It ill becomes you to reproach me like that. The day that I gave you twenty pennies it was because I had forty, and I have paid you all that I owe you during these months.
>
> For the rest, so that you will know when our account finishes, here are the proper sums and what I have given you. You know very well that I bought your picture at 2500 francs, payable at 50 a month and not a penny more. It is true that I told you that I would give you larger sums whenever I would be able. I have not been able to do it except once, last May, and you had frames made. I very much regret it, but the fault is not mine that I have not been able to do so more often. All together you have received from me since we met the sum of 980 francs, to which it is necessary to add the price of the frames and 54 francs for this month of January 1868. I have not missed a single month in giving you 50 francs. Add it up and you will know when is the end of the world.

With his letter Bazille enclosed 50 francs, and promised Monet another 50. Of larger sums Bazille would not speak, and Monet feared the wrath of his benefactor too much to protest further. The "air of charity" of which he had accused Bazille thus became accepted by Monet himself.

As dramatic tension rises and falls in the early months of 1868, some few facts come slowly into view. With Camille and the infant

Jean, Monet had settled far out on the river Seine at Bonnières, a small, pleasant town situated where the river turns off its direct course into a huge bow. Beyond Mantes, Bonnières stood on a neck formed by the river's futile evasions, affording a double view of the water as it flowed idly northward then returned to rectitude and a seaward direction once more.

These autumn sales arranged by Lejosne had enabled these adoring parents to squander money for a lavish chintz-hung cradle. In this delightful object baby Jean appeared, enormously pink and cozy, his pinwheel an elaborate festoon. Both parents derived a warm glow from the sight, for in truth, another side of Monet's nature was emerging as by pity and love he moved toward a strange new nobility. Though they managed to cohere with a surprising degree of unity, the many contradictory elements of his nature often were seen standing out in isolation. The most startling result was all that willfulness, energy, and aggression, side by side with simple paternal affection.

Monet lived on at Bonnières, looking always toward Paris to sustain his little family. Bazille's "charity," for this it was acknowledged to be, always required worry and waiting. Record of other funds is scarce, though possibly dealers purchased a few expensively framed canvases. On February 18, 1868, Boudin wrote to his friend Martin: "The two sketches by Monet have interested me very much. Your judgment seems to me severe, my good friend. One thing that astonishes me is the audacity of the composition." But in this period not only does history not dislike obscurity, it dislikes as well any attempt to dispel it. To which pictures the faithful Boudin referred, or where they had been seen, remains lost.

To reach the public, efforts of another sort were being made by Boudin himself. March 25 he held a public sale at auction of his works in Paris. Monet was active in his behalf, doing all he could personally, and through his friends Héreau, Amand Gautier, Veyrassat, Charles Jacque, and Mouilleron, to interest collectors in the sale. Always generous in his views, Boudin thought Monet's assistance responsible for the venture's modest success.

For Monet himself, however, there existed only the Salon. After three fateful battles that had resulted in two glorious but empty triumphs and one bloody repulse, Monet and the Salon now seemed ancient antagonists. To each other they represented unattainable victory and unacceptable surrender. But the rules of these yearly encounters were in process of alteration. In response to continued clamor over the harshness of juries, the administration of the Beaux-Arts announced that voting for members of the 1868 jury would be extended to any artist received at a previous Salon. An official list of nominees to the jury, bearing the same familiar names, was duly presented before this enlarged electorate.

Nothing in the regulations specifically prevented the nomination of another independent list of jurors. When compiled, a "free list" therefore named Gustave Courbet, his friends, two critics devoted to him, and selected members of the establishment who had demonstrated tolerance:

Castagnary	Jacque
Courbet	Merle
Daubigny	Ribot
Glaize	Rochefort
Gleyre	de Rudder
Isabey	Yvon

This list was distributed attached to a glowing manifesto whose idealism and innocence were bound to be remembered vividly and resentfully:

> Considering that all artists must be admitted to freely show their works at the annual Exhibition of the Fine Arts before their natural judge, the public, and that the former organization of the juries has been a serious obstacle to this right:
>
> Considering further that such exclusions as have been practiced until now, far from being helpful to the artist have had only the opposite effect of troubling and obscuring his path:
>
> That which clarifies, and that which fortifies and makes progress, is the comparison of his works with those of his rivals, the emulation of the battle, not the humiliation of refusal: . . . .

Such views, which supposed the Salon to exist uniquely for the benefit of young artists and students, were a curiously inverted form of reasoning which events cruelly magnified. For when the ballots were counted, it was found the official view had won neatly. Of the free list only Daubigny gained sufficient votes to become a jury member, and this because his name also had appeared on the official list.

More than ever it was essential that Monet renew his former triumphs. Long an audacious gambler, he courageously submitted before this pro-establishment jury of 1868 two large works specially executed while staying with his aunt at Ste.-Adresse. The first was a canvas of genuine poetic passion, representing waves crashing against the Havre jetty. The brute realism of Courbet was brought to a new pitch of emotional exuberance, expressing the reckless rage inherent in its author. His second canvas, a *Steamship*, today is unknown and impossible to judge. Like its brother, however, it surely was filled with Monet's sheer native audacity.

The *Steamship* was seen by the jury first, and by Daubigny's insistence was accepted. When the *Jetty* in turn came into view, Daubigny at once felt it was the finer of the two. To his horror the Imperial Superintendent of Fine Arts, Count de Nieuwerkerke, though himself not an elected member of the jury, said, "Ah no, we have had enough of that kind of painting," and the jury turned away.

Castagnary, a close friend of Courbet and, like him, a defeated member of the free jury list, mocked Nieuwerkerke smartly in his criticisms of the Salon:

M. de Nieuwerkerke complains of Daubigny. If the Salon this year is what it is, a Salon of newcomers; if the doors have been opened to almost all who presented themselves; if it contains 1,378 more items than last year's Salon; if in this abundance of paintings the official art cuts rather a poor figure, it is Daubigny's fault. . . . I do not know whether Daubigny has done all that M. de Nieuwerkerke attributes to him. I should gladly believe it, because Daubigny is not only a great artist, he is, further, a fine man who remembers the miseries of his youth, and would like to spare others the harsh ordeals he himself underwent.

But Nieuwerkerke's authority successfully competed with such clamors, by having the offensive works of Bazille, Renoir, and Pissarro carried to a room reserved for inferior pictures, where they were hung beside Monet's *Steamship*.

"At the Salon I ran into Monet, who gives us all the example of the tenacity of his principles," Boudin wrote on May 4. "There is always in his painting a praiseworthy search for *true tone,* which begins to be respected by everyone." More certain is that so long in opposition, these artists had become prey to delusions about themselves, their opponents, and the world about them. For the *succès d'estime* Monet experienced in Boudin's eyes was sadly unreflected by the press. The glowing tributes of former years were not penned, and with his little family Monet retreated further into the obscurity of his poverty.

11. The Knight of the Woeful Countenance

THE SALON had admitted Monet, and the result was indifference. Had his *Steamship* been attacked as a profanation of the sacred art, he would not have cared so strongly. His subject had been selected for its novelty, and as Boudin had noted, Monet's reporting had grown increasingly vivid and individual, his experiences delightfully fresh. Such work demanded notice, and the indifference of Salon and public alike dreadfully taunted a young man forced to provide for a family. That the *Steamship* was accepted proved him respectworthy, but before the crowds his achievement was slight. For another year he was merely promising.

His worst wounds always had been licked by the sea, and after that disappointing Salon of 1868 once more he made his way to the Norman coast. Perhaps he hoped his family would assist him, and probably he lingered some days in Le Havre, sketching in the basins near the Rue Fontenelle house. But Adolphe Monet remained a thoroughly desiccated soul, prissy and querulous, and unable to overlook the previous summer's duplicity. That he had a grandson moved him not at all. He saw only disgrace that "Oscar" again was living with a mistress and shamelessly carting about their offspring. Why the St.-Siméon farm was not this luckless trio's next goal one can only speculate. Always in previous years it was Monet's first thought; now one senses the soft clinging odor of debt. The last places on earth familiar to him thus closed, Monet turned his steps north along the coast road to Fécamp.

Farther up the Normandy coast than melancholy and preoccupied wanderings previously had taken him, the ancient Benedictine city possessed another port about which he could bash away at small canvases. The character of recent bold and impatient sketches done at Le Havre had been altered by his despondence. For among the squalors of poverty were anxieties and fits of turbulence and petulance that wrecked his overstrained nervous system. A year before, the ocean rushing at the Havre jetty had been painted as a glorious tumbling sea of pigment. Not only had he captured its true violent tone, but conscientiously committed to canvas the pounding surf's exact cross-pattern of currents. By the time he reached Fécamp, that unique quality of observation was gone. Persistence had left him, and irregular and grainy dots and squiggles took its place. The water he painted now contained incorrigible rhythmic inaccuracies, and the certain air of authoritative finality his works previously possessed distinctly lacked.

The studies of beached ships made at Fécamp were sober-toned and beautifully balanced snapshots cunningly arranged. But the nightmare world in which he existed too obviously had taken its toll of his will and energies. For the first time he was thoroughly beaten and sick at heart. That coarse, opulent, inimitably sardonic imagination had left a man who now produced only a minor form of art, less satisfying than that of contemporaries like Daubigny. His Fécamp sketches give nothing after their first view: no hidden facets, nor further beauties, are found on long contemplation.

He had done his best to repress the irrepressible, but now he was hurt, a cowering creature of scars and nostalgias. A fanatic and a simpleton, his lack of education spared him the painful burden of inert ideas. Even the crippling hypocrisies of convention did not sear him, though he lamented his loss of caste. The Salon's indifference he might have borne—it could never paralyze him as it did Édouard Manet. Only the conditions of varying duress in which he, Camille, and innocent little Jean were forced to live broke his spirit and sent him staring wryly into nothingness. The irreducible minimum of their needs was always lacking. Paints and canvas were equally scarce, and on June 11, 1868, Monet wrote to Bazille for colors to carry on his melancholy work: "Ivory black, zinc white, cobalt blue, lake fine, yellow ochre, brown red, yellow brilliant, Naples yellow, burnt sienna; a larger quantity of the first four colors, of the others I have less need." But Bazille had left for his summer at Montpellier and sent nothing. For two weeks Monet awaited supplies that never came, burdened all the while by an increasing din of demand from the landlord of the inn where they stayed.

Bazille's June "charity" was exhausted. No hope of funds existed until his July payment. Necessity demanded they remain at the inn, taking shelter and meals until able to pay for them. This was an old deceit, but Monet's distraught state made him unable to dissemble. On June 29, retaining this hapless trio's baggage, the landlord put them on the street. This final product of Bazille's bland pieties and the Salon's indifference was more than Monet could bear. Stranded and seeking shelter, for a moment he faced the situation with courage. Somewhere in the countryside he found a heart softened by sight of his child, and with its mother left it to a shelter.

But it is a commonplace that the physical pressures resulting from so continuous a conflict as Monet had experienced were too damaging to be borne. Since May he had compensated for this unnatural load by shrugging off tomorrow; that no longer was possible. After finding shelter for those poor unfortunates he loved, he returned to Fécamp and threw himself into the harbor. A pause full of death punctuated his anguish; then cold salt water sobered him. His act was an irrelevancy, for however much pain he bore, he *had* to provide for Camille and their Jean.

Louis Gaudibert, the Havre shipowner, long before had purchased two panels from Monet. Gaudibert also bought pictures from Amand Gautier and Boudin, in Monet's meager realm therefore qualifying as that symbolic eminence, a *patron*. To see Louis Gaudibert and make a personal appeal would necessitate a trip to Le Havre fraught with peril. He would arrive penniless, and were his family to refuse him their house, he would have no place to sleep. To Bazille he wrote:

> I write you two words in haste to ask help very fast. I am decidedly born under a bad star. I have just been put out of the inn, and stark

naked at that. I have put Camille and my poor little Jean into a shelter for several days in the country. I leave this evening for Le Havre to see if I can arrange something with my patron. My family do not wish to do anything for me. Because of this I do not know yet where I will sleep tomorrow.

Your very tormented friend.

CLAUDE MONET

P.S. I was so upset yesterday I had the stupidity to throw myself in the water. Fortunately I was not injured.

On failing strength Monet made his way to Le Havre and the family home at 13 Rue Fontenelle. From his appearance it was obvious disaster had befallen him; his somber and distraught figure was not turned away. Whether he also succeeded in loosening immediate response from Gaudibert is unknown, but the shipowner definitely was sympathetic and the visit concluded happily. More definite assistance derived from Eugène Boudin. Under the high patronage of His Majesty the Emperor Napoleon III, and His Highness the Prince Imperial, an International Maritime Exhibition was ready to open at Le Havre. Boudin had been consulted about an exhibition of paintings to take place within that larger framework, and he suggested artists whose participation should be invited. These included Courbet, Daubigny, Amand Gautier, and Carolus-Duran, in addition to himself, Édouard Manet, and Claude Monet.

Immediately Monet set about assembling an impressive display of his works. By his own means he was able to produce both large canvases submitted to the last Salon. The famous *Camille,* so admired at the Salon of 1866, but unsold, last had been seen at the St.-Siméon farm and could also be produced. For a supporting group he wrote to Bazille, with whom the masses of his canvases were stored. The request was highly specific:

[1] the two large avenues done at Fontainebleau of the same dimensions
[2] the Chinese picture where there are flags
[3] the rose bush at Guillemet's place
[4] the very white snow scene
[5] the one a little smaller with crows
[6] the marine with little blue boats
[7] the scene where one sees Le Havre from the distance with little cabins and much surf

Send them to M. Monet, rue Fontenelle, 13, at Le Havre. I am counting on you because I must strike while the iron is hot.
In haste, I shake your hand.

Quickly then he returned to seek out Camille and little Jean near Fécamp. Possessed of the few francs secured from Bazille, he brought them to a hotel, where the facts of their existence remained impressively crepuscular. His anguish was hardly diminished for all the activity at Le Havre, for in truth the situation he had contrived for himself remained an impossible one, and with sad justice he continued to be its scapegoat. The frailty of little Jean, about to celebrate his first birthday, added to the problems. An irregular life left him prone to frequent coughs, and insensitive as Monet had been to Camille's pain, those of his son were an agony to him. A further lack of promptness in Bazille's "charity" now contributed to unsettled humors.

August 6

It is well said that I cannot be the least bit happy two days in a row. I counted on receiving money from you the 3 or the 4 as usual. You surely know what harm can be done me by the least delay. Look at us, the baby sick at the hotel, and not a penny. All that costs me dear, and because I have been unable to get down to work I lose my time.

I have sent you a wire asking you to send me 100 francs. Do it, I beg of you, because otherwise I shall not know what to do, even though I am well placed for work and to live cheaply! Send me what I ask you, I will be most obliged. It hurts me always to torment you, but think of my position—an infant sick and not the least resource.

Do it, I beg of you, and with haste!

The spectacle of misery this letter brought Bazille had result. Harboring unspoken sensations of guilt over the suicide attempt to which his friend had been driven, Bazille sent the 100 francs requested. At Le Havre the Maritime Exhibition opened, and in a published jury report Monet saw himself singled out for "great truth of tone" and "indisputable sincerity of execution." The words are so nearly those of Boudin one need not look further for the influence at work, nor is it surprising that together with Amand Gautier, Yvon, Carolus-Duran, Courbet, Daubigny, Manet, and Boudin himself, Monet received a silver medal.

The portrait of *Camille,* already celebrated at the Salon, made a fortunate impression on Louis Gaudibert. Romantically glittering fabrics pleased this merchant-patron, and, further encouraged by the jury's report, he sent word to Fécamp that he wished a portrait of his wife painted in the same scale and manner. When it arrived promptly September 1, Frédéric Bazille's modest "charity" of 40 francs found Monet in a more hopeful humor. Ready to depart for Le Havre, where he must appear alone, he dispatched a further plea:

> September 1
>
> I have just received your letter containing 40 francs. I thank you, because I awaited it with impatience. My patron at Le Havre has invited me for next Monday to do a portrait of his wife. It is essential that in departing I leave a little money with Camille, and that I not be completely penniless while in the house of this Monsieur.
>
> I must beg you to send me some by return of post, without fail, my dear friend; because if I receive no letter from you by Monday morning, I will be forced to take a little money from the hotel in order to go. I do not ask a great deal of you, only enough so that Camille can await what I will send her from Le Havre, because M. Gaudibert will not delay in giving me some.
>
> My compliments on your work. I am not so fortunate.

Assisted by another 20 francs from Bazille, the first week of September, 1868, Claude Monet, Camille, and their suffering baby started south from Fécamp. At Étretat, the last town before Le Havre, quarters for Camille and little Jean were found on the Route du Havre (now Avenue George V), a principal thoroughfare whose length comprised hardly two score houses. Alone, Monet proceeded on, his short journey encompassing the distance from shabby depression to a city illumined by a fair.

Merchants lived well, and at Louis Gaudibert's imposing château outside Le Havre Monet was graciously received. Once installed, however, the production of a commissioned portrait brought on him exigencies of which he never dreamed. A part of the problem was that Mme. Gaudibert was not in her first youth. Dignified and matronly, she possessed the strong patrician features that distinguish Frenchwomen. For the portrait she proposed to wear a gown of heavy tan silk in every way equaling the green robe that was the principal feature of *Camille.* Obviously he was expected to give vent again to the fierce and absurd frenzy sweeping over that former canvas.

He flung himself into the work with disarming zest, reversing the design of *Camille,* and turning Mme. Gaudibert's head so that only a trailing edge of eyes, nose, and mouth were glimpsed past her cheek. Just as the long lines of Camille's gown had been shortened by a dark jacket, so now he draped this fashionably garbed woman in a wool shawl, cut by angular patterns of red, black, green, and white. A flowered carpet, its tone almost matching the dress, and a curtain of steel gray, completed accessories.

Abundant vivacity and resource flowed from his brush, enlivened by great charm and delicacy of color. Rough outlines of the figure appeared on canvas; the head and hands followed, each part spirited, ingenious, and prettily flavored. Patterns in the colorful shawl were developed for richness of effect, and the gown's long silk train formed an arresting linear sweep. On his canvas the silk rippled and carried, and was rich, golden, and vibrant. But precisely where this frenzy ought to have reached an irresistible climax he found its rhythms overcomplicated. To cure this ill he repainted large areas, lacking the experienced craftsmanship first to obliterate the hard edges and textures left beneath.

Those parts of the picture that comprised the *portrait* elaborated, he began to think anew of the design. And at this point the humiliating truth of his inexperience was revealed to him. To establish a background that gave proper relief he altered the hue repeatedly, each time changing fold patterns in the curtain before which Madame stood. Finally he flattened the curtain to hang in straight lines, a hint of shadow accentuating one fold at left to prevent the eye from wandering out of the frame.

As a whole this work possessed brilliance and varied incidental decorative merits. But despite the verve of painting it was wanting in pace and gusto. Employing flat tones throughout, he received no assistance from effects of light that served so well Winterhalter. The pigments grown thick on the canvas produced troubled edges against the hands gently and easily painted so long before. The head's contour also began to look brittle, and, more troublesome still, his worn brushes left a scattering of loose sable hairs. This sumptuously flabby portrait sent him spinning into renewed bouts of depression. Neither by training nor by temperament was he equipped to organize such work. Just as at Chailly, he had wandered beyond his depth, and was in danger of leaving this huge undertaking a pallid residue of tricks and mannerisms.

Gaudibert was aware of his mood when Monet ventured into Le Havre bearing his armorial bearings as knight of the woeful countenance. About his sad figure the great port presented the spectacle of a society gripped by collective mania, in the midst of which Gustave Courbet played his ponderous role of Magnifico. Louis Gaudibert himself said to Monet, "Courbet is here. Go to see him: it will distract you."

At the address given him Monet found his friend vast and dominant, fond of his young ladies and not above a pat or two. September 17 Courbet had received a letter from the exhibition committee asking if he would permit two exhibited works to be sold. No such inquiries were made after Monet's works, this renewed disappointment adding to his woeful state. Yet Monet soon learned that Arsène Houssaye, Inspector of Fine Arts and editor of *L'Artiste,* had come to Le Havre, where he was enchanted to see *Camille* exhibited. That a picture which created such a stir at the Salon should still be available seemed incredible to him, and inspired a wish to profit by Monet's bad fortune. For the derisory sum of 800 francs Houssaye offered to buy this famous work, and Monet could not refuse. In an atmosphere of forced paradox he could only hope that Houssaye's influence was a part of the bargain.

Like the exultant schoolboy he was at heart, Courbet one day exclaimed to Monet, "What shall we do?"

"Let's go to see the *père* Dumas!" he answered his own question.

The author of the *Three Musketeers* was indeed living at Le Havre. In the evening of his life, after a great popular success, Alexandre Dumas the elder had been reduced to working for local newspapers.

"I do not know him," Monet objected.

"Me neither," Courbet responded. "We have always been contemporaries, but never met."

They arrived at the haberdasher's in whose premises Dumas lived, and the problem resolved itself with style. In his demanding manner Courbet asked to see "Monsieur Dumas!"

"He is busy," came the reply.

"When he knows who asks for him, he will receive us," Courbet said confidently.

"What name shall I give him?"

"Announce the Master of Ornans!" said Courbet.

Dumas appeared immediately. Himself a giant in stature, his head crowned by frizzled white hair, wearing no shirt, he had been cooking for himself and left the stove on hearing Courbet's voice.

"Dumas!" cried Courbet.

"Courbet!" cried the author, and they fell into each other's arms.

"You must dine with me," said Dumas at last, "and the young man [Monet] too."

Because it was where Camille and little Jean were hidden, the following day Courbet, Dumas, and Monet prepared to travel together to Étretat. In his eagerness Monet came early, to find himself waiting alone with Dumas. With the author Monet then ran to fetch the Master of Ornans, whom he found in his chamber asleep, snoring mightily with clenched fists.

"I have visited kings, and they never made me wait," intoned Dumas.

At last the three departed to eat at Étretat's famous restaurant, La Belle Ernestine. Over his dinner Dumas was marvelous, speaking on art, history, politics, love, cooking, answering everything, never curt, frequently witty and eloquent. Courbet jested with him in a heavy admiring way, and when they ceased to speak both men turned to song. Monet was left a silent spectator.

Such gaiety caught the forlorn young man unprepared, and his return to the Gaudibert château provided no consolation. On sight of his huge portrait he realized afresh that the enormous risks taken with rhythms of the satin skirt had come to nothing. Carefully prepared and lavishly presented, this sharp but pastel portrait lacked the incandescence of even his dullest outdoor sketches. September was ending, and Bazille wrote to inquire where Monet wished his monthly payment sent. The reply reflects a mood of profound discouragement that had gripped him since Fécamp:

It is to Étretat, Route du Havre, that you can send me my little payment. Would you have the goodness to write to Camille, because I myself am caught here doing a portrait.

I am in a château near Havre, where I am received with over-whelming kindness. All around the country is charming. But all that is not enough to give me back my old ardor. The picture does not go, and decidedly I no longer count on glory. I am like a man going down the third time. In sum, I have done absolutely nothing since leaving you. I have become completely lazy, everything disturbs me the moment I want to work; I see everything black.

On top of that money is always lacking. Disappointments, insults, hopes, new disappointments, you see how it is, my dear friend. At the Havre exhibition I sold nothing. I have a silver medal (value—15 francs) some superb articles in the local papers, and I have made a sale which, if not advantageous in the purely pecuniary sense, seems in the right path. I sold the *Woman in Green [Camille]* to Arsène Houssaye, who came to Le Havre, who is enthusiastic and wants to launch me, so he says. . . .

From your side, do not forget me, because it is on your 50 francs that we count. And while you are about it let me know when that will finish. I lose my head when I think about that.

Deeply absorbed in the solemnity of his unhappiness, Monet was only now becoming aware of the gravest weaknesses in his portrait. Too hastily put on canvas, from the start its composition suffered from overbalance to the left. Mme. Gaudibert had been turned to face that direction, and, by an error carried over from *Camille,* her figure also had been placed too far toward that edge. A horribly va-cant area silhouetting the intricately painted shawl was fatally dis-tinct behind her, permitting the picture's strongest color note to draw attention to its serious unbalance. Made panicky by the recur-rent problems he faced, he attempted to eradicate this void by the addition of a table bearing a crystal vase and two pink roses.

The solution of this one problem produced a score more, exactly as had happened at Chailly. The table's perspective eluded him, and its edge, running dangerously close to the shawl, he timidly drew back to avoid collision. The unfortunate little gap thus created shouted his inexperience. Yet despite crudity in its execution, the table was not a hindrance but contributed to the interest of the picture and added a sense of scale. More important, a black fichu he swept onto it in sticky masses of black pigment gave new sonority and range to the color. And in fact, during all this shifting and redoing, the color fi-nally had come right. The prevailing tone had been too consistently pastel. Now it became brilliantly vigorous and diverse, jerking tired harmonic consonances back into life.

Each figure composition Monet undertook had been an extended and laborious schooling. En route there was always a repeated lurching into the commonplace and the shoddy. Yet a point came when, his problems solved, the change of climate was immediate and immensely refreshing. From all the hectic fury flowed a new immediacy, a new warmth and richness. And especially in this portrait of Mme. Gaudibert he scored richly and imaginatively, creating the finest figure composition of his early years and a picture which very properly enraptured all. Drawing upon Édouard Manet for its flat tones and arbitrary simplification of forms, its soft richness of color and rightness of effect were beyond the capacities of Manet. In an effort to emulate, Claude Monet had overtaken and surpassed his model.

As a portrait the success of this picture may legitimately be questioned, for the *portrait* element is overwhelmed entirely by fabrics. That had been the intention of Louis Gaudibert when he commissioned a picture in the vein of *Camille*. Undoubtedly he was pleased, for afterward he too was painted, and Boudin, who saw both works, thought them very fine: "especially Madame . . . very remarkable with all the éclat of color."

12. Fraternity of Vagabonds

THE ASTONISHINGLY floriated image of Mme. Gaudibert had sounded an authentic note of triumph fated to die away sadly and in discord. That Monet possessed a godly gift was increasingly clear, but the only further resemblance between that gentleman and Claude Monet lay in both having brooded over chaos. Most men in this position are incompetent; a tiny proportion may be far-out geniuses. Yet a mad and ignoble ingenuity alone can account for Monet's plight when that autumn of 1868, after closure of Le Havre's

International Maritime Exhibition, he at last was hunted down and cornered by creditors.

Cruelty, heartache, and compassion abound in events to which there is a taste of most deliberate absurdity. The pieces refuse to fit. Only a fortnight before, 800 francs had been realized from Arsène Houssaye for *Camille*. However small, the "sum of money" for which Monet had begged Bazille had come to him from an unexpected source. An equivalent sum, or more, was earned by the *two* Gaudibert portraits; and Bazille's regular "charity" could still be expected. In the orgy of sublimation following his Fécamp suicide he had acquired two important patrons and painted at least one acknowledged masterpiece. His poverty no longer was so abject, and if he remained depressed, this was not Stygian gloom.

At hand was an opportunity to preserve these funds and by a delicate stroke of irony make himself a discharged debtor. Since first it was heard at Chailly, the tale of debt had trailed him for three years. Bleak rehearsals took place at Paris, Sèvres, probably the St.-Siméon farm, and certainly the Fécamp inn from which, together with Camille and Jean, he was ejected. One doubts that even the silent passage at Bonnières was secure from such a confirmed trick of fortune. At Sèvres he had suggested his aunt Sophie Lecadre pay his debts, a plan she considered impossible as drinking the sea. Nowhere is there any suggestion he made an effort himself to deal with those who pursued him across France, until at Le Havre a stroke of illumination occurred. His moment had come and he turned at bay.

His exhibited works, including the *Steamship* and *Jetty* done expressly for the Salon, were seized for the benefit of his creditors. He perhaps foresaw this, and that by virtue of the sum realized from their sale his creditors must be legally satisfied. The greater satisfaction of being freed surely was Monet's, for at an auction attended by his Lecadre relatives and Louis Gaudibert, each of whom showed marked disinclination to bid against the other, catastrophically small prices were realized. Paul Eugène Lecadre appears to have purchased the conversation piece painted at Ste.-Adresse, and Louis Gaudibert scooped up the two large marines for 80 francs!

Louis Gaudibert then demonstrated a touching sense of justice. With vague, self-deprecating avuncularity, during the months that followed he made up the true value of his purchases in regular payments to Monet. This perhaps was the understanding under which no bid was made against him. On the small capital preserved by this most ingenious maneuver, Monet, Camille, and Jean settled quietly into a winter's nocturnal intermezzo. His debts were wiped out, and into the bargain he had confirmed a patron and converted rejected or unsold pictures into a second pension. It could hardly have been more neatly done.

That ingenious bit of spirited partisanship concluded, Monet rejoined Camille and their child at Étretat. Rapidly his nervous state, his strength, and courage, revived. He found new and quiet joy in the growth of his son, and the immediate corollary of this homecoming was a period of tranquility. For the first time he explored Étretat's famous natural bridge formations. High promontories gave extensive return views of fantastic cliffs, and for a time he wandered free of anxieties and almost literally entranced among the hills above the sea.

Freed of disturbances that had marred the previous years, every part of his life revealed Monet to be a simple man whose enjoyment of living came largely through his art. But a second recurring phenomenon immediately visible is perhaps less expected from a man so cynical. To shelter his family he rented part of a divided house, a *maisonette,* intended to house summer visitors at that famous resort. The cost was small during winter's grim season, and here, the apparition of impoverishment for the first time banished, Monet and Camille played at being gentry.

This was not the brilliance they had tasted at Trouville, though the game had delights all its own. If their stage were a trifle compact, every necessity was present for the comedy of manners into which they launched. Hung with lace curtains, lit by a glass-shaded oil lamp, their tiny dining room by night became sitting room too. Here was the cozy fire before which they sat; nor did Monet require more ample nor eloquent surroundings to induce voluptuous reverie. For if the deceits of their existence remained morally reprehensible, the reticently bourgeois exterior they gave their life is clearly recognizable.

Certain questions must immediately arise, for since the previous January, 1868, Camille no longer was a minor. With her twenty-first birthday had come freedom to marry without the consent of her parents. Vague, contradictory, their relationship still remained without benefit of clergy. From compassion for their child's illegitimacy one would have expected greater attention to convention. Surely it was not the pathetically devoted Camille who hesitated. And thus, though one admires Monet increasingly for his astonishing artistry, his perseverance and courage, again his personal philosophy becomes profoundly distasteful.

Superficially attractive, handsome, only modestly intelligent but with powers of articulation, he always began by inspiring confidence. That he demanded compassion as well was the burden of his many letters. The more one knew of him, however, the more one understood that the compassion he required from others he would give to no one. Such men are hard to love.

The shabby and unnecessary charade of a bourgeois matrimonial state continued. Camille suffered most, but the ultimate victim was Jean, now in transformation from infant to a little boy whose care and feeding consumed Camille's day. Heavier work—the washing, cooking, cleaning, and preparing of fires in the grateless chimney—was delegated to a small sour-faced servant woman. Their meals became modest imitative rituals served by this maid of all work. Lunches were broadly lit from a window. But when dinner appeared under lamplight, bizarre illumination crept over table and faces, and two small studies of these effects that Monet executed possess an original touch of lamplight fantasy impossible to dissociate from the sense of a stage.

Monet's principal efforts had followed an older habit pattern that brought him to the beach. There he created a tough, violent piece of waves smashing against towering rock formations. No more than a direct view from the town front, he made it vast and simple, the foreground held in place by figures boldly silhouetted. Here was no subtlety but a huge sense of emotional commitment. By such works as this, and simultaneous efforts to paint by lamplight, he probed, perhaps unconsciously, that narrow area between the viable and the impossible. Prodigies of ingenuity, they revealed him to be in a full flood of creative vigor.

Long winter evenings at Étretat filled Monet with the emotions of less frantic times. Mme. Gaudibert's portrait had made him aware how grotesquely ignorant he remained of the simplest technical skills available to better-trained contemporaries. Always his accomplishments were based on brute force and determination, and sometimes, as at Chailly, these had been insufficient. In the tranquility of Étretat his lack of knowledge filled him with new regret. Through his mind passed also the success and failure of past works, and their varied receptions at the Salon. Figures compelled an attention other works did not receive. His greatest notice had been gained not by seascapes but *Camille*.

In the dead of winter a new plan followed. One can only suspect the original intention was to portray little Jean and his mother in their accustomed places at the luncheon table. A secondary purpose was to extract the continual tonal radiance emitted by the undulating textures of a white cloth on that oval table. The delight of his tiny dining room was great when filled by Camille and their infant son, upon whom a special emotional glow had settled. These persons and this place brought a redemptive liberation of his spirit; never had he experienced the same contentment. Sadly, he did not understand these same human objects were infinitely less compelling to strangers, nor that to them the homely drama he proceeded to trace upon a large canvas moved into the dining room would look utterly different. Indeed, his account of the scene can be recommended to all appreciators of the human comedy for containing every farcical and hilarious element of bourgeois life.

Immediately one learns Monet's simple tastes, for he launched into a delineation of two eggs each for himself and Camille, and between them the principal dish of cheeses and sausage. A fresh bottle of wine stands beside a water decanter and his own empty glass; Camille's glass already has been filled and drunk half empty. Bread lies half off the table edge, soon to tumble on the floor. Near it are matching containers of oil and vinegar to assist the flavor of a half-hidden green salad, and nearer to Monet's plate an aspic lies covered; Camille evidently does not prize this brightly colored delicacy. The lunch will conclude with a munching of grapes.

The literalness of the subject, the unbalance of the composition, the inappropriateness of the dining room's brown walls, from the start made this venture dowdy. Camille is delicately and perceptively rendered, the leanness that crept into her features before Jean's birth happily banished, but leaving her eyes surrounded by areas of dark discoloration. Juxtaposed with this acute rendering is an image of the little Jean that suggests nothing more living than a doll. Throughout, such sadly limited proficiency coexists with masterstrokes. The result lies halfway between boredom and despair, for everything is careful, workmanlike, and badly drawn. Knowledge of the sham circumstances in which all was done transforms it into deadly satire.

Always a tireless writer of letters, during peaceful evenings at Étretat Monet penned the most extended missive of his career. No longer did he thump with words, nor pretend reticence to make demands born in despairing rage. Étretat was not unsuggestive of his Ste.-Adresse boyhood; a fusion of moods, boyish exuberance with manhood's quiet satisfactions, was apparent when he addressed Bazille:

> I am surrounded here by all that I love. I pass my time outdoors on the flint beach when the seas are heavy, or when the boats go off to fish, or I even go into the country, which is so beautiful here that I find it perhaps more agreeable in winter than summer. And, naturally, I am working all the time, and believe that this year I will do some important things.
>
> And then the night, my dear friend, I find in my tiny house a good fire and a good little family. If you could see your godson—how sweet he is at present. My friend, it is adorable to see his little being grow, and really, I am terribly happy to have him. I am going to paint him for the Salon, with other figures around him, as is proper. I am going to make this year two pictures with figures: an interior with a baby and two women, and figures outdoors. And I want to do them in an astonishing way.

The new dimension created by little Jean is notable, for if Monet still would not marry Camille, this little boy who crept about, made noises, and hammered his spoon created emotional responses with a totally authentic ring.

Equally remarkable is the persistence of Monet's few basic ideas, for now, able to work again in peace, he falls back upon thoughts expressed in 1864. After the departure from Honfleur of Boudin and Jongkind he had written that he worked better for being alone. That simple thesis is stated again, though experiences with the Gaudibert portraits and the *Luncheon* have made him newly aware of inadequate technical knowledge:

Thanks to this Monsieur from Le Havre who comes to my aid, I enjoy the most perfect tranquility. My desire would really be to remain always in a little corner of nature quiet as this. Really, I do not envy you being at Paris. Don't you agree that alone in nature one works better? One is too preoccupied by what one sees and one hears at Paris, no matter how one wishes, and what I do here at least will have the merit of resembling no one, because it will be the simple impression of my own experiences. The further I go, the more I regret how little I know—this is what troubles me most.

Entirely egocentric, he has been taught manners and realizes a letter ought not to be devoted entirely to oneself. In a random way he wanders off to speak of Bazille, but this cannot hold him long:

I hope that you are full of ardor and have become a real digger. You who are in such good conditions ought to make marvels. Happy mortal, tell me what you will have for the Salon and whether you are happy with it.

Again his own affairs engage his attention, and he asks the costly favor of shipping canvases to him, mentioning that his Paris paint dealer, Carpentier, has refused further credit. As in all his letters, one notes the disingenuous addition of "my dear friend" when he asks a service:

I recommend to you my canvases which are stored in your studio. I have lost so many that I cling to those that remain. And if you would do me a pleasure, search out from all your corners the unused canvases that I still have, and also the canvases on which there are things abandoned, like your standing portrait, and another canvas size 60 on which I have done some bad flowers. Search, and send me everything you find that can be of service to me. See to it right away, my dear friend. It will be a great favor, because I work so much the few canvases I have are nearly finished, and Carpentier has just closed my credit. This obliges me to buy for cash, and you know what that would cost.

Monet worked on in relative tranquility, drawing no conclusions and formulating no theories; in fact, doing no more than manifesting an observant eye and deluding himself that his latest efforts might turn the tide that so certainly ran against him at the Salon.

That his pictures were capable of offending and disturbing those who distrusted his flamboyant vitality and lack of technical refinement was always a fresh surprise to him.

A newly hostile element existed after Daubigny forced the acceptance of one large canvas at the previous Salon. Despite his absence from Paris, an absolute artistic integrity, and a fundamental desire to conform, Monet increasingly was a center of attention, discord, and abuse. The dichotomy so clear when *Camille* appeared at the Salon grew more pronounced. Boudin and Courbet, who, like Daubigny, were well able to judge, continued to find splendid qualities in this inventive and gifted artist. Less a matter of color or manual agility than the power of his observation, his art had an enchanting and youthful realism, shot through at last by an equally powerful youthful melancholy.

Despite a certain brutality his efforts were highly literal and fundamentally attractive to the simple bourgeois public whose intellect Monet shared. In the face of exclusion from the Salon smaller dealers showed his works in that best of all positions, their windows. "There is on display here, in a dealer's window in the rue Lafayette," noted Boudin, January 18, 1869, "a view of Paris that perhaps you have seen and which would be worthy of the old masters if the details were of the same standard as the ensemble. There is good stuff in that boy. . . . " But such prominent display also incensed the Beaux-Arts, for these tactics were of the rabble-rouser and crowd-pleaser. Had Monet a professional touch constantly and blessedly in evidence, his colleagues would have accepted him, the doors of the Salon would have been thrown ajar, and he would have found acclaim. Unfortunately he was not a byword for all-around proficiency, and the fact dealers showed his work made him seem a charlatan.

In March, 1869, Monet journeyed alone to Paris with his canvases prepared for submission before the Salon jury. Boudin noted, "Monet has returned from Étretat starving, with his ears down. . . . He still maintains that his aunt is strict with him and withholds his allowance." The journey, and frames for his pictures, weighed heavily on his finances. To live he formed the bold plan of asking Arsène Houssaye to obtain for him a job on the gang of workmen who assisted during jury meetings at the Palais de l'Industrie. Houssaye was not helpful, though he suggested Monet settle nearer Paris, where his career could be assisted—advice which did not contribute to present needs.

Paris was rife with electioneering among prospective candidates for the Salon jury. Some were able to act with a surprising light and innocuous hand Bazille could not overlook:

> March 23, 1869
>
> Daubigny has come to see me as though by chance, and [Alfred] Stevens, whom I see often at Manet's home, has invited me to his entertainments. It is curious that they can be so ambitious for so little! It goes without saying that I am going to eat Stevens' cakes and remain incorruptible.

Once it had met, however, the jury of 1869 took impish delight in its own perversity and, led by Gérôme, rejected Monet's works entirely. Stevens immediately acquainted Bazille with the result of the deliberations:

> MY DEAR BAZILLE,
>
> Your picture, *The Woman,* is accepted—I am happy to send you this good news. You have been defended (between ourselves) by Bonnat, and, can you guess the other? By Cabanel! Degas has his little portrait accepted—Fantin has a nude accepted—Monet (not Manet) has been completely refused.
>
> I must admit I am desolate for my friend Degas, whose talent and wit I admire.
>
> Regards to you,
>
> A. STEVENS

Secure in the fact his livelihood was not involved, Bazille viewed these new proscriptions from Olympian heights:

> Monet has been completely refused. What pleases me is that there is an absolute animosity against us. It is M. Gérôme who has done all the harm. He has treated us like a band of madmen, and declared that he thinks it his duty to prevent our pictures from appearing. All that is not bad.

An insult was added to this injury by the treatment accorded Bazille's single accepted work: "I went to the Salon, and am as badly hung as is possible," he wrote.

For Monet the passionate emotions of that moment created an oblivion to higher thought. Among dealers he now found those, like Cadart, who turned their backs. But that certain dichotomy already evident continued to operate. Latouche placed in his window an earlier work and found reaction less than the scream of vicious hatred he and Monet feared. "They refused his two canvases this year," Boudin noted, April 26, 1869, "but he took his revenge by exhibiting with one of the dealers, Latouche, a study of Ste.-Adresse that attracted all the artistic circle. A mob was before the window throughout the exhibition, and among the young the unexpected qualities of this violent painting created a *fanaticism*. He really made good his refusal by the Salon."

One feels that Boudin had been around filing off the thorns, for in that most essential economic sense, the great and memorable effect of that Salon of 1869 was an utter, unqualified, and complete hopelessness it thrust on Monet.

Édouard Manet had been more fortunate. Two of his works were accepted by the jury, and though roughly treated by critics and ignored by the public, he found encouragement in receiving an offer for the *Balcony*. Their personal positions before Salon and public now nearly the reverse of 1865, Édouard Manet did not object to meeting again with Claude Monet, whom he had known since 1860.

Adulation of the upper classes had not abated in Monet, and to him Manet's alert but well-bred and slightly withdrawn worldliness was highly sympathetic. "We at once became fast friends," he recalled. "At our first meeting he invited me to join him every evening in a café in the Batignolles, where he and his friends gathered after working hours, to talk. There I met . . . Degas . . . the art critic Duranty, Émile Zola who was then making his debut in literature, and several others. For my part I took there Sisley, Bazille, and Renoir. Nothing could be more interesting than these *causeries* with their perpetual clash of opinion. They kept our wits sharpened. . . . " The cavernous interior and busy, sparkling atmosphere of Manet's café could be matched only by the new and equally lavish pavilions of the Bois de Boulogne. By contrast the Café Guerbois's terrace was minuscule, a limitation caused by the narrowness of the little Avenue des Batignolles it faced. But seated at those marble-topped tables, sipping from their glasses, Monet found personalities who were a preview of the cultural landscape.

At Étretat Monet had decried just such gatherings: "One is too preoccupied by what one sees and one hears in Paris"—a statement reflecting the industrious, introverted workman he was. Yet even Monet found he could return from the Café Guerbois with a fat dossier of demolished preconceptions. To hear the most radical and appalling theories expounded suddenly amused this man who since his rejection from the Salon had suffered an apotheosis of drabness. And of particular interest is that when first he joined this company Monet already had expressed concern over the limitations of his technical knowledge, for now he penetrated into the main camp of such artists.

Édouard Manet's was another great talent imbedded in an undisciplined personality. In his Spanish phase he had spread mortarlike pigments across canvas to produce delightful tactile qualities. But often, as in the drapery of *Olympia*, when he did not succeed he plastered on more pigment. Textures then became unpleasant, as is equally notable in the nude figure of his famous *Déjeuner sur l'Herbe*: Clotted, ragged, reworked, this unfortunate body was given a final harsh outline by a dark line. Incredible failings in perspective produced the horse running about the feet of his *Espada* like a toy bulldog. His *Déjeuner* has a similar fault: Instead of bathing in a far-off stream the second woman in the composition becomes a midget on the forward plane. So compelling is this impression, one suspects she has been flipped into the air from the curiously upheld thumb of the man seated below. And just as troublesome as his craftsmanship and perspective was Manet's inadequate draftsmanship: *Olympia's* farther eye is so ill-drawn it is painful to see.

The acknowledged draftsman of this group, Edgar Degas, possessed a nervous intellectual style that at worst was an academic conjuring trick. Extraordinarily self-conscious, he worried every touch put on canvas. To vary textures his effects are gained by the brush, or quite arbitrarily with the palette knife, then left too frankly scraped, retouched, tampered, tortured, and labored. Degas could produce exquisite pencil drawings, but their best qualities never reached canvas because his Ingresque concept of a correct line ignored the grace of line itself, and the charm that comes of working freely.

In planning compositions, the portion of his art wherein he

displayed greatest ingenuity, Degas was remarkably original, but often he descended to a level of contrivance. Not above breaking an occasional rule to demonstrate with what impunity he could do so, he had an unfortunate talent for falling flat. In *The Belleli Family in Florence* he audaciously intersected the head of a principal figure with a picture frame hung on the wall behind. Vermeer accomplished this successfully, but in Degas's hands the frame becomes distinctly jarring; his intended display of virtuosity fails. Again, contrary to the basic rule of drapery painting, in the same picture one small daughter sits on a foot not indicated in the folds of her gown: The result is a one-legged girl. And since there are never two errors without a third, farther to her right in this same picture the father sits so artistically engulfed in shadow that his weight and mass are lost.

Sophisticated artists though they were, mere rudiments found these men at their weakest. Manet was unable to create perspective, nor simplify a head without distorting features and spoiling drawing. Degas could not prevent his line from growing hard, nor his surfaces from appearing worried. Renoir, at times capable of adequate drawing, frequently failed to exert himself. Pissarro was entirely a landscape painter whose figures were lamentable. And Sisley, who suffered the same limitation with regard to figures, had the further difficulty of lacking originality, instead passing through stages under the influence of each colleague.

To take this objective view is to look at significant painters from an entirely negative point of view. When the longer historic context is employed it is not entirely just to do so, for together they formed a group with remarkably virile talent whose ideas and innovations fundamentally altered the art of painting. It is equally well to remember, however, that in the eyes of contemporaries these men were individuals who created works in which basic naïveté was obvious. As a group they also suffered from something unknown to Monet: a recurrent spite against contemporaries who seem to have shown them no unkindness but adapted themselves better to the world. Drawn from the special world of the *haute bourgeoisie*, Manet and Degas could loathe with an unabatable loathing artists for whose success they felt envy. Suddenly one sees a bigness so far unappreciated in that part of Monet's own character.

Fortunately these men lived at a time when a reasonable state of

civilization prevailed. Among both artists and public were freshness,
energy, and much naïveté, and this climate proved more stimulating
to creative talent than the good sense and restraint taught in the
studios of the Beaux-Arts. By throwing in his lot with an unstable, ill-
trained group Claude Monet ran further fearful risks. He did not do
so unreservedly, for his principal personal allegiance remained to
Gustave Courbet. But on Édouard Manet he already had founded
his style of painting, and thus the die was cast. What did it matter
that in reality a man banished from the Salon had nowhere else
to go?

13. An Unlucky Chapter

THE YEAR 1869 had reached its climax in the gladiatorial confrontation of Claude Monet and the Salon. Thoroughly defeated, amazed
and incredulous that so much animosity was directed at him individually, Monet could only acknowledge how deeply hurt were his
hopes and fortunes. If at first he lingered unhappily in Paris, sharing
a few evenings of flashing thoroughbred wit at the Café Guerbois, he
could not afford to stay long in the capital nor to revel in self-abase-
ment. Summer approached, and at Étretat little Jean had begun to
toddle by Camille's side. The *maisonette* that enshrined their pretenses, as well as the candor and decency of his warmest impulses,
must be vacated to its costly summer rental.

Once more Monet, Camille, and little Jean joined the fraternity of
vagabonds. Le Havre was their first goal, but a place impolitic for
Monet to approach as an attached man. While he spoke with those
few in his native city who showed interest in his work, mother and
child waited at Octeville, a tiny village some few miles back along
the road to Étretat. His years of desperation had evolved a technique
for approaching possible patrons in a direct, nervously sincere manner: That he was so desperately ill at ease underscored his words'

effectiveness. Misfortunes were recounted frankly, followed by mention of the "fatal rejection," and a hope that they would come to his
aid. He talked so persuasively and with such desperate charm that
patrons tried to believe him and certainly shared his distress. But
neither his words nor a look of penetrating candor were sufficient to
bring business to an artist refused by the Salon: "After this blow I
must no longer pretend to do anything at Le Havre," he realized.

Only Louis Gaudibert—again—had promised the assistance of
funds to set up housekeeping in a new location. At Octeville they
paused. Where would they go? At least for as long as it required to
paint one landscape they remained in perplexity. Before the distant tower of Octeville's church Monet sketched his son, an un-
steady little boy in long trousers, holding his mother's hand. By
covering her head in a white bonnet and her shoulders by a
shawl, that girlish, impulsive, devoted Camille had accommodated
herself to poverty and the countryside. But summer crowds now
streamed to the coast, and for accommodations the only alternative
was a return closer to Paris.

Monet went to search alone and in the Paris suburb of Bougival
discovered a battered old house. Nearby, at Ville d'Avray, was
Renoir, who, equally impoverished, had proceeded to the unheard
extremity of bringing his mistress, Lise, to live at the home of his
parents. His own arrangements duly made, Monet sent for Camille
and little Jean, then occupied himself making the house habitable.
Finally he wrote to the second of his two patrons, recording in his
letter the appeal made everywhere that summer:

Paris
June 2, 1869

Monsieur Houssaye,

When I had the honor of seeing you, to ask your support in obtaining permission to work at the Salon, you gave me the advice to
come fix myself at Paris where it would so obviously be easier to
assist my little talent. My refusal at the Salon has completely decided me, because, from now on, after this blow I must no longer
pretend to do anything at Le Havre.

Gaudibert has just had the kindness again to permit me to install myself here and bring all my little family. The installation is
done and I am in very good condition and full of courage for
work, but alas, this fatal refusal has nearly taken the bread from my

mouth, and despite my not at all elevated prices dealers and collectors turn their backs on me. Above all it is saddening to see the meager interest given a work of art which has no list price [in the Salon catalogue].

I have thought, and I hope that you will excuse me, that since you have already found a work of mine to your taste, you would perhaps wish to see the few canvases that I have been able to save, because I thought that you would be good enough to come to my aid a little, because my state is nearly desperate and the worst is that I cannot even work any longer.

It is useless to tell you that I will do anything, and it does not matter at what price, to bring myself out of such a situation in order to work from now on toward my next Salon so that such things will not renew themselves.

I hope that you will pardon my indiscretion and that you will take my request in consideration.

In this hope, accept, Monsieur, the assurance of my most distinguished sentiments.

CLAUDE MONET
St. Michel
Commune de Bougival (Seine & Oise)

One suspects even this appeal went unanswered: To purchase works from outcast artists was no popular form of charity. The knives of rejection are hidden but their edges sharp, and at Bougival Monet's problem was insoluble from the start. The sequel was recorded in a letter Renoir wrote Bazille:

. . . I am at my parents' place and nearly always at Monet's, which parenthetically is old enough. One doesn't eat every day, but I am just as happy, because for purposes of painting it is good to be with Monet. I do almost nothing because I am short of paints. That will go perhaps a little better this next month. . . .

For all the members of that little fraternity the moment was dark. To assist Renoir, Bazille had pawned his watch. Because of a tardiness with rent Bazille then found himself threatened with eviction from his own Paris studio. Panic swept through them all like a rush of wind, and worst of all, it was summer, when landscape painters were obliged to prepare for the next Salon. Work went on, while all parties sought desperate remedies. Renoir sent two large canvases for exhibition at the shop of Carpentier, the color merchant from whom they all purchased materials. When he sold neither the large portrait of *Lise* nor that of *Alfred Sisley and His Wife,* Renoir next proposed to place the former in an auction.

Monet meanwhile sought the motifs for salable small pictures along the Seine. To each canvas Camille lent the charm of her presence, though to sit in the sun unconcerned no longer was easy. Jean could not be left behind, and he too was featured in a canvas, held by his mother and toddling with deceptive sureness across the Seine bridge. Equally often domestic complications intervened, preventing Camille and Jean from joining these expeditions. Alone with Renoir, Monet then tramped to La Grenouillère (the Frog Pond), close by the restaurant Fournaise, a bathing place of modish banality for tripping Parisians.

Here, wittily dappled by boats and bathers, the river presented an attractive sight. And as they had done at Chailly five years before, the two artists set to work together. Renoir was still the same nervous little figure, shrinking with the passing years like a form scribbled on parchment. From this tense physical state derived his rapid manner, facetious gaiety, and quick hand when tracing colors across canvas. But soon his sketch of the bathing place became an impenetrable jungle of colors, for that nervous, hasty artist dashed into a common fault. To distinguish between blue and green pigments on the palette in brilliant sunshine frequently is difficult. Renoir became lost, the writhing intricacies of his colors losing distinctions. The result was not merely a lack of crispness but that the entire clarity of the scene vanished.

For Monet's bolder brush no such problems existed. Color and hue were scrupulously recorded, and notwithstanding wide divergences of style it is by comparison with Renoir that one suddenly realizes how far Monet had come. After long use of flat tones he had developed a corresponding sense of flat pattern. His unforced ingenuity created a compositional center from a little island of bathers; one side of his picture was closed by a bathhouse; boats carefully filled the bottom and left; a screen of trees shutting out the rear was rendered with flashing golden impact. All parts had begun to function decoratively, and this included even the zebra stripes of water. That these mellifluous wavelets were deliberately stressed, and not inherent in the scene, is shown by their absence from Renoir's sketch. Figures Monet added demonstrated the persisting influence of Boudin, though on a forward plane the scales and trills, roulades and *fioriture* of reflections and leaves were rendered with his own instinctive strength of tone.

La Grenouillère emerged as a subject which held attention perhaps in excess of its intrinsic interest, and everything suggested a larger picture might gain great success at the Salon. Both artists made further sketches, and entertained slightly neurotic delusions about painting on a large scale. Their economic state, which showed familiar and dismal signs of regression, at first prevented any such undertaking, and when in the face of this Renoir gave himself up to despair, it was Monet who inspired his friend with new courage.

Only Bazille's small "charity" prevented starvation from entering Monet's house, and when the first week of August passed without its appearance, he was reduced to disheartened frenzy. At his parents' house Renoir stuffed his pockets with bread, carrying it to Monet, who for eight days waited fretfully to be remembered by Bazille. Then, unable to contain himself longer, he exploded into old-fashioned ranting:

DEAR FRIEND,
Do you know in what a situation I am living these eight days that I await your letter? Well then! Ask Renoir, who brings us bread from his house so that we do not die of starvation. For eight days, no bread, no wine, no fire to cook by, no light—it's atrocious!

It is truly awful of you to forget me, because, after the last letter, all this was easy to foresee. And after this one you can easily see what is ahead of me.

I have no courage to say more.

At Montpellier, where he was settled deep in his own gloom, even such a frank exhortation left Bazille unstirred. The letter went unanswered, and another desperate week followed. Morning to night it was necessary for Monet to live, assure Camille, feed Jean, and above all, maintain his own balance: Each appearance of the postman represented a fresh hope, followed by shattering disillusion.

After eight days more, each representing peaks of hope and fits of despair, Monet flung another letter into the void of Bazille's silence. Obviously it was calculated to give a sharp twinge of apprehension:

You must admit, my friend, that I have little cause to be satisfied with you after the kind of promptness you have shown in sending these unhappy fifty francs—which, had they come in time, would have avoided a great many troubles and privations, because we are dying of starvation and that is the exact fact.

It is hard to believe that what I can tell you of my situation does not touch you at all, even when I tell you that we are dying of starvation. I hope that you never know such moments of misery! Only then could you understand that you do wrong by your extreme thoughtlessness of others' misery.

Even so, I hope that understanding my position you will somehow find the means to pardon yourself for conduct so little friendly to me.

Your very faithful and very devoted friend.

Bazille responded by sending his check, but hardly a word of civility accompanied it. His was the satisfaction of mastering a patrician art, which, in his own clumsy way, Monet attempted to overcome:

August 25
It must be acknowledged that your letter has been received. I speak of the check, because you are very laconic indeed. At last we have been able to eat a little, but already we are penniless again and without doubt the same thing will recommence. I count absolutely on your money for the first or the second. Beside what is agreed I must now risk asking you for the assistance of loaning me or advancing another fifty francs.

It is obvious that had we never done business together, we would not be less friends, but, to the contrary, perhaps more. Also that in the position in which I find myself I always address myself to you first. So often you turn your back—I know it now by experience. Had I no other help but you we would die of starvation.

I am unable to paint now, having not even a smell of colors. Except for that I would be at work. Think a little of what I must suffer, and try to come to my aid!

Yet to Bazille the full weight of Monet's unblessed household was an increasing annoyance. A sensitive civilized man, he gave indications of his feelings with a delicacy that escaped the more rough-hewn Monet. Bazille's failure to communicate was a continuing protest, and this Monet, doomed to bite all the hands that fed him, refused to accept. To sympathize with him was to invite punishment, for undoubtedly he was more grasping in his demands than he admitted and a nuisance to everyone he knew. But his real tragedy was to have many gifts and to have been led astray by lack of training and mirages of easy success. Claude Monet, who despite his unhappy experiences had learned nothing and forgotten nothing, had become the great impoverished Bourbon of painting.

That September, despairing of peace from Monet's demands, Bazille at last dropped his defense of silence. Harshly he told his friend that if necessary he should go "on foot" to Le Havre, and there find employment. Emotional self-indulgence crept into the beginning of Monet's reply. But, a man of sly, devious, and contradictory wisdom, he soon betrayed another character:

> September 25, 1869
>
> This is to inform you that I have not followed your (inexcusable) advice to go on foot to Le Havre. This month I have been a little more fortunate, at least according to precedents, because I am always in such a desperate state. I have sold a still life and I have been able to work a little. But, as always, here I am stopped—for lack of colors.
>
> Happy mortal, you have gone to bring back quantities of canvases! I am the only one this year who will have done nothing. This makes me furious against everyone—I am jealous, violent, enraged. If only I could work, everything would go better.
>
> You tell me that it is neither 50 francs nor 100 which will get me out of this. That is possible, but, from this point of view, I have nothing left to me except to break my head against a wall because I cannot pretend to any instantaneous fortune. . . .

At this point Monet seems to have paused. His letter was resumed in another mood. Though his epistolary style always had been filled with extraneous excitements and cheaply emotional appeals, these disappear. One is dazzled by a lucidity of judgment and cold integrity of purpose previously hidden:

> I relish your letter, my dear friend. It is truly funny, and, if I did not know you, I would take it for a joke. You tell me quite

seriously, because you think it to be true, that in my place you would even chop wood. It is only people in your position who would believe that, and if you were in mine you would perhaps be more disconcerted than me. It is harder than you think, and I wager that you would cut very little wood. No—you see, advice is very difficult to give, and, I think, serves little purpose unless it be spoken without offense.

But after permitting such icy candor, with a cry of agony Monet relapses once more into his accustomed humor. The guileful conjuror within him then asks a new service:

All of this does not hinder the fact that I am far from at the end of my pains, probably. Now the winter comes, season little agreeable to the unfortunate. After that comes the Salon. Alas! again I will not take part, because I will have done nothing. I have indeed a dream, a picture—the baths at La Grenouillère for which I have made a few bad sketches. But it is only a dream. Renoir, who has passed two months here, also wants to do this picture.

In regard to Renoir, it reminds me that at his brother's house I drank some wine which had just been received from Montpellier. . . . Could you not send me a cask for which you would deduct the price from the balance owing to me? At least we would not drink water so often. . . . Write to me for the first.

Ten years had passed since Monet first came to Paris to see the Salon of 1859, and ever since that institution had exercised despotic control over his fortunes and destiny. Of all the rough-and-tumble lot liberated by the close of Gleyre's studio only he had achieved acclaim, and only he had been singled out for exclusion. He was blessed with a formidable array of assets, yet each year the monstrous and quixotic gladiatorial contest was renewed with a foreseeable result.

Ostracized now as a definite policy, Monet nonetheless had support of a most bracing and ironic sort. That so many knowledgeable persons believed in him perhaps was responsible for his unbending faith in himself, and for the particular form of belligerent integrity with which he failed, or refused, to reconcile his own procedures to the finely wrought finish required for a place at the Palais de l'Industrie. The "establishment" that thoughtlessly condemned him, or did so without understanding, was responsible for the continued poverty in which he eked out his sorry existence. Yet, as in all true tragedy, the contrary effect of exalting those so basely used also was present. At work Monet seemed raptly oblivious, and everything his brush touched demonstrated a sharp contrast between the routine professional smoothness of official art and his own "amateur" inspiration. How he existed ranks as a mystery in the Pyramids class, its profound depths demonstrated by the fact that no record has survived of what work he was able to prepare for the Salon of 1870.

At Fantin-Latour's Paris studio, in his own careful way that artist was preparing another group portrait. Édouard Manet was to be shown seated, palette in hand, as though in the act of painting a portrait, and surrounded by his adherents. An intimate of Manet, Bazille naturally took an important place in the composition, and he assisted Fantin by securing sittings from the others. The presence of Astruc, Renoir, and Maître made this picture almost an homage to Bazille, whose friends they were. Then Zola wrote:

MY DEAR BAZILLE,
    Tell Fantin that I will be at his place Wednesday at one-thirty.
    Your all devoted,

ÉMILE ZOLA

But no picture in which Édouard Manet was surrounded by Bazille, Astruc, and Renoir could be complete without Claude Monet, however embarrassing his inclusion to Fantin, who preferred not to prejudice himself before the Salon jury. Monet had become an outcast to that enormous degree; and at Fantin's studio he found himself hidden in shadow between Bazille's high shoulder and the picture's frame. His gaze sullen, hair matted on his forehead, Fantin's image of Monet was as undignified as his existence, in even the minor events of which the Salon held him in abasement.

Soon after, Fantin's grotesquely naturalistic image of rags and deformities was atoned for by Bazille, who that May, before vacating the latest of his studios, in the Rue de la Condamine, painted his friends in the interior. A very different Monet, sturdy, barrel chested, respectably garbed, was shown smoking his pipe behind the frail figure of Édouard Manet. "Your studio without you; it is not possible!" cried Manet, who brushed in the long form of Bazille. Typically, Manet misjudged the effect of perspective, creating a monstrously oversized figure. "I am amusing myself by painting the interior of my studio with my friends," Bazille reported to Montpellier; "Manet has painted me into it."

Discontent with the Salon was now a permanent feature of the artistic scene. No one was surprised when in 1870 another effort was made to introduce a hurriedly drawn slate of independent candidates. Proposed were Corot, Daubigny, Courbet, Millet, Manet, Daumier, Amand Gautier, and Bonvin; but Édouard Manet, who wished only to end his long friction with officialdom, resigned in horror and was replaced by Isabey. Corot and Daubigny, artists whose great popularity had been sedulously and intelligently fostered, were elected, dragging Millet behind them in accidental but inescapable triumph for Barbizon. That Courbet failed only demonstrated how strong a resistance to his brutal realism still existed.

The presence on the jury of three members from the independent slate was encouraging though overshadowed by the fact that Corot and Daubigny had been on the official list too. Their double candidacies brought them more votes than other members, and at the Palais de l'Industrie theirs was a definite mandate for change. Surely the moment had come to end that shameful ostracism to which Monet had been subjected. Daubigny, Corot, and Millet, joined by Ziem, fought their colleagues with mounting spirit, only to discover that their authority was deeply compromised by the manner of their election.

Supported by the iron indignation of Millet, this small band still insisted that at least one work by Monet be received. The usually taciturn Millet even made a personal appeal to his colleagues, stressing the great merit of Monet's canvas, but to no purpose. Daubigny, a man of uncompromising courage, resigned from the jury. "From the moment that I liked this picture I would not allow my opinion to be contradicted," he explained. "You might as well say that I do not know my trade." And in a sensational sequel that rocked the Palais, gentle and benign old Corot resigned with him!

The special ostracism of Monet, so long a smoldering scandal, now at last burst into the open. And to crown their work, the jury reserved to itself the grim pleasure of seeing a haunted, hollow-eyed image of this man peer at them from the obscurity of Fantin-Latour's large group, which they accepted and hung. "That poor devil Monet," Bazille now labeled his once dashing friend. Yet to Monet and

Camille exposure to the harsh depths of poverty for another year was depressingly unsurprising. No rein was put on their emotion, nor any limit set to its rich indulgence. They had come, at last, to the absolute bottom of endurance. Her pride as lost as that of her lover, Camille undertook to plead with those prim and haughty bourgeois who were her parents.

Part Three
MARRIAGE

The earliest known photograph of Claude Monet. (Roger-Viollet)

Monet at the time of his first prosperity, about 1873.

(Roger-Viollet)

ortrait of Monet in his Zouave uniform by Charles L'Hullier.

Monet as he came to Paris in the 1890's.

A rare charcoal portrait by Monet: Madame Hoschedé, 187(

Monet at Giverny in the early 1890's.

Monet in 1899.

Monet in his sitting room, summer of 1920. (Roger-Viollet)

Monet before the canvases in his sitting room at Giverny, summer, 1920.

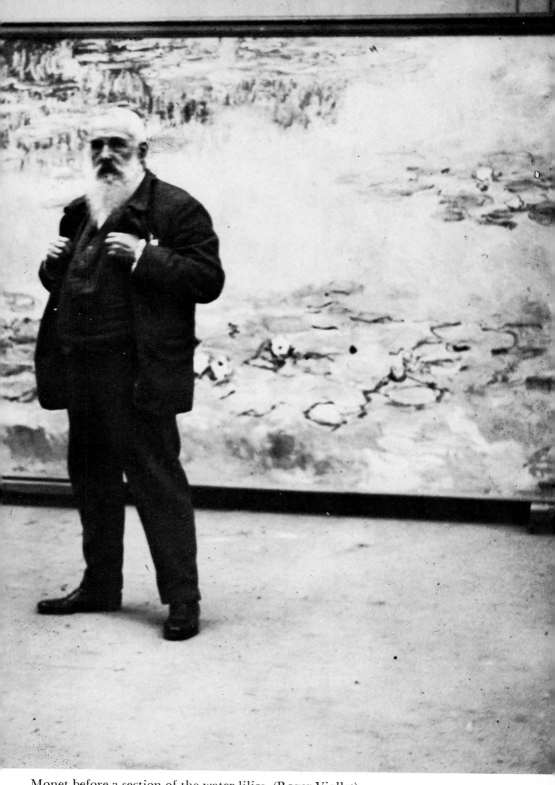

Monet before a section of the water lilies. (Roger-Viollet)

Monet beside his lily pond, summer, 1920. (Roger-Viollet)

Clemenceau surrounded by Madame Hoschedé's daughters at Monet's funeral.
(Roger-Viollet)

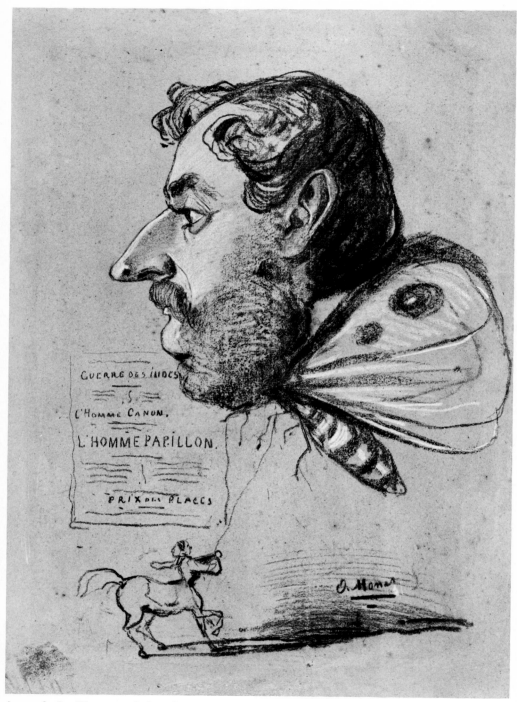

GUERRE DES INDES

L'HOMME CANON,

L'HOMME PAPILLON.

PRIX DES PLACES

An early Le Havre period caricature by Monet. (Art Institute of Chicago)

An early caricature of Alfred Bruyas done by Monet in Paris. (Art Institute of Chicago, Mr. and Mrs. Carter H. Harrison Collection)

MONET PAINTINGS
BELOW, first mock-up study for *The Picnic.* (Pushkin Museum, Moscow)

AT LEFT, the center section of *The Picnic,* now in a private collection in Paris. Courbet is at left. (Roger-Viollet)

Portrait of Jongkind.

Madame Gaudibert

Camille sitting under a lilac, probably painted just before she married Monet. (The Walters Art Gallery, Baltimore)

Earliest known portrait of Monet's first son, Jean.

One of the two lamplight studies done in Monet's combination
dining and sitting room at Étretat.

Women in a Garden. Camille in four poses and four dresses. (Jeu de Paume, Paris)

Camille in the Rue d'Edimbourg apartment shortly before the birth of her second son, Michel. (Jeu de Paume, Paris)

Windmills at Haaldersbroek near Zaandam, Holland.

(The Walters Art Gallery, Baltimore

La Japonaise, 1876. (Boston Museum of Fine Arts

Haystacks.

ection of the water lilies decoration. (Jeu de Paume, Paris)

14. The Heiress

"AT THIS MOMENT Monet stays with me, more unfortunate than ever," penned Bazille in June, 1870. "His family shows him only the most shameful avarice; because of this he is going to marry his mistress. This woman has some very proper parents who would consent to see her again, and to aid her, if she were married. It is necessary that their child eat." A supple display of delicate patrician contempt, the final phrase demonstrates to what extent Bazille's own sympathies were withdrawn from an enterprise the motivations of which made it excessively tawdry. Better than anyone, Bazille was aware that in Monet's own scheme of things marriage was still not uppermost.

Camille's father, Charles Claude Doncieux, was no less aware, and Monet was present in Paris to meet with this prospective father-in-law before a notary who would execute a contract of marriage. Dowries and inheritances, those inexhaustible sources of bourgeois drama, thus at last regaled Monet's ears. If he had learned that Mme. Doncieux, Camille's mother, had come into her inheritance from Antoine Pritelly, then at the start Monet was disappointed. Pritelly's exclusion of Camille from his testament, which in fact granted Mme. Doncieux no more than usufruct while entailing the fortune for her younger daughter Geneviève, meant that the dowry Camille could be given would represent only a minute fraction of the family's real wealth. No penny inherited by her mother could be passed on to Camille, whose portion must be drawn from her father's lesser fortune alone.

Obviously infirm and with shaking hands, Charles Claude Doncieux made no effort to hide distrust of his daughter's unconventional lover. His reservations were fortified by the absence from these proceedings of the respectable parents Monet claimed. In normal usage Adolphe Monet, or his sister, should have taken part, to represent their son's interests and in his behalf to match the sums proposed by M. Doncieux. For whatever reason they failed to appear, this omission gravely prejudiced the proceedings. Prospective husband, future father-in-law, and notary gathered as a trio of quiet misunderstanding, and things were at such a pass that whatever Monet said, he was disbelieved.

Every circumstance thus stood against Monet, whose thickened middle, broad hips, slender wrists, and small hands gave him an unprepossessing appearance. The black locks he combed forward over a receding hairline suggested his vanity, yet from certain angles he was like a red-necked peasant in fancy dress, and from others like a hefty Hasidic rabbi. Much boyish charm remained, plus boundless ambition, a feverish mind, and youthful assurance and dogmatisms both attractive and dangerous.

The confrontation took a more depressing turn when Monet realized M. Doncieux's true intentions. Twelve thousand francs had been mooted as Camille's dowry, a sum smaller than the eldest daughter of a rich family might reasonably have expected. Still, this was a definite capital, and it had elicited Monet's agreement to marriage. Now he found that by fine legal evasions these 12,000 francs would *not* be paid Camille, but must wait to be drawn from her father's estate three months after his death! While Charles Claude Doncieux lived he promised Camille only the interest on this capital sum, at 5 per cent, payable semiannually. In short, forgetting the glitter and dazzle of promises, after their marriage Claude Monet and Camille could count on nothing more than another "charity" of 50 francs a month.

The generosity behind this forced marriage was thus no greater than that of Bazille, and hardly less degrading in its terms. The curious detail that interest would be computed from the date of contract, rather than of marriage, was no consideration. And much as he entertained bourgeois pretensions, unable to contribute to this contract any material possessions, Monet was without leverage he might apply. Notable was his inability to speak the moneyed dialect of this social clique to which he thought he belonged. How could he explain to people of such a profoundly limited and parochial outlook that his poverty had become as great an enemy to him as the Salon?

An obvious example was Édouard Manet, once equally reviled, who while subsisting on his personal fortune slowly had brought the public around to appreciate his merits. Four years before, in 1866, Manet was banned from the Salon while Monet enjoyed a triumph. Now, while Monet groveled in the poverty of his rejections, Manet, elegant and worldly as ever, saw his works accepted and hung. That Camille should be given a capital of her own, sufficient to sustain them until Monet gained his feet, was an argument of both peculiar dignity and definite aesthetic appeal. Claude Monet too must become a finely modeled gentleman, able to mold the public. His gifts were incontestably greater than those of Édouard Manet, but could not be brought to bear effectively while he remained in flight from numberless persecutors and his own shabby self.

M. Doncieux's response contained a deeply nasty moral perversity, curiously parallel to that of Adolphe Monet. He proposed not that Camille receive in any degree the useful security of a capital sum, but instead, that he would make her an advance of two years' interest. This 1,200 francs, the greatest concession Monet could force, represented momentary relief to a couple who had been struggling up yielding slopes of sand. But its corollary written into the contract, that for two years after they received nothing more, meant a certain return to misery.

So long adamant for drift, decided only to be undecided in his relationship with Camille, Monet now was flung into an immensely more distasteful situation. He entered into the ritual of marriage by contract without gaining the tempting riches so briefly flashed before his eyes. The Doncieux family had deprived their daughter of the very capital she needed for an alleviation.

In the contract itself matters small and large were strangely yoked —strangely, that is, to anyone who suspected there might be some difference in scale and magnitude between crises in the life they led and to whom rent receipts were drawn. For the notary performed his function with zest, creating in the first article an entire separation of property between Camille and her husband. His only failure had been in bestowing any property worthy of separation:

There will be a separation of goods between the future couple, conforming to the dispositions of the article 1936 and following of the Code Napoléon.

In consequence there will be no responsibility for the debts of each other created before or during the marriage.

And the future wife will have the entire administration of her goods, furniture, and possessions, and the free control of her revenues.

So impressed were all by the poverty of this man to whom Camille was being married that when engrossing this lengthy document in the tiny neat indulgences of nineteenth-century script, the notary, or his clerk, showed hesitation in evaluating Monet's property brought to the marriage. A nominal sum of 500 francs was fixed for Camille, but only when the principals gathered together for signatures on June 21 was an equivalent sum added for Monet:

The future husband declares that he brings to the marriage his clothes, linens, and other wearing apparel of his personal use, the whole amounting in value *to five hundred francs.*

The future wife declares that she brings to the marriage to be constituted personally as her dowry her clothes, jewelry, linens, and other wearing apparel of personal use, the whole amounting in value to five hundred francs.

The full sting of legal verbiage appeared in the contract's fourth article, designed to protect Camille from the man she was about to marry. After providing ridiculously small sums, the provisions seemed more than adequate as barriers to nothing in particular:

The future wife will have the entire administration of her goods, furniture and furnishings, and the free control of her revenues. To this effect she is authorized irrevocably to act and direct regarding her goods, furniture and furnishings . . . make use of her rents and revenues, receive and control all accounts, dispose of her furnishings, draw all her capital, give quittances, and in general perform every act of the most entire administration, the whole without requiring the authorization or the consent of her husband.

The elusive dowry, so strangely promised yet ungranted, was memorialized in the fifth article, which by its precise terms and certainty of interest rates evokes indelibly that small world:

Pardevant M. Léon

Aumont Thiéville et son Collègue, notaires
à Paris, soussignés,

Ont comparu

M. Oscar Claude Monet, artiste peintre Demeurant à
Saint-Michel, commune de Bougival (Seine et Oise)

Majeur, fils de M. Adolphe Monet, rentier Demeurant
aux Havre, et de M.me Louise Justine Aubrée, son
épouse Décédée

D'une part

M.me Camille Léonie Doncieux, sans profession
Demeurant à Paris, boulevard des Batignolles, N.o 17,

Majeure, fille de M. Charles Claude Doncieux, sans profession
et de M.me Léonie Françoise Maréchale, son père Demeurant
ensemble boulevard des Batignolles, N.o 17, D'autre part

M. et M.me Doncieux à Paris, vouant que leur dit
M. Doncieux leur intervention à ce mari, déclarant en s'engageant
...

... pour être mariés, ainsi qu'il en tout arrêté à l'effet des dits ...
... après la célébration du mariage.

Dont acte

Fait et passé à Paris, En l'étude de M. Aumont
Thiéville
L'an mil huit cent soixante Dix
le Vingt un Juin
Et après lecture faite, les parties et leurs ... ont
... comme ... Signé avec les notaires.

C. M.
C. L. D.
L. F. M.

Claude Monet
Ch. Doncieux
L. F. Maréchale
Ch. Doncieux

Monsieur and Madame Doncieux, named, qualified, and domiciled, Madame Doncieux under the authorization which has been given her for this purpose by her husband, by these presents make to the future wife, their daughter, which she accepts and for which she thanks them, a donation of principal outside her portion, of a sum of twelve thousand francs, receivable only three months after the death of Monsieur Doncieux. This sum will produce interest at five percent each year, commencing from today.

Monsieur and Madame Doncieux, the parents, as an advance to the future wife, their daughter, and to the future husband, who acknowledge it by giving quittance to Monsieur and Madame Doncieux, give a sum of twelve hundred francs, representing the interest of two years on twelve thousand francs as promised above, beyond which last they have nothing to pay until June twenty-first eighteen hundred and seventy-two.

Starting at this last date the interest will continue to run at the same amount and will then be payable by semesters, of six months in six months, the first semester to be paid the twenty-first of December eighteen hundred and seventy-two; the second in June following; and to follow from six months to six months, until the complete liberation of the sum given.

Articles 6 to 8, which followed, presented no startling revelations nor pulled the sequence of confusing legal stratagems into any coherent form. All furniture, linen, silver, and household effects were to belong "by full right to the future wife. And the future husband will establish that any objects for which he claims proprietorship were furnished him on merchants' and furnishers' receipts." Presumably as a protection against Camille's being put in the street, even "the places of habitation of the future wife will be presumed to be rented to the future [wife] alone without any contrary indications, and all receipts for rent and other expenditures will be given in her name." If despite these efforts at protection Camille were levied for her husband's debts, the contract even provided that "the future wife or her heirs will be guaranteed and indemnified by the future husband."

On June 21, 1870, all parties to the contract assembled at 10 *bis* Boulevard de Bonne Nouvelle for the final acts of this desperate comedy. The evaluation of 500 francs for Monet's property was inserted in a bolder script than that seen elsewhere in the document, and all parties were asked to initial the passage. Unaccustomed to legal procedures, Monet proceeded to scrawl his full signature. He was cautioned, leaving a large and unfinished *Claude M.,* mingled with scratched and blotted initials by M. Doncieux, Camille's more childish marks, and the large but poorly proportioned copperplate capitals of her mother. According to custom, Maître Aumont-Thieville then read aloud Articles 1391 and 1394 from the Code Napoléon, and signed the small card acknowledging his act, which the couple were obliged to produce at the Mairie before an actual ceremony of marriage could be performed. A final awkwardness arose because Adolphe Monet was not present. At the end of the document words referring to the presence of *all* parents hastily were scratched out and initialed, following on which those present affixed their signatures.

Twelve hundred francs then were passed to Camille and Claude Monet. The largest sum they ever had seen, it was pathetically unrelated to their true needs. A playwright in fact might have characterized the entirety of this curious ceremonial as much ado about nothing.

Seven days later, June 28, 1870, these same parties minus legal advisers assembled once more at the Mairie of the eighth arrondissement, 11 Rue d'Anjou, not far down the narrow and irregular Rue de Surène from the Madeleine. Their purpose was the peremptory little ceremony of civil marriage, performed on worn carpets and in chilly rooms by the mayors of each Paris district.

Monet still appeared hesitant, as though about to commit some act for which rewards were insufficient. But quickly the routine quality of proceedings was disrupted by discovery of a lapse in his documents. Monet was unable to produce his certificate of good conduct, granted in 1862 after his separation from the army. No ceremony could be performed without this paper, and for a few morosely funny minutes it seemed the contracted marriage, for which they had received their 1,200 francs, would not take place. Then, on his own responsibility, the mayor agreed to accept Monet's word concerning his discharge, and the prescribed ritual proceeded in full obeisance to the Code Napoléon. After five years of violent "courtship" and one son, Camille at last became a bride.

The mayor then seated himself and, after copying full particulars of Monet's service onto a recruitment form, wrote a letter on the reverse:

The President of the Council
of the Administration of the
1st Regiment of Chasseurs d'Afrique,

MONSIEUR LE PRÉSIDENT,

The party named Monet, Oscar Claude, son of Adolphe and of the deceased Louise Justine Aubrée, born the 14th November 1840 at Paris, who has just been married at my Mairie, not yet having produced his certificate of liberation from the army, states that he took part in the military lottery at Le Havre in the class of 1860 and has been exonerated from service, after being incorporated in the first regiment of the Chasseurs d'Afrique.

Before inscribing Monsieur Monet in accordance with the act of the law of March 21, 1832, and under Ministerial instructions on the tables of military census for the next class, I have the honor to beg you to inform me on the exactitude of his declarations and to indicate to me exactly the date his exoneration took place.

Receive, Monsieur the President, the assurance of my very distinguished consideration.

On this inappropriate and unpropitious note the brief event concluded, leaving its own special taste of bittersweet.

The opportunity presented by this marriage and its preliminary contract negotiations was irrevocably lost. Had Adolphe Monet or his sister come forward to take part, had either of them matched the contribution made by M. Doncieux, certainly Camille's dowry would have been increased to a worthy sum. Stringent and belittling provisions might have been eliminated, and from this contract might have arisen a new career for Claude, solidly based and more possible of fulfillment. But Adolphe Monet had not come to Paris, nor taken part in behalf of his son.

Another oddity of this marriage is that the result immediately was rapturous. As ingredients, Monet and the lovely twenty-three-year-old Camille fused deliciously. The secret of their happiness lay in subtle and complex relations between two contrasting social beings entirely dedicated to each other. And a peculiarly beguiling quality resides in the sight of them suddenly relieved from their frightful

Monsieur le Président du Conseil
d'Administration du 1.er regt. de chasseurs
d'Afrique

Monsieur le Président

Le nommé Monet Oscar Claude,
fils de Adolphe et de feu Louise Justine
Aubrée né le 14 novembre 1840
à Paris, qui vient de se marier
à ma mairie, sans avoir jusqu'à
présent produire de certificat ou
de congé de libération expose avoir
tiré au sort au Havre avec les jeunes
gens de la classe de 1860 et avoir
été, après son incorporation au 1.er
regt. de chasseurs d'Afrique, exonéré

exonéré sous
les drapeaux

Avant d'inscrire le s.r Monet,
en exécution des instructions ministérielles
de l'art.   de la loi du 21 mars 1882
et des instructions ministérielles sur les
tableaux de recensement de la prochaine
classe, j'ai l'honneur de vous prier
de me renseigner sur l'exactitude
de ses déclarations et de m'indiquer
exactement la date de l'exonération
s'il y a lieu.

Recevez, Monsieur le Président,
l'assurance de ma considération
très distinguée   Le C.er d'État

Maire du 8.e arrond.t

201

vicissitudes by 1,200 francs, and—once more clad in the eye-catching trappings of success—racing to Trouville for a honeymoon.

Surely it was a brilliant example of benevolent parody, this sudden haste to break up the home that had sheltered them at Bougival, where only so shortly before Renoir had brought them pocketfuls of bread. Monet's pictures were stored partly with Pissarro at nearby Louveciennes, and partly in Paris with Bazille. Camille might almost have been compiled by a benevolent fate for the job she now did so entertainingly. Packing and preparing, providing for her newlywed husband and their three-year-old son, she also deftly drew into this party her twelve-year-old sister Geneviève, who one day would inherit the impressive Pritelly fortune.

The potential for ironies and encounters was interestingly augmented when at Trouville they came upon Boudin and Mme. Boudin, the former painting beach scenes filled with prettily garbed vacationers disporting themselves before sands and surf. "And I see you still in the Hôtel de Tivole with poor Camille," Boudin remembered in later years. "I even have saved a drawing from that time, showing you both on the beach. . . . Little Jean plays in the sand and his father sits on the ground, a piece of drawing paper in his hand . . . and does not work. . . ."

The idleness Boudin caught was momentary, for, family honeymoon or not, Monet had his painting gear at hand and made himself a common sight. Thanks to Camille's dowry, fresh clean canvases, of the fine smooth nonabsorbent quality he loved, became plentiful for him. Every care lifted from him, again shrugging off the morrow, Monet once more joined Boudin to work on the beach and near the entrance to Trouville's little harbor.

In the presence of Boudin one again becomes conscious of a persisting influence, though the works Monet undertook in those carefree weeks ranged from superficial prettiness to genuine vision. His happiness had such a pungent quality that the whiff of it is unmistakable in each small picture thrown off in casual proliferation. Everywhere his sense of pattern grew more prominent. The elaborate gingerbread of the Hôtel des Roches Noires, seen in tender halftone, was nicely balanced by clusters of Boudinesque idlers. An American flag gaily filled an otherwise vacant upper corner, a device perhaps less good than had seemed the case. Were the dark blue field set into the corner of those red and white stripes, it threatened to create too great an accent. Monet hesitated, then left an area of inconclusive bare canvas.

For the convenience of long-skirted Paris elite, a wood plankwork had been laid across the Trouville sands. On this support, equidistant from surf and seafront's fanciful architectural aberrations, Monet placed his easel for a further effort at the Hôtel des Roches Noires. As he traced out patterns, his taste and incisiveness were immediately obvious. Color was kept strong and clear, and he knocked off characteristic little figures and the heavily ornamented buildings with precision and elegance, carefully refraining from any but the boldest view. In a second study of the same scene, painted with the same glowing sense of sunlight and seaside coolness, he entirely eliminated the boardwalk's long lines, which had given a crowded appearance to his foreground.

His own personality had become so idiosyncratic that even when he directly adopted Boudin's genre, to paint Camille with her parasol on a beach chair, surrounded by her black-braided sister Geneviève, the slightly uncouth and black-garbed figure of Mme. Boudin, or little Jean dashing toward the surf, he introduced a pattern, controlled tension, and textures, which make his canvases utterly different from those of his first teacher.

An underlying cheerfulness continually reminds us how thoroughly Monet was relishing this first release from anxieties. The fascination of his own style is allowed to grow, unmolested by easy parallels to Boudin. Interesting to note is that at the end of his early years, when so much represented by the decade of the eighteen-sixties was drawing to a close, a new note was already visible in his art. For events of another largely ignored world offered unpropitious omens; a curtain was about to be drawn across Monet's youth, forever shutting it closed behind him.

Twenty-one days after that marriage at the Paris Mairie, "with a light heart" France declared war on Prussia. The Premier, Émile Ollivier, later explained that when he had said "with a light heart" he meant "with calm confidence," but his first disastrous phrase was never forgotten. Few knew, or cared, that the French Army was fatally ill-organized and underequipped, and when torchlight processions of singing, cheerful Parisians escorted newly mobilized troops to the railway stations, boulevards echoed the optimistic cry "To Berlin!"

For a fortnight this first mood of optimism endured persistent reports of disorganization and even mutiny in the army camps. On his family's estate near Montpellier, Bazille worked in peaceful isolation, writing to Maître a rare note recording the personality of gifted madness which made him so popular:

> Give me news of our friends. Fantin, has he begun something for the next Salon? I think that Manet abandons the fields of Marathon for the German provinces, to find freshness in his subjects. And Monet, is he doing a portrait of Madame de Metternich or has he gone into a hospital? Renoir must be nearly a father; will he give birth to a picture? Make no inquiries about Sisley; I know too well what he does.

Based on Monet's Algerian behavior, the gratuitous suggestion that at any hint of war he would go to a hospital was not entirely humor.

On the night of August 6, news reached Paris of two major defeats suffered by French armies at Spicheren and Froeschwiller. France was left open to invasion, and suddenly it became obvious that Paris itself was in danger of attack. Mobilization of the trained reserves, among whom Monet was numbered, immediately followed, and his first thoughts were less of France's plight than of his own. Without the discharge papers he had been unable to produce at his marriage, he was safe nowhere but might be seized and incorporated in the army. He felt no loyalty to the government of the Emperor Napoleon III, to whom he owed only his rags and exclusion from the Salon.

Every train from Paris now brought hordes of refugees fleeing to England. Those who saw the tumult they provoked at channel ports were terrified by this reflection of the continued defeats suffered by French arms. A sudden madness seized everyone. Boudin departed Trouville for Brittany, where he found shelter with his wife's family. He was followed by profoundly discouraged letters from Monet, still at Trouville. In the south Bazille, who had avoided his own military service after his father purchased a substitute, felt the moment had come to aid his country. But the awful necessity of shaving his beard was a sacrifice neither he nor his mother was willing to contemplate.

To save this manly adornment in which Mme. Bazille took pride, on August 10 Frédéric enlisted in the unshaved ranks of the Zouaves, well known for the dangerous missions they undertook.

Renoir protested Bazille's decision, and as the danger to Paris became greater, himself fled to Bordeaux, where later he too enlisted. The defenses of Paris hurriedly were put in a state of readiness, and preparations for siege included stocking the city with animals for slaughter. The Luxembourg Gardens were filled with sheep. A quarter million more, plus forty thousand oxen, were brought to graze in the Bois de Boulogne. A flour mill was set up in the Gare du Nord, the Louvre became an armaments workshop, the Gare d'Orléans a balloon factory, and the Gare de Lyon a cannon foundry. But not until September 2, when at Sedan the Emperor himself surrendered to the advancing Germans with his entire army of 84,000 men, 2,700 officers, and 39 generals, was it certain that Paris would undergo siege. The Empress Eugénie slipped away to exile in England, and inevitably and peacefully within the stricken city the empire was overthrown. Paris went wild with joy.

On September 6 the new government appointed Gustave Courbet to a commission of artists formed to protect the museums and transport works of art out of danger. German troops, and the danger they represented, daily came closer to the French capital, which took on the atmosphere of a beleaguered fortress. On September 8 Édouard Manet sent his wife, mother, and son to Oloron-Ste.-Marie, in the Basses-Pyrénées, and two days later with Degas he joined the guard formed to defend the city. Troops poured into Paris, and on the thirteenth the whole of a gigantic, untrained, ill-equipped force of 100,000 men turned out for review. It was an impressive, if disillusioning, sight. The last train left for the west during the following week, and by September 19 all remaining telegraph lines had been cut by the Germans: Paris was isolated from France and the world.

If Paris meant to fight to the death, and all his friends were mobilized for the encounter, Claude Monet showed himself considerably less fastidious. He was not, like Bazille, Degas, or Manet, one of those blue-blood-and-thunder boys whose hearts responded to high-sounding proclamations. Camille's sister Geneviève had perhaps already gone back to rejoin her parents in Paris; Camille and little Jean now were sent after Boudin into Brittany. For a time

Monet himself remained at Le Havre, hesitant. To Boudin he sent a letter for Camille, which he asked his mentor to deliver personally. Then, unconcerned with other men's fates nor that of his country, in one more desperate and paltry tactic of survival, Monet boarded ship for England with his canvases painted at Trouville. The honeymoon voyage was for one.

Unable to speak the language or distinguish himself from hordes of French refugees who crowded England, Monet immediately suffered renewed want. To Boudin he sent his address: 11, Arundel Street, Piccadilly; and his presence in London enabled him to frequent a French café, where among other displaced persons he found the recently decorated artist François Bonvin, and Daubigny, who so often and vainly had supported him at the Salon. Monet's special cowardice had brought on him further impoverishment, spiced now by that added irony of being suffered in an alien land. His own private hell had successfully crossed the channel with him.

Irony was strong during penniless weeks which soon became months. In previous depths of distress Monet never had been without the sweet assuagement of Camille. Only now, when married, had he to face despair alone. And irony, though deadly, was unruffled further to point out the hurtful truth of these months. At the start of December he read in a newspaper that Frédéric Bazille had been killed November 28, at Beaune-la-Rolande. Promoted to sergeant in the Zouaves, he had bravely led his men in an attack across snow, cautioning them above all not to fire on women or children. Two Prussian bullets caught him in the abdomen and arm, and he collapsed face down. Four hours later during a lull in fighting he was found lying in the snow, still lucid. Gathered with other wounded beside a stream, he begged that his ring be sent to his parents, and gave those who attended him the money in his pockets. The following day his long body was buried in a common grave under the snow.

Perhaps, after all, cowardice and self-interest had served Monet better, or did he reflect merely on the small balance that remained unpaid on the garden picture, resting irretrievable in Montpellier? "I suffered want" was the full extent of what he later admitted concerning this period in England, and by means of those well-known appeals, which were mostly long soliloquies, he made his want known even in London and especially to Daubigny. "It seems that Daubigny had crossed my route to be of service. From the day we met, he remained a friend faithful and sure," Monet remembered.

The charm, delicacy, and inimitable pastoral air of Daubigny's work already had succeeded in captivating England as it had France. His new canvases, produced along the River Thames, found a ready market, and, as always, that artist was deeply touched by Monet's distress.

"I see what you need," he said. "I am going to bring a dealer to you."

The following day Daubigny brought Paul Durand-Ruel, the Paris dealer, to visit Monet.

"Here is a young man who will be stronger than all of us," he urged. "Buy his pictures. I promise to take back from you any you are unable to sell, and if you wish I will exchange them for my own paintings."

Durand-Ruel did not need to be urged. He had noticed Monet's earlier works exhibited at the Salon. And despite his air of an inspired great-uncle attractively straying across the limelight, Durand-Ruel was a man absolutely serious, absolutely sincere, and a world-shaker. The fortunes of his firm had been built upon the Barbizon school. The wide acceptance that had come to Daubigny, Millet, Rousseau, Dupré, Diaz, and especially Corot, had turned his remarkable stock into a capital of enormous value. Durand-Ruel thereupon had embarked on a deliberate policy to seek further schools of art where the same miracle might be repeated.

Like many Parisians of fortune, to avoid the foreseeable horrors of siege, Durand-Ruel had sent his family to the south, then hastily packed his entire stock of paintings, the most precious first. Several important private collections were entrusted to him, and with the entire contents of Gustave Courbet's studio under his care, Durand-Ruel moved his business to London.

Too little known in England to attract crowds to his premises in Bond Street, which paradoxically bore the name "The German Gallery," Durand-Ruel put himself under the imaginary patronage of a committee composed of Corot, Dupré, Diaz, Daubigny, and Courbet, quickly adding to this list Bonvin, Ricard, and Legros, when they were discovered to be in England. If he had been able to consult those others beyond communication in wartime France, Durand-Ruel was no less certain they would have approved.

Late in January Camille Pissarro, in flight from Louveciennes before the German armies that infested Paris, brought to Durand-Ruel's Bond Street gallery a fresh canvas painted of the Crystal Palace. Durand-Ruel was absent, but on his return wrote immediately:

Society of French Artists
168 New Bond Street, London W
January 21, 1871

MY DEAR SIR,

You have brought me a charming picture and I regret not having been in my gallery to pay you my respects in person. Tell me, please, the price you want and be kind enough to send me others when you are able to do so. I must sell a lot of your work here. Your friend Monet asked me for your address. He did not know that you were in England. He himself is staying at 1, Bath Place, Kensington.

Receive, my dear Sir, the assurance of my most devoted sentiments.

DURAND-RUEL

Both thorough family men of quiet habits, and now separated from wives and children, Monet and Pissarro were delighted to find each other in England. Together they visited museums, noting with interest the watercolors of Turner, and works by Constable and Old Crome. They admired Gainsborough, Lawrence, and Reynolds, but their attention more naturally centered on English landscapists, who, living in a less sunny climate, had probed into fugitive effects of light and weather. No meticulous nor intricate study was made, but in those dreary twilight days of the English winter they entertained surprising enthusiasm for Watts, and even Rossetti.

Neither artist worked much, and what painting they did was done alone. Located in the center of London, Monet captured a distinctly British atmosphere in two studies of Hyde Park remarkable for wan poetry and a chaste, almost tender manner. Though removed from the gray sketches of vagrants and mean streets that might have been expected, Monet's smudgy urban naturalism was achieved with ease and bareness, and preserved the softness of English atmosphere. By contrast, Pissarro, who had found quarters in Lower Norwood, then a charming suburb, created scenes with the pleasant quality of making England appear typically French.

At the close of January, after four months of a siege at the end accompanied by nightly bombardment, Paris capitulated. Negotiations were held at Versailles, and an election took place to select an Assembly to ratify the peace. On Wednesday, March 1, German troops entered Paris to begin their symbolic two-day occupation. Daubigny already had returned, flushed with his English successes; and no doubt existed that Pissarro, who in England had sold nothing but two small canvases to Durand-Ruel, also wished to return home at the earliest moment. Durand-Ruel, whose own family had reached England, made a brief trip back to Paris. But on the morning of his arrival two French generals were assassinated on Montmartre, and because further insurrection threatened, he returned to his gallery in London.

Palm Sunday, April 2, 1871, a second siege of Paris began, ferociously pressed by the National Army intent on suppressing a radical Commune that controlled the city. Realizing no Salon could be held in such conditions, Monet and Pissarro proposed instead to send their works to the annual exhibition of the Royal Academy. That institution accepted the compliment in proper style, by dealing both artists the same rejections they would have received at home. In London this rejection was less crucial, for both artists continued to show with Durand-Ruel and also at the International Exhibition of Fine Arts, which opened May 1 in buildings surrounding the Albert Hall. Unable to secure cooperation from a homeland in ever greater turmoil, the French commissioner had turned over the problems of organization to Durand-Ruel, who brought forth a lavish selection of the wonders earlier shipped from France, to which he added two works each by Monet and Pissarro.

But English collectors were no more prepared than their French counterparts to accept the works of either painter, no matter how glamorously displayed. The undertones of unhappiness and anxiety always visible during this English interlude turned to disappointment, disillusion, and despair. To Théodore Duret Pissarro wrote in June:

> I am only here for a short time. I count on returning to France as soon as possible. Yes, my dear Duret, I will not remain here, and it is only when abroad one feels to what degree France is beautiful, great, and hospitable. How different it is here! One gathers only contempt, indifference, even rudeness. Among colleagues there is the most selfish jealousy and resentment. Here? There is no art, everything is a matter of business.

Again the besieged Paris capitulated, this time after being stormed by French troops who wreaked a frightful vengeance on their countrymen. A bloody peace was restored, and the dispersal of those Frenchmen who had sheltered in England began. Pissarro returned almost at once, probably in June, followed in September by Durand-Ruel. Bonvin left for Brussels, to join Diaz, Dupré, and Eugène Boudin, the latter present in Belgium with his wife since the previous December. Of those French who had crowded into England, soon only Claude Monet was left, to paint brooding autumn fog on the Thames. Because of its dreadful ending the history of his English sojourn makes a depressing story, for among those who had been in England he alone remained a practicing coward, too fearful of his country's vengeance on a deserter to venture back.

15. *Tilting at Windmills*

VANITIES, evasions, class struggles, the persistence of traditional discipline and the helpless weakness of the French government all marked the period following two sieges of Paris. Cast in the role of deserter, one expects that Monet will drown in a troubled period. Instead he bobs to the surface, puffing and spluttering and not in especially good shape, but indubitably alive and in Holland. Some accounts credit D'Esternelles de Constant with issuing an impatient invitation, twice pressed, which brought the artist across the North Sea from England. Others point to the fact Daubigny worked in the Low Countries late during that year 1871. The provenance of legends that Monet was present with either or both is nebulous. More reliable is that he faced the challenge of this new alien clime with his usual dexterity and aplomb. His dealings with Durand-Ruel evidently had supplied him with cash. At Amsterdam he sketched canals disinterestedly, and painted at least one portrait of a woman reflective of *Madame Gaudibert*.

Blue and white china he found everywhere in Holland pleased Monet's aesthetic sense, and at Amsterdam he undertook to bargain for a jug. As he hesitated, a tray of brightly colored prints caught his eye inside the case over which he stood.

He moved closer, discovering the pleasing objects were Japanese.

"If you would let me have this package of prints with the vase, I will accept your price," he said.

"As you wish," the shopkeeper replied. "They are useless to me."

This unexpected and renewed exposure to the art of Japan, in Holland, became as memorable for Monet as his first sight of such prints at Le Havre fourteen years before. Then, at sixteen, he had squandered twenty pennies each for spirited designs of parakeets and monkeys. Now his new acquisitions were the source of more subtle joy found in the bizarre restraint of a highly disciplined and civilized expression. Newly exposed to it in numerous examples, he made a special effort to understand its deceptive simplicity.

In brilliant clear weather Monet moved from Amsterdam to the more open district of Zaandam, where his first efforts were cheerful sketches of neat little houses on high banks, reflected in areas of dappled water. The clouds that at first formed an interesting patchwork across his skies soon came together solidly, an opaque background for a landscape suddenly thrown low in tone. Previously when faced with this weather he had depended on masses of pounding surf for his effects. Now he chose to be more deft and efficient, making Dutch windmills an exemplary subject for the effective employment of Japanese flat pattern.

The arbitrary violence so typical of his youthful work was eschewed in favor of a more cerebral approach, for now he thought only in terms of balances held rigidly simple. The dark silhouette of a windmill was set high on one side of each oblong canvas. Areas of clear water, muted reflections, or the lesser balance of a rowboat compensated for the bareness of ensemble. He did not force his comparisons nor make his contrasts overneat, and the fascination of this new method found him working harder and adopting an entirely new discipline of craft. Gray weather through these early winter months held low the tone of each study. Monet continued, doggedly employing an old established convention of monochrome in Dutch landscape, yet demonstrating a growing capacity and a wider range of expression than ever before.

Reflected, repeated with that emphasis gained by similarity of form, his windmills were being joined by patterned bridges too un-solid to span the flood, but skillfully linking visual imagery with brilliant design. Sails from fishing vessels joined his pictorial ar-mory. They introduced a subtle variation of shape behind upraised earthwork dikes, riding the horizon or cutting audaciously across a windmill's extended arm. Everywhere these attractive designs avoided his usual garish color jumble in secondary areas; their workmanship is fine, the ensemble ingenious, the stage sense secure. And while not reconciling perfectly all the paradoxes of East and West, or Japanese pattern with Dutch gloom, these carefully im-pasted works have a kind of confident, resolute simplicity. With equal certainty they expressed his own numbed and exhausted re-action to eighteen months' flight from other people's wars.

After the portrait painted at Amsterdam, and at least two experi-ments à la Jongkind with watercolor, during this not very protracted episode at Zaandam, measured in frigid winter weeks, Monet pro-duced sixteen known canvases. Helped by the securing of instinct, he made something unique and unequaled of them. His response to mood, the needs of pattern, and broadness of handling was unfail-ingly apt. Totally new to him, the style grew in serenity and beauty, and reached great heights toward the end. But Christmas was near, bringing thoughts of the new year, that season ever so dear to him, and the yearning for family and country grew strong.

Daubigny surely was in Holland and able to give advice. Journey-ing south through Antwerp and Brussels, as soon Monet did, he perhaps spoke with Boudin. From each he learned France had passed through so many vicissitudes of conquest, siege, and civil war that the most powerful as well as the wickedest men had disappeared from government. Little existed now to elucidate the befogged divisions between those who had fought on opposing sides. No one in author-ity questioned where a man had spent the months of ill-fated war. Monet's road was open, and by New Year's Day, 1872, he was in France to celebrate with Camille and their little Jean.

At Paris the threads of prewar confusion were quickly sorted out. From Edmond Maître, who had taken charge of Bazille's studio after his death, Monet retrieved those canvases recognized as his before Bazille's own remnants were shipped to Montpellier. From Pissarro

Monet learned that the Louveciennes house, in which had been stored the sum total of Pissarro's own production and the greatest number of Monet's works, had served as a butcher shop for occupying German troops. The many canvases had been made a useful prefabricated walk on which officers could protect their boots from the garden mud. Many more doubtless had gone to decorate Prussian drawing rooms. Despite these disappointments, Monet successfully located examples of his own work painted at Bougival and Étretat as well as Ste.-Adresse. In addition to what he had brought from England and Holland they constituted a small stock.

For a few moments more the last shadows linger, obscuring the precise location in Paris where Monet settled with his family. Boudin and Jongkind were delighted by his return, tendering him a housewarming, after which they marveled at the progress he had made, for the Dutch canvases were indeed impressive. "He is very well settled and appears to have a strong desire to make a position for himself. He has brought from the Netherlands some very beautiful studies, and I believe that he is destined to fill one of the first places in our school," Boudin wrote, January 2, 1872. By his usual keen observation Boudin had discovered a new truth. From months of exile, flight, and solitude, Monet had gained his passport to maturity. A new personality had begun to emerge, showing him more cool and detached, ironic and contemptuous. Certain of himself, confident in his future, he adopted the mantle of an infinitely resourceful, infinitely determined, extraordinarily resilient figure on the way up.

An artist in need of landscape motifs was unable to remain rooted to Paris, however. Soon again, that same January, 1872, Monet set off for Le Havre, where his quest appears to have been disappointed. Only two hasty sketches were brought away, showing a setting sun hanging over the harbor's west end. He had worked rapidly on them, summoning all his quickness of hand to express a crisis. But the result made no strong visual or emotional sense, and coming on the heels of his wonderfully controlled Dutch works, they were clearly an aberrant and retrograde experiment.

More chaste designs were sketched at Rouen, where the silhouetted city was viewed across pleasure boats moored in a river bend. Late winter views, with a solid attention to physical detail and the carefully separated and stressed value areas evolved in Holland, these were his first answer to the necessity of producing small works especially for Durand-Ruel. A certain unexpected timidity becomes obvious, the reason no less so. He had moved far from the nightmare lucidity and impetuous brushing of that purely intuitive style employed during the previous decade. Placement and a delicate control of accents now had joined with a special use of painterly circumlocution which was breathtakingly dangerous. The proper touch given a canvas kicked fantasy back into focus. But meantime the texture became starved and meager. The thin line between a visual experience that could be transmuted into his gray, reserved poetry, and that which became merely dull and ponderous, had to be learned.

Hungry as he had become for Monet's works, Durand-Ruel was in no sense confining himself to current production. Those canvases Monet had rescued from wartime oblivion began to appear at the Rue Laffitte gallery. Earlier purchases, made in England and on Monet's return from Holland, were unrecorded. "All these transactions, the exhibitions that were incessantly organized and the ceaseless coming and going of pictures sold, purchased, or shipped to Brussels, to London, or in return, would have necessitated accounts very regular and exact. Unfortunately, I was very badly seconded, my books were badly kept . . . ," the dealer apologized. In February, 1872, on his return from Le Havre and Rouen, however, Monet in a recorded transaction delivered to Durand-Ruel seven canvases realizing a total of 2,400 francs:

Marine, temps gris	*400 Frs.*
Lilas, temps gris	*400*
Lilas, soleil	*400*
Seine à Rouen	*300*
Bateau de Plaisance	*300*
Marine, Rouen	*300*
Port de mer, Ste.-Adresse	*300*

The two lilac studies, which brought higher prices, surely were painted in 1870, and the Ste.-Adresse study several years before that. Profiting from Durand-Ruel's enthusiasm, a few days later Monet brought him four more canvases, the titles of which were not recorded, but for which he received the further sum of 1,200 francs.

Everyone was pleased with these transactions, and soon after, the least disciplined of the Dutch studies, an inelegant fishing boat heading toward deep water through irregular brush strokes, was purchased from Durand-Ruel by Daubigny for 400 francs. If previously the public had approved Monet's works with a grudging, sometimes testy admiration, Daubigny's purchase was approbation indeed! Through the glistening, well-swept, and sumptuously furnished corridors of the dealer's shop Monet now perceived another alternate road to acclaim, for at Durand-Ruel's he appeared on equal terms with men prominent at the Salon. Possibly at the dealer's suggestion he also determined that the Salon, which had treated him so shamefully, should have no further opportunity to humiliate him. Notable is the fact that those of his friends in touch with Durand-Ruel followed this same tactic, for a man of genuine distinction prevented the accumulation of indignities.

Nor were omens propitious for business in postwar Paris. Among artists everything had returned to normal with remarkable speed. "[Alfred] Stevens never stops telling me he is doing masterpieces, and that this year he will easily exceed 100,000 francs," wrote an envious Edgar Degas. Manet's fortunes also changed for the better. That January, encouraged in a bold program designed to put himself in unique control of the new school, Durand-Ruel found two of Manet's works hung in the handsomely furnished Chinese studio of Alfred Stevens. Durand-Ruel visited Manet, and to the artist's delight purchased everything he found, twenty-three canvases, for which he paid 35,000 francs. Durand even asked Manet to assemble further works, and a few days later returned to make purchases valued at another 16,000 francs.

A hilarious Édouard Manet flung at the Café Guerbois, "Do you know of a painter unable to make fifty thousand francs a year from his work?" When a sneering chorus replied, "Yes, you!" he hastened to propound how wrong they were. Degas now was in contact with Durand-Ruel also, and here the first note of caution was heard: "Durand-Ruel takes everything I do, but scarcely sells anything."

Only Monet's larger Salon-inspired canvases failed to tempt Durand-Ruel, whose purpose was to create a stock of small salable works. *The Luncheon*, painted at Étretat, and preserved probably in Bazille's Paris studio, remained on Monet's hands. Yet during this same period of affluence he at last came to terms with Paillard, the landlord at Chailly, extracting from the Cheval-Blanc's moldy storage his huge canvas of the *Picnic*. Rolled up since Christmas, 1865, seven years' exposure to dampness had wreaked havoc on this work toward which, blindly perhaps, Monet continued to feel the same splendid pride of achievement.

A deteriorated section from the right end of this canvas he cut away, and for balance he cut away also a large strip from the left. Unfinished figures, which had been his greatest scourge and had grown so horribly grotesque, thus were eliminated. What remained was the portion directly centered about the picnic cloth, where a profusion of original ideas had been combined by prodigies of scintillating brushing to evoke the glitter of a forest interior.

This center of the *Picnic* contained the portrait of Gustave Courbet, which Monet seemed anxious to preserve. Unlike others, he had no desire in that postwar period to abandon Courbet or usurp his rightful place. Unfortunately, stray bits and wisps of other figures not only partially obscured Courbet's arm and shoulder but from both sides wandered into this area of the once larger canvas. Especially troublesome was a pair of Bazille's ultra-long legs, which stretched across the foreground unattached to torso or head. These Monet roughly obliterated. To explain a billowing skirt which filled the right of his scissored composition, he introduced a new head of Camille wearing a cockaded hat. This proceeded favorably, until he tried to attach it to the skirt and found they existed on different scales and different planes.

Again he stopped. Of superb richness, space, and brilliance, this large canvas after its cropping had become vast barren spaces, full of dust and bits of litter. The preserved figures stared irrationally about them, lacking the artfulness the overall structure had possessed before truncation. Disheartened, once more he put away the *Picnic*.

To the increased maturity discernible on his return to France his new sense of economic security had brought an even wider outlook, accentuating qualities which long had done him credit. The pettiness and capacity for spite that marked so many Paris artists never had been a part of Monet's nature. Now, at last, his personality included the luxury of a compassion for others granted only those whose own fate is secure.

Few in Paris retained any recollection of the recent and barbarous events of siege, the horror of streets under bombardment and the screams of terrified horses. The war was reduced to Édouard Manet's droll tales of service on the staff of the Garde Nationale at the Élysée Palace, where his colonel was Meissonier, a member of the Institute, who gave no sign of being aware that such a painter as Édouard Manet ever had existed. In return, Manet expressed disdain over the doodles his superior officer left scattered in view. But inside the Morisot family, where intimate knowledge of Édouard Manet was complete, it was heard that he had spent the time of the siege changing uniforms.

Manet, in fact, was hard pressed during this immediate postwar period to fill the Gargantuan void left by absence of Gustave Courbet. If Frédéric Bazille was the only member of this group who actually did not return from war, Courbet, that good-natured giant, also had blundered into catastrophe. During the final days of Paris' second siege Courbet had entered a bizarre political situation. Under the Commune which so briefly controlled Paris, a decree dated April 12 ordered the demolition of the Vendôme Column. Four days later the sixth arrondissement elected Gustave Courbet its Communal Councilor, and he was forthwith named delegate for the Beaux-Arts. Unable to deflect an existing order for the column's demolition, Courbet was reputed to have taken charge of the operation, unbuckling the lower plates to prevent damage. Many claimed to have seen him on May 16 in the *grande salle* of the Ministry of Justice, facing the Place Vendôme, and actively supervising the column's fall. More reliable is that, as a protest against this act he perhaps had witnessed, the following day Courbet resigned his offices.

No longer had Courbet the indiscriminating adoration of the public. And by the fortunes of war, which swept out those political allies with whom he had disagreed, then early in June 1871 brought back to Paris more distinct foes, Courbet was labeled a perpetrator of cultural depravity, whether or not he had committed the act for which he was universally blamed. He took refuge at the home of a friend, where on June 7 he was arrested.

Gustave Courbet was now in a position wasteful of his talents, involving painful consequences, and filled with ironic traps of loyalty and legality. The ridiculously sweeping charge that *he* demolished the Vendôme Column was placed against him. Only Amand Gautier never wavered in devotion, obtaining permission to visit Courbet in his prison August 16, where he executed a touching study of that vast rotund form, smoking his pipe against a simple prison table.

His hair suddenly white, his vast physique shrunken, Courbet was tried before a Council of War, and had the spirit to defend himself gallantly. No act of violence or civil disorder could be proved against him. His attorney declared Courbet's part in the fall of the Vendôme Column was a popular legend, invented and exploited by journalists.

Only the fact that Courbet briefly had taken part in the Commune's administrative system convicted him, and he was condemned to six months' imprisonment and a fine of 500 francs.

Conscious that Courbet's huge mantle as leading arch-modern now had fallen to him, and lacking in discretion and judgment, Édouard Manet made the most of Courbet's denials: "You mention Courbet," he wrote to a friend. "His conduct before the War Council was that of a coward and he no longer deserves any attention." But closer friends and kinder hearts could not dissociate themselves so easily from this amiable giant.

Gautier, himself briefly incarcerated for the offense of serving as the Commune's Keeper of the Louvre, never failed his master. His health shattered, suffering intensely from hemorrhoids, Courbet was transported from St.-Pélagie Prison to the private sanitarium of Dr. Nelaton at Neuilly, where he underwent an operation. Fearful of compromising friends, Courbet wrote to no one, but on January 2, 1872, the endearing little Boudin no longer could withhold his kind words:

> We do not wish these days to go by, days which are marked by dutiful visits to many friends who are more or less happy—without sending you, in the depths of your prison, these few words to show that we are thinking of you. We shall be satisfied if this poor token of our friendship serves to divest you of your loneliness for a few moments.
>
> Returned to Paris but a short time ago, after a long absence, we had hoped to shake your hand, but we are told it is hard to get permission to see you. I am acting as the spokesman for several of my comrades—Monet and Gautier among others—who all send you their good wishes and who are just as anxious as I am to spend a little time with you. . . .

Four days later Courbet replied. The letter was his first utterance since he had been imprisoned:

> At last there is nothing to fear. You can come in pilgrimage to a man who has served seven months in a prison cell. . . . I learn that Gautier has tasted pleasures of that sort. . . . Come if your heart tells you to, with Gautier, Monet, and even the ladies. . . .

Escorted by Gautier, Monet and Boudin visited Courbet at a moment when one dared not speak his name publicly without fear.

They found him a man vastly aged, his figure much diminished. And though Courbet had become an object of curiosity and derision, they could not help admiring his spirited efforts to disport himself in circumstances so unfavorable.

Uneasy among the guarded tautologies of which his recent canvases too often were composed, when he returned to Paris Monet happily allowed Renoir to provide a subject. From the second floor of a café overlooking the Pont-Neuf, Renoir industriously hacked out an intricate view of the bridge, the glistening lights of which he steered through a variety of unrestrained keys. His picture was a complete and thoughtless catalogue in which every window and chimney pot received its due; in addition Renoir gave a devastating account of the Parisians who passed his view in dizzying profusion. Ladies with parasols, urchins, horses and carriages, and gentlemen, tall, slim, elegant, and supercilious, were amusingly captured, not without the resourceful invention of a tactic: While Renoir dashed in figures at his window two floors above the street, his brother Edmond, posted below, stopped passers-by with some question or account vague enough to hold them still.

Here was none of the scrupulously restrained accounting Monet had brought with him from Holland and Rouen, but a brilliant and cheerfully vapid approach. If style, that ever-elusive, vital component, remained absent, the work Renoir produced was none the less as witty as the highest of high comedies. Rain fell when Monet joined Renoir at his window, and immediately an explosive scene was altered into more somber and carefully patterned prose. Renoir's quantities of hard facts changed under Monet's compelling gaze into shapes which suited the demands of his pattern-seeking eye. Renoir's gorgeous, fidgety and irrelevant ballet became an equally crowded, strongly controlled exercise in wet discomfort, so persuasive that the arbitrary style justifies itself almost completely.

More often in Paris Monet was transformed from artist to man of affairs. His days were occupied by the delivery of pictures to Durand-Ruel, tracing and recovering old canvases, and securing new supplies of paints and canvas from Carpentier's shop in the Rue Halévy. The sums of money accruing to Monet from his transactions with Durand-Ruel grew in a way unprecedented during his previously poverty-stricken existence. Again, in April, the dealer purchased a study painted in Holland, *La Maison Bleue,* for 300 francs, and in May, 1872, Durand-Ruel took a mixed group including English and Dutch works:

Parc de Richmond	*300 Frs.*
Moulin en Hollande	*300*
Pommiers en Fleur	*300*
La Grande Voile	*300*
Le Brise-Lames	*300*
Parc de Windsor	*300*
Arbres Jaunes	*300*

His rapid wet view of the Pont-Neuf is the only Paris scene Monet undertook, and soon the impracticality of living in the great city became evident. His life had been played out along the River Seine, whose charming small towns provided material for him to paint as it had for generations of landscape artists before him. As Frédéric Bazille once had suggested to him a house at Sèvres, now it seems that Bazille's close friend, Édouard Manet, suggested to Monet a house at Argenteuil, across the river from property at Gennevilliers long in possession of the Manet family.

Among Édouard Manet's moneyed and landed acquaintances was a certain Mme. Aubry-Vitet, proprietor of a small house at Argenteuil formerly occupied by the painter Théodule Ribot. One room had been darkened as a studio suitable to the umbrous moods of Ribot's Neapolitan style. Situated on the banks of the river, twenty minutes from Paris by train, everything about the little house and garden appealed to Monet and to Camille. After a recommendation from Édouard Manet, on June 14, 1872, Mme. Aubry-Vitet's notary drew up a *procuration.* By July 9 all formalities were settled. The notary issued a *décharge,* and at an annual rental of 1,000 francs the Monets took up a new abode, where they threw off the fetters of their long winter of discontent and plunged directly into an intoxicating summer.

At Argenteuil a new exuberance, and a new complacency, immediately surrounded the Monet family. No payment of interest on Camille's dowry was expected until that December, 1872, but what mattered those paltry 600 francs before the thousands Monet had earned in the previous six months? Everyone noted the new solidness of his views and aspirations. Everyone in contact with him recognized, as though it were a fresh phenomenon, that he was an ambitious man, with a passionate interest in his career, who early had tasted the excitement of being important and sought after.

And if together they seemed once more a jovial, festive pair, alone Camille remained a creature of charm, still possessed of qualities best conveyed by mention of delicacy and love. For the first time she had a comfortable home of her own, a proper marriage, and the correct routine for her day. Though the summer was advanced, her husband set about planting the garden, and little Jean, now five, was the pride of both parents as among budding plants he played with his hoop. New clothes were bought for all. Little Jean was garbed lavishly in a suit of skirted pantaloons and cockaded hat. A further burst of generosity provided him with a tricycle distinguished by a stuffed horse mounted on its front end in place of mundane handlebars. His plump legs barely able to reach extended pedals, Jean proudly rode circles into the garden path.

Argenteuil seemed, after all, the kind of place where the dogs chased the cats across the main street and both of them walked. The Monets had lived in villages far worse, and the depth of affection with which they viewed their new home derived from the sense of permanence brought to it. No doubt existed that the fearful years of the sixties had passed completely. Their house and their garden delighted them, and when, suitably attired in the tan trousers and brown leisure jacket of a country gentleman, a gay straw hat on his head, Claude Monet inspected on his front walk the large vases of blue and white Delft he had brought from Holland, it was difficult for him not to sense exultantly that the world had taken a better turn.

Pleasant, sensible, free from both the follies of adulation and the acidities of disparagement, Camille led the quieter, more sheltered existence, and at Argenteuil she resumed the daily ritual of a French housewife. As at Sèvres and Étretat, now again she rose early to provide breakfast for husband and son. Watching over her two men was a happy experience; if she was treated by Monet with good-humored patronage, and was pathetically grateful for a kind word, most happiness is the product of yearnings rather than fulfillments.

Breakfast coffee and rolls cleared away, and her husband off about his work, Camille walked through bright little streets to do her marketing. The butcher was visited, after which she chose vegetables at the greengrocer's. Farther along her route was a *crémerie,* for milk to give little Jean, and the eggs and cheese for his father's lunch. On Monday, when the butcher was closed, Camille went instead to the *triperie,* or perhaps the *charcuterie;* and lastly, before she started home each morning, she stopped at a bakery for the luncheon loaf of bread.

No detailing of her routine could convey the adorable impulsiveness of this youthful matron, the occasional melancholy of her character, or the manners that always linked the romantic and bookish girl with the Parisian lady she should have been. Marks of weariness and woe, once so noticeable, had abated, and she came back cheerfully through Argenteuil's narrow streets in time to begin preparation of lunch.

For two hours in the middle of the day her family reunited about her. That meticulously prepared repast cleared away, Monet once more went about his business: painting by the shore of the river, or taking the train to Paris with his recent labors. The care of little Jean, in additon to sewing, washing and ironing, consumed Camille's afternoon. She had a house to clean now, and, if she wished, a garden in which to work. Then at four in the afternoon the kitchen's wood stove was lit to commence preparation for dinner. Camille's hands were never still. Her active mind continued to reflect her education, and, unlike her husband, she carefully read newspapers, especially *Le Figaro,* the Paris daily. She had, perhaps, been snubbed into a subordinate wife, yet Camille's lovely thrice-scrubbed innocence remained, and she was happy at last.

By the river Monet continued the soft sketches of pleasure craft moored in the Seine begun at Rouen. Pliant and eloquent, acceptable to Durand-Ruel, they constituted an effort to continue the style evolved in Holland while his Japanese inspiration was fresh. So effective during that former period, his balances and patterning became a monotonous accentuation of foreground objects, a natural consequence of the fact that Argenteuil's sailboats and barges had not the evocative silhouettes of Dutch windmills. He returned also to still life, painting a sumptuous study of grapes, ripe autumn peaches, and a luscious melon. This attractive study was among the group Durand-Ruel purchased in September, 1872:

Arbres à Fleurs Jaunes	*500 Frs.*
Nature Morte, Melon	*400*
L'Église Près du Canal	*400*
Village dans les arbres Près d'un Canal	*300*
Promenade au bord de l'eau	*300*
Le Convoi du Chemin de Fer	*300*
La Passerelle	*300*
Entrée de Village	*300*
Bateaux Près du Quai	*300*

At Argenteuil Monet continued methodically, and with much taste and fluency, turning out simple designs with a careful notation of low tonality and no dearth of bright, neat, well-patterned ideas. The surface of his paintings became less highly wrought, more evenly and thinly spread, more and more reminiscent of the gentle atmospherics of Boudin, and wondered to where had escaped the brutal, harsh Monet of the sixties. An impulsive gaiety perhaps was felt as some glittering sail scudded past the attentive painter, who smartly impasted its clear white triangle on his canvas. Such occasional phenomena were the only exceptions in an otherwise remarkable cohesion of unassuming, quiet, Boudin-like efforts.

Alfred Sisley was among those who noted Monet's pleasant sense of prosperity. Once the smartly dressed playboy of the Gleyre studio, the war had brought Sisley a complete loss of fortune. Monet introduced him to Durand-Ruel, for whom Sisley was anxious to brush a profusion of canvases. But first he journeyed to Argenteuil, to examine more closely the remarkable phenomenon presented by Monet earning a fortune from landscapes. In the village this guest discovered Argenteuil's ancient church, reputed to have been the last reliquary of the Holy Tunic, whose slim tower he made the focal point for a composition glowing with ocherish sunlight drawn from Corot's finest Italian sketches.

But the mysterious balances and patterns Sisley saw in Monet's river views soon after drew him to that newer subject. He noted his host's broadness of vision, the trick which permitted Monet to cherish and promote the river's wealth of detail and delicacy of tone without weakening its atmospheric pungency. Together the two men stood in marshes by the farther bank, and at Monet's side Sisley captured the lyric vision he continued to deploy in studies portraying the river's more wistful moods.

The greatest merit of Sisley's canvases resides in the natural easy style he adopted. His brush slithered gently, and though by comparison with Monet's recondite visual style Sisley's river views seem unassertive and indecisive to the point of futility, the visitor demonstrated stronger lyric gifts than his host, and greater purity of tone. The soft poetry of riverbanks never had been more rapturously portrayed than by Sisley, as though to prove Monet was at his best when flushed with that more forceful temperament to which he had been born.

16. Death in the Family

OF COURSE everything was different now. At Argenteuil the vain, self-centered, ambitious man of former years allowed himself to collapse into happy uxorious anticlimax. On visits to Paris, during which frequently Monet brought Camille and Jean to visit Boudin, the latter noted "he seems content after his fashion, in spite of the resistance he finds to his paintings." For the dark shadow overhanging so much newly acquired happiness was that Durand-Ruel experienced constant rebuffs in his efforts to sell the pictures acquired from Monet.

One over whom the force of gravity previously had demonstrated little power, this dealer connection held Monet earth-bound to the little canvases of elegantly varying patterns Durand-Ruel purchased. And despite his failure to find clients for these works, in November, 1872, Durand-Ruel took from Monet another mixed group:

Westminster	300 Frs.
Cafetière et Tasse à Café	400
Chemin dans les Vignes, Argenteuil	300
Coteaux de Sannois	200
Femme en Rose	400
Usine à Deville, Rouen	300
Marine, Argenteuil	200

At Paris such canvases seemed exceedingly stylish, and a personal development. While before nature, however, the artist had constantly to restrain his natural impulse to take a more surprising harmonic twist that would match changing atmospheric conditions. Happiness soon made him more bold. The quiet care and complacency of canvases brought to Paris during the first months at Argenteuil were overcome by fresher impulses, and that ecstatic robust personality of former times again swept onto canvas, bringing a pictorial unity all its own.

For several days he worked on an explicit account of the path meandering along the riverfront near his home. Unequivocal statements were made concerning the distant Seine bridge, bathing establishments on the water, and shadows flowing down the grassy banks from a picnic ground's massed trees. Too often only neat dismissive jests, the figures he added now functioned in a tonal unity of surprising depth, holding their place in distances, and sharing atmosphere with their surroundings. Everywhere in this laborious composition is a disarming lack of presumption coupled with singular vividness of observation. By his taste and scrupulous attention to detail he formed a supreme revelation of beauty.

The experience brightened and sharpened his palette, while an easier manner flowed from his brush. He sketched bright waters of the river, overhanging trees, and fluffy clouds, all replete with decorative dabs of white sails. Everywhere in these efforts a new warmth is unmistakable; and, like the depth of greens that formed warm shadows on waving grasses, its nature reflected the painter's happy state. His house, and especially the garden which brought so much contentment, formed the newest subject for his labors. Into a vibrant study he introduced the long-skirted figure of Jean, a coquettish Camille peeking from the door behind him. Treatment was superficial and the tone facetious, fixing perfectly the quality of their pleasant existence and constituting homage to this first happiness they had known together.

Durand-Ruel meantime became attracted to Monet's earlier works, and in March, 1873, concluded a deal similar to that earlier transacted with Édouard Manet. Nineteen pictures, including everything painted prior to the war Monet had been able to gather from pawn, passed to Durand-Ruel. Among them was a large Salon piece of *La Grenouillère,* a work presumably rejected in 1870, forest

interiors painted at Chailly, lamplight studies done in the minuscule
dining room at Étretat, and the balance of his Dutch works:

Le Bodenier, Arbre de la Forêt de Fontainebleau	600 Frs.
Pavé de Chailly	700
Grenouillère, Bougival	2,000
Plaine de Colombe, gelée blanche	500
Neige à Argenteuil	500
Le Dégel	500
Moulin d'Orgemont, neige	600
Effet de Brouillard	500
Le Dîner	500
Après Dîner	500
Le Mont Ribondu, Rouen	500
La Vallée de Deville, Rouen	400
Zaandam, Hollande	400
Le Moulin de Bois	300
Marine, Hollande	300
La Lecture	500
Vue d'Argenteuil	400

The total of 10,200 francs realized was the largest sum of money
Claude Monet ever had known, and joy was unconfined. A new hat
sat high on Camille's head, the crown decorated by black ribbons and
red flowers, and its brim extended down over her forehead. New
plumage was not hers alone, for Jean's growth was a pleasing phenomenon to his parents, and with this season a great decision was
taken: Baby costumes and skirts were put away, to be replaced by
knickerbockers and a sailor suit, topped off by a straw cloche hat.
Nearly six, overnight Jean was transformed from *enfant* to little
man, bringing renewed delight to his adoring parents.

Visitors awaited warm weather before venturing down to Argenteuil from Paris. But that busy spring and summer of 1873 was little
troubled by guests, probably because the Monets were much in Paris,
where Camille's father lay seriously ill. Late that summer season
Renoir at last came to stay, an impetuous, sometimes sulky guest,
often collapsing into adolescent mirth. Immediately Renoir joined
little expeditions into the countryside, where Monet prospected for
new subjects. Her blue-lined parasol held high, and urging on little
Jean, Camille accompanied the artists to pose for necessary figures.

But the views they explored everywhere contrived to seem over-complicated and confusing: never simple enough, nor enriched by that unlooked-for strand of counterpoint which made pictures interesting. To compensate for disappointment both artists dashed in sketches of Camille and Jean knee-deep in summer grasses and flaming poppies.

For a time their attention was concentrated on nothing more appropriate than a duck pond. Each painter dabbed at several canvases, successive chopping strokes producing unpleasant scrofulous surfaces of the sort Renoir had created at La Grenouillère four years before. More bizarre was to see Monet, consumed with his passionately sincere communicator's fervor, produce confused and uneven sketches boasting little definition and only vague notions of summery reality. This fussy inadequacy and rough incomprehension succeeded the tight hard style brought back from Holland, doubtless because at last Monet had grown discouraged with a formalistic approach, openly envying Renoir's freedom to indulge a luxuriant fancy.

The countryside had yielded nothing, and subjects remained difficult to find. In colder weather Renoir joined Monet in the garden. Rather than paint the blossoming border that occupied his host, Renoir sketched Monet himself as he stood dressed against approaching autumn chill, palette and brushes in hand, his paint box spread on the ground before him. Both works produced that day recommended themselves for meticulous attention, and revealed at once a distinctive sense of tone and preoccupation with new relationships of color. Yet without a really inspiring subject at Argenteuil, Monet increasingly felt himself a peddler of artistic small change.

Quirky, perverse, a magpie collector of impressions and a conjurer of facts into fancies, at this same period when Monet despaired of finding appropriate subjects the thousand variations of color and hue delighted his eye everywhere he looked. Nothing escaped him. No guest could be served tea in the garden without the host's noting the tablecloth's varied hues. This too became a picture in which Jean plays on the ground, and mellow afternoon sunlight glitters on geraniums before finding itself reflected in a silver teapot.

Only a persisting desire to paint Salon pieces can account for the large scale on which he executed this scene, or for the quirks of technique which permitted him to lavish desperate skill, reminiscent of Chardin and Caravaggio, on the shadowed bloom of peaches. Everywhere is the magic of his vision: By a slight diminution of tone, a small accent here, a delicate pizzicato of flickering sunlight, he unfolds magical moods. But though little Jean is half dissolved in the foreground, and two spineless female figures float into view from the rear, the whole of the sumptuously flabby work is destroyed by an empty center and lack of a focal point.

The Salon still belonged to minds more systematically trained than that of Claude Monet. Still life was bright and rich and colorful in the lazy sun of Argenteuil; it was a delight to work free of anxiety and crisis. But despite the excitement of technical triumphs Monet's canvases of this period were not his best. Possessed of an attractive lyric quality, they are never expressions of an artist deeply committed. Nothing more could be expected of pictures created expressly for Durand-Ruel, for, at best, Monet's first agreeable seasons at Argenteuil had a wide streak of giggling coyness running down the center.

The bourgeois world of Paris presented an unchanging aspect, living by interminable variations on the two themes of marriage and inheritance. Without them an impoverishment of the public stock of harmless pleasures would have resulted. For those more intimately concerned, however, often it was a matter not so much for sly humor as the gnashing of teeth. Late that summer of 1873 the lurking, nostalgic conservatism and class consciousness so deeply a part of Monet's nature were revitalized by further news of the grave illness of Camille's father. Charles Claude Doncieux was transported to the Maison Municipale de Santé Dubois, in the Faubourg St.-Denis, where on September 22 he died.

The occasion was one of sadness and anxiety. Yet for the Monet family it generated rare excitement by the combination of notaries, authorizations, inventories, and Camille's dowry, the principal of which—12,000 francs—according to their contract of marriage must now be paid. Following on her father's death and funeral, Camille may actually have spent a few October days in Paris, to assist her mother to compile an inventory of property in the Boulevard des Batignolles apartment. If she did, her attention was not directed to the most important considerations. After completion of the inventory, Maître Aumont-Thieville, as notary representing the estate, prepared the customary attestation that it represented an accurate accounting of all property left by Charles Claude Doncieux. On October 16, 1873, in a lengthy interview before his own notary at Argenteuil, Claude Monet duly executed a detailed and exhaustive authorization that permitted Camille to treat for him in the matter of her father's estate. In the hands of even the meanest of provincial notaries this was a matter of some importance, demanding a prose style of unusual prolixity. Camille was authorized to:

> . . . demand the levy with or without description, proceed with all inventories and collections, and in the course of these operations make all declarations, requisitions, prohibitions and reserves, introduce all references, demand all authorizations, and act without attribution of qualities.
>
> Take *connaissance* of charges of succession, accept purely and simply under benefit of an inventory, make in this regard all declarations and affirmations necessary to the Tribunal before which it belongs, take also *connaissance* of all testaments, codicils, and donations (etc.).

Armed with this all-embracing instrument, she proceeded to Paris, where that same day the inventory was certified by Maître Aumont-Thieville. The result immediately created a widespread skepticism, and indeed, the inventory itself proved a very blackguard and entertaining document, for, if it were believed, the total value of all property left by Charles Claude Doncieux was no more than 3,196 francs. By an elaborate plan of greed Camille's mother already had gobbled everything of value left by her husband. Even the 12,000 francs promised as Camille's dowry were nowhere to be found.

A simple will, attested to be entirely from Charles Claude Doncieux's own hand, had been found and presented for probate five days before, on October 11, 1873. Written in 1852, this will took no cognizance of his children, or the dispositions of dowry so carefully made eighteen years later in Camille's contract of marriage. Under the inventory's certification another party was admitted to interest: Louis Chauchal, an architect living in the Rue St.-Petersburg, appointed guardian to Camille's minor sister Geneviève. The certification itself ended with an oath sworn by Mme. Doncieux, that she had "neither taken, hidden, nor turned away, directly nor indirectly," any property belonging to the estate. Gravely written in compact nineteenth-century script, these words bore a simper heightening their effect, for nowhere in the inventory Mme. Doncieux prepared was any mention made of the securities on which her husband had lived since his retirement.

Monet was not present at the certification of that placid and merciless inventory, but on hearing its contents he immediately intervened. The accent his tongue affected was unashamedly bourgeois, and he had the funds with which to make felt an ardent disposition. The distinguished attorney Charles Louis François Postel-Dubois was retained to act in behalf of Camille. His purpose was to discover hidden resources and secure from the estate of Charles Claude Doncieux payment of the 12,000 francs promised Camille.

Postel-Dubois acted with dispatch. Ten o'clock on the morning of November 24, 1873, at the study of Mme. Doncieux's notary, Maître Aumont-Thieville, he brought about a dramatic confrontation. Conducting his inquiry according to polite convention, Postel-Dubois obliged Mme. Doncieux not only to give an accounting of all goods belonging to her husband, but also to permit explorations into her inheritance from Antoine Pritelly. By his insistence Postel-Dubois gained an admission from Mme. Doncieux that at his death her husband had been in possession of certain securities. Unmentioned in the certified inventory of his property, these were now produced and examined, and their value declared to be 5,500 francs.

Here was renewed disappointment, for obviously this was not all Mme. Doncieux had secreted. Yet for even this she proved a tough, resourceful woman who by her own shrewdness and obstinacy struggled still to outwit them. Obliged to bring into the open these hidden securities, Mme. Doncieux now claimed they were the exact equivalent of a 5,500-franc debt her husband had owed her! Stronger action then was required. Probably by threat of a suit for the entire dowry of 12,000 francs, Postel-Dubois persuaded Mme. Doncieux to accept responsibility for a part.

In hopes that this interminable examination could be brought to an end, Maître Aumont-Thieville began drafting a document to codify their work of the day. Mme. Doncieux had promised to pay over to Camille immediately "the sum of four thousand francs, receivable as a loan against the portion of her dowry of twelve thousand francs. . . ." In return Aumont-Thieville extracted from

Camille a price: The principal sum of the dowry would be reduced from 12,000 to 6,000 francs. Therefore, "by means of the present payment it is understood that the part of the charge of Mme. Doncieux in this dowry is henceforth found reduced to the principal sum of two thousand francs."

Ferocious irony existed in the fact that Mme. Doncieux was contriving to cheat Camille of half her dowry. But argument was only now becoming heated. The unpaid balance of 2,000 francs, small as it was, must continue to pay interest, as had been stipulated in the marriage contract. Aumont-Thieville wrote:

> This sum expressly held in security will continue to produce interest on the footing of five percent a year payable by semesters the twenty-first of June and December each year.
>
> The payment of the first semester, that of December eighteen hundred and seventy-three to June eighteen hundred and seventy-four, will take place the twenty-first of June, eighteen hundred and seventy-four.

The confrontation had become a brilliant structure of collective absurdities and frustrated human purposes. With the comic eccentricity proper to his role, Aumont-Thieville attempted to force into this paper a provision favorable to Mme. Doncieux:

> It is understood that the two thousand francs will not become tangible except three months after the death of Madame the widow Doncieux.

This proved agreeable to no one, and in renewed battle Aumont-Thieville was forced to cross it through and consider new formulas. He tried again:

> With regard to the tangibility which will be given to the two thousand francs, the holding and delay of which has been consented to by Madame Monet always under the authorization of her husband, until the death of Madame the widow Doncieux . . .

Aumont-Thieville got no further. Mme. Monet did *not* agree to this sum's being retained until after her mother's death, and Monet gave her no authorization. The notary again turned back on his words, crossing out the phrase "until the death of Madame the widow Doncieux." After "two thousand francs" he inserted a mark directing the eye to a margin, where he wrote, "exaction of which is demanded now."

In the end no agreement was reached, and a flimsy tissue of words left the question unsettled: ". . . the period at which this sum of two thousand francs must be paid to Madame Monet is as will be verified to the stipulation of principal and outside the portion contained in the contract of marriage of Monsieur and Madame Monet."

So agonized had the scribbled paper become, so different in its crossings-out, marginal notes, and agonized writing, from the contract of marriage engrossed three years before in a neater version of this same script, everyone was pleased to sign and initial as directed and end the interview. For the Monets the entire question of a dowry, entered into with misgivings in 1870, now again had arisen to haunt them. Despite the skill of Postel-Dubois, in two neat cuts Mme. Doncieux first had halved, then sliced to a third, the promised sum of Camille's dowry. Only 4,000 francs had been extracted, and little hope existed they could exact one penny more.

However much such treatment had injured Camille, fortified by his own proud control of brush and patron, Monet himself could afford the luxury of contempt. Mme. Doncieux had been utterly despicable. But in two years Durand-Ruel had purchased from Monet sixty-eight canvases, for 32,250 francs. This princely income in excess of 15,000 francs a year overshadowed lesser events. At this juncture especially one wishes that Durand-Ruel's investment had demonstrated some capacity to bring a return. Instead he suffered the plight of his too enthusiastic approach in a cynical world where his treasures were viewed with something less than general delight.

Each of Durand-Ruel's efforts to show his new purchases was a conspicuous failure. The majority view at first was a mere indifference which showed no hostility, but soon a veritable campaign of protest was heard. Guilty of having presented offending works before the public, Durand-Ruel himself shared in a reprobation which made him seem a man of bad faith. His problems were intensified when simultaneously the economy of France, which had boomed after the disquieting influences of war, gravely slackened in 1873. After March of that year Durand-Ruel ceased his purchases of Monet's works. The two sources of funds on which life at Argenteuil had depended—Camille's dowry and Durand-Ruel's purchases—thus faded away together.

At the end of 1873 Monet found himself incomparably richer than ever before. At the same moment he freshly realized how little hope existed of further income. Anxious to support the painters with whom he had entered into relations, Durand-Ruel urged his clients to make purchases from them direct. Through this obliging dealer Monet thus newly came into contact with a group of collectors among whom were Faure, de Bellio, and Hoschedé. If they did not rapidly acquire numbers of his works, this group constituted his sole hope some might be purchased. With an easy guilelessness Monet therefore returned to his older habit of shrugging off tomorrow and consuming days in the rapture of his work.

Those recent trips to Paris, while details of the estate were fought out, had included visits to Renoir, and Camille had gone with her husband to see Boudin. Little Jean accompanied his parents, certain to have a wild ride on Boudin's shoulders. Another whom Monet visited was the photographer Nadar, who frequented the Café Guerbois and during the siege had been conspicuous as a balloonist. Nadar's fashionable second-floor studio was on the corner of the Rue Daunou, facing the Grand Hôtel across the Boulevard des Capucines. From these windows Monet saw eddying moods of the great boulevard below, and he began two curious efforts to put on canvas this movement seen through a screen of colored atmosphere.

Fresh clear pigments were rubbed thinly over his habitual buff-toned canvases to locate the broad masses of the composition. But on a Paris boulevard he discovered no strong pattern of the kind he had sought in Holland and Argenteuil. The result was an adequate but synthetic rendering in which solid forms, buildings, trees, and carriages, were fixed by the glow of color they effused. Reasonably brisk, not noticeably stylized or imaginative, his means created a dead-accurate rendering of damp blue haze and a bright Paris afternoon.

Only the lack of solidity was disturbing, for by bizarre reversals the city's most solid elements, its massive architecture and the Gargantuan Grand Hôtel itself, became these pictures' most liquid features. In the foreground scores of promenading figures were carefully picked out as sharp undefined accents against the bland tonality of pavement. This blend of fatuousness and idiosyncrasy makes Monet's sardonic presence felt everywhere. But all is so deft, witty, and crisp, the eye is happy to suspend unbelief. And strangely, Monet's art, long in danger of becoming lost in formulas, unmistakably showed new signs of life.

A new departure, not without beauty of color, atmosphere, and urban charm, his pictures of the Boulevard des Capucines were very peculiar indeed, full of sly jokes, top-hatted gentlemen, and peddlers selling joyful pink balloons. Immediately they raise the question whether this new, light, and somewhat frenetic style had not impulsively been knocked up to catch the attention of the clamorous and only spasmodically attentive Parisians to whom, thanks to Durand-Ruel's introductions, Monet's work would henceforth be addressed.

The great Argenteuil period, representing the first flood tide of Monet's still youthful inspiration, began only now. Two years after settling there, out of despondence and disillusionment, Claude Monet turned his attention once more to the river flowing past his door. With humor, resignation, and melancholy, he accepted the dealer's task of forcing attention from a public that had remained bewildered and somewhat revolted at Durand-Ruel's shop.

His purpose was to prove that more than a splendid collection of exotic locations was required. He knew the attention of the art-buying public to be shallow and sporadic, attracted by brightness, familiarity, novelty, fashion, and the thinnest flaunting type of theatricality. To this combination of qualities Monet addressed himself, and from them his new glittering and dazzling Argenteuil works suffered most. A shortage of hard thinking, as opposed to earnest ruminating, is striking, as well as the surfeit of bright ideas. Purists must always feel uneasy that the sudden return of liveliness to his works following the cessation of Durand-Ruel's purchases was a desperate search for novelty, a senseless and unending St. Vitus's dance. Yet the first result was an astonishing bursting forth of small works so aware, structurally so complex, they could bewilder, irritate, or entrance, but never bore.

While fresh clean canvases remained, he would lose all terror of throwing formula to the winds. Fancy could reign in a visual style more highly wrought than ever before, and if necessary, as farfetched. To assist him vary schemes on the small expanse of river, Monet planned to paint from the water as well as the shore. For this purpose he purchased a small black hull, on which he had constructed a boxlike superstructure to provide shelter for artist and materials: the same approach he knew Daubigny had adopted fifteen years before. At rear was a miniature deck, where, by folding his knees tailor fashion, he could sit with his easel beneath a gaily striped awning.

Enlarged areas of water that filled his foregrounds were an immediate advantage. A new low perspective made those areas appear vast, presenting an unbroken tonal base against which to play color chords of scattered boats, reflecting sails, and shore structures among sentinel trees. Less stable as a platform on which to work, the boat also lent extra haste to the movement of his hand. This contributed to an already notable inclination for bare buff-toned canvas to play a role in the picture. No longer did any real fusion of technique exist, except in those rare examples where greater labor brought a deliberate finish. Many sketches appeared to be only an infinity of wholly separate touches, at times applied with surprising dexterity and correctness, but also presenting much rough and scrubbed irregularity that was enthralling when it was not irritating. Renoir, who came to Argenteuil for the regatta, and joined Monet in his boat moored near shore, surprised though he must have been, quickly followed the procedures he saw employed.

The faculty of detecting exceptions, and using them as the basis for new lines of work, was essential to Monet's extraordinary goal. His pictorial thought and execution stemmed from conventions and attitudes of training. To break apart from these he sought aberrations of procedure in his own hasty sketches, allowing them to serve as starting points for new investigations. The river was his subject, but no moment was wasted on meaningless rapture, nor was he tied to his boat. Many feet had worn a path into the riverbank along which daily he plodded in search of those subjects, at once sweet and piercing, he needed to force attention at Paris. Along the entire length of this path little wildness was present of the sort he preferred in nature. Daubigny, painting untouched areas of the Oise and Somme, had been more fortunate, for everywhere at Argenteuil was ugliness, mechanization, and the hand of man.

At the uppermost end of his path the sky was rent by harsh lines of a railway bridge over which trains ground to Paris. Farther along were the symmetrical spans of another steel-girdered bridge, which shut out the equally unprofitable forms of bridges beyond. On each horizon factory chimneys belched forth their varicolored fumes. Beneath the main Argenteuil road bridge multitudes of blackened barges stood against the bank. Their cargoes were discharged slowly by laborers who painfully carried sacks of coal across planks to the shore. Only the pleasure boats dotting the river, moored helter-skelter among their attendant bait boats and boathouses, provided a light touch in a scene being snatched from nature.

Ingenuity was required to arrange compositions from such poor and ill-assorted materials. The only height was provided by trees in the picnic ground directly before Monet's own house. The ugly forms of steel bridges might be employed for this same purpose were their mechanical shapes accommodated to pictorial needs. Doubtless he was aware of London bridges painted a decade earlier by Whistler, recently displayed at Durand-Ruel's Paris gallery. That eccentric American, who had allowed a parallel taste for the Japanese to take a more rarefied route than Monet's, had rammed down the center of his canvas a single pier of Old Battersea Bridge. Its footwalk thus became an unbroken arc, running from frame to frame—an idea that recommended itself to Monet.

If he plodded through quantities of clichés to form this composition, Monet painted it with careful regard to nuances of color induced by atmospheric conditions. The effect was striking, and he began again, on a slightly wider canvas, the effect further varied by a silhouetted boathouse under one span. What at first had seemed a horrid steel bridge became a blessing for its cold symmetry, the spiderwork bringing his pictures that additional charm of easy brilliance in florid ornamentation. In bright sunlight the steel shone green, then, in less pleasant weather, inky blue. The river below picked up these varied tones and scattered them in rippling counterpoint. Pleasure boats were introduced to give new variations of shape and color; black hulls, white hulls, and long slim masts that shone orange in the sun were isolated by a sharp and discerning eye.

The blithely ecstatic growth of roughly daubed canvases encouraged him further, and whether he was creating new variations on trusted themes, simply running backward down the track of his memories, or was no less sincerely dedicated to the pursuit of new attacks on the Parisian purse, no one knew. His mind was concentrated on this fascinating game of discovering patterns that might be wrenched from nature. He climbed high up the embankment beside the railroad bridge, from where he glimpsed a new harsh linear perspective. The bridge could be brought into his picture from the upper right corner, shooting across the river and grounding itself in the earthy mass of distant shore. By day he painted this with the uneasy balance of a long triangular sail. Toward evening he did it again, softening it by a plume of darkened steam that rose from trains speeding to Paris.

Endlessly Monet walked his path along that single mile of river at Argenteuil. Varied as were his uses of material, limitations were ever present, causing him to create fewer melodies and nourish them carefully through variations. With an enchanting guilelessness he painted subjects as they appeared at different times of the day, gaining effects that bore no resemblance to each other. Always impatient with himself, his materials, the light, and the weather, now he was forced more consciously than ever before to catch effects that were fleeting, and his remarkable sleight-of-hand often made a cliché unexpectedly glitter. His inclination to rub thin washes over fresh buff-toned canvas, then touch and dab without completely covering the cloth, became more prominent. Haste was his excuse, and if his choice of means was not always infallible for quality, often it happened his least artful efforts had a ruder, more elemental strength.

Sliding rapidly from major to minor key and back again, his brush suggested the ripple of life along the river. Intensely varied in substance and shape, brush and canvas spoke his stubborn and highly personal idiom. The language itself was arbitrary, an imperfect accord between perception and intent, for as he pushed further toward the goal, he made simultaneous instinctive advances. For convenience he grew accustomed to dip his brush into alizarin and green or blue for accents which retained their force. Unmixed, but on the same brush, these complementary colors gave his sketches a strength for the most part exhilarating and amusing rather than disconcerting.

Neither a conventional effect nor one that wore thin with repetition, Monet's employment of complementary colors to form stunning darks was riveting in its freshness and originality. No one to whom he showed these canvases at first understood why they had such bewilderingly well-preserved effects when brought indoors, or why throw-away areas retained a dapper and glinting ferocity. Added to the strong individuality of motifs, this majestic use of color brought unexpected unity to hasty and uneven works.

The blacks so shortly before employed on the hulls of pleasure craft moored near the Argenteuil bridge no longer were seen. After weeks of squeezing black onto his palette, then finding it untouched at the end of the day, he ceased to force it from the tube. Rather than losing brilliance by a lack of opposition, his canvases rose in the strength of their effect. Soon he had eliminated burnt umber and ochers too, leaving himself with a selection of seven colors, from which the only darks could be formed by discordant use of blue or green with alizarin crimson. The result was a forceful pinky-purplish realism. By strange concordance of arbitrary and artificial means Monet had the sublime triumph of moving into a world of heightened reality.

Creator and chief exponent of a hastily formed new art, Monet had not welded together convincingly his various elements of elusive nuance, careful pattern, and spectacular coloristic *coup de théâtre*. A broad vein of eccentricity ran through the best of these works. Too obviously he deployed tricks and gimmicks when his profound discoveries might have been more effective in workmanlike usage. Bravura passages, dazzling though self-indulged, required taming. Had the erratic cadences of Monet's art had more dignity, it would have been no worse, and more acceptable to the same public he sought to astound. These sketches done by the river at Argenteuil, in fact, were not a great new art but the hasty, histrionic record of a man not in total command of his talent, who offered the world an electrifying spectacle.

His focus was narrow, his technical means bizarre to the point of folly, but what he put on canvas was devilishly real. It is the new power of transmission which makes works of the Argenteuil period memorable. Now and again they are humanly as well as mechanically exhilarating; in terms of achievement it is a tour de force, even if in terms of technique a *tour de faiblesse*. But what did it matter? France was not so well off for modern masters that she could afford to ignore work as inventive and accomplished as this. In less than a year of titanic effort Claude Monet had arrived at a new pulsing and trembling art that existed in an almost continuous suppurating flux.

17. A New Tactic

THE NEW KIND of painting Monet created at Argenteuil was responsible for a sequence of brash, outward-looking expressions of optimism. Hardly calculated to ease the tension of that difficult moment, they are instead the determined and protracted attempts of a highly sensitive, delicately balanced artist to force his way into the world around him, overcome his individual isolation, and bring himself into immediate prominence. Monet's newly discovered art in future years would demand its own formal resolution. Now it presented baffling and perverse elements, and had it seen these canvases, the public surely would have reacted with something of a shock to the apparent crudities.

Public reaction was sadly lacking, however, for after March, 1873, Durand-Ruel's purchases had ceased. No longer did that dealer's Paris showroom display the newest works of the artist who already had offended his essentially bourgeois clientele. The Salon was equally closed to Monet, and it was an article of faith to a man so proud that the jury of that institution must be allowed no further opportunity to humble him. To display his extraordinary new powers Monet required some fresh alternative, and thus, out of his obsessive loathing of the Salon, and frustration with dealers, he raised once more the scheme shared with Bazille and Courbet in 1867.

Those long-pent-up fantasies, in fact, had begun to proliferate earlier, when his exuberance still was supported by Durand-Ruel's purchases. The Salon des Refusés, that unexpected and inconclusive whim of the Emperor in 1863, had been reconstituted as an administrative compromise. Émile Zola's disciple, Paul Alexis, wrote in *L'Avenir National*, May 5, 1873, that this act had not altered the conditions under which French artists existed. In its place he suggested that the body of artists would have much to gain by "organizing immediately its own syndicate." This was precisely what Monet had attempted to do in 1867. His proddings and probings among friends again took more definite form, and two days later, May 7, 1873, he wrote to Alexis:

A group of painters assembled in my home has read with pleasure the article which you have published in L'Avenir National. We are happy to see you defend ideas which are ours too, and we hope that, as you say, L'Avenir National will kindly give us assistance when the society which we are about to form will be completely constituted.

The letter was published, and in support Alexis noted that "several artists of great merit" were concerned, listing Amand Gautier, Jongkind, Sisley, Pissarro, Béliard, and Guillaumin. Something more of Monet's ideas can be gained from Alexis' further comments: "Their association, however, will not be just a small clique. They intend to represent interests, not tendencies, and hope for the adherence of all serious artists." The schemes of 1867 were reflected in those last five words, but how much further these plans progressed can only be guessed. The artists soon dispersed for their summer's work, and the plan lay fallow until autumn, when Monet picked it up again with greater urgency.

What had been an interior world then quickly externalized itself. Monet demonstrated remarkable qualities of leadership, less perhaps like Moses in the wilderness than Saint Paul, who persuaded and cajoled adherence to a gospel. Converts were sought not only among an immediate circle of friends like Amand Gautier and Jongkind, but from all those artists newly represented and abandoned by the exigencies of Durand-Ruel's business. Strongly conceived and strongly made, Monet's arguments seemed to possess not only logical support but to provide the reliable alternative means of showing their works needed by all those he approached.

If in some respects the moment seemed ill-chosen, artists were freshly aware that the public was developing a taste for stronger sorts of painting. In that same year 1873 Édouard Manet had sent to the Salon a picture which revealed his recent visit to the Frans Hals Museum at Haarlem. To his friends it looked like a bowdlerized version of his own more powerful style. *Le Bon Bock*, an almost caricatured rendering of a hearty soul sitting smoking his pipe beside a glass of beer, had a considerable success. Durand-Ruel, himself unable to purchase this celebrated work, persuaded Jean-Baptiste

Faure, the Paris Opéra's well-known baritone, to do so at the very elevated price of 6,000 francs.

Manet's fame spread wide, and when one publication mistakenly printed that he was offered 120,000 francs for the work, he charged into its offices to demand "the name of the fool." His first popular success, Manet had unfortunately achieved it by a retrogressive step. Torn between his natural artistic taste and an equally natural ambition, he had followed the latter on an anecdotal road to popularity. But the nature and degree of the acclaim achieved by a man previously so reviled made everyone hopeful.

Adherents to Monet's scheme grew in number and began to represent less his own circle than the group gathered around Durand-Ruel. Renoir, Sisley, Pissarro, Manet's smoldering pupil Berthe Morisot, Degas, his friend the Viscount Lepic, and Pissarro's intimates Béliard and Guillaumin were adherents from the start. An immediate disappointment to all was the timidity of Édouard Manet, who, so soon after experiencing a warm welcome at the Salon, had no intention of antagonizing the jury. What Monet had in mind was no mere exhibition, but a highly organized and self-endowing society much like the hated Salon itself. Yearly it would hold exhibitions and, as its profits grew, would use this war chest to compete with the Salon on an even footing.

To charter such a group Monet of necessity listened to the schemes of others. Strongest among them was Pissarro's radically oriented view that the charter of the Professional Baker's Union should be taken as model. Renoir fortunately succeeded in defeating this suggestion, much to the general relief. Still, it was widely agreed that an admission fee and commissions on sales might be charged, as was the habit at the Salon, and that these would finance the new organization. Pissarro now proposed a joint stock company, and when this was accepted the newborn organization became top-heavy with regulations concerning annual subscriptions, articles of partnership, shares, and monthly installments.

Exactly at the period of Monet's greatest discouragement over Camille's dowry and Durand-Ruel, in October and November, 1873, the organization received its final impetus. The charter was drafted, signed, and dated December 27, 1873. Announcements were sent to the press, and a search began for proper rooms in which to hold its first exhibition. Fortune again smiled on Monet's plan when he learned that Nadar, the photographer, would lend his premises on the Boulevard des Capucines, which at the expiration of the March quarter he expected to vacate.

Founded by Monet, the new society soon fell into the hands of Pissarro, who placated a dissident Renoir by appointing him to the committee of management. At Monet's invitation Boudin agreed to take part, and Jongkind appears to have refused, but so long as friendship balanced what was politic, the motives of the two were interchangeable. Otherwise, deeply absorbed at Argenteuil by the most significant phase of his artistic researches, Monet took little part in the rabid search for membership conducted at Paris.

Because each artist was required to pay a participating subscription applicable toward costs, all logic supported obtaining a large membership. To do so it was necessary to go outside the little group gathered around Édouard Manet at the Café Guerbois, most of whom more recently had been in contact with Durand-Ruel. This in no way jarred with Monet's intention, which had been to found an annual exhibition roughly equivalent to the Salon, where the old establishment which had handled him so roughly would not be present. Whether the new exhibition had any special character of its own was no more important than whether the Salon did, so long as it provided a means of being seen by the Parisian public.

Degas surpassed all in his proselyting zeal, and he understood that for the fulfillment of Monet's ambitious scheme it was necessary to have every variety of painting represented. Anxious to give a "neutral" character to the project, so that it would not appear to be an exhibition of men rejected by the Salon, he suggested that the group call itself La Capucine, after the boulevard on which it would make its bow. Inappropriate to a society that hoped to hold annual exhibitions in different locations, this suggestion roused the ire of Renoir, who feared critics would fasten upon any name to denote a new school. The even more "neutral" designation of the Incorporated Society of Artists, Sculptors, and Engravers was chosen, reflecting, perhaps unaware, a similar organization which in England preceded foundation of the Royal Academy.

Degas everywhere emitted a gentle, unraucous domination, slightly lyrical in tone and self-deprecating perhaps, but no less urgent for that. His recruits included Lepic, Levert, and Rouart, as well as the Italian, de Nittis, who he insisted send an important work of the same nature he showed at the Salon. "Since you are exhibiting at the Salon," wrote Degas, "people who are not conversant with things will not be able to say that we are an exhibition of rejected artists."

Degas's tactics were equally clear in a letter to James Tissot. "Look here, my dear Tissot, no hesitations, no escapes. You positively must exhibit on the Boulevard. It will do you good . . . and us too. Manet seems determined to keep aloof. He may well regret it. Yesterday I saw the arrangement of the premises, the hangings and the effect of daylight. It is as good as anywhere. And now Henner (elected to the second rank of the jury) wants to exhibit with us. I am getting really worked up and am running the thing with energy, and, I think, a certain success. . . . The realist movement no longer needs to fight with the others. It already *is*, it *exists*, it must show itself as *something distinct*, there must be a *Salon of realists*. Manet does not understand that. I definitely think he is more vain than intelligent. . . ." Despite these elaborate efforts, neither Tissot nor Henner joined the society.

Had the validity of Monet's plan needed further support, this too was forthcoming in January, 1874, when seven pictures by Pissarro, known to be from the collection of Ernest Hoschedé, department store proprietor, patron of Manet, and client of Durand-Ruel, appeared in an anonymous sale at the Hôtel Drouot. Two among them realized prices of 700 and 950 francs. The last was considered amazing. Every evidence therefore indicated that as prices rose a favorable moment was approaching. Contrary advice fed to participating artists bore less mark of enthusiasm, though its greater wisdom could not be faulted. Théodore Duret, friend of Manet and Pissarro, wrote to the latter imploring him to abandon the plan and submit his works instead to the Salon:

February 15, 1874

You have still one step to take; to succeed in becoming known to the public and accepted by all the dealers and art lovers. For this purpose there are only the auctions at the Hôtel Drouot and the large exhibitions in the Palais de l'Industrie. You possess now a group of art lovers and collectors, who are devoted to you and support you. Your name is familiar to artists, critics, a special public. But you must make one more stride and become widely known. You will not get there by exhibitions put on by special groups. The public does not go to such exhibitions, only the same nucleus of artists and patrons who already know you.

The Hoschedé sale did you more good and advanced you further than all the special exhibitions imaginable. It brought you before a mixed and numerous public. I urge you strongly to round that out by exhibiting this year at the Salon. Considering what the frame of mind seems to be this year, your name now being known, they will not refuse you. Besides, you can send three pictures. Of the three, one or two will certainly be accepted. Among the 40,000 people who, I suppose, visit the Salon, you will be seen by fifty dealers, patrons, critics, who would never otherwise look you up and discover you. Even if you only achieve that, it would be enough. But you will gain more, because you are now in a special position in a group that is being discussed and that is beginning to be accepted, although with reservations.

I urge you to select pictures that have a subject, something resembling a composition, pictures that are not too freshly painted, that are already a bit staid. . . .

I urge you to exhibit; you must succeed in making a noise, in defying and attracting criticism, coming face to face with the big public. You will not achieve all that except at the Salon.

Édouard Manet saw the reasonableness of Duret's words, and, fresh from the success of his *Le Bon Bock,* he was content to repel every plea that he join the new venture. Among newer recruits, those proposed by Pissarro were not always acceptable to the others. He experienced difficulties in gaining admission for Guillaumin, and especially Cézanne, whose crudely painted canvases it was widely feared would outrage the public. Only because Pissarro pleaded the cause of his friends with fervor, overwhelming all obstacles, were they admitted despite the little enthusiasm shown by Degas and Monet.

Twenty-nine participants had been gathered by March, when a thirtieth appeared in the form of Bracquemond, to whom immediately Degas wrote, "We are gaining a famous recruit in you. Be assured of the pleasure and good you are doing us." Pictures began to arrive at the Boulevard des Capucines, and when Monet came from Argenteuil with his own carefully selected group, he found that Renoir, as a member of the management committee, had entrusted his brother Edmond with the task of listing them for a catalogue. Degas, who had promised many works, had sent none, and Edmond Renoir was no less troubled to find that Monet brought too many.

The similarity of all Monet's titles was another problem of which young Renoir despaired, and which appears to have left Monet unimpressed. "Why not just put down *Impression?*" he inquired, and since both rapid views of Le Havre painted on Monet's 1872 visit were present, Edmond Renoir dutifully labeled one *Le Havre: Fishing Boats Leaving Port,* and the second *Impression: Rising Sun,* though Monet might have told him that the sun, hovering over the west end of the harbor, surely was setting.

Monet's principal work was the large *Luncheon,* painted in 1868 at Étretat. So different from his more recent efforts, this probably had been selected in accordance with Degas's urging that artists send works similar to those normally contributed to the Salon. The sketch of Camille and Jean in a field of poppies had also been chosen, together with one view of that same Boulevard des Capucines on which the exhibition would take place. Representing Monet's penultimate manner, this latter had the added interest of presenting a scene visible through the gallery's windows. That no examples of his works painted on the river at Argenteuil were selected demonstrates that even Monet realized their revolutionary character. In their place he presented a group of four pastels, doubtless hoping this more attractive medium would appeal to buyers.

As Édouard Manet's closest friend in this group, to the last Degas nurtured a hope he would participate. But Manet saw too clearly the venture's futility and held back. Over and over he repeated to Berthe Morisot, Renoir, and Monet, "Why do you not stay with me? You can see very well I am on the right track." Like his friend Duret, Manet had seen the handwriting on the wall. The others blindly plunged ahead with preparations, until, as a final reservation, Manet fervently announced, "I will never commit myself with Monsieur Cézanne!" Two weeks before the Salon, on April 15, 1874, this fateful exhibition opened its doors.

And it was greeted by catastrophe. Even before the opening a bizarre interest was evidenced. Degas noted it particularly: "The newspapers are beginning to allow more than just bare announcements and, though not yet daring to devote a whole column to it, seem anxious to be a little more expansive." A large public averaging two hundred persons a day was attracted, but they came with no intention to view seriously. Critics unfortunately followed the same pattern. The outpourings of the press belonged neither to art nor literature, but that curious territory where platitude and the establishment meet.

Though Monet's works were tame and surely unrepresentative of more conventional artists who contributed the bulk of the exhibition, Edmond Renoir's frank and ill-fitting title, *Impression: Rising Sun,* was picked out by Louis Leroy, writing for the humorous journal *Charivari,* who deliberately headed his column "Exhibition of the Impressionists." He made the most of succulent opportunities in a delicious parody that introduced a character christened M. Joseph Vincent, an artist "recipient of medals and decorations under several governments," who bristled with predictable attitudes:

> The poor man rambled on his way quite peacefully, and nothing led me to anticipate the unfortunate accident which was to be the result of his visit to this hair-raising exhibition. He even sustained, without major injury, viewing the *Fishing Boats Leaving the Harbor* by M. Claude Monet, perhaps because I tore him away from dangerous contemplation of this work before the small noxious figures in the foreground could produce their effect. Unfortunately I was imprudent enough to leave him too long in front of the *Boulevard des Capucines,* by the same painter.
>
> "Ah-ha!" he sneered in Mephistophelian manner. "Is that brilliant enough, now! There's impression, or I do not know what it means. Only, be so good as to tell me what do those innumerable black tongue-lickings in the lower part of the picture represent?"
>
> "Why, those are people walking along," I replied.
>
> "Then do I look like that when I am walking along the Boulevard des Capucines? Blood and thunder! So you are making fun of me at last?"
>
> "I assure you, M. Vincent . . ."
>
> "But those spots were obtained by the same method as that used to imitate marble: a bit here, a bit there, slapdash, any old way. It's unheard of, appalling! I will get a stroke from it, for sure!"

Monet's lovely miracle of ingenuity, abounding in strange new sonorities, bore its burden of contempt as though the fundamentals of art were in some irreducible combat with experiment. A certain lazy pleasure was taken in presenting Monet himself as a corroded degenerate, and pious scavengers of the press contrived to make him the exhibition's great issue. Thus, while it overlooked that Monet had formulated the plan and persuaded the others to join him, by tarring all participants with Monet's strong brush the press with curious justice brought Monet to the front as leader. And because a term was needed by which this group could be designated, the offending word "impression," attached to one of Monet's canvases, became the too facile label.

Other newspapers and critics, *Le Gaulois* among them, took a more favorable view. A few informed critics even understood the purposes of these artists, and they gave a measured praise carefully balanced against recitals of qualities sacrificed. By contemporary standards they were correct, and even liberal, in their willingness to express balanced views. As the days passed, however, and an unfavorable tenor of response became too clear, anxiety among the painters grew. His eye fixed on the gate, Degas was pleased to find so many admissions paid. The greater damage this throng was doing their collective artistic reputations was forgotten as he wrote to Bracquemond on exhibition stationery: "Calm yourself completely. It is going very well in spite of so many abstentions. We are making 200 francs a day and the advertising was badly done. On the 1st May we shall be square."

Such pleasant words were a deception, as Degas well knew. At the very moment their fortunes were at nadir because of Durand-Ruel's crisis, by their own ill-judged efforts the painters had exposed themselves to ridicule. Critics had preferred polemic to analysis; the public came to the exhibition drawn at first by curiosity, then by an attraction enhanced by elements of comedy. Dreary and predictable conventional formulas were constantly reiterated against artists and pictures, both of which were condemned roundly for showing many signs of decadence.

The intrinsic merits of the works were not ignored by all, and a spirit of cool, skeptical inquiry was preserved by some. Castagnary, Courbet's great friend, had the paradoxical pleasure of penning angry and argumentative denunciations of those who denounced, and Alfred Sisley was able to gain 1,000 francs from sales of his pictures. A strong lead, it was poorly followed. Degas sold nothing; Pissarro's sales were only 130 francs; Renoir's 180; Monet's 200, presumably from his pastels.

Who now could doubt that in desisting from this courageous enterprise Édouard Manet had been right? Nor was any comfort found in the sad fact that Manet too had suffered rejections at the Salon, where only a watercolor and one of his three paintings had been hung. Monet's superbly grandiose scheme of rivaling the Salon stood revealed as well-intentioned, ambitious, but hopelessly half-baked. In an atmosphere alive with recrimination and sleazy economic reprisal, he returned to Argenteuil.

Benign dignity and a willingness to extend the hospitality of his river were Monet's only reactions to any assertion that he was leader of a group. Yet, unquestionably, by failing to take his knocks in the Boulevard des Capucines debacle, Édouard Manet had abdicated a position which by public consensus now belonged to the painter of the *Impression*. And the most significant fact following that fiasco was the extraordinary inclination of all the painters to gather around Monet during the summer of 1874. Like the exhibition, it was a phenomenon which imposed on them some superficial and short-lived unity that left all the roots of diversity undisturbed beneath.

Most frequent were the visits of Renoir, whose easy familiarity permitted him to join Monet wherever he worked. On each visit his friend's stronger personality affected Renoir, who, passing from Paris to Argenteuil, vacillated between a personal vision that inclined more consciously to sweetness and Monet's world of circumspect painterly illusion. The plump dark-haired girl who so long had been Renoir's mistress and model had departed his life. Earlier that same year Camille had posed for a splendid, showy composition of two figures in an opera box, which Renoir dubbed *La Loge* and exhibited on the Boulevard des Capucines. The picture's principal charm was derived from Camille's new high coiffure of center part and bangs, though for compositional reasons Renoir had softened to brown the black magic of her hair.

At Argenteuil too Camille's sensitive face, framed by a loose fringe and crowned by a high black bun, continued to intrigue the susceptible Renoir. When her household tasks were put aside, he continued to paint her. Portraits multiplied, including an almost formal treatment in which she laughed and leered gaily. Another showed Camille stretched on a divan dressed in a gorgeous Oriental kimono. Renoir painted her again sewing, her head turned down, raven lashes against her cameo cheeks suggesting still the look of "exquisite tenderness" Zola noted so long before. As others joined this band of resident Bohemians, to romp and sing and talk earnestly, Renoir multiplied his portraits further, adding Monet to his gallery, and Alfred Sisley too, when he joined them to work on the water.

A New Tactic

Soon Camille Pissarro was at Argenteuil, strewing advanced social ideas well mixed with his own common sense, tact and kindness. Like Renoir he quickly adopted Monet's new palette and dissonant accents. An elevation of key in his work was immediate, the abrupt transition lending new energy to his canvases. One misses perhaps the twin polarities of inward-turning lyricism and mordant biting harshness that were Monet's own strength. Yet Pissarro's grasp of Monet's color innovations was complete and immediately employed for a sketch of his host's son Jean riding his tricycle-mounted horse. Amid fresh and sparkling tonalities Jean's kimono-clad mother stands fixed in the distance, and the horse, once so impossibly large, now crowds Jean's knees as he furiously pedals past his father's flower beds.

What added to the sustained and coherent dramatic force of these summer months was that for the first time even Édouard Manet made the short journey from Paris. For several generations Manet's family had been proprietors of land across the river from Argenteuil at Gennevilliers, where his grandfather, Clément Manet, had been mayor during the revolution. Manet therefore had tactful excuses for his presence, and, appearing with his wife, or brother-in-law Rudolph Leenhoff, he stayed on the opposite bank at a house of his own. The reason for his visits was no less clear, especially when, his easel set beside Monet's own overlooking the river, he made depressingly unprofessional efforts to master the new manner of painting Monet had created.

Both men concentrated their efforts on depicting three sailboats moored just beyond the main Argenteuil bridge. But while Manet saw the finely modulated painting of Monet, his own broad thin color washes and occasional rough scumbles never achieved the high key his friend obtained by synthetic use of color and accent. Monet's own efforts became uneven and his all-out effects rather crude when he sought to evade black on two hulls. Manet painted them with his own quicksilver use of a black pigment; for Monet this was impossible, and, possessed of a highly precocious mind, trying out every possibility that presented itself, he daubed crusted white over both. A corollary of Monet's arbitrary approach was that he found himself under compulsion to make reflections white also, and the appropriate strength of this he was less well able to judge. Yet to Édouard Manet, Monet's flexible method of orchestrating motifs and effects seemed both assured and resourceful. Both men began anew.

Édouard Manet produced a larger oblong canvas on which for a second time he sketched the three moored sailboats. To surround the black hulls of those two foremost boats, he arranged ripples and wavelets in a mass of intricate rhythms. Determined to grasp the elusive brilliance of his friend, Manet perhaps banged the gong too hard, for the black of his hulls and the whites of his wavelets were placed side by side with little or no attempt to arrange them in an effective symphonic manner. They remain separate elements, adding up without fusing into a unit nor approaching the heightened reality of Monet.

To rescue an operation grown decidedly off-balance, Camille and little Jean were sent to stand where tall grasses grew by the water's edge. Staring idly at river and boats, by their presence they contributed necessary perpendicular forms and a touch of humanity. For the first time Camille's new blue-striped dress, surmounted by high white summer hat and black ribbons, made its way onto canvas. Yet without the synthetic strength of color Monet employed on this same riverbank, Manet's tone remained disappointingly low, his vigorous brushing far less scintillating than the crackling touch of Monet.

A special care was exerted to cultivate Manet, and bring him closer to that little group of artists which so earnestly desired his adherence. In retrospect, the exhibition on the Boulevard des Capucines had succeeded in bringing to them all a new attention. If they were infamous, at least they were known. New exhibitions were planned, for in the purely financial sense from gate fees and commissions on sales the society had earned its expenses. Another year, with higher attendance and more sales, they could do even better. And perhaps Manet, who had been roughly handled by the Salon jury, now would consent to join them.

His proud, rather irritable nature gave something of a peacock's air to Manet. Short rather than tall, dressed with the fastidiousness of his class, in his dashing air and erect stiff-necked posture he reflected perfectly the dandyish atmosphere from which he was drawn. Hovering over him always was a suggestion that a man with diversions and companions straight out of fashionable gossip columns rarely digs below the surface of either life or art. The curious manner in which he had elected to battle for a higher tone without accepting, or understanding, the deeper significance of Monet's new discoveries supported this suspicion. For though Manet was fully charged with the extraordinary energy of that age, he was a figure curiously lightweight, and not free from inclinations to conventional respectability and hypocrisy.

The synthesis of pigments Monet had discovered, and Renoir, Pissarro, and Sisley had adopted immediately, Édouard Manet either rejected or failed to grasp. Yet Manet in years past had astonished the world, and, like Bazille, he exerted on Claude Monet the fascination of belonging to a world of fashion. The easier mode of life Monet had experienced since his marriage, even the finery in which Camille garbed herself, surely reflected Monet's pretensions to respectability, which never had left him even in deepest poverty. Bazille, and now Manet, were the sort of people with whom Claude Monet felt he belonged. Concentrated efforts were made to bring Manet closer, artistically and personally, and to ensnare him in the web of Argenteuil.

For painting on the river that summer of 1874 two boats were in use. While Monet and Camille nestled with easel and canvas on the afterdeck of their own specially fitted craft, Édouard Manet drifted nearby, working from another. He rendered Monet the homage of a sketch showing him seated at his work. The classic purity of Monet's profile was well suggested, but Manet's use of color demonstrated still his conspicuous refusal to integrate or venerate the lessons abounding at Argenteuil. The hard shell of Manet's ideas was not wholly pierced, though what he observed ferociously dented it. While Monet and Renoir trudged off to paint matching canvases of a little pier to which they had tethered a boat with spread sails, Édouard Manet began work on two larger compositions intended for the Salon.

Before the vast panorama of riverbanks and moored pleasure craft, Manet posed his wife and her brother, Rudolph Leenhoff. Plump and bizarrely dressed, before a background with which they little sympathized, Manet seated them on a bench cutting across the first plane of his picture. Everywhere in this canvas he sought lightness and brightness. All was glare and contrast, and unconvincing, for rapidly Manet slid into hollowness. His overcrowded canvas showed objects whose spatial collisions jarred, and a river pasted to the backs of his figures. Manet suffered further from the insurmountable disadvantage that the simple thinly applied blacks and browns he employed for darks had not the strength to throw forceful light tones into relief.

If Manet continued expending his labor and skill for a meager result, he remained undaunted, and in a second effort posed Rudolph Leenhoff by the tiller of a small boat. Here the background was no more than water, reflecting the sky's clear blue. For even greater brilliance Leenhoff posed in white undershirt, wearing still his fashionable straw hat. This performance was in disputable taste, and surely as an afterthought Camille again was borrowed to drape herself across the foreground, supported on her elbows. Her blue-striped dress, worn in Manet's earlier study by the riverbank, now was seen cutting off the foreground, and the same high white summer hat, marked by trailing black ribbons, brought dash to a composition whose brushing lacked interest.

Curiously Japanese in flatness of color and form, this second large effort by Manet shared the curious anomaly of the first. Although it was cunningly devised to provide a maximum of effect, its level of invention high, conventional darks of burnt umber again failed to hold their place or create modeling. Mistakenly Manet had dismissed as intrusive the imaginative vision of Claude Monet. By a strange reversal his own pictures thereafter lacked the persuasive truth of Monet's, for at Argenteuil Manet was unable to create the probity, and plain emptiness, Monet wove into profusions of canvases. Indeed, in retrospect Manet's whole endeavor seems absurd and agonizing, like playing the harpsichord in boxing gloves.

His workmanship proved more sound in the garden of Monet's house, and there, expending his efforts on small figures in landscape, Édouard Manet demonstrated clear mastery that came as a vindication. Camille had donned a white suit and sat under a tree wearing her matching white bonnet. In her hand she held a fan, and to complete the composition, little Jean, grown plump and healthy at Argenteuil, sprawled beside his mother's outstretched skirts. Quietly watering his plants, Monet himself looked on, occasionally forced to chase hens that wandered into the carefully devised scene.

Soon Monet grew restless in his passive role. With easel and canvas he deployed himself on Manet's right, concentrating his fire against the profiled figure of Manet himself in long coat and broad-brimmed hat, at work in the shade of a flowering tree. Renoir arrived, his presence constituting a new tactical diversion as he too took a small canvas and, unable to resist the scene, found another position on Manet's right.

The artist for whom Camille originally had taken this pose, Édouard Manet, was obliged to continue his operations despite unexpectedly heavy fire from his colleagues. Though Camille's face showed no definite character in sketches he previously had made of her, now it assumed a sharp likeness to his former pupil, Berthe Morisot. Around it Manet arranged a sequence of refined textures, highly colored yet sparse, so that perspective was properly created and everything was clearly visible in its own plane. In secondary portions of the sketch, such as the delineation of hens and Monet's bent figure, he showed stunning technical virtuosity.

From the corner of his eye Manet continued to watch Renoir, who, motivated by pure enthusiasm, had given no attention to the grouping of figures. On his canvas Camille's skirt flowed awkwardly, while the feet of little Jean struck the edge as though specially truncated to do so. When nearly finished, Renoir retrieved the unbalance by happily dabbing a rooster into the vacant right side, accomplishing his object with irresistible charm and dexterity. A mysteriously grotesque travesty of proper and orderly working methods, Renoir's little coup clearly displeased Manet. When he took aside Monet, he allowed his annoyance to be seen. "You, who are close with Renoir," Manet said, "you ought to advise him to turn to something else. You can see that painting is not for him!"

18. A Peddler and His Wife

"IMPRESSIONISM" had been born, cynically baptized, and by the river at Argenteuil Monet had instructed his three principal disciples. As they went forth to become fishers of men, immaturity and inconsistency still marked the new art. Yet already the brushes of Monet, Renoir, Sisley, and Pissarro were producing original beautifully conceived pictures with an audacious purity of color and style. What in the dim past had begun as Monet's own childish, self-indulgent and self-defeating rejection of disciplines had developed not only into unchallenged ascendancy over his friends but a wholly fresh art whose unexpected shifts of harmonic support created majestic new conciliations between the traditional elements of painting.

A new epoch had dawned. But secure within its palace on the Champs-Élysées, the artistic establishment was able to commit the atrocious *faux pas* of ignoring the four-headed meteor about to burst over its skyline. At Argenteuil that enormously significant summer of 1874 passed, and a man who, working alone, had accomplished the impossible saw his fortunes dwindle still further. Durand-Ruel's purchases were reduced to 1,300 francs during the whole of that momentous year 1874. Camille's mother showed no inclination to part with the 2,000 francs remaining of her dowry; no legal means existed to extract the money. Autumn arrived, then winter, and after the new year the Monet family faced anxious prospects.

Gripped in an overall mood of despair, Monet did as he had done at the St.-Siméon farm before Jean's birth, moving out to work in fresh snow. Pigments at first were heavily applied, a dense layer of paint simulating the blanket of snow. His new synthetic color then asserted itself, emitting lovely nocturnal music and producing delicately toned, pale scenes of snow filled with stylized shadows of human emotion. Moral courage and physical effort were required to perform this exhausting and frigid task. But throughout life he had followed the same pattern, assuaging anxieties in the absorption of his chosen labor.

Renoir, who paid a frigid winter visit to Argenteuil, found Monet immersed in an atmosphere of guttering candles and snuffed oil lamps. The high Delft pots containing overgrown garden plants had been moved indoors against the cold, and from behind a screen of these Monet, an illusionist collaborating with an enchantress, attacked a scene of the dimly lit Camille seated at her dining room table. Dressed in an Eton collar, navy jacket and knickers, Jean was stationed in the foyer to provide a focal point in the middle distance of his father's canvas. Renoir joined the work with a new portrait of Monet that no longer was the patient pipe-smoking figure that previously had twinkled with a look of stolid and menacing benignity.

Warmly dressed, a hat on his untidy head, his coat pulled tight against winged collar, Monet was a man obviously oppressed who proposed to Renoir that they organize a sale of their works by auction. A method of selling pictures adopted by Boudin since 1868, sale by auction earlier had been mentioned by Théodore Duret as an alternative to the Salon. Quickly the plan was joined by Sisley and Berthe Morisot, who, though not in need herself, anxiously supported her friends in every extremity. Her substitute marriage to Manet's brother Eugène, in December, 1874, was perhaps not a source of great happiness. Increasingly she allowed her friends' struggles to absorb her sympathies.

These four once more girded their loins, to prepare pictures for the dreadful fall of the auctioneer's hammer. Advance notice in the newspapers was essential, and because Édouard Manet had brief acquaintance with Albert Wolff, the eupeptic, beardless critic who held forth in oracular, witty, and disquieting style for *Le Figaro*, Monet, seconded by Berthe Morisot, pressed him for an introduction. Manet obliged, perhaps awkwardly:

> March 19 [1875]
> My friends MM. Monet, Sisley, Renoir, and Mme. Berthe Morisot are going to have an exhibition and sale at the Hôtel Drouot. One of these gentlemen is to bring you the catalogue and an invitation. He has asked me for this letter of introduction. You do not as yet, perhaps, appreciate this kind of painting; but you will like it some day. And it would be very kind of you to mention it a little in the *Figaro*.

Wolff granted Manet his wish, but in a derisory fashion: "The impression which the impressionists achieve is that of a cat walking on the keyboard of a piano, or of a monkey who might have got hold of a box of paints. Perhaps there is some good business here for those who are speculating on art in the future." Against this cacophony the friends brought to the Hôtel Drouot seventy-three paintings, of which Monet contributed twenty.

To the public assembled on March 24, 1875, it was unavoidable that so many brilliantly colored canvases should have been indistinguishable from each other. A cycle of changing seasons, ranging through an astonishing variety of emotions, they were considered jokes. Shrewdly or otherwise, the sale catalogue drew attention to the fact that these paintings were among those that had appeared at Nadar's studio the previous year. Durand-Ruel was present, to render the only service he could as an expert. A few friends, including Théodore Duret and Gustave Caillebotte, a neighbor of Monet's at

Argenteuil, came in hope of bidding up the prices. Quickly the futility of this was established. Gripped in a mood of hilarious obstructionism and exasperated by passionate pleas from the artists' few friends, the crowd hooted at bids, eventually forcing the auctioneer to summon police, who prevented scuffles from becoming open violence.

Unable to make purchases himself, Durand-Ruel was a sad witness to this new catastrophe which befell artists with whom his fortunes so intimately were linked. He assisted them to buy back a few canvases that threatened to be lost for less than the cost of their frames, but the total effect was a new and more odious fiasco. The best prices were received by Berthe Morisot, whose works adhered less rigidly to the gospel of Monet. For all four artists the total amassed was only 11,496 francs, including canvases bought back, from which Monet's share was 4,665 francs, or an average of 233 francs each. When costs incurred for shipping were deducted, in addition to sales commissions, it became a mystery how he would pay for the frames.

Springtime arrived again at Argenteuil and found Monet bitter and betrayed, yet imposing even in an hour of decline. On the river he was summing up two years of the most intense experimental activity, producing works that combined a bold and successful originality of design with the new triumph of his synthetic colorism. That he should have done so while slipping further into need exposed a monstrous anomaly of that affluent century. Always resourceful, he continued to turn over plans in his mind, though now their scope was smaller, dedicated less to the advancement of his career than to his survival as a person.

As once he had turned to Frédéric Bazille, so now, in circumstances sadly similar, Monet labored systematically to make a confidant and help of Édouard Manet. That haughty Parisian was aware of his renewed plight, but even more than with Bazille, Monet found it an exhausting exercise in tact to remain on good terms with Manet, who displayed with equal abandon both an inveterate waspishness and a quick eager affection.

Fortunately, too, Monet was blessed with a lavish imagination, and as at Le Havre he once had turned his debtors to disadvantage, now he addressed himself to obtaining from Mme. Doncieux the final 2,000 francs of Camille's dowry. His efforts became a saga of audacity, and his instrument, when all others failed, was Marie Charles Édouard Carpentier, the esteemed color merchant from whose shop in the Rue Halévy, beside the new opera house, for years Monet had obtained the paints and finely woven buff-toned canvases that were the essentials of his trade.

A plan offered Carpentier was the purchase of Camille's dowry, a handsome investment guaranteed to pay 5 per cent. Carpentier showed definite interest. Monet wrote immediately to Maître Aumont-Thieville, demanding a copy of the document Camille signed in November, 1873, setting forth the sums due to her and the interest they would bear. Despite brevity his letter had a tone of urgency, and the reasons are all too clear, for that same day he was obliged to write as well to Manet:

Monday morning, 28 June [1875]

MY DEAR MANET,

It is becoming more and more difficult. Since the day before yesterday, not a penny left and no more credit, neither at the butcher nor the baker. Though I have faith in the future, you see the present is very painful. . . .

Could you not send me by return of post a 20-franc note? That would help me for a quarter of an hour.

With regards,

CLAUDE MONET

Vague and inconclusive discussions concerning the dowry continued into summer. Meanwhile happiness at Argenteuil, which had started so grandly for all, petered out too soon. Lacking funds for any purpose, they remained under constant surveillance and knew pressures from all those who had extended them credit. Especially this was true of merchants in the village, to whom daily Camille went for the food they ate. Courage was required now to face this indignity; and country justice, where all one's neighbors sit in judgment, could be fast and merciless. A week later the blow fell:

Argenteuil, 8 July 1875

MY DEAR MANET,

If it does not inconvenience you too much, would you again advance me the feeble sum of 60 francs. I am between the paws of a country bailiff who can do me much harm. With this sum I can make a part payment with him. He has given me until tomorrow at noon. Try to help me out of this.

I will pass your house tomorrow morning or I will send someone between 10 o'clock and noon. If the thing is not possible for you, send me immediately a word so that I can search elsewhere.

With regards,

CLAUDE MONET

The only discernible salvation during the crises of that summer, Édouard Manet accepted an unsought burden with remarkable aplomb. In addition to the small sums of money he loaned Monet, Édouard Manet sought patrons for his friend, and when possible he made personal introductions. The first, and forever the most reverberative of these, was to Ernest Hoschedé, director of Au Gagne-Petit, a department store on the Avenue de l'Opéra. Enormously heavy, with straggling beard, squinting eyes, and bulging lower lip, the ugly and exuberant Hoschedé had thrust a taste for contemporary paintings deep into his bustling executive's existence.

Like Durand-Ruel, from whom his pictures were bought, Hoschedé had felt the depression of 1873 keenly. Speculations had become a part of his existence, and perhaps to camouflage losses which never were regained, in January, 1874, and again April 20, 1875, he sold at auction his large holdings of Barbizon works. Since he had acquired them the value of these pictures had appreciated enormously. In 1875 his collection of sixty-six paintings, including fifteen by Corot, ten by Courbet, and two by Daubigny, brought the very large sum of 227,215 francs, with which he plunged into purchases of impressionist pictures.

Whether it was true love that motivated Hoschedé, or a desire once more to profit from augmenting values, his initial choice fell upon Édouard Manet. From Durand-Ruel he purchased the largest among appealing Spanish-period canvases, including *The Street Singer, The Woman with Parakeet,* and *The Spanish Majo.* Hoschedé then cultivated the artist himself, who that summer was invited to his estate at Montgeron to paint a portrait. Hoschedé still possessed too great an abundance of those extrovert qualities associated with tycoons, and due to his constant absences at Paris the portrait did not progress. The conditions of that visit are reflected by the tantalizingly brief and scrappy works Manet produced.

Already Hoschedé had bought from Durand-Ruel's stock one of Monet's London scenes, *The Houses of Parliament in Fog,* whose flat tones and coloristic reserve made it not unrelated to Manet. The earlier view of *Saint-Germain L'Auxerrois,* painted from the Louvre balcony, also had joined Hoschedé's collection, and he added to it a Rouen scene of *Ships at a Quay.* None of these demonstrated a taste of great adventurousness, and perhaps the only work he purchased that showed Monet as a colorist was a study of the *Beach at Trouville.*

Monet himself then was asked to Montgeron. Honored frequently by painters of fashion, such an invitation was new to his quiet life, and doubtless he was attracted by the elegance of surroundings. The Hoschedé children had been forewarned that a great artist with long hair was expected. Though on his arrival they surely noted the only long hair decorated his chin, the younger girls especially found that he was inclined to display much interest in children and tease them jovially.

Though a plain woman, Mme. Hoschedé proved an agreeable hostess. Matronly of proportion, the same age as Monet, Alice Hoschedé's presence was much blemished by a mouth that too noticeably deviated from the horizontal. Apprehensions always were caused by an appearance that at first seemed sneering. But these were discarded on realizing that she was instead a person of gracious charm, well endowed with the indispensable skills to keep guests comfortable and in good humor. And like any personal disfigurement, once overcome, the impression caused by her expression created a bond of sympathy and a sense of intimacy. Fortunately she also possessed a warm uncoquettish smile and an almost therapeutic maternal quality, which, radiating over her abundant progeny, appeared to light on every living thing it encountered.

At Montgeron Monet experienced a world almost of fantasy, in which inanimate objects and persons were equally tinged by the pervasive air of unreality. And though during a visit that grew to extended length he did much small-scale sketching of autumn landscapes, his principal purpose was to produce a large decoration of novel character. Never before having turned his hand to such problems, he produced a work of unexpected beauty. Embodied in a thicker impasto that drew from a single tonal radiance an extraordinary variety of color, atmosphere, and emotion, his huge evocation of a forest interior with hunters accommodated newly extended technical resources to an elusive enchantment. Textures were heavily daubed, yet interspersed with the glow of multitudes of quarter shades and half tones through which tingled an autumn woodland.

Capable of much perceptive sensibility, Madame Hoschedé was aware of Monet's strained and collapsing circumstances, making herself miraculously gentle and sympathetic. Possibly at her urging, as well as that of Manet, Ernest Hoschedé made further purchases, now direct from the artist. As an obvious speculative venture he acquired the already legendary *Impression*. Quieter, more elegiac moods were what attracted Hoschedé, and he purchased as well an Argenteuil snow scene and a study of the railway embankment in sunlight. As a souvenir of the visit he added to these a curious garden scene in which a group of his elegantly clothed children disport themselves on the lawn.

Introspection that marked so many earlier works had been banished at Argenteuil, until now at last it reappeared. Not that Monet failed to muster the fullness and ripeness of tone required for these works he was creating. The climactic canvases of his Argenteuil period were indicative of individual progress toward self-fulfillment and self-expression, in terms that were increasingly original, economical, and uncompromising. But now the massed blooms by the riverbank were seen in brooding melancholy, expressive of a more tender and sensitive poetry. Particularly revealing was that his internal struggle against pessimism was abandoned, and his work took refuge in it. His art became the vehicle for thwarted human feelings as visions of the river were bombarded with moods drawn from his loneliness and sensitivity.

Of special significance is that when in the company of Camille he remained emotionally more firm. For it is no accident that the parallel series of gardens in which Camille appeared with her parasol are a joyous outpouring of light and color. An absolute technical control of his newly devised medium, and the final victories of his synthetic colorism, are celebrated in these dazzling canvases lit by the brutal harshness of pure sunlight. His stubbornly optimistic gaze lit on clumps of gladiolas, chrysanthemums, and massed dahlias, all of which the new technique permitted to shine forth undiminished. Doubtless he was himself caught up in the gaiety of his vision and achievement, enjoying the sinuous convolutions of pigment commas proliferating before him. Blistering in their intensity, one cannot escape a suspicion these brutal heroics are the works of a man nearly blind with panic and proving his courage by self-dramatization.

Two of these most recent works, *Dahlias Beside Water,* and the stupendous *Young Woman in a Massif of Dahlias,* were directly purchased by Ernest Hoschedé. By now Durand-Ruel also had sold a score of Monet's works from his stock. Decidedly a small group of hesitant *amateurs* was forming, and each time he completed new canvases Monet made an effort to have them seen by these individuals. Among them was Faure, the baritone, another of Durand-Ruel's clients and already a notable collector of Édouard Manet's works. Like Hoschedé's, Faure's taste and his connoisseurship were open to dispute. Too obviously he liked having things both ways, finding pleasure in a saucy dash of charlatanry against a moderately reassuring background. But Faure had made the interesting discovery that if skepticism were suspended much enjoyment could result from Monet's canvases, and at Durand-Ruel's urging he began purchases with an early Courbet-inspired Ste.-Adresse beach scene. To this he added a choice group of six dizzying Argenteuil river and bridge scenes. Unlike Hoschedé, Faure's boldness was genuine.

Greater numbers of important collectors now were purchasing Monet's canvases than ever before. Yet the sales remained too small to affect his exposed and vulnerable position. On October 2, 1875, therefore, he took a more hurtful step. Once more at the Paris study of Maître Aumont-Thieville, Claude Monet and Camille entered into another of those lengthy documents whose monothematic gloom and insistent meter marked their downward path. The sense was tediously contained in the third paragraph:

> By the terms of an act received by Maître Léon Aumont-Thieville and his colleagues, notaries at Paris, the twenty-fourth November eighteen hundred seventy three, registered, Madame the widow Doncieux has paid to Madame Monet, who has given quittance, the sum of four thousand francs drawn from the portion of the dowry of twelve thousand francs constituted for Madame Monet, the which dowry, as has been shown, is at the charge of Madame Doncieux reduced by half or to six thousand francs.
>
> It results therefore that Madame the widow Doncieux owes still to her daughter the sum of two thousand francs as her portion of the dowry. In regard to these two thousand francs there have been the terms of a

TRANSPORT

These facts exposed, Madame Monet wishes to transport with all guarantees and promises of payments by default of Madame the widow Doncieux, the debtor . . . to Monsieur Marie Charles Édouard Carpentier, color merchant, residing at Paris, rue Halévy, number 6, who is present and who accepts,

The sum of two thousand francs which is owed by Madame the widow Doncieux, her mother, from the six thousand francs remaining in the charge of Madame the widow Doncieux from the dowry constituted for her by her father and mother.

Monsieur Carpentier, by these presents, will be enabled to demand and receive from Madame the widow Doncieux, the said sum of two thousand francs . . . and he will have rights to the interest of the said sum from this day. . . .

The present act is made by means of the sum of two thousand francs which Monsieur Carpentier has paid to Madame Monet, which she acknowledges, in cash notes of gold or silver or notes of the Bank of France. . . .

Whether Camille had been paid all the 2,000 francs in cash, or whether in reality this sum was discounted by amounts owed Carpentier for colors and canvas, the outrageous, sinewy, educated piece of comedy which had surrounded her dowry now was finished.

Of no weight in herself, charming, feckless, capricious, but singled out by that passion which created her place in history, Camille set her signature to paper for the last time known. How bizarre, then, that in giving up the sad remnant of her dowry, and the final connection with her youth and family, she forgot the name of the man she so tragically loved, and signed herself *C. Doncieux.*

Among conscientious liberals a strong inclination existed to applaud experiment, and sometimes naïveté, for its own sake. Any bright cocky style was certain of a degree of attention, provided the public could be made aware of it. Therein lay the great problem. If Édouard Manet's spontaneity did not flow quite like a limpid brook, he alone brought to the great Salon public a reflection of ideas found among his friends. At each Salon that special public attentive to him marveled at new turns of what seemed an inexhaustible fancy.

To forestall rejections, in 1875 Manet submitted to the jury only one canvas, painted at Argenteuil. Featuring his wife and brother-in-law, this work was hung, to receive the usual rough handling from critics. Manet, however, continued to forge ahead, for he had a definite following and patrons who paid thousands for his pictures. Comparison with Monet's completely outcast state had its own tragic eloquence. And no matter how strong a man's convictions, the time must come when he will realize that he is trafficking in dangerous, even lethal, delusions. By the end of 1875, unable to exist on private sales at wretchedly poor prices, forced constantly to beg from friends, surely this had dawned on even Claude Monet.

After the fearful reception of their works at the Hôtel Drouot, all plans for the group's second exhibition were abandoned. Ruminating over the futility of that first venture on the Boulevard des Capucines, the fiasco of the sale, and the abandonment of plans for further exhibitions, Monet at last accepted that Édouard Manet had been correct not to join them. However tortuous the path he was forced to tread at the Salon, that institution surely represented the only hope of a better future. In recognition of this fact Monet stirred himself to plan the sort of brilliant figure painting that once, early in his career, had brought overwhelming acclaim.

Ten years had elapsed since that flattering reception granted *Camille,* a period during which his earlier self, the bluff and unscrupulous soldier of fortune, had experienced profound changes. Youth had been replaced by a quieter maturity, and years by the river at Argenteuil had separated him from the flat tones once his delight. But his weakness for Oriental design, visible everywhere from Camille's blue kimono to the prints and fans hung on his walls at Argenteuil, was widely known. Monet recalled, of the friends who urged this new course on him, "They tempted me by showing me a marvelous [Oriental] robe on which certain gold embroideries were several centimeters thick."

Entertained over this ultimate turn in a bizarre course, he prepared to express his taste for artificiality on a large scale. He would attract attention by some serpentine flourish of posing, then divide his picture into rough thirds. The lowest would become a floor covered by the repetitious designs of a grass rug. The upper portions he expected to serve the more elaborate purpose of generating rhythmic vitality by forcing the eye to move over a scattering of thirteen Japanese fans.

Communication on a wider basis always was granted any daring theatrical creation. Unaccustomed to dramatic contrasts of shadow in figure painting, sheer theatrical effect was not possible to Monet.

Camille fortunately made good her husband's deficiency by stepping into the spectacular scarlet gown with her head thrust high, sweeping a fan through the air in elaborate coquetry. By that highly exaggerated flourish her eyes and chin conveyed an equivalent of drama, though the gown itself contributed a flavor that somewhat inclined to run together, like dissolving Neapolitan ice cream.

Camille was competed with, and upstaged, by a ferocious sword-bearing Japanese warrior who inhabited the robe's intricacies. Gesturing and grimacing astride a wounded dragon, he formed awkward juxtapositions and implausible folds. This well-entrenched assailant fought furiously against every effort by artist and model to control him. Finally, to swamp him entirely, Monet made the leer of Camille's face too blatantly obvious, as though she suffered not merely from overt suggestibility but an unnecessary lewdness. This he further reinforced by an untidy mass of blond hair, which, by concentrating attention, drew the eyes away from the squirming samurai.

This amalgam of styles and intentions nonetheless flowed together with astonishing smoothness. Monet's new synthetic use of color, perfected on the river, showed remarkable capacities indoors, contributing greatly to a work of immense strength and coloristic splendor. Structural weakness in the face was perhaps too obvious, nor was the robe itself entirely persuasive. Especially where an arm of the samurai lay flush against a contour fold, it assumed a three-dimensional existence of its own that destroyed the robe's illusion. And the fact that this large, heavily gowned figure cast no shadow to either side startled the eye accustomed to naturalistic conventions. Damned with enormous intensity of temperament, but no density of character, this uniquely flamboyant creation seemed to erupt in berserk symbolical fantasy.

While at work Monet was also obliged to think of more pressing problems:

Argenteuil, 23 January [1876]

MY DEAR MANET,

I ask you to pardon me for appealing to you so often, but what you brought me is gone. Again I am without a penny. If you can, without its inconveniencing you, advance me 50 francs at least, it would render me a singular service. I am awaiting a collector, the dentist Verdier, who will certainly purchase something from me.

Also I am working hard so that he will find something to his taste.
My wife will pass your house tomorrow morning between 10 and
11, assuming it is not weather unfit for a dog. If so I will come myself.
It would be very good of you to oblige me in this way.
With regards,

CLAUDE MONET

Implicit in this letter is the belief that gentle, obliging Camille, so
often an uncomplaining model to Manet, could not be refused at his
door. First-rate as the mocking charmer of the Japanese canvas, she
also was cast in the role of blushingly uneasy beggar. The resourcefulness of Monet's mind was present at each turn, sometimes whimsi-
cal, sometimes severe, and, as this letter also implied, willing to
indulge in hopeful illusions based on a collector's expected appearance.

Through Manet and Durand-Ruel he had made the acquaintance
of every collector he could. To these, in repetitious and renewed
interviews, he attempted to sell his pictures by a fine blend of shrewd
appraisal and personal reminiscence. A continual veering and shifting of tone is apparent, but the utter lack of histrionics, and the
obvious hints of embarrassment and despair, are very nearly as
shocking as the demands once made on Bazille, and clinically far
more intimate. In February, while crisis hung heavy over Argenteuil, this was notable when Cézanne proposed to bring to lunch
Victor Chocquet, a minor customs official.

The days of entertainments at Argenteuil had passed. The squire
had retired to his former occupation of shaming people into purchases of his pictures. Armed probably with loans from Édouard
Manet, Monet wrote to Chocquet on February 4: "I have promised
Cézanne that he might come to lunch with you tomorrow, Saturday.
If it does not frighten you to have a very modest luncheon, it will be
a great pleasure for me, because I will be most fortunate to have
made your acquaintance. . . ."

Agonizing corners had been turned through the years. In a professional sense Monet often had taken one step forward and two back.
More recently he had gone through periods when his own introspec-
tive tendencies had been weighted down by the need to appear
positive. By personal insistence he was now selling pictures, often to
distinguished patrons and collectors. But prices were small and

quantities insufficient, so that despite this minor success his life remained a writhing account of exposure to loneliness and fear.

The wearying combination of physical strain and psychological anxiety varies with the degree of risk and the time it continues to be run. Its effects, however, are cumulative, producing a sense of hopelessness and frustration. Activated by his need, early in 1876 Monet again became articulate, hoping to revive the private exhibitions. He was able to indicate eminent new patrons attracted to his works since the last exhibition, but time and experience had punctured his principal arguments. The task of organizing painters as demoralized as himself was beyond his energies, and hope no longer was firm. The very thesis of an opposition Salon was abandoned, and in April, 1876, the thirty participants of the first exhibition drastically shrunken to nineteen, a second exhibition was held directly under the banner of Durand-Ruel at his gallery in the Rue Laffitte.

Édouard Manet loaned Renoir's 1867 portrait of Bazille to the exhibition, but refused to join himself. To display the fact that his works were being purchased by distinguished collectors, Monet borrowed no fewer than nine pictures from Faure. One other was given by Chocquet, who, loaning as well six works by Renoir, ceaselessly prowled the gallery collaring visitors he might convert to his own faith. Among those caught by this spry, benevolent, white-haired gentleman unfortunately was Albert Wolff, critic of *Le Figaro*, who on leaving the gallery demanded his 50-centime entrance fee refunded!

From every quarter of the press the murderous howl of two years before again was heard. After reading Albert Wolff's taunting and patronizing article, Manet's brother Eugène, Berthe Morisot's husband, had to be dissuaded from challenging him to a duel. Bad publicity and the less central position of the gallery naturally produced a lessened flow of visitors. For those who did attend, Monet's screaming figure piece, now entitled *Panneau Décoratif: La Japonnerie*, was the major attraction, and before the exhibition's close it was sold for the astonishing sum of 2,000 francs.

Even a sum of this magnitude no longer was capable of refloating Monet's economy, which, if anything, and despite his sales, sank at an increasing rate. He counted his patrons almost compulsively, and for a man sinking ever more deeply in debt, he sold surprising quantities of pictures. Durand-Ruel noted with approval his success in this department, but though he was the last to care, at least in this regard Monet's integrity had fallen to shreds.

The most recent link in Monet's chain of collectors was an eccentric Romanian herb doctor, Georges de Bellio, whose unsavory French and heavy accent created an unforgettably trenchant personality. De Bellio immediately had been touched by the dogged determination of the painter, and as their personal acquaintance grew, Monet, with his practiced and well-calculated skill, succeeded in entangling de Bellio in his private affairs. Seven weeks after the close of the exhibition Monet wrote:

June 20, 1876

DEAR MONSIEUR,

Since your visit I have done much work. I have [completed] a series of new things which are quite interesting, I think. You could have first choice of a canvas if you wished, and if by chance you were attracted by another canvas this would be a very good moment, because I find myself again once more brutally interrupted in my tasks by an accursed question of money. . . .

In any case I owe you a canvas. Come choose it and do not forget that you have promised me your professional care and that you must cure me.

If you have nothing better to do Thursday the noon train will bring you here exactly at lunchtime, and if Callot was free I would be very pleased to have him accompany you.

Awaiting the pleasure, receive my best compliments,

CLAUDE MONET

P.S. Come Wednesday or Friday, but come.

De Bellio was not able to visit Argenteuil, but Monet's letter was not unfruitful, for this patron sent the price of a second canvas, which he promised to come select.

Frequently Monet also took the train to Paris with canvases under his arm, trusting in his ability to force them on some unwilling collector. Whether with blushing urgency he called unexpectedly at their doors, or they were induced to take the train from Paris, at each confrontation Monet oversold himself heavily. He fixed his piercing eye of innocence upon them and assaulted them with barrages of preformed pleas calculated to the last wan smile. The trials of his poverty were an essential ally. A powerful appeal to parties

First page of Monet's letter of June 20, 1876 to Georges de Bellio.

already persuaded of his talent and his need, he transgressed brutally against their friendship and produced an effect curiously embarrassing, even compulsive, but for the wrong reasons.

His technique was so exquisitely primitive each repeated effort alienated sympathy. Yet those he approached, often conscious of his trickery and purpose, could not help liking the monster and believing in him. And even those who realized the worst of the truth—that Monet merely had hit upon a successful formula for selling pictures—could with unexpected swiftness be disconcerted and reduced to quivering jelly by the receipt of a letter recounting some real disaster that had befallen him. For every outside resource was exhausted now. The dowry was gone, no relatives of either party assisted them, Durand-Ruel purchased nothing, and the entire structure of life at Argenteuil rested on these urgently foisted sales of canvases.

Too often while giving voice to his unhappiness and his needs Monet reduced a desperate battle to moaning. On July 25 he wrote again to Georges de Bellio:

> It is with a broken heart that I am writing to beg you, if you have a moment for that, to come choose the two sketches that you wanted to buy from me and paid me for in advance. I can do no business, my creditors show themselves intractable, and except for a sudden appearance of rich collectors we are going to be thrown out of this nice little house where I have been able so well to work. I do not know what is going to happen to us. . . .

The well-groomed appearance of Camille hid to what degree she shared the emotional strains of her husband. At Argenteuil her patience always seemed a rich commodity shared by all, though her charm and gaiety were slightly urban and her speech retained its hint of Lyon. For eleven years she had lived with the difficult artist in what seemed a state of complete harmony. Sheathed expressively in many costumes, she had been an ornament and a convenience, exuding always that attractive sensuality felt by all who surrounded her. No woman ever commented on Camille, but the esteem of men is found in every portrait painted by her husband's circle.

While Monet became a valiant, insistent, and emotionally overwrought beggar, with the lover's self-annihilating sensibility Camille granted him those gratifications in her power. The strangely haunting beauty of this relationship never was more touchingly apparent than while she permitted the last bittersweet ecstasy to be wrung from her affection. From this tenderly devoted wife he drew peace and renewed strength. But now, nine years after the birth of Jean, Camille herself became aware of the mysterious forces inhabiting them both. At twenty-nine, she contributed to the hopeless disorder of their lives the painful assurance that she would bring forth another child to share their agonies.

From a key of dedication and rich sentiment her love modulated quickly into darker tones of tragedy. The state of affairs was scarcely conducive to poise. Already emotionally overwrought, if Monet did not refuse to accept this new reality, he exhibited a remarkable degree of reluctance. Camille's personal dilemma became even more strikingly acute until, in a piece of arbitrary violence, she decided, or was persuaded, that this unwelcome pregnancy must be terminated. Her craven husband too irresolute to save her, a ponderous episode on which hung the convoluted pattern of her short life was inaugurated. Camille, submitting to ordeal secretly and at unskilled hands, sustained a torn womb that refused to heal. Pain and discomfort were intense, while all about her the pattern of life at Argenteuil, so completely dependent on her, stopped to await a recovery that seemed delayed, then unwilling.

Camille's strength to face the persistent elusiveness of Monet's fortunes had failed. No one was more shaken than Monet himself, whose letters transmitted images of a gaping wretch seeking any possible salvation. The doctor called to treat Camille at Argenteuil expressed little hope for improvement. He made the signal mistake of speaking of an operation, a suggestion which terrified Camille still further. To outflank this, Monet wrote to Georges de Bellio, whose nonmedical cures were a sudden hope:

Argenteuil, Saturday night

DEAR MONSIEUR DE BELLIO,

A new misfortune has overwhelmed me—I have not had enough of being short of money. Because my wife is so sick the local doctor wants to have the opinion of another doctor. I am very much alarmed because the gravity of the illness is not hidden from me.

We will be very lucky, my wife and I, if you would give us counsel, because there is talk of an operation which terrifies my wife. I cannot tell you the exact nature of the malady, but it is something like an ulceration of the womb. For the rest I will take the liberty of coming to see you tomorrow morning (Sunday), and if, as I hope, you will give me your advice, I will give you the necessary explanations.

Until tomorrow then,

With best wishes
CLAUDE MONET
5 Boul. St. Denis, Argenteuil

As her health drained away, Camille suddenly looked aged, bleached and wizened. The erotic stimulation she had conveyed by every glance disappeared. Around both wife and husband daily anxieties amid pressures too painful to bear, in addition to their shared burden of guilt, produced a small, closed, neurotic household in which the outside world seemed more and more menacing.

Because Monet was unable to leave Camille, or to peddle his pictures among even those few in Paris who might possibly buy them, the autumn quarter of the rent introduced a new crisis. Camille's situation grew more grave; Mme. Aubry-Vitet, the landlady, discouraged by repeated delays on the part of her once-prosperous tenant, became more dogged in determination to have her rent. After a period of rumblings the volcano erupted. Her demands forced Monet to go to Paris, where he no longer sought purchasers for his canvases but outright loans. He failed, and returning home found Camille in greater pain and graver danger. An appeal was sent Manet:

MY DEAR MANET,

I am heartbroken. Last night, on returning, I found my wife very sick. The doctor was obliged to come many times. I saw my landlady this morning, and it was only by much pleading that I obtained her consent to wait until Monday. Friends are rare when one is in distress. Even so, would you be good enough to come to my aid—I am going to beg you not to abandon me.

I have run around all day to find someone who would loan me the money, but without success. Unable to find a single moment to come see you, I address you these few lines begging you to find in your turn some means, because I have a fear, a terrible fear, of being unable to find any and if the catastrophe must take place I really do not know if my wife would be able to endure such a trial at this moment.

It is bothersome always to hear complaints from others. Excuse me, and try to assist me if you possibly can.

With regards,

CLAUDE MONET

A detail from Monet's letter to de Bellio, explaining Camille's last illness:
". . . mais il s'agit d'ulceration de la matrice."

The prose style he so long had favored, littered with awkward images and unhappy metaphors, had gone. Monet's words give the uncanny impression of a man in agony watching himself writhe.

Though willing to help, Édouard Manet himself lacked the means and sought delay. At mention of Manet's name Mme. Aubry-Vitet held off her demands, then, infuriated once more, at an early hour the Thursday morning following she burst renewed crisis over the heads of Monet and his agonized Camille. In a pathetic gesture, Monet hurriedly sent a messenger to Paris bearing the sketch of Manet he had made two years before in the Argenteuil garden:

MY DEAR MANET,

This morning at seven-thirty Mme. Aubry presented me with her quittance. Because I awaited you I said to come back toward noon— but there it is. My debt is 250 francs and I have no more than 200. Try somehow to find the other hundred and send them to me. I will beg Mme. Aubry to wait until tomorrow or even the day after.

With regards,

CLAUDE MONET

Manet was unable to honor the forced sale imposed at his door. Whether he noted the obvious discrepancy in Monet's figures also causes wonder. Embarrassed by the payment of his own rent, he did the best he could by sending the messenger and canvas to Théodore Duret with an additional note:

Thursday

MY DEAR DURET,

Here is a letter that I receive from Monet. My rent has cleaned me out. I am unable to do anything for him. Could you give the hundred francs to the bearer of the picture?

Regards,

ED. MANET

But this too failed, and one suspects it was Édouard Manet himself who again momentarily redeemed Monet's peace at Argenteuil.

19. Forbidden Love

ARGENTEUIL had been a brief and beautiful pipe dream in the middle of a nightmare. The mysteriously grotesque parody of reality that nightmares suggest settled about them now permanently, tapping private guilts and exteriorizing obsessions with savage harshness. In the autumn of 1876 the town itself assumed a sour presence. An invalid who knew constant pain, Camille was transparently shielded by her husband from the bailiffs who called and from Mme. Aubry-Vitet, who demanded her rent in repetitive rituals of fury. Constant journeys to Paris on which he peddled pictures from door to door among his patrons, and the inexorable flow of letters whose pithy phrases were handled with greatly increased freedom, all suggested the time had come to abandon these spoiled pastoral entertainments for Paris itself.

To gather funds for this move and find accommodations, that December Monet spent a desperate fortnight alone in Paris. Not only was he unsuccessful, but almost stranded. He wrote to Renoir's patron, the publisher Georges Charpentier:

> I am going to ask you if you would loan me five or six louis—I am terribly troubled at this moment.
> For ten days I have been in Paris without being able to find a penny and I am unable to return to the country where my wife is so ill. You would render me a great service in giving this sum to the bearer and as soon as I have returned definitely to Paris I will come to see you and reimburse you either in paintings or in money.
> I hope you will not refuse me.

Matters were no more hopeful at the New Year. To be rid of her troublesome tenant Mme. Aubry-Vitet gave Monet an added two weeks in which to vacate her house. On January 15 he was required to settle his debts and depart. A climax of remarkably sustained fury took place in the first days of 1877 as he concentrated the robust vigor of his demands on already browbeaten patrons. One, new among them, who obliged, was sent a note January 8:

> DEAR MONSIEUR [Murer],
>
> Would you, I beg, excuse me for not yet having come to thank you for your graciousness, but for the last ten days I am on hot coals. My wife suffers greatly and the little boy also is not well. Before us is the prospect of moving on the fifteenth, without yet knowing to where we will go, or even whether I shall be able to conclude my affairs at Argenteuil. As you see, there is much reason to lose one's head a little. . . .

A timeless effect of uncanny intensity surrounds his appeals, sent in masses to people who otherwise were sensible and fastidious, but who yet were mesmerized by his impetuous attack and the dramatic clarity of his letters and presence. In adversity he was an astonishing mover of men, who released from the shackles of their own mediocrity the tens of persons who contributed to this move from Argenteuil. His sights were set on the not inconsiderable sum of 1,500 francs. Cannily he allowed no one to realize the full nature of his need lest it dishearten them. In appeals that for all their emotional intensity were really demands, each in turn was asked for the sum he might possibly provide. It was the old rule: from each according to his means to Monet according to his needs.

By his style of common but furious verbal energy, by forcing pictures on unwilling collectors, and by extorting "loans" which really were cash contributions, he succeeded in raising the greater portion of his goal. Mme. Aubry-Vitet extended his time by two days, to January 17, and with a Paris studio discovered in the Rue Moncey, he set about to find the last sums necessary. Georges de Bellio, who had been consulted concerning Camille's condition, and more recently had contributed 200 francs to this vast enterprise, was sent a further appeal just before the deadline.

> DEAR M. DE BELLIO,
>
> In two days, that is to say, the day after tomorrow, we must leave Argenteuil. To do this I must have paid my debts. I have had the good luck since I saw you to realize 1200 francs. No more than 300 francs now are lacking to be able to pay some last things and be ready to depart.

Would you do me a *last* service and advance me again 200 francs, because I am absolutely unable to find it. You already have done so much to pull me out of the embarrassment I have been in the last two weeks that I hope you will not abandon me just at the moment when I reach port. I am able to say to you that it is a last service because I am going to find myself disembarrassed of all my creditors and finally will be able to devote myself to serious work.

You know all the efforts I have made for that. You know the position of my wife. Make a last effort and I will not be the only one grateful to you. Send me a few lines in response, to the rue de Moncey, so that I can find your answer tomorrow morning. But do not abandon me, I beg of you.

Believe me, your all devoted,

CLAUDE MONET
Tuesday, the 15th January

Even this was insufficient, and finally Mme. Aubry-Vitet agreed to keep the *Picnic,* painted at Chailly, against the balance. Thus, in a reiterated and harshly underscored irony, the *Picnic* once more was put in pawn, while a strident processional scene of furniture and canvases was formed and directed toward Paris.

On January 17, 1877, with their son Jean, now a darting lad of ten, Claude Monet and Camille arrived together in Paris for the last time. At 26 Rue d'Edimbourg, near the Rue de Rome and the Gare St.-Lazare, they took a small apartment which their furnishings brought from Argenteuil made seem more than adequately respectable. Draperies and lace curtains quickly covered the windows, carpets the floors, and in the sitting room Camille was able to rest on their flower-covered chaise longue. Everywhere in this new abode the eye was caught by the decorative glitter of well-framed paintings, Japanese fans, and even the occasional luxury of blue Delft on display.

Perhaps the ceremonious clutter of more typical nineteenth-century interiors was lacking. But if so, this was the only indication their apartment expressed a degree of quick adaptation and adjustment, rather than settled bourgeois ease. For again in departing Argenteuil Monet had wiped away his debts. And however distasteful the means by which he gathered funds, even at this disastrous period his income of 3,000 to 4,000 francs a year far exceeded emolu-

First page of Monet's letter to de Bellio, asking one last favor. "Voulez-vous me rendre un dernier service . . ."

ments received by most civil servants. In a society built upon many such dismal enclaves the true level at which he was starving comes sharply into view. Creatures of destiny, unfolding still their tale of forbidden love, and Camille's condition filled the curiously comfortable, uneasy, ironic situation in which they found themselves with sadness and distress.

Easels, stocks of canvases, and paints were carried to the little studio at 17 Rue Moncey, where Monet seems to have considered it possible to attract portrait orders. An example of his abilities was necessary for display, and here too he brought the dying Camille, once more to serve as model. The effort he made to control his technique was bold, multicolored, and widely expressive, Camille's fixed eyes drawing all attention from a naïveté of structural workmanship so disastrous as to be almost lovable.

Monet's creativity had not survived triumphantly, for he was prey to the chaos of his own emotions, and while hoping to attract portrait orders from persons lured to the Rue Moncey studio, little else in a wintry city excited his ardor. Then, just as he had sought attention at Argenteuil by presenting an absurdity and leaving it, in an equally bizarre end-of-tether inspiration he settled on the great St.-Lazare railroad station. The forms of steel and iron structures already had presented extraordinary opportunities for contrapuntal pattern. New possibilities of an equally off-key nature were suggested by the station's grouping of mighty engines under colossal steel-and-glass sheds. Everywhere drafts of steam and luminous wisps of black, white, and gray smoke swirled into Paris's misty winter air.

From the Rue Moncey Monet walked daily with his canvases to the Rue d'Amsterdam, down whose inclining slopes he came to the Gare St.-Lazare. His easel placed on the quay, and frequently the tracks themselves, he turned a horribly world-weary gaze upon the great triangular shed filled with darting colored vapor. And just as with the Argenteuil bridges, he proceeded to exhaust the possibilities of pattern by exploring the materials before him from every angle in every condition of atmosphere.

That he labored in conditions of wretchedness and self-distaste is reflected in the inequality of the work he did. All of it fell short of the complete spontaneity achieved at Argenteuil. And even allowing for interludes of lassitude, one becomes conscious of his own disquiet over subject matter and whether his technical equipment was suitable for static, reflective scenes peopled only by movements of vapor. The impact created by pure novelty must be translated into something of enduring artistic value. Through repetition, and cunning placement of key pieces and textures, he organized the railway station into satisfying pictures.

Thin slabs of color flowed smoothly from his sable brushes, coming together loosely on the canvas between a buff-toned webbing of bare cloth. At times the paint surface, hammered at by a steady crescendo of strokes, linked up into a unified globulated whole, achieving a new and varied beauty of shimmering, coruscating, or crystalline texture. The often disjointed sketcher's technique seen at Argenteuil showed signs of developing further into a heavily daubed, floating, diaphanous surface, weaving a kind of descriptive orchestral tapestry that evoked place and atmosphere, light and shadow, so vividly that each scene was presented to the mind's eye in all its subtle detail.

However fertile and original, methods of painting canvases were only a portion of Monet's task, for he was equally fertile and original when evolving methods for their sale. Even before completing his canvases at the Gare St.-Lazare he established afternoons in the studio to which his patrons were invited. A letter written for this purpose carefully shielded the nature of his new subject:

DEAR MONSIEUR CHOCQUET,

I wanted to come myself to say that after tomorrow, Friday, I will always be here from one-thirty until four o'clock. But to my very great regret, I had not left enough time to go as far as your house.

If however you have a moment to spare tomorrow, I will be very happy to see you and to show you 2 or 3 canvases that I have just done and of which I shall not have more for several days. It would also give us the greatest pleasure for you to meet M. Bellio, who has promised me a visit.

Receive also for Madame my many compliments.

CLAUDE MONET
17, rue Moncey

Whether or not Chocquet honored this invitation, he appears not to have purchased any of the Gare St.-Lazare canvases. Georges de Bellio was more obliging, choosing an atmospheric study of smoke wisps rising past engines beneath the Pont de l'Europe. Ernest

Hoschedé followed by purchasing *two* of these electrifying canvases. But the largest and most elaborate was acquired by Gustave Caillebotte, former neighbor at Argenteuil, sailing enthusiast and painter of talent, who exhibited with the group Monet had formed. Monet's hours passed waiting in the studio were well employed also, painting still lifes. One of these, a basket of flowers, was given Charpentier in repayment of his "loan" of the previous December.

For a time the fervent Victor Chocquet remained an untapped resource, a situation to which meticulous attention was given. After completion of the St.-Lazare series, Paris had little to offer an artist feeling the repressions of his own sullen indifference. He visited Chocquet, who with his heiress wife lived in an attractive apartment high up over the Rue de Rivoli. Chocquet's windows caught morning sunlight filtering over the roof of the Louvre, holding it until evening, when the sun was ready to set over Ste.-Clotilde's twin spires. The curious downward perspective of rays falling on the Tuileries in that early springtime was not an overwhelming subject, but Monet sought permission to paint a view so familiar to Chocquet. Three canvases that resulted, dull greens in hazy sunlight unrelieved by anything but distant grays, were devoid of the distinction with which often he had invested even failures. But these muted commentaries were attractive to those familiar with what they represented. Chocquet obliged as intended; de Bellio bought a second.

For pure landscape the only resource near that section of Paris where Monet resided was the Parc Monceau. Though this flower-bedded preserve daily was crowded with nursemaids and carriages and children wandering free, Monet brought Camille there as soon as her strength seemed sufficient. By the end of March he produced several studies, one of which had been ceded to de Bellio, and another, of Camille in sunlight, to Hoschedé. Offering fewer opportunities to work, Paris in recompense brought Monet an advantageous proximity to his clients. A new feature of his life was dinner invitations which brought him to the well-furnished tables kept by Charpentier and Hoschedé. By these means he sold upwards of seven canvases during the first three months at Paris, realizing approximately 2,000 francs.

Into this profitable springtime came also, at Easter, a second invitation to visit with the Hoschedés at Montgeron. In the luxury of their estate he produced another large decoration to match the earlier woodland interior. Beneath a sky that was one of his infallible glowering performances, Monet employed familiar boldness and incisiveness to disport an extraordinary composition of turkeys. The decorative potential of barnyard fowl had been demonstrated by the printmakers of Japan, yet never had they attempted any work displaying such large-scale technical command or haunting rustic beauty. Neither relieved by any dramatic contrast nor leavened by changes in pace or palette, fifteen white birds pass through slow variations, their colors and textures beautifully balanced.

To achieve purely decorative purposes Monet subdued his brutal forward-driving style. Awkward passages of drawing surrounding the birds' heads, and the arch of backs and tails, are chiseled out with almost ostentatious clarity and display. Most remarkable again was how well his technical resources, evolved in small scale, were suited to a work of such size, creating a decoration that is totally unexpected and most carefully put together. In spite of the decorative lack of real substance, its coloring, design and technical acrobatics make it fascinating.

By April 1, when a third group exhibition opened in an apartment Caillebotte rented for the purpose at 6 Rue Le Peletier, close by Durand-Ruel's gallery, this elaborate composition of turkeys was not yet completed. Pleased by his own success, Monet, who worked on the hanging committee, saw that it was hung, the catalogue carefully noting its incomplete state. After the opening Victor Chocquet played his usual role, wandering the exhibition with an air of mock politeness, permitting his opinion to be attacked in hope his fervent replies would convert the foe. Chocquet's adversaries rarely had the last word, yet if the artists had hoped that by repeatedly showing themselves to the public they would be greeted by a lessened antagonism, they were fearfully wrong. *Le Charivari* published cartoons of a policeman advising a pregnant woman, "Madame, it would be unwise to enter!" and of a rich patron surveying a canvas, exclaiming, "But these are the colors of a cadaver!" Like pious Methodists on a tour of the Vatican, the mood the public showed was still compounded of derision, disgust, and sheer fascination. They appeared to be holding themselves back from exploding, though whether with mirth or indignation was beyond the disheartened painters to judge.

Camille's health remained uncertain, her strength never sufficient for a normal life. That the essential gratifications she had so long provided her husband were impossible is reflected in the repressed tensions gnawing at him all the previous winter, which were visible in the laborious and contrived textures of his works. By spring of 1877 the worst of her pain appears to have subsided; and, once more feeling stronger, able to take the air occasionally in the Parc Monceau, Camille resumed her compassionate role. The heroism of ordinary acts achieved an uncommon tenderness in this beautiful sunset mistaken for a dawn.

At the Parc Monceau Monet worked again with an immense flexibility of approach, focusing a clean, bright, expertly scintillated tone, supported by his own synthetic harmonies. All trace of the gravelly texture and disjunct approach that abounded earlier disappeared. Through the summer he produced pictures of the simple greenery, trees, and flower banks, seen in heat and sapping intensity. The insinuating sweetness and sensuousness again present in both the luxuriance of pigment and the lushness of his vision perhaps were drawn equally from the frequent presence of Mme. Hoschedé, who, bringing her younger children to the Parc Monceau, allowed a delicate sentiment to grow up between herself and the artist. Affectionate indulgence was obvious on her side, pity and liking on his. The period encompassed numerous changes of mood and tempo. More than half Monet's time was passed in the Rue Moncey studio, awaiting calls from patrons, writing letters, intriguing for the sale of his canvases. Other intrigues were present also, and of Alice Hoschedé's visits to that studio explanation can perhaps be given.

Camille's particularly delicate illness had made other women alluring but troublesome to Monet. Toward Camille he bore an affection which veered between protective infatuation and panic-stricken responsibility. She knew his needs and satisfied them like some fragile princess in a fairy tale. This grim, impassioned, unsmiling, uncharming man in the presence of his wife thus stripped from himself his shield of invincibility and indestructibility.

Herself therapeutically maternal and proud of it, Alice Hoschedé was surely aware of serious dislocations in the life of this powerfully built artist, two years younger, and physically far more active, than her own vastly overweight husband. She shaped the sympathetic relationship with tenderness and occasional rapture, nor did she encounter opposition from a man as well disposed as Monet toward the opposite sex. The same age as Monet, her figure inflated, the mother of six children, soon Alice Hoschedé jealously cherished and guarded Monet, holding him in a grip half embrace, half bear-hug, as living proof that she was not a middle-aged matron but something more volatile and feminine.

Camille's health continued to cause concern, despite which she performed her tasks and comforted her husband with all the devotion of her love. By that August, 1877, she became certain that the dreadful circumstance of the previous year had recurred. Her magnanimity had led her back to the edge of the precipice, and now, in the reduced state of her health and strength, no interference with nature could be considered. The situation was tragically unreal, yet required the most earnest decisions, for, if she could, Camille must be permitted to bring forth this new child.

The timing of these events made them doubly unfortunate, for over the summer Monet's socially elevated clientele was absent from Paris in places of fashionable resort. For months he had done no business, and by October, spurred by renewed anxieties, his tone once more grew shrill:

Thursday, 25 October 1877

Dear Monsieur [Chocquet],

I am abashed and ask of you a little indulgence for a man who is penniless. But really, I do not know which way to turn, and I am going to ask you to take from me one or two daubs which I will let you have at any price you set on them—50 francs, 40 francs, whatever you can pay, because I cannot wait any longer.

I will be at home tomorrow, Saturday, 17 rue de Moncey, from 3 o'clock, and I very much hope that you will not fail to come!

Excuse, I beg you, my indiscretion and believe my sincere regards.

Claude Monet

Georges de Bellio was the next to hear from him in the same vein of frantic pleading. Camille's pregnancy had pricked the bubble of illusion more swiftly and surely than anything else. Sad realities were accompanied by a decrease in the willingness of his patrons to buy. This was reflected by the disastrous fall in the prices he was demanding:

Saturday morning

DEAR MONSIEUR [de Bellio],

I have not dared to write to you before, fearing to abuse your kindness. But I am in a terrible fix without an accursed penny, and do not know where to find one any place. I spent all day yesterday without turning up anything. It is for that reason I address myself to you again, begging you to forgive so much indiscretion.

Two sketches of the kind and dimensions of your bridge for 150 francs. The same two you admired so much. And that for my part I will consider to be good business at a time like this.

Excuse me for not having come myself, but I am afraid of abusing and I am a little ashamed. Be good enough to give your answer to the porter. . . .

Forgive me.

With best wishes,
CLAUDE MONET

Equally astonishing is that having satisfied his Argenteuil creditors, and earned at least 2,000 francs before the summer, already he was so disastrously in debt. For years embarrassment and poverty had been the mainstays of his pleas. Yet never had they been urged with such neurotic abandon, nor had their compulsive power reached such heights as in a note sent Émile Zola, friend of Manet and Bazille, whose recent successes as a novelist brought him again into Monet's view:

Can you and would you come to my aid? If I do not pay 600 francs by tomorrow night, Tuesday, our furniture and all I own will be sold and we will be out on the street. I do not have a single penny of this amount. None of the transactions on which I have been counting can be concluded at this moment. I would be desperate to reveal the situation to my poor wife.

I am making a last effort and approaching you with the hope that you may possibly lend me 200 francs. This would be an installment which may help me obtain a delay. I do not dare to come myself. I would be capable of seeing you without daring to tell you the reason of my visit.

Please send me word, and in any case do not speak of this, for it is always a fault to be in need.

One suspects that Zola did not oblige. To obtain 200 francs Monet had spoken to Zola of needing 600; to de Bellio he next proposed an astonishing scheme based on a figure of 500 francs:

I could not be more unfortunate. I am going to be sold at the very moment when I hoped to arrange my affairs. Once on the street and destitute there will remain only one thing for me to do—to take any job I can get. It will be a terrible blow for me. I cannot believe it and am making a last effort. *With five hundred francs I save the situation. I still have approximately, in my house, and at M.S. . . . twenty-five canvases. I will give them to you at this price. In doing this you will save me.*

That Édouard Manet received no appeals during this desperate season hinges less on their proximity in Paris than the alienation that had come between them. In return for the Renoir portrait of Bazille, found exhibited at Durand-Ruel's gallery, Bazille's family the previous year had sent Manet from Montpellier Monet's enormous *Women in a Garden.* Édouard Manet happily conserved this huge canvas until in a fit of pique the two artists exchanged words.

"You have a little study of mine at your home," Manet snapped. "Return it to me. For my side, I will send back your big picture, for I want nothing of yours!"

Monet took Manet at his word, sending the study of Camille and Jean made in the Argenteuil garden. In return he found himself once more in possession of the huge garden picture.

What had occasioned Édouard Manet's wrath is unknown, and gives rise to wonder, for a popular odium surrounded Claude Monet that autumn. Whether or not it derived from his association with Alice Hoschedé, it contributed strongly to his reduced fortunes. By begging, wheedling, demanding, and lowering his prices disastrously, but above all by endlessly running the streets of Paris, canvas under arm, Monet held on through the autumn of 1877. What underlines the tragic intensity of his problems is that conditions cruelly deteriorated. Among regular clients, Hoschedé and Faure had ceased to buy and Chocquet was definitely more interested in Renoir and Cézanne.

His prices reduced to half, a third, sometimes even a fifth, of previously modest levels, Monet brought himself down into the realm of lesser figures who bought from Pissarro and Renoir. Among them was the pastry cook and writer Eugène Murer, who on December 20 purchased four canvases at 50 francs each. The basic economic dilemma was never resolved. Always Monet was forced to improvise among short-term measures. Two days before selling his works to Murer, he had written to Murer's friend, the Auvers physician Paul Ferdinand Gachet.

MONSIEUR,

If you had the time, and if you really wished to come see me, I would be at home, 17 rue Moncey, tomorrow, Wednesday, from 10.30 to 11.30 and from 1 to 2.

I would be happy to let you see what I have, and if you find something to your taste you will find me very accommodating, and the more so when a financial embarrassment is upon me which I must discharge tomorrow without fail, under pain of the most grave consequences.

I hope therefore to see you tomorrow morning.

Believe my distinguished sentiments,

CLAUDE MONET

Tuesday, 18 December 1877.

Christmas, and the New Year, that season to which he always had been so sensitive, sharply outlined his tortuous state. When a more gracious Édouard Manet paid a seasonal call at the Rue d'Edimbourg apartment, he found Monet in complete despair. Desolated as he was, Monet was ready to propose a scheme parallel to that previously offered de Bellio. The next day Manet wrote to Théodore Duret, the only person he thought might be interested:

Wednesday

MY DEAR DURET,

I went to see Monet yesterday. I found him quite broken down and in despair. He asked me to find someone who will take ten or twenty of his pictures at 10 francs each, the purchaser to choose which he liked. Shall we arrange the matter between us, say 500 francs each?

Of course no one, he least of all, must know that the offer came from us. I had thought of some dealer or collector, but I foresaw the possibility of a refusal. It is unhappily necessary to be as well informed as we are, in order to effect in spite of the repugnance one may feel, an excellent business transaction, and, at the same time, to do a good turn to a man of talent.

Answer me as soon as possible, or make an appointment with me.

Kind regards,

ED. MANET

Though Duret already possessed a few examples of Monet's work, he did not take part in Manet's proposal. In his place Manet next approached Ernest Hoschedé. To reveal to this important patron the plight to which Monet had fallen, or the severely reduced prices he would accept, was perhaps not discreet, especially because Hoschedé's interest in Monet had abated. Whether he knew of, or resented, the artist's closeness with his wife, or merely was feeling the extent of his own financial reverses, is uncertain. With bland man-of-the-world skill Hoschedé pushed the burden back onto the shoulders of Édouard Manet by sending him part of a small balance: "Here are two hundred francs which came to me yesterday by magic. Have you an absolute need of the other hundred this morning?"

Unwilling to participate, Hoschedé took delight in implying that Manet should proceed alone. "Could you not by chance negotiate the two thousand two hundred francs in goods that Zacharie Astruc [owes] you without a hullabaloo? You said, it seems to me, that you have a banker who discounts your note." The precise transaction to which Hoschedé referred is as obscure as the action Édouard Manet took is clear, for nobility of sentiment was not absent from his frockcoated breast. Unwilling to allow the New Year to pass without granting Monet an alleviation of his suffering, Manet executed a note in his favor, which was brought to his bank to be discounted:

On the fifteenth of March following I will pay M. Claude Monet or to his order the sum of two thousand francs, against merchandise.

ÉDOUARD MANET

49, rue de St.-Petersburg

Paris

Whatever popular odium operated against Monet continued still in its work. The shrill call of the begging artist was all that issued from his pen. That secondary surprise, always occasioned by the disappearance of sums as large as that given him by Manet, was lost in the din of his anguished cries. Something uniquely pathetic exists in a man who has called wolf too often, and whose most heartrending sufferings go unheard. Monet had put himself in that bizarrely unhappy situation. Only those who had not suffered from the continuous crises at Argenteuil could still be approached. These newer purchasers unfortunately dealt only in the smaller sums for which he had been forced to take up begging. Gachet was among them:

> 17, rue Moncey
> Saturday night, February 9 [1878]

DEAR MONSIEUR GACHET,

I am going to tell you my embarrassment courageously, and ask you a new service.

The doctor who visited my wife today, announces to us the event for tomorrow or the day after. I am all in panic because I have not a penny and we lack even the things of most pressing necessity. Knowing your kindness and your interest in my welfare, I have thought that in such circumstances I could again address myself to you even though I am already in your debt for one hundred francs.

I have already so much tormented my usual patrons that I do not know to whom I can address myself.

Would you again advance me one hundred francs and come to see me soon at Paris so that I may pay you in paintings. In that way you will render me a great service and at the same time contribute to the courage and security of my poor wife who torments herself for not having necessities for this great event.

A word of response by post, and excuse me without ill feeling.

> Regards,
> CLAUDE MONET

In response Gachet followed a normal pattern by sending half the sum asked, an eventuality for which Monet had compensated in advance by asking 100 francs for a canvas he was then selling at 50. After three years of abusing his victims by these tactics it was undeniable that he had become an even more pathetic ogre, whose baleful glance was now bereft of its magic power to frighten patrons into a state of charity.

20. *The Last Favor*

CAMILLE'S BRUISED BODY, insufficiently strong for this ordeal she was about to undergo, in February betrayed further signs of weakness which the doctor interpreted as the onset of birth pains. This proved incorrect. Pale, weak, with darkening patches spreading across the hollows of her eyes, she carried her unborn child into March, 1878. Finally, on the seventeenth, she was delivered of a fine healthy boy, who on entering the lives of his parents, complicated beyond measure their already meager existence.

The birth of a son was worthy of congratulation, and at the scene of delivery, in the Rue d'Edimbourg apartment, Édouard Manet dispensed witty good cheer. In company with another well-wisher, the composer Alexis Emmanuel Chabrier, Manet then went to the Mairie of the eighth arrondissement where he registered and attested the birth of Michel Jacques Monet. Whatever comfort she derived from these proud scenes, Camille was unable to recover. On April 7 a call went out to Émile Zola:

> Can you help me? We do not have a single penny in the house, not even anything to keep the pot boiling today. On top of this my wife is ailing and needs care, for, as perhaps you know, she has given birth to a superb boy. Could you loan me two or even three louis, or even only one? . . .
>
> I ran around all day yesterday without being able to find a penny. . . .

Thoughts of painting were abandoned while Monet, assisted by little Jean, cared for mother and infant. "I am unable to work as much as I would wish," he apologized to Eugène Murer four days later, unable to give him canvases for money advanced. "One day it is the weather which is not propitious, then the household tasks recall me to reality. Then, as perhaps you know, my wife has been delivered of a beautiful boy, and for two weeks I have had to look after the patient. Impossible to think of painting at such a time." A month of pain and tedium passed. Camille's condition showed no improvement and Monet was unable to leave her. On May 16 words of embarrassed pleading went out to Georges de Bellio:

> It is not because you have had the graciousness to tell me that you will always have a louis at my disposal that I am coming to you to ask for it. . . . I do not wish to abuse and I assure you that it is only because I am very much in need today that I ask it.

Ernest Hoschedé's unwillingness to assist Monet was a confirmed principle. Stories had spread about his financial reverses, which for some time he had been hiding. No one, however, was prepared for his sudden bankruptcy, or the ensuing sale of his collection, which took place at the Hôtel Drouot, June 5 and 6, 1878. At disastrously reduced prices five important works by Manet, twelve by Monet, and examples by Berthe Morisot, Pissarro, Renoir, and Sisley were thrown on the market. Of Pissarro's nine canvases only one reached 100 francs. Eight hundred was the highest figure realized by Manet. Monet varied between 60 and 250 francs, the early view of *Saint-Germain l'Auxerrois* alone fetching the higher sum of 505 francs. Georges de Bellio profited by purchasing the famous *Impression* for 210 francs, and other canvases among those that failed to reach 100 francs may have been bought by Eugène Murer.

Ernest Hoschedé himself took leave of that scene of public and domestic drama. Departing France alone, he opened a new business in Brussels, where he retired into an amalgam of myth, personality, and legend. At Paris his wife carried on without him, existing on the limited resources provided by her dowry. Plucky and resourceful, Alice Hoschedé became a dressmaker to those she formerly had entertained in regal fashion, assuming responsibility for the education of four daughters, an older son, and the year-old infant, Jean-Pierre. But the departure of her husband left her exposed to scandal, and from a climate of wagging tongues, now fully unleashed, Monet was forced to consider retreat. In every way his return to Paris from Argenteuil had been disastrous. But after the too obvious freedom of Alice Hoschedé contributed new fuel to dangerous gossip, to tarry further in that barren city became reckless.

Anxiously weighing departure, at the end of June Monet was still in Paris, where gaudy decorations rose into place for the first National Festival since an ill-fated war. Marking also the opening of an International Exposition, astonishing displays of flags changed the city's aspect. They created a climate of jollity and affection and, in their hearty—indeed, positively boisterous—style, became a direct inspiration to paint. So rarely free to exercise his skill, Monet set out with his equipment down the Rue Montorgeuil. Huge crowds made it impossible to set up his easel: "The street was decked with flags, but swarming with people. I spied a balcony, mounted the stairs and asked permission to paint. It was granted. . . ." In the next days he repeated this procedure in the Rue St.-Denis, twice creating garish rapid sketches containing many incidental beauties apart from their strange bursting momentum.

A last effort to portray the moods of his "native" city, these sketches were followed by wild unconsidered flight. Nor had he even the funds sufficient for that. A note of warning was dispatched:

DEAR MONSIEUR MURER,

Two words only to forewarn you that I will come to see you tomorrow, Saturday, in the afternoon, towards 4 or 5 o'clock.

Perhaps I will have a service to ask of you.

Kindest regards,

CLAUDE MONET

Friday night

But on this visit he never found courage to tell Murer the purpose of his trip. Sunday morning, his furniture being carried to a van, he was forced to write again:

DEAR MONSIEUR,

As I wrote to you, I came to ask another service yet did not dare— and here I am in a cruel situation, our furniture loaded on the wagon, but nothing with which to pay the moving man, not a penny.

Would you render me the greatest service, and advance me one hundred francs, without which I do not know what to do. If you do not have this sum, give the messenger what you can, but try to make the hundred francs.

I hope that you will not refuse me, and I thank you in advance. My best to you,

CLAUDE MONET

Sunday morning.

Brokenhearted, unable to refuse her husband the consolation he sought, at thirty-one Camille had been worn down into an old woman without ever managing to find security. Her impending end was a matter for much sadness and heart-searching as for the last time she accompanied her husband on a journey. With Jean and three-month-old Michel, they may temporarily have halted at Argenteuil, but finally, that winter of 1878, arrived at Vétheuil, on the river loop that flowed north past Bonnières. Here again they became established in a tiny house facing the river, but with none of the optimism that had accompanied their earlier arrival at Argenteuil. The six years between had seen the wreck of every hope, and the dissipation of every resource.

Hardly were they settled when it became necessary for Monet to begin long journeys back to Paris, adopting always the same shabby tactics that forced pictures on unwilling patrons. When they learned who was at the door, people often sent out word they were not at home. This may have been done by Charpentier. Monet wrote to him:

> I came to your house this morning in the hope of doing a little business, just so that I would not have to return without money. I was not able to see you and regret it very much. I am sending you a canvas that I think should please you. I ask you 150 francs for it, and if that should seem too high, 100 francs, which I hope you will be able to send me at Vétheuil, Seine et Oise.
>
> If the canvas does not suit you, when I come back I will make an exchange.
>
> My thanks in advance. With regards,
>
> CLAUDE MONET
>
> P.S. I believe I can ask you this because it is such a long time since you gave me hope you would buy something from me.

His visits to Paris served other purposes too, for Alice Hoschedé remained there with her children. That he saw them is certain. The exact date of one call, December 31, 1878, is inscribed on the sketch portrait of Jean-Pierre he presented to Alice Hoschedé for his New Year gift. As her life ebbed away, Camille's place was already ceded to another, in whom her husband found that same blend of earthiness and sophistication compounded in fascinating proportions.

For a short time that winter he even took heart. Was it Mme.

Hoschedé, with her sound department-store training, who reproached him for permitting prices to fall? Through all the years of his relationship with Camille his price structure had been haphazard. But when unexpectedly Dr. Gachet and Eugène Murer arrived at Vétheuil, to demand canvases for which they had paid in advance, he was inclined to reproach them in terms never before heard.

Vétheuil, December 18, 1878

Monsieur Murer,

I was surprised, I admit it, to see you accompany the doctor because I was actually thinking of writing to you. But that particular day I was so despoiled of canvases that his visit disconcerted me. I put no blame for that upon you, please believe me, and am enchanted that even so you have each found a canvas to your taste.

Only, I will be very obliged if when you will see Monsieur Gachet, say to him, that on my first trip, if it is a little more fruitful than this last, I will return to him the hundred francs that I still owe him. It would have been in bad grace for me to refuse him a canvas, but I could not give him two others in these conditions.

I have already done myself much harm by not selling them more dear, and in these conditions it is certain that I must resign myself to dying of starvation. With you it is another thing because it was agreed and accepted in advance, but would you not wish, the next time you choose, to look among canvases of smaller dimensions. This present occasion, having so few things among which to choose, I was not able to make this condition, even though I ought to have made you wait.

You will understand this, I hope, because you would not put me in the position of making you a gift.

Believe in my distinguished sentiments,

Claude Monet

P.S. I have not been able to come to you. I was already on my way when your letter arrived.

What broke the back of his brave new resolution is that a Vétheuil "period" never got started. Through the late autumn he had made despairing efforts, painting at least one still life in which chrysanthemums found stunning balance before the less vivacious flowers on wallpaper. On his unexpected visit Dr. Gachet had carried this off. And though the Argenteuil studio-boat had miraculously reappeared, Monet's further efforts were snow scenes that sounded tones of personal lament. Everything became monotones of gray, the colors of cigarette ash and mashed newspapers.

Stalking across the river on broken ice, overwhelmed by the friendless winter landscape, his own pathos was painted into the declining ball of the sun. Snow scenes always had represented the ultimate scope of his own desolated emotions. At the New Year Monet wrote to Georges de Bellio:

> I have come to an age when I am no longer a beginner, and it is sad to be at my age in such a condition, obliged always to ask, to beg sales. My misfortunes weigh on me doubly at this time of the year, and 79 is going to begin just as this year has finished, very sad above all for my family, to whom I cannot make even the most modest present.

The months of winter and spring passed. Once fresh and youthful, shy and loving, Camille declined in a sickening intensification of symptoms. Unable to look after her sons, that task fell to her husband, on whom descended a final, full realization of her fate.

He understood at last that everything for which they had worked and hoped through fourteen years was ebbing away in tragicomic self-deception, pointless suffering, and death. Once a common sight on the streets of Paris, come to town with a canvas under each arm to be forced on unhappy collectors, now he ceased to be seen. Occupied by the care of an infant and his stricken wife, he also ceased to work. Utter demoralization followed, introducing a mental state in which he abandoned the outside world, which, in turn, left him on the periphery of events.

He saw no one; letters remained unanswered. Camille's last bits of jewelry were pawned, including the gold locket she wore at her throat. Even the call to a new exhibition of the impressionists failed to rouse him. Sisley and Renoir already had announced their abstention because they wished to submit to the Salon. Unwilling to leave Monet unrepresented, Caillebotte made the enormous effort of gathering together twenty-nine works. He attended to their framing, and shipped them to 28 Avenue de l'Opéra, where the exhibition was held. That one of the earliest works was borrowed from Paul Eugène Lecadre raises hope that in this extremity Monet's family might again have re-established contact with him. But they did not.

Immediately after the opening, April 10, 1879, Caillebotte wrote

Monet eager, approving, half-jocular letters, intended to bring good cheer to Vétheuil. "We are saved. By five o'clock this afternoon the receipts were more than 400 francs. . . ." "The receipts continue good," Caillebotte wrote again, May 1. "We now have about 10,500 francs. As for the public—always in a gay mood. People have a good time with us. . . ." The exhibition, in fact, seemed unusually well attended, and after expenses were paid, an excess of over 6,000 francs remained, for division at 439 francs each among the sixteen participants. Monet's share was increased by half the sum due Mary Cassatt, an American who had taken part, and who purchased one of Monet's works.

Such mild hope could bring no alleviation of suffering to that bleak house at Vétheuil. Monet never left to see the exhibition. His state of gnawing, ever-present misery found no consolation from any source. One had always believed that his most striking feature, and greatest strength, had been that he never at any time felt a tremor of affection for any other human being. All that was overcome. His emotions first had strangled him, then left him in a state of obsessive, almost hallucinatory fatigue, tired of life, struggle, misfortune, begging, and want.

There was no hope; everything was an illusion. The life he too long had led, the prolonged torment of Camille, who now seemed unacceptable either to life or death, had shattered and overwhelmed him. To de Bellio he wrote bitter lines:

March 10, 1879

I am completely demoralized from this existence that I have followed for so long. When someone is like this at my age there is nothing more to hope for. Unfortunate we are, unfortunate we remain.

Each day brings its pains and each day there surges up some difficulty from which we can never escape. I give up the struggle and all hope of arriving and no longer feel the strength to work in such conditions.

Repeated inquiries from Charpentier finally brought response:

I hardly know what to say that you already do not know. That is to say that for a very long time I have been in misery and found it impossible to work, and all my time is passed in taking care of my wife and our little baby. You know all that and that I have not been able to exhibit a single new canvas and that for a long time I have been unable to show anything to anyone. You must also know that it has been impossible for me to leave here, not even to see our exhibition. I am in the wrong with your letters, but I have had so many torments and anxieties that I perhaps lost my head. . . .

Through the summer of 1879 Camille's life ebbed away. Early the morning of September 4 her husband looked at her, and found that she was dead. At daybreak he began to sketch the silver mask of death formed by her rigid, grotesquely emaciated features. The open jaw betrayed a low glint of irregular teeth, and mechanically he sought the sequence of tones across her forehead. His obsessive task nearly was done before some outer reality caught him up. With sudden horror he realized in what act he was engaged, and that he had become a prisoner of his visual experiences, whose lot was no better than that of a beast in a treadmill, forever running forward.

Whether he ever had truly loved Camille in life, it was undoubtedly true that he loved her now. The sympathy which in her lifetime had been hers thus flowed to him after her death when he was tortured by remorse. Grief-stricken and alone, that same day he summoned the courage to write de Bellio: "What a sad situation is mine, alone with two children, without resources, without a penny before me—and what is to become of me if someone like yourself does not come to my aid."

And though this was only one more among hundreds of supplicating letters he had written, that day also he thought of the life from which Camille had come, and the agonized death to which she had gone. The burial she would have on what money he could beg in every respect would be unworthy of her. He thought too of a locket he had taken from her, to pawn in Paris, and the following day, September 5, 1879, wrote again to de Bellio: "I am going to ask of you a new service, to get back from the Municipal Pawn Shop the medallion for which I send you the ticket. It is the last souvenir my wife had been able to keep, and I would like to put it around her neck before burying her."

Camille was laid to rest in the little walled cemetery crowning the hill at Vétheuil. There summer suns, the rains of autumn and winter snows still beat on her, though precisely where she lies is lost among broken and unmarked graves. Should reflection fall on that half of Camille's dowry her mother had found means not to pay, or that Mme. Doncieux lived on in a condition of impeccable bourgeois luxury, an inescapable and eerie sensation arises that Camille's death at thirty-two was the unnecessarily barbaric ritual murder of a girl who by her love had offended the standards of her class. Nor perhaps should it be ignored that by her long and painful death Camille Léonie Doncieux rendered one last service to the man whom she so dearly loved. Her final act of parting left Monet free to attach to himself another woman with dowry, as he did within the year.

Entr'acte

Impressionism: A Definition

THE LACK OF CONVENTION in Monet's training and youthfully un-disciplined personality allowed him untrammeled freedom to in-dulge in breathtaking harmonies and modulations of color. Deliber-ately pushed to their utmost limits at Argenteuil, these created such tension that they produced a wholly new technique. "Impressionism" was only a derisive and haphazard title given this art, but soon it was accepted and nailed to the masthead forever.

Public and critics reacted savagely, but what exact qualities set apart these new pictures eluded the nineteenth century just as it has scholars, critics and writers since. Definitions that abounded, be-cause they lacked technical understanding, inclined to be mere descriptions. Castagnary's effort was no more efficacious than "They are impressionists in the sense that they render not a landscape but the sensation produced by a landscape." Corot, Daubigny, Turner, or even Fragonard, all of whom at times gave this sort of evocation, might equally well have been in his mind, though demonstrably none of them were impressionists. Renoir's friend Georges Rivière made another attempt: "Treating a subject in terms of the tone and not the subject itself, this is what distinguishes the impressionists from other painters." Closer, surely; but by following this descrip-tion it becomes impossible to distinguish a late Velasquez or an atmospheric Guardi Venetian scene from an impressionist picture.

Nor was impressionism any use or new stress laid on local color, as has been suggested more recently. The presence of olive in the flesh of Byzantine mosaics, as a half tone associated with the more conven-tional pink, was a formalized carry-over from ancient paintings, where local color had been noted and employed to bring greater reality. It is equally present throughout works from the late Italian Renaissance, and descriptions of Titian's finishing pictures with his fingers verifies that it was these small modulations of hue he sought to capture.

In fifteenth-century France Corneille de Lyon painted heads (like that of Louis de Rieux in the Louvre) with half tones of strong blue. The effect is stunning, and later Rubens and Van Dyck also employed areas of blue in flesh painting. Jacob Jordaens similarly made regular use of purple as his transition into shadow. Studying the example of Van Dyck, Sir Joshua Reynolds, Gainsborough, Romney and Lawrence made the habit a normal usage in England, and Gilbert Stuart brought it to America, where by eliminating brown from his visible color components he advanced halfway down the road to impressionism. Certainly no one in the nineteenth century reacted very violently to local color, and the further failure of this theory is that the impressionists obviously were dealing with generalities and broadness of vision rather than perception of hue changes in small areas.

Yet the impressionists were not uninfluenced by the new movements and dogmas of their century, and the discovery of varied tones within color areas previously been considered a single hue was establishing new trends. Commissioned to do a ceiling for the Louvre in 1835, Léon Cogniet painted Napoleon inspecting finds of Egyptian art made by his army, creating an extraordinary study of light and irradiated desert haze. Troops, tents, statues, and the forms of landscape are all dissolved. Nearer to the foreground amber draperies under which Bonaparte stands turn orange in folds and ocular gray-blue in cast shadows.

A perfectly trained academic artist like Michel-Martin Drolling, who in 1850 painted murals for the church of St.-Sulpice, also could brush extraordinarily naturalistic sunlight. Under its rays solid stone turns the color of warm cream, and clear blue shadows abound. Color, and the true color of all things in nature, carefully examined and carefully painted, by the middle of the nineteenth century was part of established procedure. Impressionism, therefore, was not local color, the painting of sunlight, or any degree of concentration on these. Nor was it division of color, which Monet never employed; nor in 1880 had Monet yet concentrated upon ocular phenomena, though this later became a part of his practice. A workable definition does not lie here.

Impressionism, though it grew out of materials and concepts present everywhere in the nineteenth century, can only be understood as the creation of one man. Had Claude Monet not developed it, undoubtedly this art would have come into existence without him. Nor can one avoid the feeling that in other hands its birth would have been less clouded by difficulties, for the same components might have been joined together differently. As historical fact, however, it was the chance combination of four factors—(1) the new chemically created colors available to artists in the nineteenth century, (2) economic pressures on Monet, (3) Monet's personal inclination to attract attention by shock tactics, and (4) Monet's special genius with color—that forced the coalescence, perhaps prematurely, of this forceful new art. And the character of impressionism bears the mark of its creator.

For years in advance Monet's canvases had contained ravishing passages of poetic feeling, beside areas crudely impasted and unfelt. Sheer enthusiasm and extrovert dash had accounted for the best of his painting, though everywhere are warm, melodious, and genially tempered passages. His larger efforts were suitably lavish and ingenious, without ever reaching stylistic distinction, and frequently they are blemished by faulty control of technique and basic naïvetés. Characteristic of Monet's inclinations and economic circumstances is that, constantly working out of doors with the stronger colors provided by nineteenth-century technology, he sought methods leading to a fluent, accurate, and exciting manner.

It was the arbitrary limiting of colors on his palette that forced Monet into a position from which he made startling discoveries. Without black and brown he required an alternate means of creating the strong tones and accents they alone had supplied artists for centuries. From such alternate methods impressionism was born. The actual chromatic development is clear from a comparison of colors Monet requested from Bazille in 1868 (probably incomplete— note the absence of green) with the notation: "Send me quantities of the first four colors, it is of these I have the most need":

ivory black
lead white
cobalt blue
fine lake
yellow ocher
burnt ocher
brilliant yellow
Naples yellow
burnt sienna

and two available lists of the colors he used for *impressionist* painting as preserved by, respectively, Tabarant and Gimpel:

white lead	cobalt blue
cadmium yellow (light, dark, and lemon)	ultramarine blue
ultramarine lemon yellow	violet
vermilion	vermilion
cobalt violet (light)	ocher
superfine ultramarine	orange
viridian	dark green
	another green (not light)
	white

The second of these, representing what Gimpel recognized on Monet's palette in 1920, understandably is less accurate in names. However, comparing these two lists with the first, it becomes clear that black, burnt sienna, burnt ocher, and possibly others in that same dark range have been eliminated. On both these later lists are found the synthetic colors with which chemistry had equipped Monet's generation: cadmium yellow in three grades (probably including what Gimpel listed as "orange"), cobalt violet, and viridian. Examination of Monet's pictures implies that some strong synthetic red also was employed, probably alizarin. This and other observations are verified further by the list of colors Monet sent Georges Durand-Ruel in 1905.

Briefly I serve myself with lead white, cadmium yellow, vermilion, dark madder, cobalt blue, verte émeraude, and nothing more.

Comparison with Pissarro's equally simplified palette, showing the same absence of black and brown and predominance of synthetic colors, only stresses the point:

white lead
light chrome yellow
Veronese green
ultramarine or cobalt blue
dark madder lake
vermilion

Monet's world-shaking discovery was the entire realm of high-keyed synthetic coloration that from this point evolved on his palette and proliferated on his canvases. Where burnt umber traditionally had provided somber contrasts, now chemically created dark madder or alizarin crimson (or dark madder lake for Pissarro; Renoir used superfine carmine, Venetian red, French vermilion, and madder lake!), when taken onto a brush already loaded with ultramarine blue or chemically created viridian green, gave a new effect that crackled electrically. Because brown and black no longer were present to sully the clarity of colors, the tone of his painting rose astonishingly. And the constant necessary improvisations of color developed in Monet a new mastery that produced harmonic changes of extraordinary ingenuity. After centuries of dominance by gray or brown gammas, pictures now sang in clear tones of green, lavender, or pink. They also gained an evocative new atmospheric power, and Monet's canvases greatly increased their power to transmit searing images.

Impressionism thus was a complete break with the basic brown or gray tonality common to all painting for nearly five hundred years. And the blaze of color was decidedly shocking, for this new tonal language accomplished the impossible. It broke through barriers to an art totally new, producing pictures whose unexpected reality and hallucinatory power persuaded the world it was undergoing a revelatory experience.

Unlike other epoch-making discoveries, impressionism has never been fully dissociated from the man who created it, and ever since it has been confused with the personal mannerisms of its creator. Because Monet's wasted youth had left him a poor craftsman, because his drawing was weak, because canvases were developed by planes instead of lines, he inclined to be hasty in execution, was more a sketcher than a painter of finished works, and worked predominantly out of doors, these have been considered the basic features of the art. In fact they are only Monet's scrappy and ill-assorted usages of a transcending discovery whose capabilities they limited rather than exploited.

Renoir soon showed the further potential of this art by demonstrating its capacities in portraits and figures. By bringing to it his own marvelous craftsmanship, in the eighties John Singer Sargent demonstrated its fullest capacity and forced it directly into the academies. That Sargent did so while employing Monet's own limited palette, and synthetic coloration, proves that only Monet's inferior craftsmanship had made his stupendous discovery unacceptable from his own hands.

Impressionism was so badly received at its birth not because of the originality of its achievement, nor because of Monet's own superior creativity. Indeed, that quality alone was to save him from extinction. It was his wasted youth—his failure to acquire competent craftsmanship, his inability to paint with even the minimum proficiency possessed by Beaux-Arts students—that was responsible for his continuous rebuffs. Monet's greatest failure was that while deploring the training of his contemporaries he never learned to control his own brush. He wasted his genius by not disciplining his style nor acquiring real craftsmanship, and the paradoxical conclusion was that when he made discoveries of magnificent and shocking power, public and critics alike were unable to distinguish between them and the crudities of his personal style. That condition still exists.

Separated from the clutter of Monet's personal manner of painting, the essential components of impressionism are:

(1) the elimination of black and brown from the palette
(2) the development of synthetic accents of greater strength, from combinations of the new chemically produced colors available in the nineteenth century
(3) the creation by these means of pictures entirely formed of clear colors and their mixtures, with a consequent increase in color strength, purity, and brilliance

The definition of impressionism is: An art employing chemically constituted pigments to create a synthetic coloration and more powerful accents without the use of black or brown.

Part Four

AN

INVERTED

MIRACLE

21. Joint Ménage

CAMILLE'S DEATH marked a midpoint in the life of Claude Monet. It occurred when he was thirty-nine, and had reached almost halfway in the long span of years allotted him. It came at a time when he had reached lowest ebb, and shortly would shoot upward like a meteor. It ended one phase of his existence and clearly began another. More precisely, it provided the final titanic shock which wrenched from him the psychological bonds that had both provided the basis of his art and prescribed its limits. For if his special genius had been formed in pain, anguish, deprivation, disgrace, and despair, it was renewed through this death and the torments of remorse that followed.

The long ordeal had created psychic disturbances too deep for him to cope with ordinary reality. Alice Hoschedé saw this fearful circumstance, if not its full proportion. Warm in her sympathies, she eased his situation by taking his two sons to Paris, where they were fed and cared for in the companionship of her own children. Alone at Vétheuil, Monet was gripped in a state of numbed shock too enveloping to report the death, or remember correctly on what date it had occurred. Only this suggestive detail externalizes his traumatized condition. All else is shrouded in silence: He saw no one, wrote no letters. He passed his days consumed by a remorse shared only with the bleakness of early winter.

From these months of intense self-hatred and the frozen, helpless rages of a man reduced to a pathetic hulk by suffering arose the permanent impairment of his human resources. An essential part of his personality had died with Camille. The young, hardy, luckless artist, painting his crude but marvelously inventive canvases, had disappeared into the grave with her, never to re-emerge. After that devastating autumn and winter of 1879, by a fantastic exertion of will, Monet shook off external symptoms of his state. What then emerged was another man, battered and shrewd, who viewed the world with feelings profoundly corrupted. By Christmas this new Claude Monet picked up the career of the old, rebuilding it on a distorted basis of tragedy.

For the first time in a year he ventured outdoors to paint, making a focal point of the church beside which Camille lay buried. Direct emotional linkage with his subject found further expression in empty foregrounds, and the vacant quality of an unusual upright composition built of river weeds and trees wobbling into Japanese balance. Developed of close harmonies, and so expressive of isolation, only his suppleness and control, and an insistence on dappled and bouncing banks of cloud, prevented these canvases from sounding a dirge.

His further effort was a large still life, and when this appeared successful, he would surely have done more had not a new storm of debt, stored up since the previous year, broken over his head with threats of seizure and expulsion from his house. One expects that he will topple again into helpless gloom. Instead he responded nearly as of old. Renewed crisis coincided with a strong desire to pass New Year's Day with his sons. To this end he gathered strength and found older canvases for a desperate campaign. His methods would be the only ones he knew:

Vétheuil, December 28, 1879

DEAR M. CHOCQUET,

I am going to pass two days in Paris. I bring a certain number of new canvases which I will be very happy to show you.

If therefore you have a moment free, you will give me much pleasure to come see me at 20 rue de Vintimille, where I will be tomorrow, Monday, and Tuesday, from 1 to 3.

Believe in my best sentiments and pray remember me also to Madame.

Best wishes,

CLAUDE MONET

The same hesitant air fills another note dispatched to Charpentier:

I am going to arrive with a certain quantity of canvases. Will you refuse to come see them? I hope you still bear me enough interest and sympathy and that you will answer my appeal by coming to see me tomorrow, Tuesday, 20, rue de Vintimille. I will be there until five o'clock.

His mornings were kept free for visits to those who failed to call on him. Then he employed his eloquent, intense performances, contrived to create a pity that loosened purse strings. Many doubtless felt he was melodramatic; more in Paris experienced a distaste at receiving this strange painter whose dalliance had destroyed the Hoschedé marriage. Certainly Faure, the baritone, approached once more by this shabby artist surrounded in unchaste rumor, found no other means to treat him than with the dreariest of comic affectation.

"I am glad to see you, dear friend, above all if you are bringing me a masterpiece," that elegant celebrity began.

"I do not know. I have done my best," was the artist's reply. His initial reaction was one of incredulity mixed with despair, for his dramatic air made no impression on the singer.

"Let us see. Ah-hah!" said Faure, looking over the proffered canvas with his connoisseur's air. "But that will not do at all, my dear boy. If I buy your pictures without bargaining, they must have some paint on them. You've forgotten, obviously. Nothing but canvas. That's not enough. Take it away. Put some paint on it and I will buy it, maybe. . . . You see, I'm a good fellow, eh?"

The air was thick with deliberate Philistinism, a harsh discord against Monet's enervated presence. Faure sensed the false note he had struck, and in a slightly more serious tone asked, "As a matter of fact, now, can you tell me, what do you think that represents?"

Monet's effort to reply without betraying his irritation was not entirely successful.

"I do not think. I know that it represents sunrise in the fog at Vétheuil, on the Seine. I was out early in my little rowboat, waiting for the effect of the light. The sun appeared, and I—at risk of your displeasure—I painted what I saw. This is perhaps why you do not like it."

Faure weakened, but his resolve not to be played upon by Monet's dramatics held him firm.

"Ah! Ah! I understand very well now. You have to know. Ah, yes.

"N'ayant pas reçu ce matin de réponse . . ." Monet's ordeals are visible in the deterioration of his usually bold script.

The Seine. And the mist which at first rays of light muddles the view. You cannot see very well. But that is the fault of the fog, is it not? . . . Just the same, there is not enough paint on it. Put a little more paint on it and I might very well buy it."

Of those patrons among whom formerly he had been able to make his rounds only Georges de Bellio remained, and to him a note was dispatched.

> I am going to propose something to you—three canvases that I will let you have for 200 francs, of which the first, Le Dégel, is one of the best canvases that I have brought back. I would also let you have them for 150 francs if it is necessary.

Even de Bellio, whose Romanian accents seemed always to be proclaiming a breadth of sympathy that had vanished elsewhere in Monet's relationships, failed to reply. By Friday Monet could wait no longer, and wrote again:

> Friday 1.30
>
> DEAR MONSIEUR DE BELLIO,
> Not having received a response by this morning to my letter I must press on in all haste to supplicate you not to abandon me, but I have not the courage to present myself before you because at bottom I am in a more pitiful state than you think. It is most unfortunate but do not refuse me because I must return immediately to Vétheuil, otherwise I lose all courage and there is nothing more than an intolerable existence.
> With thanks . . .
>
> CLAUDE MONET

De Bellio came to the Rue de Vintimille address, and when he did, combining generosity with nobility of spirit, he had the grace to refuse his advantage. Among three canvases offered him he found one view of Vétheuil most pleasing, and for this he gave Monet the 150 francs asked for all three.

An efficient style of villainous salesmanship no longer was possible. All the self-dramatization of the past years had numbed his collectors to further pleas. Bourgeois values also were arrayed against him, for his role in the frightful Hoschedé marital fracture had made him socially unacceptable. Even when mixed with the new stridency—which, however unintentionally a guide to his character and conditions, was at times unfortunate—the old tactics of personal assault and pity-seeking were useless.

Shattered by the indifference of all those on whom he had counted, Monet realized that new methods were required. To improvise them was less facile, and in his uncertainty, for the first time since before 1870, he exerted himself to contact dealers. Among these was Arnold & Tripp, at whose premises he was left to stand in a vestibule while the two partners and their staff examined his canvases.

"These are by Monet, the impressionist. Is he not absurd?" he heard them laugh aloud.

The curtain was lifted for curious eyes to peer at him before his works were returned.

A man of greater discernment and more sound business sense was Georges Petit, Durand-Ruel's principal rival, whose reputation he plotted ceaselessly to destroy. Petit expressed willingness to make purchases from Monet on the double condition that he submit to the Salon and maintain a level of prices. Durand-Ruel's contrary method of advancing his artists by private exhibitions, and avoiding the Salon, had proved fruitless. His large stocks hidden away and now out of date, he had succeeded only in isolating the impressionists from a great new wave of patronage sweeping France.

Petit immediately purchased from Monet two canvases for 800 francs. In return Monet adopted the new philosophy entirely. His private patronage gone, Durand-Ruel useless to him, he saw himself in a position of non-alignment, unenvious and unenvied, inoffensive, but ready to consort with all parties to assist in his sales. The upheaval in his ideas was unconstrained, but did not offer the consolation of greater intellectual credibility. A not especially illuminating account was penned on his return to Vétheuil:

Vétheuil, January 8, 1880

DEAR M. DE BELLIO,

I am going to tell you some good news—I have sold to M. Petit at the price of 500 francs the still life that you saw, and also a snow scene for 300 francs, with promises of new purchases. It is a good thing, because M. Petit has found my canvases to his taste. I must only warn you that he has strongly recommended to me no longer to sell so cheaply. It is on this condition that he will do new business with me.

It cuts me to be obliged to say this to you who have been so helpful to me, but you will understand yourself that at the prices at which I have sold my canvases it would take me four months to begin to make a living and to pay for my canvases and colors. You have a nice enough collection of my pictures so that in future you can buy a few less and pay a little more. You will always remain the first to whom I will show my canvases because I will not forget how often you have pulled me out of embarrassment.

I cannot refuse you the other pleasure of selling you that view of Vétheuil for 150 francs and I do not regret it, having suffered myself to see the best and most important of my canvases sold at such low prices . . . but all that will be nothing if, as I hope, M. Petit will give me a pat on the shoulder.

We have had here a terrible ice jam and naturally I have put in motion some things that I will offer you on my next trip.

Please accept my many compliments and all my best wishes for the New Year.

With regards,

CLAUDE MONET

The incidents of this period are small, hardly dissociated from the tenor of what had passed before. But already they exemplify Monet's habit, abundantly illustrated later, of identifying the good not with an objective principle but with his own personality and material requirements. This included the habit of adopting a cynical, almost malicious attitude, and was unprettily expressed to an impatient patron (probably Dr. Gachet) who during the previous winter had advanced him sums totaling 400 francs:

There is a very simple way to have your canvases if you are apprehensive that I myself will not hand them over to you. It is to give the matter into the hands of a bailiff. I am stunned that you have not had that idea. But I will freely spare you all such bothers as soon as possible. It is therefore absolutely useless for you to take the pains to stop at Vétheuil . . . not being in my house it will be impossible for me to receive you. And it may be that way because I am in the midst of so many troubles I never know where I will be the next day.

The important thing being for you to have your canvases, it will suffice you to know that I will see to it that they are given to you with all possible speed, in order quickly to make an end to relations between us.

This same inflexible new order in Monet's affairs was illustrated by two related episodes. Like Renoir and Sisley, who since 1879 had renounced participation in the impressionist exhibitions, Monet was heard to speak uncharitably of new members introduced by Degas and Pissarro. An embroilment thriving on frantic invective and obscure animosities was magnified when it became known that Monet had submitted to the Salon. Degas's contempt grew heated, and Monet complained to Duret that he was treated like a renegade. A certain latitude surely might have been allowed a man who so recently had passed through appalling miseries, but this Degas did not grant.

Surveying the awesome wreckage of the impressionist exhibitions, Monet now serenely absolved himself of any flaw in strategy, any unwisdom in program, any imprudence in the many arguments that persuaded others to join him. Nor did he grant that Manet and Duret, who so vehemently had counseled against the plan at its inception, had been correct. But the founder of the impressionist exhibitions, aware that they had failed in their principal purpose, nor even become established as the opposition Salon he so grandly had wished to form, abandoned them.

Though Monet himself felt immaculately untouched by any trace of error, either by forming the group exhibitions or abandoning them, the same parties who opposed his plan at the start now magnanimously rushed forward to receive him. Accompanied by an eight-page essay from the pen of Théodore Duret, and a heavily stylized ink sketch of Monet done at Charpentier's request by Édouard Manet, an exhibition of eighteen canvases opened June 7, 1880, in the offices of Charpentier's illustrated journal, *La Vie Moderne*, at 7 Boulevard des Italiens. Devoted to his recent production, for the first time seen as a group, Monet's works created new interest. His vehemence was shown in force, coupled with all his abundant resource of synthetic coloration and flair for piquant moods in nature. A strong contrast existed between the livelier and reflective aspects of his art, and many who came to giggle remained to gape.

An interview was arranged, and with ill-chosen ingenuity a writer from Charpentier's journal asked if Monet, creator of impressionism, had ceased to be one of the impressionists whose exhibition he had not joined. The reply was cutting: "Not at all. I am still and always intend to be an impressionist . . . but I see only very rarely the men and women who are my colleagües. The little clique has become a great club which opens its doors to the first-come dauber. . . . " Aimed perhaps at Gauguin and others of Pissarro's friends, whose talents were primarily decorative or gymnastic, this barb was felt by all. It added to a growing sense of envy and to the howl of criticism with which his sudden and unexpected advance was watched.

To pocket every vagrant penny, Monet began systematically raising his prices. A large canvas of breaking ice floes at Vétheuil, not unlike the work shown Faure six months before, was exhibited at *La Vie Moderne* bearing the not inconsiderable price of 2,000 francs. Monet was delighted to receive a letter from Mme. Charpentier herself:

Paris, June 22 [1880]

MONSIEUR,

I know that my husband very much wants your large picture of the Débâcle. I would like to make him a gift of it on my savings, and as much as I would detest to bargain with a man of your talent, I have not the means to pay 2,000 francs. As you have not yet sold it, perhaps you would accept my conditions: 1,500 francs payable in three installments—500 francs on October 15, 500 francs January 14, 1881—500 francs April 14, 1881.

Excuse me, dear Monsieur, for seeming to bargain with you, and accept the assurance of my most distinguished sentiments.

MARG. CHARPENTIER

In the background of events lingered always the plump and matronly form of Alice Hoschedé. So soon after Camille's tragic death this relationship was logically wrong but emotionally right. At forty her bulging loins had given up their abundant fertility, but retained powers of healing. Alice Hoschedé's therapeutic abundance comforted Monet's nervous ills, and she brought him also the additional strength of another firm hand to control and occasionally tame his heroic lunacy.

That her husband still lived, most of those in Monet's circle were aware. In a vague way Ernest Hoschedé remained in contact with the artists of whom in better times he had been the principal patron. Even in exile he possessed numerous examples by Édouard Manet, Monet, and others, and as he continued to live abroad, from evident choice, Hoschedé's absence took on an appearance less of economic necessity than of disapproval of his wife's notorious unfaithfulness.

Alice Hoschedé continued to go her separate way, from her dowry providing for her own six children and the two sons of Monet. But her efforts to fashion a new life were not successful. Bourgeois Paris, convinced of its own moral rectitude, bestowed only tentative concessions on such an unruly matron. Fallen from an unshakable height, she found herself the center of scandal, with disapproval and ostracization never far. Monet, suffering from isolation and loneliness at Vétheuil, living still in the house where Camille died, seemed intent on observing a full nine-month period of mourning. This elapsed during the upswing of his fortunes, and following on the new status he gained from the *La Vie Moderne* exhibition, Alice Hoschedé abandoned her efforts to appease bourgeois values.

Since the death of Camille they had acted with discretion. Now this forty-year-old mother of six made the journey to Vétheuil, and the children of both parties shared their atmosphere of bedroom flutter. No less remarkable was that when she installed herself in Monet's little house at Vétheuil, at least five of her six children accompanied her. The step was an enormous one in that age when divorce was almost unknown as a remedy. While Ernest Hoschedé lived, marriage to Monet would always be impossible.

The poignant love story of Camille seemed to have been exchanged for a happy bedroom farce played by overblown juvenile leads. However amusing this impression it was far removed from fact. Earlier dalliance had generated a passionate prelude, to which now was added a glowing sensual fulfillment, coupled with obvious domestic felicity. A conventional triangle had been formed into two overlapping idylls. Alice Hoschedé had not the gazelle-like form of the youthful Camille, nor could her round face and fractured smile suggest beauty. But for what she was, happily and completely she put herself at the disposal of this man.

The effort was successful beyond all expectation. Attractive summer images issued from his brush, everywhere touched with renewed and lilting brilliance of color. They flood irresistibly into the heart. Never did this often disorganized, profoundly injured man trip so gently over visions of soft clouds, rippling foliage and water, nor the devastating gaiety of a careless countryside. Whether they picnicked across the Seine from Vétheuil, permitted the hordes of children to paddle boats, or sent them gathering blossoms in the fields, the bright humor of every episode was set down in bold and vigorous canvases, shimmering and rippling under fluent strokes.

Alice Hoschedé's dowry, which Monet never forgot, gave all those who settled in her sphere a new sense of security. To that degree it was once more the story of Camille, for again Claude Monet had found a woman able to support him. The likeness ended there. Granting that integrity is a prismatic concept, meaning different things to different people, it entered into this unblessed union. Whereas Camille's defeat had been the direct result of her attitude of mind, fearful always of losing her lover, Alice Hoschedé had a superior hold on this self-deluding, morally arrogant man. The plump wife of a successful merchant, accustomed to the gentle life she had known, surrounded always by the grace of her own cultivated ways, she took control of Monet as Camille never had been able to do.

Her own finances held firmly in hand, Alice Hoschedé was able to assure Monet that he always would have materials for work and never would know starvation. Her patrician virtues of thoroughness, dedication, and detachment all served him. Immediately the disgruntled, furiously bellowing and pleading artist of former years disappeared. He ceased to pay calls on patrons with canvases; no begging letter ever again issued from his pen. All the outrageous implausibilities of his former way of life promptly ended.

Spurred by the new interest in Monet, Paul Durand-Ruel, with the backing of Feder, director of the Union Générale bank, recommenced the plan formed a decade before. New purchases were made from all the impressionists, and from Vétheuil on February 15, 1881, Monet wrote that after two months of illness he now would bring to Paris the canvases requested earlier. Regular purchases were inaugurated, and by June, 1881, when accounts for the first four months were settled, Durand-Ruel had taken from Monet thirty-seven canvases for the sum of 7,500 francs.

To provide the variety of subjects that Durand-Ruel once more demanded, in March, 1881, Monet departed alone for Fécamp. The prosperous, confident man who painted seascapes was not recognizable as the haunted young artist who in that same harbor had essayed suicide. And new assurance was seen everywhere in the canvases he produced. The previous June Émile Zola had published stinging comments on Monet's art: "Monet has given in too much to his facility of production. Too many informal drafts have left his studio in difficult hours, and that is not good; it pushes an artist on the slope of unworthy and cheap creation. If one is too easily contented, if one sells sketches that are hardly dry, one loses the taste for works based on long and thoughtful preparation. . . . "

The truth Monet recognized in these criticisms he acted upon with surprising alacrity; the new order entered into his imaginative but ungrammatical art. Nor did he seem troubled by his own intractable nature. For though he continued to employ clean attack and solid tone, and his works of this period express bright motifs, amusing effects, bright ensembles, and unflagging high spirits, they gain a new depth. Sailing into uncharted regions, it was necessary for Monet to answer every question for himself. There were no rules but only principles, as in morals. The homogeneous nature of these newer canvases throws an aura of tentativeness and experimentation over those done at Argenteuil. The faltering, searching quality of those works no longer appears, making itself more evident where it exists.

For the first time one notes letters exclaiming that he required time "to make some retouches," and in consequence, through added cerebration and more careful development of a thickened texture, his works find the integrity of their own style. Nor could that great dramatist of his own emotions help investing his pictorial components with living, passionate human qualities. Returned to Alice Hoschedé and the seven children who awaited him at Vétheuil, a series of sumptuous oversized still-life compositions followed, their colors vibrantly set forth in areas of related hues stunningly calculated to make them sparkle. Sunflowers and chrysanthemums became a waltz of dragonflies, and the less naturalistic his approach the more convincing and intense was the impact. Unmatched for clarity, coherence, and grandeur, his evocations of dancing blooms in sparkling atmosphere contain passages of exquisite sensibility and simple lyrical beauty. No artist had conveyed this same feeling of swimming luxuriance, or symphonic wholeness and unity. Even the handling of pigment, previously the weakest part of any painting by Monet, suddenly acquires new beauty as the eye follows brush rhythms with fascination.

The vision of this man's incredible will power, which enabled him not only to survive the incredible blows of previous years but expand his career and his capacities in middle age, is awesome. In his still-life paintings a new intensity is present: Views of the town of Vétheuil, painted from the river's opposite bank, are equally ravishing, and brushed with an irresistible lilt and subtlety. The short dabs of his sable brushes, everywhere brilliant and efficient though seldom witty—now straight, now comma like, now smoothly flowing into thin impasto, now roughly placed atop dry surfaces—conveyed the new quality that had come to Claude Monet himself. He had summoned up complete control, a new assurance, and a new fertility, the catalyst of which was Alice Hoschedé.

It was, in fact, as if Baron Scarpia had taken the marschalin to wife, then discovered that she had been raised in a countinghouse along the Danube. Despite her accommodating impulses, Alice Hoschedé remained five feet of relentless will. And though their eccentric middle-aged household, blessed with its surplus of children, gave offense to more sanctimonious Parisians, Alice Hoschedé retained always some suggestion of a stalwart nanny. In middle age she was being heavily wooed, an experience she did not regret. But she was no appealing and sensitive Mélisande, but a woman able to switch magically from romantic sighs to hard good sense.

Hints of the department store are never distant. In the poetic intensity with which he gave voice to banalities Monet himself has no modern rival, but the prose of his letters now often demonstrated a harshness of tone most unexpected. Even relations with Durand-Ruel had been resumed with a polite civility suggesting unforgivingness over that dealer's failure to support him in the previous decade. This might be ascribed to the peasant shrewdness he always had demonstrated, a part of which was his ability to forgive former enemies but not former associates. With the increasing range of his business affairs, however, something new is detected, for suddenly he displayed an expert knowledge of merchandising procedures which brought him remarkable success.

Again in 1881 he refused to join the impressionist exhibition. He did not contribute to the Salon either, and by this point, two dealers copiously supplied with his works, it is evident Monet was content to rely on merchandising skill alone for advancement. Of Durand-Ruel he could inquire whether 2,000 or 2,500 francs could be sent him, at the same time making note that he had refused an offer from Charles Ephrussi. The interest of this patron formerly would have been an event of importance. Now, finding the offered price too low, Monet gave a cavalier refusal. So pleased was he, he did not scruple to ask Durand-Ruel if he had not done well.

The little house with scant garden at Vétheuil grew inappropriate for this blithely elegiac painter. No return to Paris was possible for a compromised family trailing its assortment of children. Undesirous of that monstrous bourgeois scrutiny, in November, 1881, a move was made to the Villa St.-Louis, at Poissy, where life continued as before. The following March it was Monet who supplied funds when Alice Hoschedé's youngest child, Jean-Pierre, took sick. By that date too there could be little question that he had become true head of this household and master of its purse. For, though less than two years before he had accepted Alice Hoschedé for the benefit of her dowry, now it was Claude Monet who contributed the principal sums to support of her family. In June this numerous tribe journeyed together to Pourville, from where Monet reported to Durand-Ruel they were "all enchanted to be here. The children are all in perfect health; and as for myself, after a few good walks, I am going to work with new ardor."

Pleased, and feeling himself a success at last, he continued to write to Durand-Ruel in a unique blend of candor and caginess, inquiring about sales and urging alternate exhibition schemes. Underneath the new manner and merchandising zeal remained his sharp, disillusioned mind, which had begun to grope in other directions. "Now that we are well known, it is the moment for a great blow. We must do things with audacity," he counseled—and Monet became the first to take this advice.

22. The Salesman's Game

THE MASSIVE HEAD, the titanic sneers, even the increasingly sly expression centered about Monet's eyes had begun to project an irrefutable imprint of greatness. Triumphs of the will could be read in the noble crag of his profile, his robust frame suggesting the utterances, manners, and man of an Amos and the martial vigor of Joshua. To these he added a petulance that was entirely his own.

His youth had been expended peddling dreams pathetically un-illumined. Now, in middle life, Claude Monet suddenly had come into step with his times. Without adequate explanation for the astonishing changes, audibly purring with satisfaction, he was sud-denly a man of destiny whose least worthy aspirations and most in-credible fantasies coincided with those of a whole generation. Over-weening ambition remained, but he did not permit the rewards of success to become merely monetary. Instead they provided the long-sought opportunity to practice his art most effectively, to project personality, elaborate his private vision, indulge in an unemphatic but totally unrepentant aestheticism, and in a series of highly idio-syncratic canvases make coherent what formerly had been a lucky-dip assortment of new ideas, effects, and moods. Most important of all, an immense new conviction and authority was brought to an eccentric creative genius anxious to seek further conspicuousness through defiance of conventions.

This massive new drama, so unlike that which had been its prologue, required a complete new cast of characters, for whom the stage quickly was cleared. For a wistful Camille substitution already had been effected of a buxom matron whose buoyant voice had an engaging hidden chortle. Nor did the scenes of triumphal procession about to unfold retain a villain's role: Adolphe Monet, that erstwhile monument to terror, wandered quietly into the wings, his death leaving no record. The acutely theatrical force now in command then decreed that his sister, Sophie Lecadre, also must come off stage. April 22, 1882, at the age of sixty-eight, she died at Le Havre, in the same Rue Fontenelle house that had been so much a part of Monet's youth. Aunt Sophie's husband, Adolphe Aimé Lecadre, survived his wife only nineteen months, abandoning a cramped and applauseless supporting role on November 20, 1883.

The pace and structure of this new drama permitted Monet by sheer force of his emphatic personality to reform the impressionist exhibitions into an expression of truly *impressionist* vision. "It is well understood, is it not," he wrote to Durand-Ruel on February 24, 1882, "that I will not exhibit without Renoir, and that no other painters among those we have named will take part in the exhibi-tion." He tried to select a strong group of his own works by post, but,

unable to remember his pictures from the titles, took the train to Paris.

"Are you really Claude Monet?" a tall, bearded young man called to him urgently in Durand-Ruel's shop. Already he had evolved from unknown quantity to demigod, and this young man of distinguished bearing was Sargent, Carolus-Duran's favorite pupil, himself at twenty-six a maker of headlines.

A perfectly trained and highly gifted young artist, Sargent had been "bowled over" by "for the first time coming across a picture that looks like nature and gives the sense of living." Already acquainted with Édouard Manet, who had given him a watercolor sketch of irises, Sargent invited Monet to dinner. From the Café de la Paix, near Durand-Ruel's gallery, they proceeded at Monet's suggestion to the Café Helder, off the Boulevard des Italiens, where a private dining room was available. Quantities of Monet's own canvases in the restaurant filled him with shame lest Sargent, and numerous friends who accompanied him, might think he had suggested the Helder for that reason.

From Sargent's youthful enthusiasm, beneath which lay much poise and detachment, it became clear Monet could influence a new generation of highly skilled professionals.

For the headless torso of impressionism Monet determined to provide strong leadership, and the perverse law of compensation that drove him on urged him to show an audacity truly remarkable. Already at Pourville he had begun to push further his personal vision. The dazzle of light had obscured accurate observation, creating an effect of half blindness in which a cliffside cottage and the sea were reduced to floating diaphanous textures. Not content to capture the transient in nature, he had delved into these bizarre optical effects.

The sole advantage of Poissy lay in adequate schools for the children. This fruitless area provided only one sketch of fishermen, and constantly Monet seemed to be escaping to Fécamp, Pourville, Varengeville, Dieppe, Le Havre, and Étretat. For him to exercise his talents of illusion nearer home another location became urgent, nor did he require the most grandiose scenery in nature. His life had been passed in the villages and hamlets of the Seine Valley. There he had fought his decisive battle; he would not abandon it now.

In rapid gestures and taut flourishes Monet's thick hand scrawled a new demand to Durand-Ruel: "I count on going into the country today to find a house, because in ten days we must leave Poissy. . . . I must speak frankly of what this will cost me; and I ask you to respond to me in the same fashion. . . ." Four thousand francs was the figure he asked the dealer to send him in two installments. His letter completed, Monet left for Vernon, near Vétheuil, a region he had found fertile in landscape motifs. There he learned of a farmhouse available at Giverny, four miles distant.

At first sight Giverny was more barren even than Barbizon, a line of dreary farm dwellings scattered on one side of the road and railway embankment which separated them from a marsh. The peasant's house to which he was directed faced these railway tracks from behind a barren orchard, its simple oblong interior divided into low-ceilinged, cell-like rooms. A graceless veranda wrapped around the exterior, and slightly lower, at one end of the structure, stood a carriage house. Surely only haste and necessity made Monet accept this excessively humble accommodation, which lacked running water and whose plumbing was outside. The venture gained a comical air when on his return to Vernon the train, hailed by a village wedding, stopped in mid-route, permitting the entire party to climb on board, led by its fiddler.

"I am still at Poissy, but up to the neck in packages. All week we are going to be moving . . .," he wrote April 15, 1883. "Our packing is not yet finished," Monet explained fourteen days later, obviously dismayed by the quantities of garments possessed by Alice Hoschedé's daughters, three of whom were in their teens. "Finally I leave this morning for Giverny with a few of the children, but we are so short of money that Madame Hoschedé cannot leave and she must quit the house tomorrow before six o'clock. . . . " Funds from Durand-Ruel quieted the alarm, and on April 30 the family completed its move to Giverny, where a letter waited with news of Édouard Manet's death. Monet wrote immediately:

May 1, 1883

DEAR MONSIEUR DURAND-RUEL,

I have just learned the terrible news of the death of our poor Manet. His brother counts on me among the pallbearers, and I must be in Paris tomorrow night. . . .

Your all devoted,

CLAUDE MONET

The dramatic framework was thus simplified by one last stroke just as Monet took his final place at Giverny. The curtain slowly ascended.

Burdened by expensive tastes and school fees, this family of seven children and two adults required 1,500 francs a month. In part this was provided by Alice Hoschedé's personal income. The bulk, however, derived from the sale of Monet's pictures. He had come a long way since at Vétheuil three years before he had painted a portrait in exchange for a pair of boots. He still found it necessary to work with a spade in Giverny's poor clay soil, planting flowers destined for still-life compositions, and hoeing a vegetable garden to which each evening he sent the children with watering cans. A similar spirit of Spartan good will motivated Alice Hoschedé, who, surrounded by her four daughters, set to work cooking, marketing, and cleaning.

The boats in which he painted were brought from Poissy, necessitating construction of a shelter. To Durand-Ruel he wrote again, June 5, his letter not notable for delicacy of phrasing: "I am counting strongly on your promise. I have not wished to say that you are going to abandon me. . . . As soon as I have some good things I will send them to you; now I shall be able to think of nothing but painting . . . I will no longer leave my brushes and I will give you some things that will please you. Meanwhile, I ask you not to forget me, because tranquility is the first consideration in order to work well."

Such demands were of little service to Durand-Ruel in a period that had become difficult. His happy arrangement with Feder, director of the Union Générale, had terminated abruptly the previous February when that bank failed. A general financial crisis followed, continuing into 1883. Embarked on his ambitious new program, and obliged to return much of the capital Feder had put at his disposal, Durand-Ruel struggled to carry on. Of all the crosses he bore, surely the heaviest was Claude Monet, whose frankly commercial instincts came increasingly to the fore. Inclined to be edgy and unrealistic despite his occasional elaborate civility, not even a special exhibition of his works arranged by Durand-Ruel in the early part of 1883 pleased him.

Camille Pissarro considered the affair "a great artistic success, very well organized, not too many canvases, forty at most, and well spaced.

It is a well deserved success, for Monet has shown some marvelous things. . . . " Monet's own view contrasted violently, and revealed what his criteria had become: "Do not think that I aspire to see my name in the newspapers. I am very much above that, and do not care for the opinion of the press and the self-proclaimed critics of art, each of whom is worse than the others. No, from the artistic point of view it means nothing. I know my value. . . . But it is from the commercial point of view that we must see these things. And not to acknowledge that my exhibition has been badly announced, badly prepared, is to be unable to see the truth."

Pronounced with explosive abandon, his views proved curiously correct, for sales were disappointing. And though he continued to give opinions to Durand-Ruel, his letters communicating them beard, thunder, and all, privately he was aware of the situation that dealer faced, and counseled others that "this is just a bad moment that must pass." Dealers and private purchasers were shown a stiff attitude even after Georges Petit began to experience parallel problems. Pictures were sold, but for the most part business remained enervatingly slow. "I am still very annoyed with the way business is going. All those whom I ask for help tell me to wait. That is easy to say," complained Durand-Ruel, who practiced his own form of tact with difficult artists. "The Gallery keeps me extremely busy but all I earn is trouble. I wish I were free to go live in the desert."

Monet, playing his own keen game, was a match for him. His letters cut Durand-Ruel to ribbons like an avenging sword; others more obsequious and sympathetic alternated: "I am always afraid to bother you, and then, as you have said, my demands for money are a burden on you. I have complete confidence in you, and I know all your devotion to our cause. I assure you that I have never doubted and I would be desolated were you to believe the contrary." Such magnanimity by the side of constantly elevating prices made Monet seem a character whose parts were not quite connecting. The 300 francs he was glad to receive for each canvas in 1881 had now become 400 and 500 francs. By the spring of 1884 a price of 900 francs was heard, and works carefully selected for the special honor were priced at 1,200.

The qualities most desirable for success had taken a form both singularly unattractive and singularly antisocial, and in his total concentration he sacrificed not only character but also something of his intellect. A profoundly ambivalent character, Monet sought advantage where it could be found. If it suited his present purpose, he could even advise against shipping his pictures to America, Durand-Ruel's latest and most farsighted venture: "I avow that certain of these canvases I will regret to see depart to the land of the Yankees and I would like to reserve a selection for Paris, because it is only there that a little taste remains."

These corrosive words were not mere tactics, for he honestly preferred his latest, most daring, and in some degree most attractive works were shown in Paris. His reasons were unrelated to Durand-Ruel's fiscal anxieties, nor had he any special distaste for Americans. The proximity of Paris to Giverny merely brought him personal advantage. Once a new genre of picture was shown by Durand-Ruel or Georges Petit, those most impressed with his dazzling conjuring tricks could make purchases direct from the artist. Always present, such ulterior motives made Monet's policies with dealers remarkably restrictive and doctrinaire, though some things he reserved to them exclusively. In November, 1885, he chanced to see his name advertised in *Le Figaro* among a list of pictures being auctioned: "Get busy," he wrote to Durand-Ruel, "because at this moment above all it would be very bad to let it sell cheaply."

In January, 1886, began a distinctly new phase in Monet's relations with dealers. He long had been critical of Durand-Ruel's American venture. Now he took a stronger tone, questioning the whereabouts of canvases he desired to have shown in Paris: "What remains in France?" he asked directly, "because I would very much like to be known and to sell my pictures here." Infuriated by the vagueness of Durand's son, and the lack of money paid him during the father's absence in New York, Monet demanded an account of recent sales. "I remain stupefied by your indifference," he wrote to Durand-Ruel in America, accusing him, with that long-favored word, of *abandoning* him.

For his part, Durand complained to others that Monet treated him like an enemy. Whatever he hoped to gain by this, Durand lost completely. With the crushing observation that he preferred his works to remain in France, Monet returned an advance sent him for pictures routed to America. Never having faced such an unprecedented situation, Durand-Ruel launched a halfhearted counteroffensive, sending back certain canvases with a request that they be retouched. Monet parried this thrust by refusing alterations and making an offer of other canvases in their place. For a short time the situation remained equal. Then in a fit of moral fervor Monet turned the tables on Durand-Ruel by returning a 1,000-franc advance, demanding a statement of their accounts, and informing the dealer that henceforth they would do their "modest affairs" for cash.

What gave Monet this extraordinary scope for maneuver was the constant market for his works presented by other dealers. And independent of them all he continued to make private sales at Giverny, where his own strong and picturesque personality was brought to bear on patrons. Other satisfactions also strengthened his policies, for in the spring of 1887 nearly everything exhibited at Petit's was sold, and a third dealer, Boussod & Valadon, for whom the young Theo van Gogh was manager, soon was stocking canvases by Monet and Degas, and asking for others by Sisley and Renoir.

Stories spread, and improved in the spreading, about Monet's sardonic humor and a streak of ruthlessness in his business arrangements. Even among those who had known him in less exuberant times, his glance suggested sincerely evil leers. "I ran into Monet at Durand-Ruel's. For some reason or other he always seems to have a sly look," complained Camille Pissarro, who, like all Monet's associates, was astonished at the unprecedented strides he made. Durand-Ruel one day took Pissarro aside, and in "a tone almost of accusation" asked whether he had sold to Theo van Gogh of Boussod & Valadon. Pissarro replied affirmatively, at which Durand shot back that he must not give pictures to "a person like that! Bring them to me." For van Gogh to have them "is bad for my business and keeps me from selling." Ruminating over such developments, Pissarro's observations were brief: "Unquestionably there is bad blood between Durand and van Gogh; the former is furious about the deal with Monet . . . Monet plays his salesman's game, and it serves him."

23. *A Public Figure*

ONE EXPECTS to be refreshed by changes in Monet after the fearful difficulties under which he had existed so long were ameliorated. But with his problems largely solved, an appalling lack of change became visible in him.

"I have received a letter from Monet, who is in despair because he has not succeeded with the canvases on which he worked most furiously . . . ," wrote Pissarro. It is not a new note but, as time passed, one that grew more insistent. The anguish he derived from his work took a new precedence over purely material cares, and he explained disarmingly, "I have more difficulty today doing the things that formerly I did easily." In part his developing critical sense was responsible. Continually he apologized for slowness of delivery, his tardiness a direct result of new technical procedures.

Durand-Ruel had advised him the untidy finish of his pictures was the principal cause of earlier unsuccess. The rough, uneven, broken paint surface was repellent. "Regarding the finish, or really the polishing, because that is what the public wishes, I will never agree with it," he insisted, at the same time inaugurating processes that would essentially alter his surfaces. More robust impasto was a first means employed; an immediate result was creamier surfaces. Pictures of this time were carried through before nature at one session, the paint heavily applied and the result intensely vivid. Attractive as this approach was, it lacked flexibility, for Monet's art no longer was that of a sketcher.

The veteran anarch at last had come to blows with the technical limitations so long imposed on himself. A more stately and elaborate art was glimpsed, before which he expanded his resources. Never would he abandon his desire for every canvas to seem an instantaneous encounter with nature, but already he was demanding too much diversity from the unsophisticated framework of pictures produced rapidly and in uncertain open-air conditions. Since moving to Giverny he had adopted Corot's method of retouching sketches in a studio. A wider dynamic range, greater chromatic intensity, and genuine passages of fortissimo and pianissimo were developed from the chaste outdoor notations.

Once they entered the studio at Giverny, canvases were treated as abstract patterns, worked over, improved, or, in some few cases, ruined, on the principle that a picture must be more than merely a divine trifle chopped from nature. Each new canvas he placed in a frame, the better to judge its effect. In this manner those painted at Étretat were drawn together, altered, and finished. None of the ecstatic, ornamented combinations of sun-drenched mountains and sea recently undertaken on the Riviera was shown before undergoing this same process. His immensely absorbed labors at Giverny strengthened their original melodic incantations of the Mediterranean coast with harmonic implications as unfamiliar as they were momentous.

"I have decided to enlarge my studio," he informed Durand-Ruel at the close of 1885, "and I am going to have to pay more than 400 francs for this." Walls were cut so that the old carriage house was entered down a few steps from an inside corridor. Where large doors had been hinged, a many-paned window was installed. In this specially constructed room Monet continued to refine canvases brought from outdoors. Already matured as an instrument, his art achieved a new brilliance that astounded Eugène Boudin: "That fellow has become so daring in his tones that one can see nothing after him. He overpowers and makes old-fashioned everything around him. Never has painting been more vibrant nor more intense. . . . "

Nor had it ever been attacked in the same way.

Perhaps Monet's dealers were not the demons he made of them, nor was he the slippery customer they sometimes supposed. Prodigal genius and prudent commerce do not marry happily. However deplorable his means, Monet succeeded in making all other forms of landscape painting seem hopelessly romanticized and out of date. He had himself become a legend, and never was he so aware of this as early in 1886, when Émile Zola sent him a copy of L'Oeuvre, his newest novel. Though its narrative was too subservient to the allegory, and the action so poorly paced it is dangerously slow at first and wildly improbable at the last, Monet was deeply hurt to discover in L'Oeuvre crudely caricatured events from his own life.

Zola's hero, Claude Lantier, was a composite drawn as much from Cézanne and Manet as himself. The first masterpiece of this hodgepodge artist was recognizable as Manet's *Déjeuner sur l'Herbe*. Lantier then went to live Monet's existence at Argenteuil, painting canvases whose descriptions made it certain they were his. In view of this revealing fact, Lantier's tragic death by suicide, morbid images drawn of the funeral, and a final estimate of complete and insane failure seemed deliberate unkindness. High artistic intentions coupled with bad faith and lack of scruple had led Zola into a morass of pseudo-profundity. Prodigious in energy, curiosity, prolixity, and with a sure instinct for the middle-class mind, the author had wandered into areas of judgment for which he was unequipped.

Zola's novel also revealed the extent to which Bazille had recounted Monet's most private affairs to the prying author. The frail and lovely Camille, whose memory still was fresh, became heroine of this tawdry romance. Their unmarried liaison, the birth of their first son, even a tasteless betrayal of Monet's mixed emotions at the marriage, filled the pages of a mechanically contrived fable. Every detail of the little ceremony at the Paris Mairie was suggested, its location hidden only by altering the number to that of its nearest neighbor. Positive identification of the characters was possible from numerous clues: Claude Monet had become "Claude Lantier," Camille was "Christine," and their son Jean was "Jacques." The reader was even told where to look: "How odd! Claude and Christine. We both start with the same letter!" the pseudo-Camille exclaims early in Zola's pages.

A further revelation existed in passages where Sandoz, a character who represented Zola, watched Christine analytically, and felt deeply moved, "for he saw in her a woman in love he would have liked to portray in his books." Here was outright admission that Zola had used his intimacy with Monet and Bazille to gather material for this book. The treachery was long premeditated. Doubtless the youthful Monet would have flown into a rage at this public insult to himself and the memory of his dead wife. The man who had emerged from the sufferings and privations of Vétheuil had reactions more restrained, even cautious, lest he bring attention where it was unwanted. To Pissarro he addressed a question: "Have you read Zola's book? I am afraid it will do us great harm." The response betrayed no hint that Pissarro had recognized Camille, and though Renoir, had he read the book, would surely have done so, Monet was reassured. An evasive acknowledgment was sent Zola:

April 5, 1886

MY DEAR ZOLA,

You were good enough to send me L'Oeuvre. I am very grateful to you for it. I have always enjoyed reading your books, and this one was doubly interesting because it raises questions about the art for which we have been fighting so long. I have just read it and I am worried and upset, I admit.

You were purposely careful to have none of your characters resemble any of us, but, in spite of that, I am afraid lest our enemies among the public and the press identify Manet or ourselves with failures, which is not what you have in mind, I cannot believe it.

Forgive me for telling you this, it is not a criticism; I have read L'Oeuvre with great pleasure, finding memories on every page. Moreover you are aware of my fanatical admiration for your talent. No; but I have been struggling for a long time and I am afraid that, just as we are about to meet with success, our enemies may make use of your book to overwhelm us.

Excuse this long letter. Remember me to Madame Zola, and thank you again.

Devotedly yours,
CLAUDE MONET

Surely it was only to register protest in the name of a cause that Monet wrote. For his feelings over this shoddy exhumation were far stronger than he permitted his letter to reflect, and from the publication of *L'Oeuvre* dated an estrangement with Zola.

Despite the unfortunate nature of Zola's attack, and much exquisite jealousy on the part of masters decorated at the Salon, Monet had reached the top of the greasy pole. His insistence on the importance of his ideas, and the momentousness of his discoveries, proved how shaky the whole setup remained. An additional embarrassment was that Ernest Hoschedé had returned to Paris, where he appeared at an artist's dinner and "made a little speech and drank to the honor of the old Impressionism. He seemed to be criticizing Monet, Sisley, and Renoir; there is something besides art in his criticism, I fear, for he is generally eclectic . . . ," Camille Pissarro noted.

Yet the legend of brilliant and intransigent Claude Monet continued to spread. He was widely known to entertain unflattering views concerning the artistic establishment, and in 1888 these came fiercely into view, when the government attempted to bring him into the official camp by award of the Legion of Honor. Monet indignantly refused. Scornfully he failed even to answer letters from Rodin, who proved less strong before this same temptation. "The Minister is not accustomed to responses of that nature," commented Monet's friend, the author Octave Mirbeau. The uproar dramatized Monet's singular but defiantly negative position in France. Sargent then provided him with a more affirmative cause that could be taken before the public.

Though at first he had seemed a cultivated Parisian, on further acquaintance John Singer Sargent proved an American born abroad who retained the special gifts and tastes of his forebears. In his hands the striking portrait techniques of Carolus-Duran had developed into a visually superb art with the unique ability to disembowel pictorially. Possessed of impeccable taste and well-forged craftsmanship, Sargent easily absorbed the characteristics of Monet's impressionism. He created a recognizable idiom of his own, expressed in those broader, juicier textures produced by the bristle brushes newly introduced into France.

At the Galerie Georges Petit, Sargent yearly exhibited beside Monet and made for himself a special place in the modern movement, until his career suffered an equally extraordinary collapse. Scandalized by a portrait, all marble arms and black velvet, which seemed to ridicule an eminent lady's supercilious bearing, rouged ears, and obvious cosmetics, Paris turned its collective back on Sargent. Shortly before a permanent move to London he paid a last visit to the widow of Édouard Manet, who lived still at Gennevilliers in the little house now filled with her husband's works. Hung over the piano Sargent found the famous *Olympia*, and its tremendous impact on him he never forgot.

This turbulent early section of Sargent's career soon passed. In 1887 he exhibited at the Royal Academy a figure composition related to the outdoor works of Manet, and created by use of the impressionist palette of Monet. By this canvas pure impressionism of the variety Monet had taught to Renoir, Pissarro, and Sisley was carried into the academies, and received with surprising acclamation. *Carna-*

tion Lily, Lily Rose was purchased for the Chantrey Bequest, after which Sargent himself briefly visited France. At Giverny he became enamored of a study of sea and rocks painted in Monet's more violent mood. With his habitual growl Monet commented, "I do not share your admiration."

"What talk!" said Sargent, who purchased the picture and, once returned to London, claimed to be in raptures before it. "I could stay there for hours at a time," he wrote, enclosing his check, "in a state of voluptuous brutishness, or of enchantment, if you prefer. I am delighted to have such a source of pleasure in my house."

On both sides of the Atlantic Sargent enlisted adherents to his specially indulgent views of Claude Monet. Durand-Ruel profited from increased American sales, and Sargent's visits to Paris produced an impressionist fanaticism among the American element, who in 1889 purchased the entire series of works Monet painted in the Creuse Valley, one canvas among them for the astonishing sum of 9,000 francs.

On this same visit to Paris Sargent learned that Mme. Manet, forced to sell the works of her husband, was about to allow the *Olympia* to go to an American. At Giverny, where he worked beside Monet with astonishing effect, Sargent suggested a subscription to save this special example of Manet's skill for France. On his own initiative, in July, 1889, Sargent made soundings among artists in Paris. "Apropos of Olympia," he wrote to Monet, "I have seen Boldini who will give a thousand francs. A friend of mine spoke to Roll and [illegible]. The two approve and Roll would like to give something but says he is unable. I have not seen Duret in person. . . . " But on July 24 Roll himself wrote to Monet, promising to give 100 francs and congratulating him on the idea. Promise of another 1,000 came from Georges de Bellio, and Jacques Émile Blanche sent his offer of 500 together with a list of persons he proposed be contacted.

The availability of funds made it imperative that the Manet family be committed formally to the plan. Monet contacted Berthe Morisot, sister-in-law to the dead artist, outlining a plan to purchase *Olympia* for presentation to the Louvre. Fearful that governmental agencies might be opposed to this bold scheme, Berthe Morisot consulted Puvis de Chavannes, whom Sargent would shortly recommend for a Boston mural commission. "You do not know how officious and complicated he is," she wrote back to Monet when Chavannes counseled that Manet's friend Antonin Proust, Minister of Fine Arts, should be sounded. She herself meanwhile expressed to Monet what had become the general view: "You alone, with your name, your authority, can force the doors if they are forceable."

Until November no word of the project had reached Mme. Manet herself, who wrote to Monet with much pleasure: "It is with profound emotion that I have just read your letter announcing to me what you, Monsieur Sargent, and some friends, will do for the memory of my dear husband. It is so handsome, and I am so touched, that anything I would be able to say to you would be still beneath my true sentiments. I was unaware of this project of sympathy, and the Olympia in the Louvre is the height of my wishes. . . . "

Begun with much good will, the plan did not succeed without moments of drama. Antonin Proust at first had promised 500 francs to the subscription. Then, in an article that appeared the following January, he declared the idea unfortunate. On the ground that Manet never had solicited the state, Proust stated his name ought not to be associated with "a request he would have reproved." Manet's family demanded rectification, and Monet wrote to Proust, alleging offense to the widow, and asking that a retraction appear in *Le Figaro,* where the original injury was printed. Proust's tart response gave a dangerous twist:

January 27, 1890

MONSIEUR,

For three days the newspapers have attributed to me an initiative that came from you. You remained mute: that was your right. I have spoken: it was mine.

You think today that my words have been unkind to you. If you find yourself offended I await your friends. As for the role of spokesman for Madame Édouard Manet that you take, I do not know that you have been authorized to take it.

I have, Monsieur, the honor to salute you.

ANTONIN PROUST

The terms of this slight were sufficient for Monet to consider the proffered duel. In Théodore Duret and Gustave Geffroy he found seconds, who called on Proust while Monet awaited them in a café on the Boulevard Haussmann. More inclined to diplomacy than assassination, Duret and Geffroy arranged for a pacific encounter at which Monet and Proust arranged their differences.

Collection of the subscription continued, and Proust was not the only friend of Manet to entertain reservations. Monet was plainly stupefied by Émile Zola, whose letter suggested "that collectors are syndicating to raise the prices of an artist of whom they have canvases, I can understand; but I have promised myself that I, a writer, shall never become involved in this sort of affair. . . . " Despite such futile and petty derisions, the enormous success of the subscription might have been best ascribed to the all-around brilliance of the occasion; those few who objected were swept away by the fulsome tide of contributions.

At the start of February a goal of 20,000 francs was fully subscribed. Monet wrote a formal offer to the government, appending the list of subscribers. He and Sargent each gave 1,000 francs, de Bellio and Théodore Duret joining them in the amount of their generosity. Jeanniot scraped together only 50 francs, nor did Pissarro, Chabrier, Geffroy, or Renoir do better. Degas, Manet's closest friend, obliged only to the extent of 100, in which he was outdone by another of Manet's friends, Sargent's teacher, Carolus-Duran, who gave 200.

In answer to official questions Monet explained that the gift was conditional upon acceptance of the picture by the Louvre or the Luxembourg Gallery. Gustave Larroumet, Director of Fine Arts, negotiated the point, outmatching even Monet in sanctimonious subtlety. Monet never relaxed his condition: The picture must not leave the Luxembourg Gallery unless for entry into the Louvre. Larroumet insisted this was impossible because the Luxembourg Gallery was essentially a museum of passage whose collections changed constantly. But he assured Monet that in direct compliance with the wishes of the subscribers the picture would remain in Paris, and on display.

When Monet sought to bind Larroumet to these terms, the latter excused himself by passing the correspondence to the higher authority of his Minister, Léon Bourgeois, who wrote that the *Olympia* could be accepted only if it were given without condition. It would be the intention of his administration, if possible, he said, to keep it in Paris and always on exhibition. This was the final agreement. At

Vernon, August 26, 1890, Monet's notary wrote an official donation, which was transmitted to the Council of State. In response, November 17, 1890, the President of France signed a decree accepting that earthly parable without a heavenly meaning in behalf of the nation. Sargent permitted all credit to flow to Monet, who assumed a position in French art far beyond any Courbet had occupied. At fifty, a public figure who suddenly lived in a state of premature deification, Claude Monet was almost an emperor and not quite a gentleman.

24. *The Fiery Angel*

FOR MONET audacity had become a way of life from which evolved a new, brilliant, unboring but ferociously ephemeral art. A distinctive flamboyance was present in the dramatic intensity brought to visual experience, and it was expressed with an equally novel but absolute technical control and an impeccable artistic syntax, which made the countryside so rich in its meanings, its implications, and its resonances that it provoked, stimulated, and satisfied to a degree beyond reach of less theatrical entertainments. That a man of Monet's withering experience in life should finally have settled on this dramatic expression was altogether just. His art continued in this direction, wandering at first, until it found increased momentum and progressively and consciously he pushed it further.

A rich and fruitful period continued with only occasional lapses natural to the rhythm of production. Subjects were everywhere, each offering Monet the opportunity to adjust his flaming vision and elaborate a reaction to form and color that was absolutely particular. One evening behind the house at Giverny his eye lit on a progression of haystacks, each shaped like the thatched huts of tribes indigenous to darkest Africa. In the darkening murk, their curiously formal, unpicturesque, and unemotional progression suggested a picture.

The following day, assisted by Alice Hoschedé's second daughter, Blanche, Monet made his preparations to work. Wheelbarrows, in which his materials were habitually transported about the working area at Giverny, were brought out and loaded. Once in position, Monet saw the haystacks take on colors to match the modulations of light in their extensive field, and he experienced the delight of a satisfactory sketch growing under his brushes. Another day, returning to the site, he saw the effect had altered.

"Would you go back to the house, and bring me another canvas?" he called to Blanche Hoschedé.

Again he advanced a work of exquisite beauty and mellow tone, until once more altering conditions of atmosphere made the effect too different. A second time he sent Blanche Hoschedé back to the house for a fresh canvas. Exemplary in terms of poetic expression, his studies, each representing some separate effect that appeared with the flight of the sun across broken heavens, continued to multiply. Each change in the day, and each new day, presented an altered atmosphere and gave a changed appearance to these haystacks, which, like a mirror, reflected everything about them.

Subtle blues invaded from the sky, to be overwhelmed by the heightened color of the straw itself, reinforced by the glow of earth below. In the intensity of light centering on his retina strange unexpected tones of red were born. Refracted in their brilliance against the sky-blue falling from above, these reds lost themselves in a perturbation that created violet, which, itself shattered in brilliance on the human eye, carried overtones of green. To capture the overwhelming splendors of these effects by means of the simple palette he employed, Monet's synthetic coloring reached new heights of complexity in which something hallucinatory began to develop.

Yet pure technical dexterity was never allowed to substitute itself for sheer blood-and-thunder theatricality: Scarlet haystacks, violet fields, and yellow sky were appearing with an overwhelming sense of truth; limpid yellow haystacks and equally limpid fields were marked by sky-blue shadows; quivering sanguine haystacks stood floating in fields totally dissolved by amber light. Monet continued, commenting cheerfully on colors unseen to anyone but himself and skimming an arena of half blindness in which the solidity of objects was reduced to floating diaphanous textures.

Autumn found him hard at work, still multiplying the permutations of his astonishingly variable subject. In October he wrote to

Geffroy: "I am digging away very hard, stubbornly doing a series of differing effects, but at this season the sun goes down so fast I cannot follow it. . . . I am back at the sluggishness of work that leaves me despairing, but the further I go, the more I see it is necessary to work very hard to render what I seek: 'the instantaneous,' above all the visual appearance, the light scattered on all sides—and never those things that come easily and leave me disgusted. . . ."

A simple haystack in an empty field at one part of the day seemed to burn, and at another turned to ice. For each effect, lasting so short a time, it was necessary to have a new canvas at hand, and each canvas had to be kept near awaiting a reappearance of the effect. The autumn season wore on; the sun dimmed. Wintry haze through which shafts of brilliant sunlight cut their way settled over Giverny. At arm's length from his easel, quickly dabbing his touches, Monet worked on and the months passed.

The *Haystacks* burst upon Paris as a well-calculated sensation. The cause of this was twofold. His vision had gone further than ever before, creating more arresting effects. But also, no canvas of the entire group was permitted to remain an expression of ordinary casual vision. Monet had consciously limited himself to portraying fantastic, ephemeral effects, impossible for the untrained eye to see. A fiercely competitive contemporary artist, he had devoted himself to symphonic arrangements and Wagnerian blasts, to the exclusion of simple truth. "For the moment people want nothing but Monets, apparently he cannot paint enough pictures to meet the demand," observed Camille Pissarro as the *Haystacks* began to appear. The astonishing éclat of these works overwhelmed all who saw them. It was the value of shock, and Monet rode the crest of its wave. "Worst of all," Pissarro commented, "they all want haystacks in the setting sun! Always the same story, everything he does goes to Americans at prices of four, five, and six thousand francs."

The audacity so apparent in his vision, methods of work, and relations with dealers now took a new form. Dealers displayed his works from all periods combined with those of other artists, a system that retained too high a proportion of calculated anarchy. He himself no longer bred random jumbles of art, nor did he see advantage in permitting his pictures to become part of such an arrangement after they left his studio.

In the face of extraordinary demand Monet played a new card. At

his instigation Durand-Ruel, with whom he once again had consented to do business, but on his own terms, collected an exhibition
devoted to *Haystacks* alone. Repetition and similarity were to be
made a virtue, the violent effects of light and color, the annihilation
of substance, fiercely compared and contrasted. "I saw de Bellio
yesterday . . .," reported Pissarro. "He mentioned that Monet was
going to have a one-man show at Durand-Ruel's, and exhibit *nothing
but haystacks*. The clerk at Boussod & Valadon told me that the
collectors want only *Haystacks*. I do not understand how Monet can
submit to this demand that he repeat himself—such is the terrible
consequence of success!"

The sheer improbability of such an exhibition added to its amazing effect at the opening, May 4, 1891. Huge throngs realized how
correct was the idea behind the venture, for the emotion from each
canvas reinforced the others, producing a more overwhelming final
assertion than was possible from separate works. The gesture perhaps was lacking in that final courage necessary to an overwhelming victory—only fifteen canvases were shown—but despite elevated
prices crowds who attended purchased them all within three days.
The *series*—always present in Monet's works, and founded on his
fundamental disinclination to give up a good motif once discovered
—at last had become consecrated itself as an artistic technique.

Prosperity mounting about him ever higher, in October, 1891,
Monet proceeded to purchase his house and the surrounding property at Giverny, for the purpose demanding funds from Durand-
Ruel: "I am going to ask you to take measures to give me the sum
of 20,000 francs, which I need for the 25% for the purchase of my
house. If able I will come for it myself this week, but I can never
be certain because of the weather. Since your last visit I have had
some disappointments and problems. . . ."

A reversion to bourgeois values on a scale far more immense
than ever before lit the scene at Giverny. The days when Alice
Hoschedé cooked and her daughters cleaned, helped with household chores, and watered the garden had been left behind like some
petrifying impertinence. The house now had a married couple as
staff, the woman to cook, her husband to tackle heavier chores.
Over both Alice Hoschedé presided in constant demonstration of
her skill as organizer and housekeeper.

The barren orchard long since had been covered with flowers, and it was tended by two or three gardeners, one of whom was head gardener. *Vignevierge* grew in twisted ropelike stems across the veranda, and over his paths Monet systematically erected iron trellises on which to throw festoons of roses. On all sides walls and gates were raised around· the property. So long deprived of everything worldly, Monet showed traces of a possessive mania, dominating Alice Hoschedé, his own sons, and her daughters in a frantic grip that was the last remnant of his former insecure truculence. One could not overlook that, surrounded by his two silent sons, he was a grand pasha isolated in a walled garden with five plump females, to none of whom had he any clearly defined relationship.

Still considered a stranger to Giverny, and making every allowance for the ingrained antipathy of villagers slightly scandalized by his way of life, Monet could become impatient over delays with his ironwork. One day he appeared at the blacksmith's shop, grumbling and growling over "these filthy workers." A stiff Norman named Tellier, the smith took off the cap from which a French artisan never parts, and retorted, "M. Monet, filthy workers wear a cap." A small occurrence, it was illustrative of relations between Monet and a village suspicious of outsiders and slow to accept anyone scandalous and new to its midst. As time passed and it was seen that he gave out work to local tradesmen, paid good prices, and was as generous on this level as he was avaricious on his own his position in the community grew to one of baffled respect.

The garden Monet created before his house was a decor in uniquely execrable but torrential style, where many flowers were closely packed into a display of color that ignored rules. Whether of enigmatic curvilinear patterns, or simple balance and synchronization, all sense of plan, or desire for vistas, was absent. Instead Monet had sought, and achieved, a wild profusion of blooms scattered without formal relationships. Even this bizarre garden did not absorb him entirely during those first years of residence at Giverny. Constantly he drew on the meadows and surrounding hills for his subjects.

The *Haystacks* had been only a commonplace scene in the fields behind his house; nothing could disguise the blazing flare of theatrical genius that had transformed them into ambitious tinkerings with illusion and reality. When exhibited together at Durand-Ruel's Gallery, fifteen *Haystacks* not only showed the rhapsodic side of his talent to greatest advantage, but the total effect of this gigantic symphonic unity was of an unparalleled orgiastic splendor. Giverny itself immediately was able to provide him with the glittering lure of another such spectacle.

Combining the gifts of Ceres and Midas, this fifty-one-year-old artist had turned to gold the crops growing about him at Giverny. The result had been magnificent, and surrounding him was an unaccountable aura of radiance. All his forces had blazed up in final dazzling power when, on his way to the station, Monet saw poplar trees winding beside the little river. Many painters before him had eked out expressive cantabile passages from such long lines of poplars, though none were able to add the subtly dissonant harmonies of which the mature Monet was capable. The sight itself, nonetheless, was neither sensational nor electrifying. Only the remarkable development of this second half of his creative life, sprung from the earlier empirical discovery of a new method of painting, had prepared him to create from such trees another extravaganza hardly less arresting and more immediately attractive than the *Haystacks*.

Unfortunately these balding trees were "ripe," and, as was the French custom, soon would be felled for lumber. Younger trees would replace them, yet these present tall, mature, windswept poplars were the more perfect medium. With them he could deliberately plumb the depths of his art by every conceivable mutation and metamorphosis of design, lighting, and color.

The commune of Limetz, to which the trees belonged, already had offered them for purchase. Monet interviewed the mayor, who, though understanding his request, was unable to retard an announced sale. "You are going to pay dear for this fantasy, my good man," said Monet to himself. Next he approached a wood merchant who was a prospective purchaser. By agreement the merchant made the purchase with backing from Monet, on condition that the trees would be left standing long enough for his visions to be completed.

This time Monet began his work with the deliberate intention to paint a series. The *Haystacks* had sold well individually, but when grouped together at Durand-Ruel's they had opened new frontiers in his art, and received the best prices. Such a confluence of events could not be ignored. In the poplars he selected perhaps the most appropriate subject of his career. A sinuous curve of bright festooned treetops wound down his canvas, linking the irregular progression of parallel trunks. The recurring phrases, loops, and parallels acquired strong poetic significance as they were wrought upon canvas after canvas in altering atmospheric conditions.

In those views which took a more broad view, the winding river produced a second loop of treetops halfway down his canvases, its new snaking rhythm answering the primary bend above. From the start his grouping was tight and compositions perfectly balanced in the true manner of Hokusai. As he progressed, his view inclined to a further limitation of area that tightened the trunks within a narrowing frame. Like poems concerned with approaching dusk and night, occasionally illumined by the blinding flashes of a distant bathing sunlight, the imagery of these poplars prompted a subtle and restrained execution. Permutations of atmosphere and color were exploited by the pizzicato brush technique that gave personal character to pigment applied without liquid medium. Fat and pasty textures were woven into an atmospheric unity spellbinding in its melancholy eloquence. The effect was often haunting, and made vivid contrast with more conventionally noted passages of foliage and cloud.

Perhaps because now he had a composition that in itself was a thing of beauty, and subject to those subtle variations of placement at which he was so adept, these pictures, unlike the *Haystacks,* are not all glaring spectacles. The effects at which he aimed were simpler, easier, and far less extravagant. By their sustained lyricism and concentrated emotion they evoke a different, less antagonistic world where the conflict between demons and angels of light for the *Haystacks* has been given an armistice.

Instead Monet has contented himself with a stunning academic lesson. Few standard progressions or cadential clichés are left unemployed or unrefined, and most are robed in elaborate harmonies. The theory of progressions familiar to every architect is vastly expanded and brought to a point of expression incapable of further development. Pathos and excitement, deep personal expression, and wild orgiastic abandon are woven into it, the sense of eeriness heightened by ascending and descending rhythms and harmonics.

Arrangements for the correct marketing of this new artistic triumph Monet kept in his own hands. To recoup his costs the trees themselves were felled without remorse. A few canvases were seen at Boussod & Valadon, to prepare the public while the last of the series were completed in his studio. Instructions for an exhibition of the entire group, as a unity, went out to Durand-Ruel February 23, 1892: "You can send the invitations that you can make in my name (the opening Monday, 29 February). And, if you think well of it, place an announcement of two lines only in *Le Figaro*, indicating the date of the opening and that the exhibition closes March 10."

So deliberately arranged according to Monet's own scheme, the event itself was an immediate success. "I am leaving," said Degas, when Monet met him at Durand-Ruel's Gallery. "All these reflections in the water make my eyes ache, and then I have a feeling there is such a draft. Very nearly turned up my collar."

Even the village of Giverny was caught up in wild adulation of Claude Monet. No longer a stranger, he was accepted as the local celebrity, the *grand Monsieur*. Frequent waves of American visitors who passed the inn on their way to the master's house were viewed with interest and pride. The first of these to remain had been Theodore Robinson, for whom Monet and his family developed a genuine fondness. "You see, nothing has changed. Sometimes in the village one sees some unknown faces. They are your compatriots who come to see if spring has arrived . . .," he wrote to Robinson during the *Haystack* success.

Only a few weeks after this letter something of great importance *did* change. On March 18, 1891, Ernest Hoschedé, long-estranged husband of the woman who so long had presided at Giverny, and the father of her many children, died. By some curious amalgam of sentiment and bourgeois respectability, Monet permitted his mistress' husband to be brought to Giverny, for burial in the churchyard only a few steps from his own door. There Jean Louis Ernest Hoschedé was given a handsome tomb, and a monument bearing his name emboldened across its ornaments. The fixed period of mourning was nine months, after which Alice Hoschedé at last would be free to marry Monet. For the second time in his life, typically, Monet drew back. Of all the fears endemic to his nature, that of marriage was the greatest.

What forced his hand was the maturing of the children. Suzanne, next to cadet daughter in age, was nearing twenty-four, and had formed an affectionate relationship with Theodore Butler, an American from Ohio. For a year Butler had absented himself from France, then in 1892 returned to Giverny with an earnest proposal of marriage. As Grand Pasha in his walled garden Monet felt disconcerted at the prospect of losing a member of his household. An obvious and typically bourgeois fear overcame him concerning the marriage of Suzanne Hoschedé with someone of whom he knew so little. Despite his wide acquaintance with Americans, Sargent was unable to shed light on Butler's family. Fortunately Sargent's friend at the Carolus-Duran atelier, Carroll Beckwith, was native to the same Ohio city of Columbus. This amiable friend of both parties vouched for Theodore Butler's respectability, smoothing Suzanne Hoschedé's path to the altar.

Shortly, however, Monet began to wish Beckwith had been less obliging. Preparations for the wedding were vast, complicated, and completely deranged his household. Worse than that, in the many formalities that preceded it, his own position began to appear a trifle unorthodox. What was he to this girl? For twelve years he had acted as her father; suddenly he found he was not even a relative and possessed no voice in the proceedings. To a man so completely master of his household this was too vexing to be borne. Thus, in July, 1892, after twelve years of liaison, and merely because of the stupidities of other people's affairs, Claude Monet and Alice Hoschedé were quietly married.

A blushing bride at fifty-two, and a pound overweight for each of her years, Alice Monet accepted her new position with aplomb. At Giverny the happy and satisfied tenor of life saw no change. To a few old friends Monet was obliged to mention the state of affairs, lest they not realize the new protocol in force. In reply Boudin wrote:

> Let me congratulate you on your marriage and to congratulate Madame Monet, whom I used to have the pleasure of seeing in those days when she received artists with so much affability and so graciously. For many years the chance conditions of existence, the urgent demands of life, have undoubtedly separated us, but they have not prevented me from taking part in your struggles and your success. . . . I have followed your bold experiments with interest, your experiments which ever have been so daring, but which have given you honor and renown. What a long time since we went to paint landscapes in the valley of Rouelles. . . .

Like Louis XVI, Monet accepted his marriage reservedly and with the same laconic word *rien:* "Nothing really new to tell you," he penned to Durand-Ruel, "except that the house is very upset because of the next marriage of Mlle. Suzanne Hoschedé with a young American painter. I have not been able to get back to work."

A month later, July 20, 1892, Theodore Robinson wrote in his diary: "A great day, the marriage of Butler and Mlle. Suzanne. Nearly everybody at the church, the peasants—many almost unrecognizable. The wedding party in full dress; ceremony first at the Mairie, then at the church. Monet entered first with Suzanne, then Butler and Mme. Hoschedé. Considerable feeling on the part of the parents. A breakfast at the atelier lasting most of the afternoon."

Giverny presented the unique sensation of a village sustaining a coterie and a discipleship drawn from distant lands. "The Monet boys are present in force," noted Carroll Beckwith after serving on the jury of the National Academy in New York. A Frenchman who once poked his nose into Giverny's Inn wrote that it was like being dropped down *"en plein Middle-Ouest."*

The center of so much adulation, Monet himself retained a curiously modest manner, a happily dedicated man using the walls of his garden to parry all unwelcome obligations and proceeding from discovery to discovery.

In the *Haystacks* and *Poplars* series he had reached the peak of his powers and developed a uniquely characteristic manner, exuding an immense warmth and dramatic intensity that fully exploited his earlier technical discoveries. His art had become a magnificent sidewise look at the world. Deliberately he was limiting his subject matter to small areas, exploiting fully what for others might have been only a single aspect. In the process, as strokes built their unique, foaming, coral-like surfaces of pigment, consonance and dissonance, tension and relaxation, no longer could be defined as opposites, but merely the amalgamates of his inventive and strangely imaginative art.

The *Poplars* in particular were a summit and synthesis of everything Monet had achieved. Here his special technical discoveries in color, which were Impressionism itself, had married perfectly with his new medium-less employment of pigments. The lyrical sweetness of so many early Argenteuil works is married to the somber expressionism of beach studies painted at Ste.-Adresse. The delicate exoticism of *La Japonaise* and Zaandam combines with the harsh brutality of Sargent's *Rock,* while over all a grandeur of conception reigns that was only dimly heralded in the big, confident proportions of the *Picnic* unfinished at Fontainebleau. In the dimensions and range of its idiom the *Poplars* towers over all predecessors, and the vastness of all landscape painting, for never before had a suite of paintings in series expressed one man's vision of a single subject.

No wonder there was an exultant note in his fifth decade; the long years of patient exercise at Ste.-Adresse, Bougival, Argenteuil, and the Gare St.-Lazare had borne fruit. Poverty and death had been no wasted ordeal. His absolute unshakable confidence in himself had prepared him to reveal poetry in every triviality. The formulation of this into a new system, and the canvases produced by it, make it impossible for him to be compared with anyone at all, unless it be Wagner, who also had broken out of the encumbering frame of composition that shackled predecessors by demanding four nights on which to perform an opera. The series became not only Monet's perfected quintessentially theatrical illusion but the fundamental document of his art. For in the series, as nowhere else, he developed the crucial debate between image and idea.

It is at once surprising, yet inevitable, that even before the *Poplars* had undergone their retouching and finishing in the studio, Monet's natural pragmatism sought justification in yet another step. "Monet has been in London since yesterday," Pissarro noted; "He probably went there to work. Everyone is awaiting with impatience his series of London Impressions." More likely the fact that his son Jean was at school in England had occasioned Monet's journey to a city he was inclined to enjoy. But he was prospecting for another motif too. On returning to Giverny for Christmas he wrote to Durand-Ruel, ". . . I will apply myself to finishing your pictures [the poplars] which I count on delivering to you very soon, having the intention, if the winter is not very interesting (by which I mean dry or snowy), to return to London to work there. . . ."

Despite his announced intention, early that February he found another motif nearer to hand, at Rouen, and it was the great Gothic cathedral that he fixed on for his next vast effort. His reasons for this choice are not apparent but require no close examination, for it was a period of unusual schematic fertility, and he had chosen wisely among the ideas that came to him. The great stone front of the cathedral presented a convenient subject to be turned to fantasy while he rode out every digression of light and color with fine histrionic force and the full flood of his torrential talent. His final point of view was found on the second floor of a novelty shop

owned by Édouard Mauquit, at 81 Rue du Grand-Pont. A room
was put at his disposal, and amidst accumulations of canvases and
paints he began to work through the open windows as the great stone
structure gleamed in winter sunshine.

From quarters in Rouen's Hôtel Angleterre he directed his *Poplars* exhibition, hurrying to Giverny to expedite the delivery of
canvases.

Their sensation was immeasurably greater than the *Haystacks*.
Crowds left with spirits gladdened, and the mind and imagination immeasurably enriched, to find the stunning achievement standing out stereoptically in their recollection. The *Haystacks* triumph
had perhaps been more for dramatic than artistic content, but
that of the *Poplars* was unimpaired. From Rouen Monet wrote
that he was "very well satisfied with what you tell me of my
exhibition. From different sides I have heard that the effect was quite
grand."

But in this same letter were other matters. With regret he informed
Durand-Ruel that though he gave him a definite preference in the
choice of his works, when other dealers came to Giverny he did "not
wish to show these people the door; finding it absolutely unlucky and
bad for an artist to sell exclusively to one dealer . . . I cannot refuse
to sell to others." Even at Rouen he was visited by the representative
of Boussod & Valadon, to whom he was forced to confirm what he
already had said to others: "I do not wish to sell at this moment."
News of his *Cathedrals* had got abroad, and amid expectations of this
new series, desires to purchase them reached fantastic urgency.

25. *The Engulfed Cathedral*

IN THE BRILLIANCE of an unbounded success, the sprawling, melodious career of Claude Monet completely obscured his colleagues'.
After 1882 he took no part in their displays, and without him, except for one revival in 1886, the impressionist exhibitions ceased.

Alone, Monet's advance continued, with astonishing results. After a visit to America the painter Raffaëlli reported being told, "Monet is so great that all the other painters ought to paint Monets." And if as a hero of the age Monet were deplorable, it was equally true that, influenced by his second wife, he had brought his art to a unique flowering, which a Midas instinct turned to gold.

The honest talent of those other impressionist artists retained a touchingly naïve character. Though frequently given prominence by Monet's increasing fame, in the contrast of styles Pissarro, Sisley and Renoir seemed irretrievably uninteresting, and the works of lesser followers actually repellent. "I feel so puny and mean next to that robust artist!" exclaimed Pissarro, and this psychological bond triumphed over him as it did the other impressionists, whose relationships to Monet, if stilted and altogether absurd, were both poignant and consoling.

Among those who had joined with Monet in the first 1874 exhibition, Edgar Degas alone became an artist with a public. By surreptitious insistence on the qualities of his academic training, by appealing subject matter and the production of occasional clever portraits, Degas had been the first to find regular sales. This position he never lost. Off in his own corner, cryptic and rebellious, untouched by the development of impressionism as a limited palette and a self-exclusive art form, Degas trod the lonely path of an iconoclast academic.

Renoir's place in public esteem underwent severe alterations during the 1880's. An inability to balance his bright, external skills at painting with an easy clarity of draftsmanship forced him into probes that were a form of personal soul-searching. Labored and hard-edged pictures issued from his studio, lacking the limpid purity of earlier periods. This extended soliloquy lost him much of his previous popularity, and he ceased to receive the portrait orders that had been his livelihood.

Most thoughtful and experienced, and oldest of the group, Camille Pissarro permitted his theoretic turn of mind to lead him into adoption of a petit-point system propounded by a younger artist. The empiric impressionism of Monet was to become an exact science, with reference to learned treatises by eminent physicists. When he laid siege to Monet, Pissarro met with complete rebuff and much anger. A further result of his new style was that Pissarro remained the last of the impressionists, able to make sales only when the tide ran high. "I was penniless . . .," he reported in May, 1891, as Monet experienced his great *Haystacks* triumph at Durand-Ruel's. "As a last resort I wrote to Monet, who promptly sent me a thousand francs."

Alone among his associates in following still the original path of impressionism taught at Argenteuil, Alfred Sisley also failed to meet with success. Lyric and charming, his works lacked all the spectacle that Monet employed to force himself on the public. Lax in ensemble, lacking in drama, and artificially optimistic, Sisley's works lacked an emotional intensity sufficient to raise them from what seemed triviality. Whether passionately felt or profoundly wrought, they represented a minor episode of impressionism before Monet gave it another fervent and impassioned character. As such they were a respectful, almost apologetic solution which was no solution at all.

Toward these colleagues of his youth and unhappiest hours Monet felt a deep bond expressed in alternations of secretiveness and assistance. Frequently gruff, plain-spoken to the point of rudeness, a bully demanding unconditional surrender from family, dealers, and friends, he could be diffidently sympathetic and infinitely patient with those in real distress. His pattern of existence operated along a rigid system of thought that was non-compromising but very broad. Loans of cash he was willing to make, aware how such help had come to him. The vagaries of his own bewildering course among dealers also frequently provided voids for others to fill. Early in 1890, after Monet deserted Theo van Gogh at Boussod & Valadon, the gap was closed by a Pissarro exhibition. The following year when Montaignac, a representative of the Galerie Georges Petit, expressed interest in Pissarro, Monet quickly conveyed the news.

"This is a bad moment for me; Durand does not take my paintings," Pissarro admitted only shortly after. "For the moment people want nothing but Monets." To obtain Monets it remained essential to approach directly, or through dealers, the sly man at Giverny, who relentlessly continued his game of forcing up prices. Every advantage was watched and his personal renown carefully nurtured. When Sargent and Rodin had been decorated with the Legion of Honor, Monet grandly refused the honor. His remarkable rebuff to an officialdom responsible for the suffering of his early life created a stir, but rebounded to his disadvantage when shortly after he sought a public commission.

Due to his health, and the numbers of his other commissions, Jules Breton, who had received an order to provide panels for the Hôtel de Ville, renounced this task in November, 1892. In his place Rodin proposed Claude Monet. Few then realized Monet's powers as a decorator, but the nomination was a farsighted one—which the commission dishonored by awarding its contract to Pierre Lagarde. The reversal touched Monet deeply, generating the sort of reaction typical of him in earlier years: He set his face and determined never again to seek public commissions or honors.

Episodes of this sort demonstrate that behind the public face of Monet remained another depth. The wounds of his past had thinly knit but not disappeared. They were responsible for the benevolent-sardonic minor-prophet personality which masked a happy home life, for, as Pissarro observed of his art, "these canvases breathe contentment." Monet no longer was an unhappy man, but discontent never was far and it roused griefs that might otherwise have lain dormant. Among fellow impressionists he experienced a sniping criticism that too often reflected envy of his success. Increasingly he turned to people outside his own field, to sculptors, politicians, poets, and writers, for the intellectual companionship he sought. That this world of persons equally famed was opened to him was one of the pleasanter increments of his own position. The inestimable tribute of unassuming sympathy and conviction was keenly savored. He accepted equally a blistering hero worship from the coterie of Americans gathered around him at Giverny, aware that by both these means his name was carried farther and higher than ever before.

Among artists Sargent alone remained an openhearted champion. Himself rapidly expanding into a colossus that would dominate the English-speaking world, he remained a loyal and staunch ally. From him Monet received a deference that was sincere, and the recommendation of many new purchasers. Periodically Sargent arrived at Giverny, as when early in 1893 he came to select one of the *Poplars* and a Creuse Valley study, for a patron of his own. But whether on occasional visits to Giverny, or in America or England—where Sargent soon dominated the Royal Academy—the force of his belief was turning Monet's name to magic.

A subject of unparalleled complexity, Rouen's great Gothic cathedral found Monet an uneasy suitor. To avoid an overelaborate realization he concentrated boldly on what had become the true purpose of a series: the progressive fragmentation of human vision and its endless ambiguities of perception. In this optical experience he sought drama by evocations of the *instantaneous* at the expense of clarity.

For such special purposes his second-floor window was well chosen. At noon each day the sun's force gradually attacked the cathedral façade. The building's vast insubstantial wraith could be seen moving in and out of shadows with supernatural regularity and ease. Encumbering veils dissolved individually, but following predetermined architectural patterns. Revealed singly were startling details of delicate tracery and filmy screenwork, bony systems of architraves, and disguised statue-laden buttresses. As they captured each new area, blasts of light in turn were magnified by the shrouded gloom of the room from which Monet watched. His system of observation thus presented its own pattern of distortions, of both scale and focus.

In two previous series his field of vision had successively narrowed. Now the window itself imposed physical limitations by decapitating Europe's most famous Butter Tower. The window's restricted width likewise prevented him from seeing the lower sections of both towers at one time. Rather than sacrifice an essential unity of effect, the towers were eliminated from his design, a decision whose eccentricity robbed him of the characteristic contour of a Gothic cathedral. Left with only the rump of a façade, he grouped the three great doors flush against the bottom of his canvases. A balanced and effective pattern emerged, but one singularly pedestrian for being deprived of any hint of the structure's soaring grandeur.

On this remaining third of the façade he concentrated the full force of his withering vision. The fiery angel that had contributed so strongly to earlier series provided new revelatory experiences, for while creeping across the bolder architectural forms, the sun struck at larger protrusions first. The conscious stylist and pattern maker always within Monet created sharp, precisely formed light images, knit by rhythms always violently alive. A joyous spectacle filled with throttled ambiguities took form, then grew in intensity through the gradual corrosion of an elaborate network of shadow relationships. Caught in the deepest of recessed areas, these provided complicated color intermezzos to punctuate and comment on the more violent drama surrounding them.

Midway through the sun's advance across the façade, four encrusted and ornamented architraves stood illumined in seas of darker color. The effect was voluptuous and dramatic, its frenzies generating a momentum which projected magic into luminous areas of colored shadow. Monet responded with eagerness and style, not quite unblemished but still immensely rewarding. Blazing areas of light now predominated. Deposits of color that formed his shadows grew more luminous, subtle, and varied, then, in the final works, faded away until the deeply recessed portals alone sheltered them.

Only now did the great superspectacle at which Monet aimed emerge. He followed the tongues of light that licked at exploded remnants of shadow, forcing their entire dissolution into a sheet of uniform glaring light. The cathedral was fixed on his canvas by a blazing area of brilliance, but almost every trace of Gothic form was lost in vibrations that shimmered through the air. The vast hulking structure stood irradiated on its site, a vision held to earth by penetrations of blue sky between truncated towers.

As this series evolved, it became equally certain that Monet was advancing yet another step by aiming at a wholly artificial concept of art. This series was itself an alliteration, superbly expressive, and containing much ravishing color. If it was more remarkable for glitter than architectural incisiveness, that was perhaps expected of Monet. More solemnity and grandeur existed in these performances than in his previous series. But totally unexpected was that they were images that belonged to a nightmare, filled with skeletal suggestions, effects of color impossible to attribute to atmosphere alone, sensations of frightening, painful semiblindness, and the sick fear implicit in moving in darkness.

The angel of fire had grown dominant, her hysterical obsession infecting every work with satanic mania. This was not even poetic drama or high romance, for though eager to suggest poetic and philosophical overtones inherent in the flight of brilliance across his cathedral, Monet had become caught up in staggering implausibilities of structure. It was less that his bizarre visions lacked the brittle hard polish of the cathedral inspiring them than that the corrosive legacy of his desire to push ever farther into the intangible had left him a romantic egotism encased in a cathedral of churning cotton wool.

To force into paint an imaginative process natural only to the eyes, the very method Monet employed on earlier series had altered.

Deeper accents and tones defining architectural forms were systematically omitted, making the canvas a record of the uniform film of light bouncing off the Gothic structure. It was an orgy of virtuoso vision, even if the mysterious shimmer that remained was such as was seen only in wilder dreams. Spectral and groping rather than palpable and real, these pictures replaced the gentle perceptions of his earlier years by a tumult and a shouting, a fanfare of trumpets and a clash of cymbals. Because he himself saw everything so irradiated, so magnified, his self-hypnosis was transferred to canvas, rising to a truly terrifying and shattering climax.

Through two winters he concentrated on the mesmeric task, repeating his one composition with variations of effects and canvas sizes. From February, 1892, through the end of that April he remained at Rouen. The following year he returned: "Useless to tell you that I am profiting from this beautiful weather. I work until I nearly drop from fatigue—it is always in this way that I have the best results. Also I wish for a continuation of the weather," he wrote to Durand-Ruel, March 23, 1893. "I work very hard, but could not dream of doing anything but the cathedral. It is an enormous project," he added seven days later.

To Geffroy he wrote with greater intimacy of the personal problems and decisions faced by such daring innovations: "My stay here advances, but that does not mean that I grow close to finishing my cathedrals. Alas! I can do nothing but repeat myself: the further I go the more painful it is to render that which I perceive; and I tell myself that anyone who says he has finished a canvas is very arrogant. Finished means complete, perfect, and I am working very hard without progress, searching, testing, without accomplishing great things, except my own fatigue."

Late in the spring of 1893, the many canvases accumulated in his room above the novelty shop finally were transported back to Giverny. On leaving the premises that had seen the birth of such vivid and abundant imagery, he growled a laconic "It's finished" to the proprietor. But a second stage had only begun.

Monet's sardonic mind and stagecraft had fashioned works which, once returned to Giverny, daunted even him. Both biting and brilliant, his cathedrals concentrated on harshness and angularity in subject and harmonies, nor was he certain that this combined well with their booming rhetorical style of composition. These were the works of a fanatic, a man with blazing eyes and a voice like doom, and there was a distinct danger that the immense good will and affection collectors felt for his recent series might wilt before his further advances into an actual destruction of vision. Had he perhaps toppled over into the ridiculous? Would his views of the cathedral not appear to Paris like something more in the nature of a fit than of ecstasy?

Through the year 1893 he reworked the cathedrals in his Giverny studio. What he did is unknown, though doubtless they emerged from this renewed onslaught with greater uniformity of finish, an enriched color, and corrections to the structural framework of the building itself. Plans for the exhibition matured while Monet still pondered the problem, uncertain of his solution. "Your son must have told you that he found me a little discouraged," he wrote to Durand-Ruel, February 20, 1894. "I am enough so to be on the point of canceling the exhibition of cathedrals, which still do not please me. At the end of the week I will write to you whether it is yes or no, but I think it will be no. Time passes and I make no progress with them."

He continued to work, and during the summer of 1894, more than two years after its commencement, he came to final terms with the series. Whether the cathedrals pleased him in an artistic sense it is impossible to know. His instincts, and the reactions of his own little circle, persuaded him they had a distinction based not on ordinary considerations but on the obvious superiority of his nerve and skill. Though an occasional hint of real style crept through their novelty, spurious glamour was their true hallmark, and this was appropriate to the economic circumstances that began to intrude into their history.

Monet had determined to employ this series for a further great advance in his structure of prices: 15,000 francs each was first heard in May. Durand-Ruel protested; Boussod & Valadon quickly removed themselves from consideration. "If anyone asks me for the cathedrals I will not sell them except at the price I have asked you," he wrote Durand-Ruel, May 7, "except on the condition that they remain in France a certain time, to make an exhibition at the proper moment."

Private clients always had been Monet's extra strength, and he summoned their legions to Giverny. To gaze on the new series, so talked of but mysteriously unseen, was sufficient inducement for the journey. The leap Monet had tried to take was too large even for him, however: "I have not seen everyone, but when I have we can reconsider this delicate question," he told Durand-Ruel on the twenty-first. "Here is what I intend to do. To put aside a certain number of cathedrals, those to which I attach the most importance and which will not be sold for the moment at less than the full price. This will permit me to sell the others more cheaply. I believe that this is the best solution. . . ."

Summer advanced while Durand-Ruel made tentative offers to purchase the entire series. After quarrels that were gossiped over throughout Paris, he proclaimed that Monet's unbudging attitude made this impossible. "The collectors say Monet is wrong," wrote Pissarro in October. "For example, people want to see the paintings before America gets them." But Pissarro's information already was out of date. In September, at Giverny, meetings were held at which—speaking separately to the representatives of Boussod & Valadon, and Georges Petit—Monet agreed definitely to lower his price from 15,000 to 12,000 francs. This bargain rate established, the dealers made their selections.

Count Isaac de Camondo was brought to Monet's studio by Manzi, and this distinguished collector, deeply impressed by the spectacle he found, purchased four *Cathedrals* at a price of 50,000 francs. Those he chose, showing the great Gothic hulk covered in gray mist, dull morning light, and tentative sunshine, prove Camondo to have been a cautious man despite his magnificent gesture. "If it is your intention to have some (I speak of the cathedrals)," Monet wrote to Durand-Ruel, "you had better disengage yourself from your understanding, otherwise you risk arriving after everyone already has chosen."

What Monet's battle against the dealers, and his final victory over them, had cost became evident only when peace was declared. In April he was forced to ask Pissarro for the money previously loaned him to buy a house. But reunited at Durand-Ruel's gallery May 10 to 31, 1895, the great series of cathedrals proved its ascendancy over the more heroic and straightforward themes common to painting. Fresh, powerful, and striking, often brutal and barbarous in their strength, the scenes constantly alternating in effect and dramatic structure,

"Si donc vous êtes dans l'intention d'en avoir (je parle des cathédrales) vous ferez bien de vous dégager de votre entente . . ."

they were hailed as an artistic triumph. And though the basic message of Monet's fractured vision was swamped in smartness, and one felt bombarded in chic, Monet's vision communicated itself to the public, who cheered with him over his wildest ecstasies.

Reservations were expressed too. "They have been attacked by the younger painters and even by Monet's admirers," Pissarro noted during the exhibition. "I am carried away by their extraordinary deftness. Cézanne, whom I met yesterday at Durand-Ruel's, is in complete agreement with my view that this is the work of a well-balanced but impulsive artist who pursues the intangible nuances of effects that are realized by no other painter. Certain painters deny the necessity of this research; personally I find any research legitimate that is felt to such a point."

And yet, in retrospect, though an extreme triumph, the cathedrals also represented a new variety of defeat, for Monet had overreached himself in every respect. Of the forty or more canvases begun at Rouen, only twenty were shown in Paris. Many more remained at Giverny, discarded in incomplete states from which Monet felt unable to rescue them. At the exhibition one canvas was sold to Gonse, of the *Gazette des Beaux-Arts,* and a second to an unnamed American. Sargent made a noble effort to interest Mrs. Jack Gardner of Boston: "I am so glad you want the Rouen Cathedral. It is the white one or rather the rosy one, not the green one," he told her. "I remember your mention of it when I saw you last, and that I had told you it was sold to the Prince de Polignac, and wired you on hearing it was still to be had." But Polignac *had* bought this picture, and Mrs. Gardner did not select another.

Of the twenty *Cathedrals* exhibited, twelve were therefore stripped of the frames specially hired for the exhibition, and returned to Monet at Giverny. Three years later, in June, 1898, he was still able to exhibit seven of these at the Galerie Georges Petit. The shouting and the tumult had produced little of substance. No new series was undertaken. The path that had led to this shattering theatrical illusion was abandoned.

The temporary check to his career that Monet experienced from the *Cathedrals* was without lasting effect. His other works were widely sought, and already infrequent opportunities to acquire his earlier pictures were creating astonishing prices. On March 18, 1894, the collection of Théodore Duret, containing six Monets, was sold at auction. Sargent wrote to Mrs. Gardner in Boston: "There are some beautiful Manets, I believe, and a famous old picture of Monet, *Les Dindons Blancs,* which is exquisite. I have no idea what it would fetch, but eight or ten thousand francs might get it, to judge by his present prices." Painted at Montgeron for Hoschedé, this work surpassed expectations by reaching 12,000 francs.

And as Monet came to understand better the nature of his public, new series of a quieter more poetic nature made their appearance. The same capacity to express the fragmentation of human vision before variations of atmosphere was present in twenty-four canvases of the *Cliffs* series, shown at the Galerie Georges Petit in June, 1898. But now, instead of dawdling over favorite themes, or going at his canvases like a brash steamroller, in a second series of eighteen *Mornings on the Seine* he showed an artistry less severe and brusque than before. Without stylistic retrogression Monet was prepared to explore the softer, quieter episodes of nature.

Mornings on the Seine were suggestive of a new attitude of affectionate detachment, demonstrating how much his continued success had altered and broadened Claude Monet. At the end of his fifth decade there was an obvious regeneration. The marks of his earlier self never were effaced; neither the marble look nor the snake's half-smile was eliminated, but the good years had altered his nature. His voice still could have a searching, restless fret, and letters were written with biting heaviness. But in equal measure his personality was tinged by the aura of radiance that glowed from within. Dedicated from birth to pursuit of an art, he had been taken up, as if by angels, into a realm where others could not follow.

How much of this was due to the reformative influence of Alice Monet's fractured smile can only be surmised, though her part in shaping his later years must not be minimized. To her is attributable the warm, closely knit family life by which he was surrounded, the remarkable solidity of which was most apparent in 1897 when Camille's son Jean married Blanche Hoschedé, two years his senior. Together the couple departed Giverny's walled garden to make their home at Rouen, where Jean was employed as a chemist by his father's brother Léon, who operated a dyeing and weaving plant at Maromme-Les-Rouen.

Monet had neither lost a son nor gained a daughter, and this tightening of family bonds contributed to the stability of his humor and the growth of his personality. His life had grown full of wholesome material comforts, among which he ate, drank, and smoked rhythmically around the clock, yet not immoderately, in a state of continuous blissful ingestion. His fits of petulance and bad temper were short-lived and seemed reserved for the purchasers of his pictures and recollections of the unhappy past. To the present he brought a bigness, a generosity in spirit as well as material things, on which his friends learned to rely.

In earlier years Monet had shown no warmth toward Cézanne, but by 1895 he had purchased paintings by the man from Aix, adding them to a personal collection that included Manet, Renoir, and Henner. He grew fond of confounding visitors to Giverny with this collection, Cézanne's works especially, and on one occasion in the nineties he invited Cézanne for a visit. Monet's intention was to introduce him to his own circle, whose acclaim might build self-esteem, but the visit proved unpleasant. In that strictly bourgeois household Cézanne's gaucheries were difficult to overlook, especially when, after Rodin took his hand, Cézanne exclaimed, "He shook my hand! And he is a man who has been decorated!" Unable to accommodate himself to the situation, Cézanne finally fled, leaving to Monet the task of collecting canvases abandoned in his haste. Unsettled and distrustful, Cézanne then turned on his friends: "Pissarro is an old fool, Monet a cunning fellow, they have nothing in them. . . ."

More sophisticated than the painter from Aix, Pissarro also flitted between envy, criticism, gratitude, and admiration. "Monet, who has always been so kind to us . . ." is found in a letter to his son. But acute awareness of their economic differences created a source of irritation nothing could mellow. "It is said money is scarce, but that is only relatively true; does not Monet sell his work, and at very high prices—do not Renoir and Degas sell? No, like Sisley, I remain in the rear of the impressionist line."

Through years of continued privation such thoughts affected Pissarro's vision, producing a puzzling alternation of sentiments: "I saw the Monets, they are beautiful, but . . . while good, they do not represent a highly developed art. For my part, I subscribe to what I have often heard Degas say, his art is that of a skillful but not profound decorator." Relying more on feelings than on thought,

Pissarro equally often contradicted himself: "The *Cathedrals* are being much talked of, and highly praised too, by Degas, Renoir, myself and others." And the most reliable indication of his belief is that he too followed in the path Monet pioneered. A year after Monet he too worked at Rouen, quoting Monet's methods: "You will remember that the *Cathedrals* of Monet were all done with veiled effects which give a certain mysterious charm to the edifice. . . ."

In common with Monet and the other impressionists, Pissarro harbored resentment against Émile Zola. Monet's distaste was perhaps more acute, and more hidden, for Zola's treachery to the dead was impossible to forgive. A further irritant, and a painful epilogue, had been presented by Zola's willful misinterpretation of motives during the *Olympia* subscription. These sins weighed less on Monet's mind after Zola became involved in the Dreyfus affair. Together with Geffroy and Clemenceau, he took the writer's side vociferously: "I watch from afar and with passion this ignoble trial. . . . More and more I admire Zola for his courage," he wrote. And ten days later, February 25, 1898, "The wonderful courage of Zola! It is an absolute form of heroism"; despite which the treachery of an earlier date had been too severe. Artist and writer never met again.

Though the ideas with which he had been associated often had been arraigned, as the decade of the nineties advanced Monet rarely suffered attack. Older than Courbet or Manet lived to be, he combined the positions of both men to emerge as the most respected of senior artists. Few examined whether he was a saint with chance devotion to art, or a hypocrite able to shake off and disavow errors of the past. Was he cunning or merely weak? Did his complete disavowal of theory permit him ever, in any real sense, to know what he was doing? Surrounded by this mélange of conflicting opinion, the rootless Bohemian artist of a former age found acknowledgment as the greatest single influence on his century.

Indicative of the respect in which he was held was that on his deathbed it was for Claude Monet that Alfred Sisley sent, in January, 1899, when—disappointed with life and resigned to death—he realized his end was near. That personal warmth which attached friends to Monet in the days of his youth had returned. And in its sober modesty his conduct in the years of his success was an example to all. His decision to remain clear of official honors was adhered to with stoic firmness. So strong were his feelings that in August, 1900, when Renoir accepted a decoration, he wrote to Monet apologetically: "I would not like this little piece of ribbon to change our old friendship. Tell me this is stupidity, the most disagreeable words, I shall not mind. But do not be ironic because whether I have done something silly or not, I hold onto your friendship. As for the others I do not care."

Monet's reception of the news bore an air of melancholy. Renoir's abandonment of the strange principle left him alone, the last intransigent just as he had been the first. His reply brought from Renoir further expressions of faith: "You have, you, an admirable line of conduct. Me, I can never know one day what I am going to do the next."

26. The Patriarch

AT 9 Rue Lamartine, Paris, on March 4, 1903, Mme. Doncieux was discovered dead in her apartment. To write a certificate of death, consultations were held at which no one could supply her Christian name, nor that of her husband. That she had been mother-in-law to the famous Claude Monet, and was grandmother of his sons, remained unsuspected. Since the death of her younger daughter Geneviève, May 15, 1894, Mme. Doncieux had lived alone, rigorously preserving the two fortunes her rapacity had denied Camille. That such a lethal malevolence at last had been turned on herself, and that she had gone to her death unreconciled, unabsolved, and unabsolving, was exquisitely ironic.

With Mme. Doncieux perished a last link to the past, and the last recollections of Camille, save for those rattling within the brain of an artist deliberately cloaking them in silence. Since her death twenty-four years before, Monet never had mentioned her name, except occasionally to acknowledge that she modeled for a Renoir portrait hanging at Giverny. Nine years after her death he had comforted Boudin on the decease of his wife: "I share your sorrow. I have gone through all that, and know the void such a loss leaves. Be strong and brave, that is all I can say to you, while sending you my sincere condolences." But at Giverny the hope in Camille's smile, the submission in his dismay, her sweet childish ignorance lightly sequined with a fetching sophistication, never were mentioned. Michel, child of her deathbed, grew up unnecessarily burdened by a belief he had caused his mother's death. And except for her Christian name, attached to a few pictures, all substance vanished. Camille Léonie Doncieux became a shadow that once had crossed the life of Claude Monet.

He was a great traveler now. Norway, Madrid, and London saw his corpulent little figure and oddly tailored clothes. A series of the Thames was in progress almost simultaneously with another at Lavacourt, across the Seine from Vétheuil. In good weather his huge Panhard-Levassor automobile was rolled out, and amid much smoke and fumes an overstuffed chauffeur drove him to the vacant summer villa rented for this winter work. Installed in a second-floor room facing the river, large glass doors opened onto a balcony, Monet again painted Vétheuil. Two decades had passed since Camille was laid to rest beside the church at which daily he peered, and still her grave was unmarked.

The amount of visual energy exploded by these projects was fantastic, yet, even carried on simultaneously, they were not sufficient, for his largest interest had become the creation of a new garden. Giverny itself had given rise to the first two series, the *Haystacks* and *Poplars*. The third had been provided by Rouen, not far away down the Seine. Madrid had given him nothing to paint, Norway produced few canvases, and London, his series of which occupied him still at Giverny, was distant. It was Giverny—his own garden, in fact—which would provide him with the motif for a last series fated to occupy him for the balance of his long life.

A strip of land across the railway tracks from his front gate had been purchased during the nineties. First he experimented with unsuccessful boating scenes on the stream running through this property. Later he had the stream diverted and set men to work digging a pond. Two small concrete sluices were installed to control the flow of water, and when ready he examined a seed catalogue for varieties of plants and water lilies. The house staff was increased by an extra gardener in whose charge this water garden was placed, and then, after the beginning of the new century, Monet enlarged the pond until it reached the entrance gate of its little property. To gain access a small arched bridge in Japanese style was constructed across the water's tapering neck. Close by he planted a thicket of bamboos, under whose delicate leafage the outlet ran, and bowers of roses deliberately hid the whole of this compact but luxurious garden from the eyes of those passing on railway or road.

From the moment Claude Monet devoted himself to sketching in his water garden, his existence lost normal confines of time and gave instead the impression of unfolding in one unbroken arc. Quite uncoordinated with any action but his own, Monet drifted on, a living triumph over ingrained prejudices, able to ignore all convention whether personal or artistic. Time's numbered units passed at a most unrefined gallop. They succeeded only in moving him beyond sight of criticism into realms of pure acceptance that scarcely any other artist attained.

Everywhere the poetic impulse prevailed in a lyric art that no longer attempted to stun with huge climaxes and violent outbursts, but preferred to demonstrate how richly colorful and continuously interesting were impressionist procedures. Canvases peacefully boiled over with pinks, yellows, and art-nouveau purples, all spumed over pale green by some obscure emission of the pond's depths. And everything he touched was lit by that mysterious extra something that is more than flawless instinct, more than pious attention to nature, more than the stored experience of a lifetime growing luxuriously long.

The fiery irascibility he formerly displayed had been tempered; he was more sage, more restrained, but complete master of a house where he had created an ambiance in which he could practice the self-indulgent asceticism common to the small-scale tyrant. Everyone surrounding him was forced to serve his psychological needs at their own expense of spirit. Life whirled with unabashed dedication, suiting every function to his convenience; dinner was prepared at the hour when he finished work, lunch was coordinated with the opening of the water lilies, and everyone gathered when expected.

Dominance was so complete his son Jean was unable to escape

even through marriage to his stepsister and a home removed to Rouen. For whether by his own wish, or that of his wife, every weekend Jean with Blanche returned to Giverny. Never during his father's lifetime did Jean's younger brother, Michel, reach a state of independence sufficient to marry. And surrounding Monet were always the Hoschedé daughters, visibly growing more plump, and ripe with nubility to the point of rotting like medlars. Suzanne, because of whose marriage to Theodore Butler Monet's own nuptials to her mother took place in 1892, died in 1899. But even this emotionally crucial situation was not permitted to alter a rigorous family unity. Suzanne was laid to rest in her father's tomb behind Giverny's little church. Then, to care for her two young children, Butler married her sister Marthe Valentine, four years older than the deceased Suzanne.

The new century thus altered and hardened a ritualistic aspect in life at Giverny. After the first years Monet rarely worked mornings but, like his water lilies, greeted the day when the sun had half crossed the heavens. Dressed in his specially arranged costumes of heavy boots, fashionable *demi-sussarde* ankle-buttoned trousers, and frilled shirts with great pleated cuffs, daily he was seen to dab and scrub at variously shaped and proportioned canvases. Balanced on a barstool under umbrellas of generous size, or walking vigorously back and forth, on both sides of him he strewed quantities of matches and half-smoked cigarettes.

His white beard had grown to Mosaic proportions, and so thoroughly did it hide shirtfronts that, unless he was going to Paris, Monet never troubled with a tie. This was his only concession to comfort, for, conscious of his neat classic profile each week he had a barber visit to crop his hair close to the head. More conventional attire—a dark suit and carefully starched collars, or *boulevardier's* checked trousers and walking stick—was worn to Paris, nor did he scruple to hang a gold watch chain across his ample vest. The bourgeois ethics of Alice Monet are seen here, refashioning a rebel into a merchant prince. But Monet too was of bourgeois origin, and the respectability of these later years was a reversion to patterns into which he was born, and which at earlier moments of his career he had himself essayed less successfully.

The cultivated habits of his wife were surely discernible in other respects, however, for Monet had become a great reader. That he concentrated on the works of acquaintances shows what immediate impulses spurred him, but he also ranged afield. Often in the evenings he read aloud to his family, a practice facilitated by a spacious new sitting room created from the first studio. Though wicker chairs were in evidence, deeply cushioned and tufted couches and a chaise were present too. A writing desk decorated with photographs of himself and friends served for his voluminous correspondence, and on the walls four rows of unframed canvases spelled out the history of his labors. To replace this necessary work space, in a farther corner of the garden a specially designed structure rose up crowned by towering pagodalike source of light. This was his new studio, ample in space and amenities for the finishing of series.

Enclosed in this walled domain of his own creation, Monet was accepted passively by those whom he bent to his will. Uniformly he impressed them as modest and businesslike in his application to work, a silent, dedicated man. Perhaps it was his lofty, unshaken, and unassailable position, both in the outer world and his own patriarchal domain, that was responsible. Perhaps only that he remained a most industrious, mysterious little man, and his sense of the madness and fitness of things became theirs.

Full of an unobtrusive good sense, he applied that increasingly rare commodity to the affairs of younger generations gathered about him. Though he bitterly had opposed Durand-Ruel's American policy two decades before, it had been his salvation. For Theodore Butler he demanded of Durand-Ruel whether the New York gallery could not be "engaged to exhibit a certain number of canvases? As I have told you, he has need of encouragement, and by helping him a little over there, you would be doing us a favor, my wife and me. . . . We would be greatly obliged if you could give him a pat on the shoulder in New York." Nor did he forget obligations to the dead. In Paris one day he visited Clemenceau, who had become a Minister, reminding him of the years passed since Édouard Manet's death and that the *Olympia* by right should be hung in the Louvre. In three days it was done, a happy culmination to the task undertaken with Sargent eighteen years before.

Much in society when she lived with her first husband, Alice Monet retained her gracious ways, and distinguished guests seemed always to enjoy the reception they found. Each Sunday the family increased by the presence of Blanche Hoschedé and Jean, and it was then that Clemenceau often appeared, Durand-Ruel arrived, or distinguished collectors shared lunch. Accustomed to American pronunciation of the English language, Monet showed much amusement when visited by Sargent's British friend, Mrs. Charles Hunter, whom the American artist, a sepulcher of respectability in London, frequently traveled with on the Continent. A fine-looking woman wearing fussy costumes that contributed to her tremendous bearing, Mary Hunter spread her tennis-club English about Giverny to the delight of Monet, who beamed at her gimlet-eyed as though she were a private joke on Sargent.

The dining room was low of ceiling, longer than wide, and painted a startling canary yellow. All appointments were of the same color, making simple rustic furniture and cane-bottom chairs fairy-like: an idea originated with Whistler when the artist had decorated his Paris apartment. Frame against frame on the walls, cramming every available space, were a selection of Monet's Japanese prints. And curiously, among these his choice fell on figure studies demonstrating the Japanese skill with bodies that leap about, wiggle, or bang into each other across blank paper, in place of the stylized renderings of landscape.

Alice Monet was careful to prepare specialties for each of her guests, whose preferences she noted. Clemenceau ate nothing but baked potato; Sargent followed Monet's own example by heartily enjoying elaborate preparations. Woodcock was a favorite of the master himself, whose son Michel each year presented him with the first bird he shot. It was a table where one spoke of the dishes, and where the serving of a cake could find Monet questioning a guest: "Do you like rhubarb?"

"Devil!" he answered himself. "That is the secret of this magnificent cake. . . ."

Michel discovered that it had the flavor of wet straw—"like the straw on old bottles," he refined his estimate.

"Improved by three years in the cellar!" called another.

But no jest spoiled the pleasure of Monet, who again complimented the cake. "Go on, pour some *muscadet,* as recompense for the rhubarb," he suggested.

The wine had been stirred by its trip to Giverny. "You should drink this *muscadet* in my own district, by the banks of the Loire, with two dozen Brittany oysters, sea-flavored and pungent," the guest responded.

Monet was practiced at gustatorial bargaining. He struck back. "I once ate a fish previously extolled to me as one of the most delicate dishes of Nantes: a lamprey. A friend had sent it with instructions that made my mouth water. But it was odious. A sort of hard gut, revolting, ran from one end of the fish to the other. The recollection is not a happy one."

"That is because your lamprey was what we call 'corded,' that is to say, it was not spawning. Except in February and March lampreys are not edible. They are seasonal fish. But do you know our white butter?"

"Ah! Ah! So you fall back on your white butter!" cried Monet, pleased to have demolished all other defenses. "I wish you would give me the recipe."

"There is no exact recipe. It is a sort of sleight-of-hand a few old women at riverside inns achieve when a fish dinner is ordered. All that is necessary is to cut up some garlic heads, cook these over a very slow fire in a wineglassful of white wine, until they are reduced to a good consistency. Then, always stirring, and never allowing it to boil, drop in the butter, bit by bit. The sauce must be thick and unctuous. It can be flavored to taste with pepper and salt, and served very hot with a fine fish cooked in bouillon, preferably a pike. . . ."

Monet looked straight before him, a slight smile creasing the corners of his eyes.

"We must try it," he said.

Come to purchase a picture or write an interview, the casual visitor to Giverny found a different man. One critic was struck by three things: a unique presence, searching eyes, and immaculate linen. Little profundity existed in such observations, for though chosen with elaborate care, his clothes were never a particularly good fit, nor particularly elegant. More significant was that when confronted in this way Monet's memory played bizarre tricks, and those who expected to hear from him the unvarnished truth were from time to time disappointed.

His characteristically amiable, semiarticulate interviews were in fact clumsily self-promoting. By rambling dissertations he constantly endeavored to establish who and what he was, to underscore heavily his own importance at earlier periods, and to assemble the components of his being into some definable entity. This amounted to an obsession, and because the image he sought to create by postulating an omnipotent and omniscient self was beyond him, he developed a mild line in compulsive boasting.

One visitor of this special sort, Wynford Dewhurst, saw Monet in a genial humor as he strolled through his property. To be seen in the character of a country gentleman, surrounded by the good and substantial things brought by his success, pleased Monet now no less than at Argenteuil thirty years before. For Dewhurst's edification he discussed the grafting of plants and other agricultural mysteries with numerous blue-bloused and sabotted gardeners. Himself dressed in soft khaki felt hat and jacket, lavender-colored silk shirt opened at the neck, drab trousers tapering to the ankles and secured by big horn buttons, and a short pair of cowhide boots, his appearance was decidedly quaint, but with a well-considered smartness.

"Yes, my friend, today I cannot paint enough, and make probably fifteen thousand pounds a year; twenty years ago I was starving," he enjoyed remarking on such occasions.

Forty years of an unfortunate and turbulent lifetime had elapsed since he entered Gleyre's studio, and they improved considerably his impressions of what took place there. The seventeen months of study were telescoped to a brief fortnight; on meeting with Sisley, Bazille, and Renoir, "I forthwith preached rebellion to them. The exodus being decided on, we left, Bazille and I taking a studio in common." In the next years his story grew further, until he recounted how the four had "banded together, we grumbled. It was enough for a single word to declare open revolt. . . . I avow that I pronounced it, that word. I led my friends and we quit Gleyre's studio. . . ." So definitely the leader of impressionism when he spoke, he liked to imagine he always had been so.

Nor had the dramatics of which his life had been so full departed from him. Though less visible to his family, who daily saw him work in the garden with silent devotion, to a guest the great authority and emotional range he brought to his role created an overwhelming presence. From steps inside a rear gate where customarily they stood after presenting cards to Sylvain Besnard, the terrible-tempered porter and chauffeur, would-be callers might on occasion spy Monet himself. An aged squat little figure, crowned by a peasant's straw hat, he bore down in a state of exasperation. Here was the master himself, superbly on stage, larger than life, playing to the gallery in a manner suggesting a mixture of Rasputin and Svengali.

"Gentlemen," he said, "I never receive when I am working. Never. I am lost if I am interrupted while I am at work. You understand, gentlemen, I pursue a patch of light. It is my fault; I want to seize the intangible. It is terrible, this light which escapes one, taking color with it. Color, any color, lasts but a second; sometimes three or four minutes, rarely as long as that. What can one paint in three or four minutes? They are gone so quickly and then one must stop. How I suffer! This painting, how it makes me suffer! It tortures me! It hurts me!"

The hero left his guests excited, satisfied, astonished, and profoundly moved. Fulsome in his adulation of the people he approved, those he did not were fortunate to get off with no worse a description than "constipated" (Fantin-Latour), "dauber" (Gauguin) or merely "wretch." Constantly spilling over into declamation and exclamation, he seemed in fact to practice a certain ambivalence toward even those of whom he approved. Views of Corot, from whom he had derived his method of retouching sketches from nature, came forth colored by an impressionistic sense of truth. "He was the greatest landscape painter in the world. . . . I ask myself how Ruisdael with his black tones can have seen nature. I cannot even understand Hobbema. Hobbema sometimes understood light, witness his *Allée* in the National Gallery. I repeat, Corot was the greatest landscape painter the world has known."

But when someone casually remarked, "The good Corot, as everyone called him," Monet's face changed and reddened. Praise of another stung him, and he swung around to disagreement with no fear of inventing his facts: *"The good Corot;* I do not know about that. I do know that he was anything but good to us, the impressionists. The wretch! He barred the doors of the Salon to us; he hunted us, and prevented us from exhibiting. He swore that we were malefactors, yes, actually malefactors. . . ."

Provocative creator, craftsman, salesman, merchant, propagandist, Monet's position continued to expand; his frequent exhibitions suggested a sea of triumphs on which his name rode ever higher. Durand-Ruel continued to take the lion's share of his produce, in response to which, when interviewed, Monet never failed to credit this dealer with saving the impressionist movement from starvation. If such acknowledgment suggested he had mellowed, it is equally certain that nothing had separated him from those rigorous methods of merchandising he had evolved in the previous century.

At his preposterous worst Monet could pen to Durand-Ruel such words as "You should know me well enough to know that I am not a man interested in money—is it not so?" Such bizarre self-appraisal had all the form of deliberate wit, despite the insecure sense of humor. But it was not, and the truth was he retained still a vicious, driving greed. In the first decade of the new century he was able to render to Durand-Ruel bills high as 247,000 francs against delivery of seventeen pictures. On a Sunday, viewing works at Giverny, Durand-Ruel might choose canvases valued at 113,000 francs.

Though overinclined to exploit the ultimate commercial value of his abundant productivity, Monet remained in every sense a functioning artist. In March, 1901, Sargent laughed to see ninety canvases littering the room Monet had taken at London's Hotel Savoy. Each was a separate record of some momentary effect over the Thames. But when the effect repeated itself, and an opportunity arose for further work, the atmosphere generally had changed before the particular canvas was found. Eventually Monet gave up, and asking Sargent to obtain a photo of the Parliament buildings for him, he had all ninety essays transported back to Giverny.

"I cannot send you a single canvas of London," he told Durand-Ruel two years later, in March, 1903, "because to work as I do it is indispensable that I have all of them before me, and it is also true that not a single one is definitely finished." Another year passed before he felt able to exhibit a London series and sent instructions to Durand-Ruel: "Would you come next Wednesday or Thursday to make your choice of London views which I am at last near to finishing. . . . I expect to be able to show from 35 to 40, and we will be able to open the exhibition for the sixth of May." But while the *Londons* still were hidden at Giverny, Paris filled with the rumors that entwined themselves into the growing legend of Claude Monet. Count Isaac de Camondo, who had purchased four *Cathedrals*, visited Giverny to purchase a *London*, and stories spread that he had gobbled up the entire series.

When exhibited in 1904, the London series proved to be a uniform evocation of fog and mist over the Thames. Well presented, vigorous, omitting fussy inessentials, they were a curiously empty but comprehensive account of the English capital. A mood of ecstatic adoration was induced in entire crowded audiences, and Durand-Ruel sold one a day during the first ten days of the exhibition, at *20,000 francs each*. Monet was outdoing himself.

Yet when this series was exhibited in England, for the first time Monet's methods became suspect. Aware that he had asked Sargent for photos of the motif employed, William Rothenstein and others questioned the propriety of this procedure on the part of an impressionist. Scandal was in the air, and as reports reached Monet, he moved startlingly to uncontrolled rage. He knew neither Rothenstein nor anyone else mentioned, "but only Mr. Harrison, whom Sargent had charged to make for me a little photo of Parliament which I have never been able to use. But it is of no importance whether my cathedrals, my London, and other canvases are made after nature or not. . . . I know so many painters who work after nature and do nothing but horrors. That is what your son must respond to these persons. The result is all."

The following day he proposed writing direct to Sargent, "to whom I owe a response, how certain of his friends are acting towards me. . . . I would like to know also whether Sargent has come many times to your exhibition, and if your son has not found him slightly hostile himself, because he has written to me in terms so singular in the view of many of us that I am wondering if he does not watch our success with a jealous heart." But Sargent's generosity and championship withstood unwarranted suspicion, and soon Monet was overjoyed by the success of the exhibition: "It is an excellent thing to have made such a decisive blow at London, and I congratulate you," he told Durand-Ruel.

In England, as in America, Sargent remained Monet's most potent champion. The attention of his superior intelligence was directed to definitions of his friend's art, and deliberately Sargent produced formulas excluding all but the remarkable spectacle Monet created. Only occasionally did his ideas reach paper: "I dare say I muddled what I said about impressionism last night and perhaps this is a clear definition of what I think Monet would mean by the word: 'The observation of the color and value of the image on our retina of those objects or parts of objects of which we are prevented by an excess or deficiency of light from seeing the surface or local color.' " That Monet had regaled the world with spectacles as a deliberate economic policy was neatly passed over in the mention of "excess or deficiency of light," a phrase that ingeniously welded the series to the main body of impressionism.

By Sargent's influence visual and optical phenomena employed in Monet's later works became the only pure *impressionism,* a word to which no other form of painting could aspire. Even Sargent's own impressionist works of the eighties found themselves outside the new exclusive criteria he created. That they were actually the truest form of this art, and Sargent himself an early impressionist, were quietly sacrificed. To a writer on art he propounded the doctrine forcefully: *"Impressionism* was the name given to a certain form of observation when Monet, not content with using his eyes to see what things were or what they looked like as everyone else had done before him, turned his attention to noting what took place *on his own retina* (as an oculist would test his own vision). It led to his doing 50 pictures of the same subject under varying degrees of light and the phenomena which he recorded would be more or less apparent when there was excess or deficiency of light. . . ."

Nor would Sargent permit development other than Monet's unique vision to be classed as impressionism. "The habit of breaking up one's color to make it brilliant dates from further back than impressionism," he wrote again. "Couture advocates it in a little book called 'Causeries d'Atelier,' written about 1860. It is part of the technique of impressionism but used for quite different reasons. Couture, Delacroix, Orchardson break up their color, but they are not impressionists."

At Sargent's Chelsea studio Monet had walked past masterly portraits with unseeing eyes. From impressionism Sargent had learned to paint flesh with astonishing brilliance, and to catch that same *instantaneousness* in expression that Monet sought from atmosphere. But for *studio* work Sargent had also adopted a classic tonality, and at this Monet refused to look. His offense was so obvious that Sargent himself had to restrain angry friends: "You do not understand, he does not like this kind of painting." Only Sargent's brilliant landscapes, their bristle-brush textures built to more feverish heights than Monet's own, gained approval, and Monet showed himself especially pleased by the watercolors of Venice that Sargent created with dazzling spontaneity and good humor.

To paint in Venice himself now passed through Monet's mind,

and an invitation to stay at the Palazzo Barbaro, home of Sargent's relative Daniel Sargent Curtis, was duly arranged for October, 1908. But Mrs. Curtis' high and dry formality failed to recommend itself to an artist equally exigent toward his work. With his wife Monet moved to the Grand Hotel Britannia, from where he inspected the water city for effects inevitably transient or deliberately provocative. He found himself under no necessity to wander from the center.

Sargent had sketched his watercolors from a gondola on the still waters, but Monet preferred solid ground under his feet. "I am lost in admiration of Venice, but unfortunately cannot make a long *séjour* . . .," he wrote. Meanwhile three or four locations appropriate to his needs were discovered, and from these obvious positions he launched a campaign. An isolated *fondamenta* near the Campo San Maurizio yielded a variety of architectural subjects along the Grand Canal. Opposite was the Palazzo Mula in morning's blanketing shadow; later in the day he turned his view to the Church of the Salute, its domes and minarets seen through mooring posts before the Prefectura. From another opening onto the Grand Canal he sketched the Palazzo Dario, but it was from the extended prominence of the Dogana, or Custom House, that Monet was best able to employ stylized techniques calculated to project his hypnotic vision of a city that had unexpectedly overwhelmed him.

First by weeks, then by months, the stay was prolonged. His sixty-eighth birthday was passed in curious rejuvenation, dabbing canvases of San Marco from Venice's Custom House and the island of San Giorgio. For once his honest and sufficient craftsmanship brought pleasure as it extolled an air more radiant than any he had known. In sunset views of San Giorgio seen from the Via Garibaldi his extraordinary facility expended itself not in opulence of effect but in strange exaggerations and juxtapositions; yet to those familiar with Venice his efforts possessed considerable truth and depth. On December 7 he wrote Geffroy, "I console myself with the thought of returning here next year, because I have been able to do nothing but preliminary efforts and starts. But what a misfortune not to have come here when I was younger! When I had all my audacity! . . . But I pass some delicious moments, almost forgetting that I am as old as I am!"

27. Valedictory

VENICE witnessed the smoldering blaze of a fierce sun about to go into eclipse. Months were passed in audible ecstasy, but with whatever hopes of returning Claude Monet departed, his future held only the peace of Giverny, the scent of roses, and the lapping of water in his pond. At Christmas his wife Alice became ill and unable to leave her bed. Monet acted as though he were the afflicted, raking doctor and family with ravaged eyes, and searching distractedly for a comfort that was not found. He was unable to work. His unwillingness to work became a symptom of relapse into earlier crude melodrama, and soon the foreboding this aroused was justified. Once again he accepted fate with that same irrational blend of stupefying complacency and mordant delight in his own pain.

Pan is not lightly ensnared; this threat to a union that had endured thirty years was eclipsing in pathos and collapsing dignity. A most unwilling and most naturally uxorious of men, Monet's gray, battered, oddly woebegone visage again expressed grief. Threatened with further sessions of imbecile idolatry, he refused to give the morosely funny interviews he so enjoyed: "I have asked him to be good enough to postpone his visit" was the polite formula of March, 1909. By July it had grown more firm: "I must say that if M. Brinton wishes to write an article about me you [Durand-Ruel] possess enough of my paintings from all periods to inform him sufficiently, and otherwise, as you know, I do not wish to take part personally." Retirement behind his walls at Giverny became complete.

Years passed while his exhibitions, his sales, and the visits of his dealers continued, each episode marked by an enormous new sensibility and an unwillingness to face the world for any purpose. Only the fierce necessity of extracting sympathy, a motive always so prevalent, forced him to raise his pen:

Giverny, May 18, 1911

DEAR MONSIEUR DURAND,

I give you some very bad news. My dear wife is in her last extremity. It is no more than a question of hours. You know through what anguishes I pass, especially the last fifteen days. I am at the end of my strength and courage.

Your all devoted

CLAUDE MONET

If this revived recollection of earlier letters in the same mood, that was extinguished the following day by a telegram: FATAL DÉNOUEMENT THIS MORNING FOUR O'CLOCK.

To provide Christian burial a priest was brought to Giverny, where for many years none had been resident. But the sight of his wife lowered into a tomb marked *Ernest Hoschedé* stung Monet. The dead seemed at last to have reclaimed its own, a thought too abominable to be entertained. The tablet placed on the tomb therefore read: *Alice Monet, died May 19, 1911.* Nothing more: Neither her birth, her maiden name, nor her relationship to the man in whose tomb she lay and to whom she had borne so many children was permitted by Monet's jealous and possessive wrath. For all the ages she became his alone.

Deep shadows had fallen over Giverny. The whole kingdom contracted in one brow of woe, its undisputed monarch a curious bundle of contradictions: shrewd yet naïve, humorless yet capable of relating funny anecdotes, masculine in his appetite for possession yet feminine in his partisan ferocity and love of pain, bold on canvas yet increasingly unsure. About him life continued in the ordered pattern established by his second wife. He remained the man she made of him, and her children, fathered by Ernest Hoschedé, surrounded him still, exercising a nicely judged blend of sympathy and calculated self-interest.

But the shadows remained. A portrait Carolus-Duran had painted of Alice Monet in her youth was purchased and hung in Monet's little bedroom. Jacques, oldest son of its subject, and never a part of the family at Giverny, importuned his stepfather for restitution of his own portrait by Édouard Manet. After eight months of bereavement he wrote: "These days of festivities at the end of the year have been very painful to pass and resulted in a redoublement of sadness, lowness, and complete discouragement. I am going to get control of myself and take up again my brushes that I have abandoned, and I hope soon to have finished my canvases of Venice"—which had lain three years in the studio.

Probably it was true that Monet's recollection of his intentions in the Venice works had dulled through a period of extended anxieties. Though successful, their exhibition in May, 1912, was not greeted with entire acclaim. Sargent urged the president of the Brooklyn Museum to purchase a blazing view of the Doges' Palace, but some critics spoke of a decline. The truth lay elsewhere, for while finishing them Monet had become disturbed over the quality of his vision. August 1, 1912, he informed Durand-Ruel, ". . . the specialist that I saw in Paris has confirmed what was said by the doctor at Vernon. But he has given me a treatment which can retard the progress of the evil and by consequence the operation—not because it is grave, but because it will have the effect of changing my vision totally."

His age he had spoken of at Venice only to say he felt younger. Suddenly, the death of his wife left him an old man, and at seventy he experienced the ravages of time. Often he had written that courage abandoned him, yet in the face of increasing physical handicaps his gallantry of spirit was marked. A "front" was presented to the world, whose incidental intransigence and occasional waspishness were forgiven out of admiration for the indomitable resolution of which they were the necessary safety valves. As a practicing artist however, it was generally agreed that his career was finished. His brushes lay forgotten in the studio, where since his return from Venice no new work had been brought.

The ending of splendor is always sad, and the superbly eccentric artist-pirate of previous years now amused himself by expanding his collections of Delacroix, Cézanne, and Renoir. He ceased to travel, remaining remote and unseen behind his walls at Giverny. But in February, 1913, he returned from a trip marveling at all he had seen, and ". . . all disposed to return next year to work in that admirable country." The hand of tragedy gripped him too firmly for such an enterprise; this time it was his son Jean whose serious illness snuffed out courage. Earlier a quarrel between Jean and his uncle Léon Monet at Rouen saw him depart that employ for his own, at Beaumont-le-Roger, farther up the river Epte near Giverny, where Jean organized a trout farm.

To recognize this unfortunate child of unmarried parents, whose birth had been aided by Bazille's charity, might now have been impossible. At forty-seven Jean Monet possessed not only the views but the virtues expected of a son of a manse. Industry, fortitude, resolution, appetite for knowledge, and self-control all marked him, and his death, on February 9, 1914, struck at his father fearfully. Like all the major events of six years past, this too enhanced a sinister aspect of the earthly scene at Giverny. The Hoschedé tomb again was opened, and when his composure was regained, the bereaved father wrote, "I knew my son incurable, but it is no less painful for me and his poor wife. . . . Our consolation is to think that he no longer suffers, because he was a true martyr."

Emotionally unstable before the event, filled with forebodings of his own end, Monet suffered grievously. Jean's widow, Blanche Hoschedé, the most artistically inclined of her family and an incarnation of the married heroine's moral virtues, now took her mother's place at Giverny. Nearly fifty, her life was given over to her recluse father-in-law and stepfather, whose shadow she became. A determined woman in the house was something for which Monet always had been grateful. Blanche assisted him to continue in the old patterns, her ministrations and care easing without erasing the sadness with which he greeted each day. To an even greater degree he began to insist on his own importance, to think with the perspective of one who had already passed into history, and to secure his place.

"My memories of study are not long; I passed perhaps fifteen days altogether with Gleyre," he would say now, and to his few visitors he seemed decidedly older, his step less firm, his personality more thoughtful and fretful. With pride he spoke of many homages received, and of his early struggles. But accounts he gave of those years were even more exaggerated. "You sometimes change the pictures that you have on your walls? I see two or three new ones . . ." he was asked one day.

"These are old memories" was his amiable response. "I hold onto them; I like to see them around me. As much as possible—and it has not always been easy!—I have retained a work from each stage of my life. . . . See the Norman beaches, England, Norway, Belle-Île, the Seine. . . . John Sargent lived in Paris . . . he had a great admiration for my paintings, so much that he made fanatics of the American colony. An entire series went to America!"

Over a bouquet of marigolds, brought to be disposed in a vase, he then turned pensive. "Mirbeau loved flowers too," he murmured of the dead author.

The habit of making remarks with conscious dramatic content suggests Monet was aware of their effect and the place they would take in his legend. At bottom he was an actor still, though posing before the wider audiences of history. Yet so many pronouncements poised uneasily between the colloquial and the rhetorical were an index to his mental state. Like those gathered closest about the retired artist, Georges Clemenceau was aware of an urgency in getting him back to work, lest synthetic drama and compulsive stridency replace the balance of his reason.

Earlier Monet had suggested to the critic Roger Marx the possibility of decorating a Salon with the theme of water lilies: "carried along the walls, its unity, enhancing all the panels, would give the illusion of an endless whole, of water without horizon or bank," and thus exploit still further a vein that had proved so fruitful. No patron had appeared to commission this extraordinary scheme, and like other plans from his years of physical exuberance, the sadness of life left it unexecuted. After his son Jean's death, Clemenceau comforted the confounded painter, and heard again this unique decorative idea.

"It is superb, your project! You can do it still . . .," he urged.

And at this point Monet's life, which many thought nearly over, doubled back on itself to teach a lesson about salvation. For that cagy resolute crank determinedly struck a defiant attitude. No one expected from him more than an intermittent vitality, sparking on and off in bursts of painterly rhetoric. Instead he boldly embarked on the largest and most protracted work of his lifetime. At seventy-four, the threat of blindness through cataracts hovering over him, he thought in terms of a valedictory: a decorative ensemble that would be a mighty drama of light and color over his lily pond.

Neither his first studio, now his sitting room, nor the second nearby in the garden, could accommodate this vast project. A gigantic interior was required with a plentiful and even light, where panels painted at his pond could be seen together and worked over. For this exclusive purpose he planned a new studio 50 feet by 70, its skylight supported on steel girders rising 50 feet off the floor. Designs were drawn and construction fixed for August 1, 1914, when Germany intervened by launching her attack on Russia. Two days later

France answered with a declaration of war which brought rapid German invasion through Belgium.

The north overrun by Germans, a British Expeditionary Force in everlasting retreat, the studio was overshadowed and did not progress. Concerned over his son Michel, who was engaged in fighting, Monet nonetheless resumed his labors beside the pond: "I am as well as possible, and my vision seems good. Thanks to work, the great consolation, all goes well," he wrote. Slowly he also was able to force the new studio to rise in his garden. Workmen were scarce and materials scarcer; Clemenceau, who provided his cigarettes, probably saw that other necessities were forthcoming, and by 1916 the studio was completed.

Something quite different from the gentler, more diaphanous performances that for more than a decade had been shown in Paris was meantime evolving by the lily pond. From the beginning his efforts were broader, rougher, and the result of a good deal of labor, painted on canvases one meter by two, or twice the size of his previous water gardens. Contributing was the fact he had adopted Sargent's example by working with bristle brushes, to which it was necessary to habituate himself. But also there was a jar of originality, distinct and audacious, about these new efforts of a mischievous old visionary.

Daily his gardeners carried the large panels down the center path of his garden, across road and railway embankment, which to his lasting sorrow cut his little world in twain, then placed them on easels beside his pond. There, seeming shorter and more paunchy than formerly, his head thrown forward on bent shoulders, Claude Monet worked. His hands remained powerful and firm, his use of the brush suggesting athletic vigor. An unpleasant scraping sound filled the air as each fresh white canvas disappeared under colors applied in large circular movements. His concentration was so intense he seemed unaware if Blanche, or even his grandson Jimmy Butler, yet another artist in the family, worked near him. For life at Giverny had become exhilarating again, and everyone present began consciously to bask in the sun of an Olympian old age.

Radiating zest, stealing darting mutinous looks at the occasionally cloudy heavens, Monet gave himself over to the moods and humors of his pond and the thrilling excitement of its spirit. Dappled by beams of light, covered by the decoration of its lily petals, he saw it as a mirror on which to glimpse the reflected world of trees and clouds overhead. Their shapeless splendors were in endless transformation, only occasionally swiveling back into the objective from dream orgies of diffused color. Everywhere were rhythmic incidents that fleetingly evoked the world of reality imprisoned within the colors' seething incoherent revolt. But the surface texture of the water itself, played on by the winds, broken by ripples and lapping currents, he avoided. For that predictably flamboyant impresario had determined to project the shock effect of a watery world without actual water.

As evening approached, the panels were carried back to the studio. Set on wheeled easels, they began to accumulate around the vast interior. A heavily built table in the center of the floor held his brushes, boxes of paint, a bowl of spotlessly clean brushes, and other utensils he employed. His wide-brimmed hats joined the mélange, and a tiny bottle of turpentine, intended for the cleaning of brushes, seemed to last forever. No oil was employed, nor dryer, nor other ingredients to thin his impasto, which spread over canvases with the distinctive corallike texture that was his trademark. Any tube of color containing too much oil he spread on blotting paper, sheets of which also were found on the table, to make the paste as thick and hard as possible.

Colors were placed on his palette in unctuous ridges, and so heavily that they threatened constantly to smudge his sleeves. Even when he was first sketching on canvas, his habit was to rub with a stiff brush and color rather than employ turpentine washes. And when by necessity his brushes were laid down at dusk, the painter ran to his flowers, or gladly settled himself in an armchair or on the single couch his studio boasted. Eyes partly closed, arms hanging limply, motionless, he sought after the movements of light that had escaped him. Harsh meditations on the futility of his labors often followed, and were anyone present he found opportunity to libel himself and his abilities. Thus life at Giverny moved on.

As a subject the water lilies possessed a subtle charm and beguiling modesty which might seem to flourish best in a precisely ordered framework, not in inflation. Yet Monet had always demonstrated an inclination to carry every new element, whether of idea or of technique, further and further until it reached an ultimate extreme. An artist who constantly had transcended the conventions by the power of his brush, he continued to expand the size of the individual panels painted before his pond. After 1917 his gardeners were ultimately tasked to carry canvases 17 and 19 feet long, on weighty stretchers; and over these, by the same scrubbing processes, larger vistas of reflecting water were evoked.

Where at first his dehumanized canvases had seemed to avoid all emotional appeal, he was proceeding to call forth a universality of feeling. Scumbled by the circular motion that described the limits of his reach, canvases became notable for the violence or morbidity of their mood, expressed in audacious imagery, or elaborate conceits of obscured reflections. Impressionism found new integration of its basic tonal, discordant color structure, for no longer was there any taste for economy in texture or statement. His tone was high-pitched, unsubtle, megaphonic; but the documentation was superb, retaining lingering visual touches and enhancing mundane realities with selected palette phrases of exceeding delicacy and warmth.

That inimitable tonal language, sparse yet resplendent, hieratic yet sensuous, became more beguiling than ever. At its core lay a prodigious concentration of thought, enlivened as never before by thrusting quicksilver rhythms. Obscure hubbubs built up, suddenly releasing an energy that lurched abstract forms into an uncannily real life. For too long he had slogged along in his prime with puritanical distrust of the recherché stroke and only very occasional rhythmical passages. Now the balletic rise and fall of his sweeping brush plunged and charged to drums and trumpets. Provocativeness had begun to take the form of fluent and compassionate painting, to create diverting surfaces to be watched with keen and fascinated admiration.

The day of the armistice in November, 1918, was a happy one at Giverny. Monet, the father, felt relieved that his son Michel would come home safely. Elsewhere Georges Clemenceau, Premier of the victorious France, thought of the quiet of that pool at Giverny. Bringing with him Gustave Geffroy, Clemenceau came down to make a selection among the enormous canvases arranged in the studio. As head of the French government, he had decided that the state would install the vast panorama in Paris, at the Orangerie: No place else, and no other recipient, could properly show them.

But the water lilies had yet to be completed in the studio, and at the age of eighty, his sight weakening, Monet worked on. "The old man is so blind now he sees nothing but color," Sargent observed, and Monet was no less aware that this was true. An air of bittersweet became more prominent; forty years of prosperity, honor, and fame had not eradicated the fifteen early years of poverty, to which his conversation constantly returned. Camille's name was never mentioned, though she was remembered with obvious warmth: "This canvas was done in 1872 at Argenteuil, where I lived. The personages are my first wife and friend, the man a neighbor . . .," he scribbled in pencil to identify an old work.

A slightly senile nostalgia seized him at times, and a giggling prurience, curiously shot through with the innocence and the tremulous sadness which afflict all who live in the treacherous and irrecoverable past. To advance his delicately evasive and pious biography of Monet, Gustave Geffroy was forced to beg Blanche for cooperation: "I understand very well that Monet does not like to rummage in his papers. It is always melancholy, but surely he does not think useless the researches that I have to make. . . ." Begun so well, the years of the water lilies had become concerned not with happiness but with the ending of happiness.

On Sundays carefully screened visitors were permitted to call, and he showed an eager delight when they recognized his merits. Clemenceau frequently took lunch with the family that day, his specially prepared baked potato still considered a sacrilege in that food-loving household. Each a veteran of many battles, the two old men then went to sit beside the lily pond, where in graceful long-breathed meditations they talked philosophy, visual phenomena, love, and good eating, reminiscing the days of their youth and avoiding all references to the state of the world.

No one better understood the stubborn self-critical artist than this senior statesman who sought to exorcise his horror of increasing blindness. Monet at times pummeled himself violently, swearing his life had been a failure and all that remained was for him to rip his canvases to pieces before disappearing himself. Studies filled with delicious rhythmic frenzies fell victim to fits of temper-driven despair. Many were saved by Blanche, whose helpful ministrations never left him, and who even fished from the pond his brushes thrown there in a moment of tragic self-doubt. In such a fit two self-portraits perished. In another he spoke harsh words to Clemenceau concerning a third. As the old Premier was leaving, he ran to

"... cette toile a été faite en 1872 à Argenteuil ..."

find it, throwing the canvas into his carriage, calling gruffly, "Carry it off with you and let no one speak of it again."

To an occasionally risked opinion on the progress of the water lilies, Clemenceau might receive a growl, assumed to mean "Wait and see." At other times only silence answered him. Clarity of vision belonged to an earlier period of Monet's life. Could he be represented by work done when he was in visual decay? History was strewn with answers, but the question haunted him, his vision too inadequate ever to provide personal assurance. Clemenceau continued to insist on the valedictory gesture, persuading Monet to go to a notary's office in Vernon, where, April 12, 1922, a formal donation was signed. In characteristically repellent fashion Monet had not been backward about making conditions: The panels were to be permanently housed in a building constructed to the design he had approved; no other works of painting or sculpture might be added; they were to be displayed in the order he indicated; the panels were never to be varnished.

Yet most uncharacteristic was that he signed over this most extended work of his lifetime to the French state *without recompense of any sort.* The valedictory on which he already had worked seven years, at vast cost, became a free gift to the land of his birth. When the document was signed, the old man was seen to have tears running down his cheeks. Emotionally exhausted, uncertain, anxious, he said, "It is a great arrogance to make such a gift. What will people say who come after me?" The state of his vision played on him with malicious mockery, and he never considered the *Nymphéas* were finished.

Meanwhile his oppressed eyes grew more dim. By February, 1923, they reached such a bad state that unable to see certain colors, unable to work, threatened with complete blindness, in the presence of Clemenceau the eighty-three-year-old artist underwent surgery at Giverny. A fortnight later at a clinic in Neuilly a second attempt was made, again with Clemenceau present. The old Premier had urged the most radical treatment, but Monet, fearful he might lose even what vision remained, refused to risk total blindness. After twice undergoing surgery he therefore was left in a state of half vision.

Friends and family now begged him to consider the *Nymphéas* finished, to which he shook his head without answer. Neither the admonitions of the surgeon nor the more strenuous commands of Clemenceau prevented him from resuming work on them, too soon.

Less than six months later a third operation became necessary, and was performed at Giverny once more in the presence of Clemenceau. Monet was compelled to remain quiet, until, after a sufficient interval, again he was squeezing paints onto blotting paper and scumbling them across the canvases. The terrible tragedy of absolute blindness had been averted, but Monet's eyes remained veiled.

A general reaction of exasperated pity surrounded him, occasionally relieved by reluctant admiration for the courage of this man who suffered so much. But all were aware that anxieties were driving him to a state of unbalance. By 1924 he admitted freely to callers that he could get no clear idea of his work. That he was waxing desperate, ruining both strength and health, was equally certain: "I no longer sleep because of them," he admitted. "In the night I am constantly haunted by what I am trying to realize. I rise broken with fatigue each morning. The coming of dawn gives me courage, but my anxiety returns as soon as I put my foot in the studio. . . ." When at last he wanted to burn the *Nymphéas,* Clemenceau stopped him. "Monet—you cannot do that. You are pledged!"

Legal ownership of the panels residing in the French state, all had indeed become irrevocable. But while Monet lived, he refused to part with them. Clemenceau and all at Giverny trembled for the result. Gently the old Premier watched over the moods of his friend; a letter from March, 1924, began: "My poor old lunatic, I think I am fonder of you when you are stupid. But in spite of the pleasure it is to like you, I wish it would not happen too often." Another, from October of that year, carried the same blend of docile respect and haughty command:

DEAR OLD SOUL,

Your letter has given me great pain. Not that I believe what you say against yourself, for you never did a masterpiece without damning it. What hurts is that you are so unreasonable in your reasoning. Old folks should be excused like children as much as possible; but there is a limit to everything.

First you wanted to complete the unfinished parts. It was not really necessary, but understandable. Then you conceived the absurd idea of improving the others. Who knows better than you that the impressions of an artist change every moment. If you were put with your canvases before the Cathedral of Rouen would you find nothing to change?

You have a justifiable ambition to outdo yourself, *and you have done it.* . . . Do you think that I care less for your honor as a painter than yourself. No, but you think that I and those that say the same to you are bad judges. Well, I answer that you are a bad judge of your judgment and that it is folly to begin again on completed work.

But the old artist's insistence was too strong, and despite his clumsy darkened vision and owlish spectacles he worked on.

For the great living and dead of Monet's generation an inevitable flow of books had commenced. Geffroy's volume was followed by another in 1924: *A Giverny Chez Claude Monet* recounted the frequently truncated conversations that took place when its author, Marc Elder, had visited Giverny in behalf of the Nantes Museum. Intended as a dealer's puff, and written with fulsome genuflections, it nonetheless contained curiously revealing hints that would have pleased Freud.

In May, 1926, a year following the sudden death of Sargent, his friend Evan Charteris contacted Monet. While working on a memorial volume dedicated to the great American, Charteris had been surprised by definitions of impressionism he found in Sargent's letters. Provided with an introduction from Paul Helleu, Charteris made the journey to Giverny, where in an afternoon of broad sunshine he found the aged, Mosaic, and shrunken Monet conversing in his garden with visitors from Japan. Presently they took reverential leave, and after perusing Helleu's letter Monet extended a cordial invitation to enter the house.

Such occasions stimulated the old man, and before the rows of his canvases in the sitting room, the scent of his garden and the hum of bees entering through an open window, his benevolence was impressive. Through magnifying lenses he gazed out with candor, not at all the fretful man known to intimates, but impressing his guest by the strength of his compact frame, the vigor of his voice, and the alertness of his mind: "at once gay and kindly, wholly simple and unaffected, with something rustic in his bearing."

But an accurately prepared translation of a Sargent letter Monet seemed not to understand at all. He asked that it be read to him a second time. Obviously flattered now by the references to him, he remained unable to recognize his work in Sargent's definition. "It is all much simpler than Sargent thought," he murmured, as indeed it was. All professions are a conspiracy against the laity, a context in which Sargent's remarkable propagandistic success is less than surprising. The art of Monet was worthy of such efforts. Sargent realized that if occasionally Monet was boring about his *Poplars* and his *Lily Ponds,* even his most obsessed passages were consistently relieved by sharpness of thought and rare freshness of perception.

That this was achieved by anything other than fresh painting in a limited dissonant palette Monet himself inclined to deny. The effect was to make him seem even more wayward and inexplicit than he was. Except when he had sent a list of colors to Durand-Ruel, or said mockingly to an interviewer, "My secret is that I never use black," he had failed signally to provide an accurate definition of his art. And though what distinguished his technique could easily be established, Monet seemed to believe that "impressionism" was indistinguishable from his own personality.

Even the word "impressionism," which throughout the English-speaking world bore Sargent's special meaning, had itself become an irritation and an offense to Monet. Following Charteris' visit, his eyes too weak for him to write, Monet dictated to Blanche: "After having reread your letter and that copy of Sargent's, I must avow that if the translation of the letter of Sargent is accurate I could not approve of it because Sargent has made me greater than I am. I have always had a horror of theories, and have only had the merit of having painted directly from nature, seeking to render my impressions before the most fugitive effects. And I am desolated to have been the cause of a name given to a group of which the larger part were not Impressionists." Two months later the word still rankled. August 26, Blanche Monet again wrote to Charteris: "He is more and more desolated to have been the involuntary cause of the name Impressionism."

Such modest claims as Monet made, and the nature of his feelings toward an errant word, throw a curious perspective upon the vast accomplishment of his lifetime. He was a man who had not merely manipulated events but created history by wrestling with his times and imposing his personality on them. And it was his personality itself that was a most astonishingly pervasive factor in the world's art. One forgot that the Salon still existed. Housed since 1900 in a newer, and smaller, palace on the Champs-Élysées, yearly it continued some-what perfunctory displays. Soon it would withdraw onto a balcony, while below an exhibition of automobiles, or children's toys, drew the vast throngs that once the Salon had reserved to itself.

The decisive nature of Monet's victory over a system had opened the door to new ideas and principles, new patterns of success, and new artistic creeds. Because his own position had been achieved not only by the most significant artistic discovery of the nineteenth cen-tury, impressionism, but also by a process of clever dealing, and by forcing the public to take notice by a succession of shocks, he pointed a way that others followed into a blind alley of irrelevant vogueishness. Art became the bastard calling for which no creden-tials or examinations were required. Frightened by their abysmal failure to recognize the impressionists, critics abdicated any func-tion beyond indicating what was *new,* permitting systematic judg-ment to disappear before a criteria of novelty. Curiosities, and in-tellectual conundrums, were transmuted into examples of art by an abundant verbiage. To call attention to oneself by being worse than anyone has yet dared to be is all too easy, and to this absurdity the success of Monet over the Salon had led in a straight path.

In the twilight of his years Monet was able to ask Durand-Ruel 170,000 francs for four old canvases long at Giverny. Yet around him public assurance was melting away in direct ratio to the vanishing esteem of the Salon. As standards perished, anarchy within the arts created a babel into which only the wealthy eccentric, the speculator, or the self-styled intellectual risked entering. Aware of this, Monet himself answered with trembling emotion, "Those who bought us loved us. They sometimes tried to help us . . . they never dreamed to play on our chances. . . ."

How paradoxical that this was happening at the precise moment that benevolent anarchist showed himself so completely and remark-ably altered. The greatest work of his lifetime was being quietly donated to the nation; that Sargent exaggerated his greatness was not denied; he claimed only the virtue of having painted directly from nature. Overwhelming changes in the man's fundamental character were surely due to something far more potent than the reformative incapacities of age. In his eighth decade he was not only the dominant artistic personality of his country—for *all* new art was called impres-sionism—but a regenerated man. Fortunately his unregenerated days already had produced that body of great painting without which we scarcely would have heard of the good and aged squire of Giverny.

"One morning recently on going out I realized that my vision had returned with a perception of tones and tints as in previous times. Because of this I am at work," Monet had said to conclude his interview with Charteris. Beside his pond he began new canvases of strained overcolored reality; in the studio he again scoured and scribbled across the panels of his mighty aquatic drama, forcing it to unfold in two arcs that never broke into sections. Peering harshly, as though in an attempt to caress with his eyes tissues that evaded accurate vision, he seemed profoundly inept, and his work at times became ornate and pretentious. The surfaces already were crudely labored, and Monet scumbled on in blind hope. Finally, he took Clemenceau's hand to lead him before the huge canvases on which was spread the completely realized spectacle of light on a stretch of sleeping water.

"Well, what do you say to that?" he cried mockingly. "You never dared to give me criticism. But I knew well enough that this water was pasty. One would have said it had been cut out with a knife. All the lighting had to be done over. I did not dare it. And then I made my decision. . . ." And the fact was that whether or not he succeeded entirely, the illusion had become complete. Quintessentially theatrical, it had been achieved by a man nearly blind employing the deliberate simplicity of means evolved in his own superbly strong youth, and not least by imprinting his own unmistakable personality on the result.

The effort had been frightful. Henceforth until his death Monet's vision, perhaps the most luminous of anyone of his race, was extinguished, and he lived on in darkness, though in physical tranquility. "It is all over," he said to Clemenceau. "I am blind. I have no further reason to live. However—you understand—so long as I am alive I will never allow these panels to leave the studio. I have reached a point where I fear my own criticism more than those of the most qualified eyes. There is every chance I have attempted something too big for me. Well, I am willing to die without knowing what fate has reserved for me. I have given my pictures to my country. Let her judge me."

The loss of all reason to live saw the start of a gentle decline which continued through the autumn months of 1926. In November he ceased to rise from his bed. Clemenceau remained close and was present the morning of December 5, when Claude Monet died.

The only time in his life Georges Clemenceau collapsed from emotion was at the grave of Claude Monet, the friend he loved best. "I walked at my own funeral," he said; and such was the importance of the occasion few noticed the ironies. No priest officiated at the solemn burial, and so great was the importance of the man interred in Giverny's little churchyard, it was not remarked that like his wife, Claude Monet had been laid to rest in the tomb marked *Ernest Hoschedé*.

Notes

THE SALON

The history of the Salon is well known, though never before seen in this affirmative character except in passages written a dozen years ago for my biography of *John Singer Sargent*, New York, 1955. A description and measurements of the Palais itself can be found in K. Baedeker's wonderful old guide to *Paris*, 1865, which has been useful in many other ways. Descriptions of the jury at work are based on Émile Zola's novel *L'Oeuvre*, published in 1886, which exists also in an English translation as *The Masterpiece*, New York and London, 1950 (the translation by Thomas Walton). It is notorious that Zola gathered much real data for this work, and that notes on jury conduct were provided for him by a member, Antoine Guillemet. Unfortunately Zola refers to a period somewhat later (1882–1885) than that at which I have placed this account (1859); and one can only pray that changes during those twenty years were not more noticeable than they have seemed. They may not have been; from my work on Sargent I have an older familiarity with the Salon, an opening of which (1884) is well caught in a letter written by Ralph Curtis. Varnishing Day is also nicely described by Will Low, *A Chronicle of Friendship*, New York, 1908.

Jules Grun painted the central garden of the Palais de l'Industrie, where sculpture was exhibited, at a period again slightly later than that of Zola's account; his picture is in the Rouen Museum. Another large picture depicting the Palais in the course of its demolition (1900) hangs over the stair in one of the many Paris Mairies I visited. The flurry of sticks at a jury meeting, probably that of 1885, is the subject of a fascinating picture by Gervex exhibited at the Salon of 1885. Recently rediscovered from an old reproduction in *Paris-Salon*, 1885, it appears in Hans Platte, *Les Impressionistes*, Paris, 1962. The original picture remains lost.

Chapter One
LIKE A MOTHERLESS CHILD

The many photos of Monet, almost all taken in later life, show a man of small stature. I was able to arrive at a more definite measurement in talking with his "grandson," Mr. James P. Butler, whom I interviewed May 26 and July 14, 1956, and who asserted that Monet was approximately the same height as myself. His olive skin in boyhood is mentioned by Marthe de Fels, *La Vie de Claude Monet*, Paris, 1929, in a recollection quoted from an unidentified Le Havre schoolmate. Monet's own impressions of the 1859 Salon are from his letters to Eugène Boudin, found in Gustave Geffroy, *Claude Monet, sa vie, son temps, son oeuvre*, Paris, 1922. The works he failed to notice, a matter of equal interest, from the Salon catalogue, 1859.

That Monet's mother had died when he was about twelve was the impression of Mr. Butler, and is verified by Monet himself, who is quoted to this effect by René Gimpel, "At Giverny with Claude Monet" in *Art in America*, June, 1927. Unfortunately the heavy bombings of Le Havre in the last war destroyed most such records; those concerning Monet's family which have survived are specified further on in these notes. Mr. Butler also spoke about Monet's brother, whose certificate of birth is on file in Paris.

Quoted references from Monet relative to his youth are from an interview he gave François Thiébault-Sisson, published in *Le Temps*, Paris, November 27, 1900. Extracts from the original French text are also found in Fels, and the whole of the interview was reprinted by Durand-Ruel, New York, in a good English translation. I have employed all these, altering the well-known translations whenever I have felt some other words might express more exactly Monet's nuance of meaning.

Monet's traditional birth date, given in Thiébault-Sisson, is verifiable only by a *reconstituted* record of birth preserved in the Paris archives. Monet, who provided this information, is thus the only authority for the date of his birth, and, as in the interview, the address is limited to "rue Laffitte." Data here given on Monet's brother, mother, father, aunt, uncle, and grandfather are drawn from records of their births and marriages found in the Paris archives. The birth date of Aunt Sophie Lecadre's daughter is from her grandson, M. Maurice Thieullent (letter, April 13, 1965).

Adolphe Monet's embarrassment concerning his parentage would appear to have been acute. At the time of his marriage in 1835, he recorded his mother's name as Catherine Chaumerat, adding the all-important words which normally complete that line in every French document, "his wife," signifying a legal and recorded marriage. His bluff held good for many years, until in 1871 the Paris City Hall and all its records were burned. Under a law passed February 12, 1872, an effort was made to *reconstitute* the destroyed records by interviewing persons able to provide information. A section of the commission sent to Le Havre called Adolphe Monet before it August 13, 1877, and at this late period in

his life (he was seventy-seven), after he had severely castigated his son for a liaison, Adolphe Monet was forced to admit that his parents had not been married. The reconstituted report of his birth executed on that date thus does *not* end with the essential words *his wife*: *"L'an mil huit cent, le trois février, est né à Paris Adolphe, du sexe masculin, fils de Pascal Monet et de Catherine Chaumea."* Note also that in this record the spelling *Chaumea* has replaced *Chaumerat*, which Adolphe Monet gave in the record of his marriage forty-two years before.

Monet's boyhood home at Le Havre, 13 Rue Fontenelle, no longer stands. The city suffered severely in the last war, after which the entire square of houses was razed to make way for a parking lot. Only No. 33, actually in the next street, still stands to show what the Rue Fontenelle houses were like. The Bassin de Commerce is now the yacht basin, but unchanged. The death certificate of Louise Justine Aubrée Monet appears not to have survived the last war; at least my efforts to discover it were not fruitful.

Monet's school at Le Havre is identified by Fels, who also sketches M. Ochard's appearance from Monet's caricature. This drawing is in the Chicago Art Institute, which is fortunate to possess ten of the thirteen known Monet caricatures. Three more are in the possession of the artist's son, Michel Monet.

Boudin's relations with the framing shop and the Municipal Council from G. Jean-Aubry, *Eugène Boudin, d'après des documents inédits*, Paris, 1922, and Ruth L. Benjamin, *Eugène Boudin*, New York, 1937, where a photo is found of Boudin at work. Boudin's less typical early work of this period is well represented in the Musée du Havre. His influence on Winslow Homer, like their crossing of paths, is entirely inferential. Homer was in France from the autumn of 1866 through the summer of 1867, and worked in areas where Boudin was present; see Lloyd Goodrich, *Winslow Homer*, New York, 1959, and Albert Ten Eyck Gardner, *Winslow Homer*, New York, 1961. More important, however, is that on his return to America Homer's fashionable young ladies seen at Red Bank, N.J., resemble closely Boudin's painted at Trouville, and habits of composition and tonality are shared.

Monet's first press notice is quoted in Geffroy in such a way one cannot be certain whether an unflattering opinion has not been chopped off one end or the other. Geffroy's volume was published during the lifetime of Monet, and his was a diffident attitude toward a subject from whom all his materials were obtained. This is illustrated by letters he wrote to Blanche Hoschedé-Monet, while the book was in progress; see Jean-Pierre Hoschedé, *Blanche Hoschedé-Monet*, Rouen, 1961.

Discovery of the Daubigny was recounted by Monet to Marc Elder, who had the resource to write his book *A Giverny Chez Claude Monet*, Paris, 1924, from the frequently fragmentary conversations of a few visits. Adolphe Monet's letter addressed to *Monsieur le Marie/ Messieurs les Adjoints* from Jean-Aubry, who found it and its sequel in Le Havre archives while they still existed. That Monet submitted a still life is mentioned in Minutes of the Council Meeting, quoted in Fels. John Rewald, *The History of Impressionism*, revised and enlarged edition, New York, 1961, reproduces a still life (page 41) which he says is "possibly" the one submitted. No information exists on this point, and the same claim could be made for any authentic still life of this period.

Chapter Two
PARIS BY PLAN

That Monet stayed at the Hôtel du Nouveau-Monde is known from his letter of May 19, 1859, to Boudin. I have called the railway station "St.-Lazare," as it is now, though at the period it was still the Gare de l'Ouest. The hotel address, and further details of changes being wrought in Paris, from the wonderful information Baedeker supplied his readers in the 1865 guide to *Paris*. Further insights from Georges Laronze, *Le Baron Haussmann*, Paris, 1932. Monet's visits to artists from his letter to Boudin of May 19, 1859. Physical descriptions of Troyon are from Marthe de Fels, *La Vie de Claude Monet*, where Napoleon III's comment is also found. Monet's second, and equally important, letter to Boudin, dated June 3,

1859, is from Geffroy, *Claude Monet, sa vie, son temps, son oeuvre.*

For further accounts of the long and arduous examinations required for entry into the École des Beaux-Arts, see my *John Singer Sargent*. For references to Amand Gautier, see *Bulletin des Musées de France*, No. 8, October 1932; also Paul Gachet, *Deux Amis des impressionistes: le Docteur Gachet et Murer*, Paris, 1956. Gautier's picture *La Promenade des Soeurs* and the portrait of Dr. Gachet (the latter except for its greater finish much resembling Whistler) both in the Musée de Lille. Monet evidently mentioned in a letter, now unknown, his admiration for the *Promenade (Bulletin des Musées de France)*.

Geffroy, page 14, quotes Monet in later years as realizing that his period at the Brasserie des Martyrs "did me the greatest harm," and by inference one must suppose he extended this regret to his entire "idle apprenticeship." My details of Monet's participation at the Brasserie from Geffroy, who also supplies the party at Courbet's studio. The drawing Monet made of Alfred Bruyas belongs to the Chicago Art Institute (C17315), Mr. and Mrs. Carter H. Harrison Collection, where it has remained unrecognized. Boudin's encounter with Courbet at Honfleur from Charles Léger, *Courbet et son temps*, Paris, 1948.

Minutes of the meeting of the Le Havre Municipal Council from Fels. The probably apocryphal exchange with Adolphe Monet from Thiébault-Sisson (interview in *Le Temps*) November 27, 1900, who one can only hope did not interpret as a verbal exchange what Monet meant was written. After taking part in such interviews one cannot vouch for the accuracy of a journalist transcribing notes. It is also notable that in recounting these events at that later period of his life (November 1900), Monet both telescoped and expanded the time sequence to improve his story. Among other things, he imagined that his year in Paris had been *four* years, and that during that time he frequently visited Le Havre.

The fascinating postscript on his June 3, 1859, letter to Boudin makes clear that he had received the bad news of his rejection by the Municipal Council while in Paris. Also that while still there he had made up his mind to remain. This checks well with the elapsed time sequence between the Council Minutes (May 18) and the body of Monet's letter (June 3), at the writing of which he was unaware of the Council decision and his father's unwillingness to assist him further. Only in the postscript is he aware of (1) the Council's rejection and (2) his father's unwillingness to continue his allowance. Therefore in these seven elapsed days since he had written the body of the letter, Monet had received the bad news and had a further exchange with his father.

My treatment of events surrounding the Daubigny is the best reconstruction possible from events known. Monet told Thiébault-Sisson that during his stay in Paris he frequently visited Le Havre, and since he surely had not taken the Daubigny with him on a short trip to see the Salon, yet had it in his room when writing to Boudin February 20, 1860 (Geffroy), one comes to the inescapable conclusion he had been back to Le Havre, fetched the Daubigny, and possibly had the quoted altercation with his father.

But then again, Monet's exact reference to this picture—". . . the little Daubigny in question is entirely mine. It hangs [*est pendue*] in my room"—could also mean that it still hung in his room at Le Havre. Monet's letter of April 21, 1860, from Gustave Cahen, *Eugène Boudin, sa vie et son oeuvre*, Paris, 1900, page 36.

Monet's letter of February 20, 1860, is dated 1856 in Geffroy. By the internal evidence this becomes a too obvious absurdity, and the proper date of 1860 has been recognized by Étienne Moreau-Nelaton (*Jongkind*, Paris, undated), Jean-Aubry (*Boudin, d'après des documents inédits*), Rewald (*The History of Impressionism*), and Raymond Régamey ("La Formation de Claude Monet" in *Gazette des Beaux-Arts*, February, 1927).

Pissarro's manner of painting at the period of the trip to Champigny can be established from a landscape now in the Budapest Museum of Fine Arts (No. 377B).

It is significant that the name Oscar, or "O. Monet," appears on the earliest of the caricatures, and that these are the more carefully developed works in charcoal and white chalk. In Paris Monet begins to sign his works "Claude Monet," and such later caricatures are hastily contrived by comparison with those done at Le Havre.

Chapter Three
A COMPLACENT APPRENTICE

Comparisons of Monet's personal appearance before and after his military career can be made from the photo of him "at sixteen," and the small full-length portrait *en Zouave* painted by Charles Lhullier on Monet's return from Africa. The portrait could well have been done at Le Havre, thus showing Monet before he was actually separated from the service. In it the long hair of the photo has disappeared, but the upper lip has once again become dark and one sees a suspicion of that hirsute stripe which in the photo had marked his chin. For a swarthy young man Monet's beard was slow to sprout. Even at twenty-five, when he was painted at the Chailly inn by Bazille, it covers his chin and jaws without having reached his cheeks.

Monet's own account of his military career is from Thiébault-Sisson's interview in *Le Temps*, November 27, 1900. His tales unfortunately do not check against the military dossier preserved at the Ministère de la Guerre (1er *Régiment de chasseurs d'Afrique*, 18° volume — n° 7225). Here there is no mention of an illness, or of a furlough, and under its terms Monet was exonerated from service in Africa. Constructively, of course, this would be true, as he was gazetted to Africa, wherever he may physically have been on leave. The fact that Monet was painting in the open at Le Havre while "convalescing" suggests good weather and summer; having been at Le Havre in many seasons, I believe it improbable that he could have done this, or sketched a cow grazing, or eaten out of doors with Jongkind, after the period of his recorded exoneration, November 21. Thus it becomes inescapable that he did in fact have a long leave at Le Havre *before* his actual separation from the army.

His illness, if he had one, may well have been malaria, of which he had a recurrence some years later. Supporting this is the Thiébault-Sisson reference to a fever. The wildest embroideries have appeared: Georges Besson (*Monet*, Paris, 1951) is certain it was "anaemia"; François Fosca (*Claude Monet*, Paris, 1927, page 16) with equal certainty suggests typhoid.

The Englishman who so providentially introduced Monet to Jongkind has never been identified. Monet recounted this story to several persons, and it is printed by both Thiébault-Sisson and Marc Elder (*À Giverny Chez Claude Monet*). Jongkind's bizarre appearance is mentioned in Rewald's *The History of Impressionism*, and in Georges Besson's *Johan-Barthold Jongkind*, Paris (undated). A photo of him is published with my own article "A Monet Portrait of Jongkind" in *The Art Quarterly*, Winter 1958, where Monet's little portrait of him is also seen.

That Monet now adopted Jongkind's manner of painting we must accept on the authority of his own declaration to Thiébault-Sisson, for aside from the still lifes no work from this period has survived. However, the words of his aunt Sophie Lecadre to Amand Gautier (quoted in Régamey's "La Formation de Claude Monet," in *Gazette des Beaux-Arts*, February, 1927) imply that it was the irregular surface adapted from Jongkind she was characterizing as "appalling daubs." Jongkind's strange debut in the Monet home was told to Elder (and repeated by Fels), who also recorded Monet's further observations on Jongkind's character, and his love of marionettes.

The relationship with Toulmouche from Elder, who recorded that Monet remembered Toulmouche's "delicious" wife Marie as late as their interview, in the 1920's. Monet recollected his own excitement while working on the still life painted for Toulmouche (Elder), and from his description of the components one is certain that the picture is the one now in a Hamburg private collection (13 by 18⅛ inches, reproduced in Elder and Rewald).

The interior of Gleyre's studio is well known from its appearance in *Trilby, A Novel*, by Georges du Maurier, where it is called "Chez Carrel." Three illustrations by du Maurier himself, contained in the London edition of 1896, give his recollected impression of the interior.

The mutual acquaintance of Monet and Bazille is given as "Wanner" by Gaston Poulain, *Bazille et ses amis*, Paris, 1932, page 24, although no such Le Havre artist is known. Monet's enthusiastic work on his first study in Gleyre's studio he mentioned himself to Thiébault-Sisson, to whom he also recounted Gleyre's criticism and the effect it had on him. Gleyre's criticism of Renoir is from A. André, *Renoir*, Paris, 1928; also mentioned in François Fosca, *Renoir, His Life and Work*, Englewood Cliffs, New Jersey, 1962.

When both men recounted these events, they had entered their years of glory and developed the curiously untrue thesis that they had rebelled to the extent of departing Gleyre's studio. According to contemporary documentation, Monet, though discontented, attended Gleyre's studio for seventeen months. Renoir was even more docile. This is treated more thoroughly in later chapters. *A Corner of a Studio*, in the Louvre, would seem to date from this period, and demonstrates that Monet had acquired a certain proficiency in a conventional approach to painting.

Much confusion exists in all accounts of these years, due to unfortunate errors in the order of letters published by Poulain. A convention has grown up that supposes Monet to have made a trip to Chailly-en-Bière, near Barbizon—in company with Bazille, Renoir, and Sisley—at Easter, 1863. If the letters found in that volume are read in proper sequence there is no possibility that such an excursion took place. Monet is first mentioned in Bazille's letters on page 24. The author explains, without supplying an exact date, that this letter is written "at the start of 1863, in the neighborhood of four or five months after his [Monet's] entry into Gleyre's studio." Bazille's own entry into the Gleyre studio is already established on page 16 as having taken place in November, 1862: "Four or five months" therefore brings us to the period March–April, 1863.

Thus Monet has just entered Bazille's letters at the very period when this trip is supposed to have taken place (Easter). The balance of Bazille's activities for that year are summarized in a long letter given on page 32: he recounts returning to Paris after his summer holiday at Montpellier, and speaks of plans for the winter ahead. Obviously no trip to Chailly has taken place. It falls more logically into the following year, 1864, when the Gleyre studio has closed, and all the painters concerned (Monet, Bazille, Sisley, and Renoir) were decidedly free.

Many other confusing errors in the order of letters are noted in their proper sequence in these notes. Among the most significant is Édouard Manet's exhibition at the Galerie Martinet, which took place in March, 1863, and which Poulain (page 36) would make the following year, after the close of Gleyre's studio.

Chapter Four
THE NEW FREEDOM

The incorrect and frequently reversed arrangement of letters already noted in Gaston Poulain's *Bazille et ses amis* extends into this period and produces a situation where everything has become doubled. Monet, Bazille, Sisley, and Renoir are said to be at Chailly in 1863 and again in 1864. Bazille is present with Monet at Honfleur early in 1864, then Monet is said to escort him to Honfleur a second time!

These errors I have attempted to correct from the information included in the letters themselves, as they appear in Poulain. Probably the reader will not be aware that scholarship in some hands is made a cutthroat business. After I had traced the originals of documents contained in Poulain (with the kind assistance of M. Gaston Poulain himself, and M. Jean Claparède, Conservateur of the Musée Fabre at Montpellier), I received a flat refusal from M. Gabriel Sarraute, who would not permit me to see or employ them in any way: *"Je ne dois pas vous communiquer ces lettres, pas même des photos fragmentaires des lettres déjà publiées"*; his letter dated December 1, 1964.

Monet's superiority to his friends at Chailly is entirely a matter recorded in letters written to Montpellier by Bazille. None of Monet's studies from the Gleyre studio now survive. Some were possibly destroyed when he stored his canvases with

Pissarro during the War of 1870. But it is also likely that in his desperate need during the years following, Monet painted them over. Canvases from the late sixties frequently have more than one picture on them; in the portrait of Jongkind we already find Monet doing this. However, the fact that so many of Monet's seascapes from the later part of this year are extant inclines me to the view that at least some of his earlier Courbet-inspired canvases have found their way into the *oeuvre* of that artist.

Toulmouche's caustic intervention from Régamey's "La Formation de Claude Monet," *Gazette des Beaux-Arts,* February, 1927. M. Régamey mentions that he has been permitted by Robert Rey to employ copies of thirteen letters from Monet and Mme. Lecadre to Amand Gautier. Unfortunately the only quotes he gives are from Mme. Lecadre's "idiots" letter and the exchange between Monet and Toulmouche. Bearing on Monet's laziness, there is also the phrase "one must force him to work seriously," but it is used so cryptically that it is not clear whether this is a quotation from Mme. Lecadre or represents an observation or an instruction to Gautier.

Today the letters are lost. See my special pleading on this subject in "A Monet Portrait of Jongkind" in *The Art Quarterly,* Winter 1958, page 390, note 13. M. Rey, in a letter to me dated December 15, 1956, stated that all his notes on this subject were kept "at La Charité aux Loire. In 1940 the Germans occupied that house and they scattered all those papers." The letters had also been used by Mme. Aline Bloch, a student of M. Rey at the École du Louvre, for a thesis on Amand Gautier presented in 1932. (For a report of this, *Bulletin des Musées de France,* No. 8, Octobre 1932, page 136.) According to M. Rey, Mme. Bloch was "arrested by the Germans in 1943, transported to a camp of death and killed by them," and no copy of the thesis is known to exist either in the Louvre or elsewhere.

Monet recollected his meeting with Millet while speaking with René Gimpel ("At Giverny with Claude Monet," *Art in America,* June, 1927). The incident was said to have taken place at "the Robinson Ball," and though it has been convenient for me to employ it in this context, the dating may be different by some years. Millet lived until 1875.

Bazille described the trip by river steamer to Le Havre and the stop at Rouen (in Poulain). Monet's shore picture belongs to the Minneapolis Art Institute; Jongkind's picture containing a similar rowboat, painted that same summer, can be seen reproduced in Georges Besson's *Johan-Barthold Jongkind*, plate 16. Bazille's larger version, which timidly copies the Monet, is in the collection of Pierre Fabre, Ste.-Comes, Gard, France; Rewald (*The History of Impressionism*) first realized the relationship and reproduces both pictures (page 110, 1961 edition). References to Boudin's visiting Monet at the St.-Siméon farm are found in Ruth Benjamin's *Eugène Boudin*.

"The very fishing vessel that had appeared in Édouard Manet's picture" is in Monet's *Le Havre: Fishing Boats Leaving the Harbor*, Hill-Stead Museum, Farmington, Connecticut. Identification of Monet's first sketch portrait as Jongkind appears in my "A Monet Portrait of Jongkind." Monet's letter is from Benjamin. Amand Gautier's connection with Louis Gaudibert doubtless derived from the fact that both men were of Lille origin: See Paul Gachet, *Deux Amis des impressionistes: le Docteur Gachet et Murer*, Paris, 1956.

Chapter Five
A NERVOUS WINTER

The date of Monet's return to Paris can be established from Poulain's *Bazille et ses amis*. He had surely arrived before Bazille gave notice at the Rue de Vaugirard in November, 1864. The actual address of the studio they took together is 6 Rue de Furstenberg, the entrance falling in the Place Furstenberg. Delacroix had died fifteen months before, August 13, 1863. His studio in a garden pavilion, attached to his bourgeois apartment by a specially constructed staircase, is now the Delacroix Museum. Monet recounted his meeting with Courbet to Marc Elder (*À Giverny Chez Claude Monet*, page 27).

Descriptions of Camille are drawn from the many pictures of her Monet painted in the period immediately following their meeting. Émile Zola left more studied impressions in notes (prepared for his book *L'Oeuvre*), preserved at the Bibliothèque Nationale. Her smile, so carefully characterized in *L'Oeuvre*, is unfortunately found elsewhere only in a less successful Renoir portrait reproduced in Marcel Zahar, *Renoir*, London, 1948, plate 13. From this it is possible to see that Camille posed for Renoir's more famous work, *La Loge*, Courtauld Collection, London.

When my researches into the relationship between Monet and Camille were undertaken, no more was known of Camille than her Christian name. Recognition that "Christine," heroine of Émile Zola's admitted *roman-à-clef*, was in fact a representation of Camille, opened the path to the rediscovery of many documents. "How odd! Claude and Christine. We both start with the same letter!" Zola permits his heroine to say (page 31, English editions), thus providing the key to their identities. When introducing their son, he carried this further by making Jean into "Jacques."

An essential caveat is that Zola has made use of only the personal life of Monet and Camille. The picture "Claude Lantier" paints at the same moment is certainly Édouard Manet's *Déjeuner sur l'Herbe*. Yet everywhere Zola demonstrates a deadly accuracy when dealing with the personal relations of Monet and Camille. He was perhaps not aware of Camille's bourgeois origins, attributing her refinement to a convent upbringing. But the fact that he does not make his Christine a Parisian implies that he heard the trace of Lyon in Camille's speech.

For methods by which Zola's many clues led to the discovery of documents, see my "New Materials on Claude Monet: the Discovery of a Heroine" in *The Art Quarterly*, Winter 1962. Despite its date, this issue of *The Art Quarterly* appeared in 1964, following on which I received a letter dated November 26, 1964, from Professor Rodolphe Walter, complimenting me on the researches it contained and asking the name of Monet's notary at Argenteuil. Well he might compliment me, for Professor Walter had failed to mention that he pillaged that article without remorse or acknowledgment for one of his own in *Extraits des Cahiers Naturalistes*, No. 26, 1964. In a further letter of April 7, 1965, he pretended to be unaware of any obligation to acknowledge my materials.

Individual documents by which this portion of Monet's life with Camille has been re-established are mentioned in their proper sequence. That Camille was tall is mentioned by Zola, who himself was short, in *L'Oeuvre* (English editions, page 37). Her height is difficult to judge from the paintings, and no photos are presently known, though some may exist. When painted beside Bazille, however, Camille does appear to come up high against his tall figure. Probably she was the same height as Monet, or about five feet seven inches.

That Camille was born at Lyon, January 15, 1847, is specified on the record of marriage, as is that her father, Charles Claude Doncieux, was retired—a *rentier*. Between the time she ran off with Monet to Chailly in 1865 and their marriage in 1870, the Doncieux family moved to 17 Boulevard des Batignolles, at a yearly rental of 1,070 francs. From the inventory of M. Doncieux's estate, drawn up in 1873, one can establish the exact furnishings of this apartment, and the value of every object. One also finds the wages of the single servant: 35 francs a month.

Camille's younger sister, Geneviève, had been born in Paris in 1858. That the Rue de Furstenberg was the place of Camille's seduction is logical, but would be merely conjectural had not Zola described the entrance to the studio so accurately (*L'Oeuvre*, English editions, page 20). Probably for motives of delicacy (or libel —Monet was still alive at the time of publication) he located this entrance on the Île St.-Louis.

That Monet still received an allowance from his father is necessary to his ability to accept responsibility for half a rental with Bazille. His only known sales prior to this date are those of the previous summer to M. Gaudibert. As he had never exhibited in Paris, it is unlikely he had any income other than his allowance during this winter. After being sent away by his family, he had specified to Bazille, "*Je crains même de ne plus reçevoir d'argent; pourtant, avec le mal que je me donne, ce serait bien mal.*" Thus the allowance had not yet been cut off at this period.

Concerning Bazille's experiments with beards, at least one portrait of him exists, by Monet, in which he is clean-shaven except for a mustache. This picture, full-length, in which he carries a dark umbrella, is at the Kunsthaus, Zurich, and is mentioned by Monet in a letter to Bazille found in Gaston Poulain's *Bazille et ses amis*, page 132: "And if you would do me a pleasure take a look in all your corners for any blank canvases I still have in your place, and also the canvases on which there are things abandoned, like your standing portrait. . . ." In the so-called "self-portrait" (21¼ by 18⅛ inches) in the Frédéric Bazille collection, Montpellier (actually painted by Monet), the beard is being grown principally on the cheeks, and has not yet concentrated on his chin, as it does in the Renoir portrait (Jeu de Paume) dated 1867.

While planning to stake everything on his acceptance at the Salon, Monet was certainly aware of the greater leniency of the new jury system adopted since 1864. The proportion of rejections had declined sharply, though it was no less an irrational hope *for Monet*. Bazille's letter concerning his intense application is from Poulain, page 48.

The first study for Monet's landscape motif at Chailly is now at the Metropolitan Museum, New York, where it is called *Le Pavé de Chailly* (38¼ by 51⅛ inches). Though now somewhat darkened, this picture surely shows the sparkling effect that Monet sought for his huge work. Two other smaller, less adventurous and more labored studies from this period, quite similar to each other, exist in the Jeu de Paume and the Hansen Collection, Ordrupgard, Denmark. It is more than likely that all three were employed by Monet for the assembly of his final compositional sketch, now in the Museum of Modern Western Art, Moscow.

Chapter Six

THE MASTERPIECE

Baedeker's 1865 *Paris* is specific about the length of journey by rail from Fontainebleau to the Gare de Lyon (page 210), and, in its interesting description of the

Fontainebleau area, mentions the artist colony at Marlotte but omits Chailly entirely (page 216). That Monet met Courbet again at the Salon of 1865 he recounted to Elder (*À Giverny Chez Claude Monet*, page 27). When he told Thiébault-Sisson (interview in *Le Temps*, November 27, 1900) of Manet's indignation at this same Salon, Monet inadvertently said it was the Salon of 1866, and his picture the one exhibited that year. Because Manet was not represented at the Salon of 1866, nor Monet in 1867, this incident could have occurred only at the Salon of 1865. The interesting sequel, and Astruc's offer, also from the Thiébault-Sisson interview. It should be noted that in this instance, and others, there are honest errors of memory on Monet's part. However, he gave a slightly different account of this meeting with Manet to Elder, page 27.

The more important picture Monet exhibited at the Salon of 1865 was the *Embouchure de la Seine*, 35½ by 59 inches, now privately owned in Paris: this is established from his sketch published in *L'Autograph au Salon*. Many wild guesses have been made about the identity of the second marine painting shown. The title listed in the Salon catalogue, *La Pointe de la Hève à Marée Basse*, would appear to fit only one canvas, 16 by 29 inches, sold from the Norman B. Woolworth collection at Christies', June 19, 1964, No. 45. In the catalogue of that sale it was definitely claimed this picture was number 1525 at the 1865 Salon; on what grounds is not stated. Even so, the contention is logical and probably correct, despite the fact this picture does not represent low tide. (Rocks which emerge from the water at Ste.-Adresse at low tide are of an ugly dark tone, and Monet seems to have avoided them deliberately in all his works painted there.) Bazille's letter concerning Monet's success is from Poulain.

Geffroy, in *Claude Monet, sa vie, son temps, son oeuvre*, page 29, identifies the seated male figure at center of the sketch for the *Picnic* as Lambron. Monet's summonses to Bazille from Poulain, *Bazille et ses amis*, where one also finds his arrival by midnight train, the rain which followed, and Bazille's letter: "Monet, who is working fast. . . ."

Monet told Elder (page 27) of Courbet's great interest in the *Picnic*. The advice itself Monet recounted verbatim to Elder (page 52) and in slightly different words to Trévise ("Le Pèlerinage de Giverny" in *Revue de l'art ancien et moderne*, February, 1927). It must always be remembered that variations in wording can frequently be ascribed to the reporter, whose memory and sense of language can produce alterations. Monet claimed later that he had not accepted Courbet's advice about undercoating the canvas, but examination of his pictures of that period proves he did.

Though the substantial shape of outbuildings at the Cheval-Blanc, Chailly-en-Bière, has not altered in the last century, much rebuilding has certainly taken place. A part of the stables are now garages; more have been converted to chalets and a hall for use during busy summer months. Observation suggests, however, that no section of the stables available to Monet in 1865 was large enough for a canvas of the size he worked on, were it stretched and on an easel in the normal way. More than likely, Monet gained added space by nailing the canvas directly to a wood partition.

Courbet's extraordinary success of this period is discussed in Gerstle Mack, *Gustave Courbet*, New York, 1951; Marcel Zahar, *Gustave Courbet*, London, 1950; and Robert L. Herbert, *Barbizon Revisited*, New York, 1962. Boudin's part in this meeting at Trouville is found in Jean-Aubry's *Eugène Boudin*, as well as Ruth L. Benjamin's *Eugène Boudin*, from which I have extracted Courbet's letter of invitation.

That Monet's father had stopped his allowance is made clear by hardships encountered at Chailly that autumn. But exactly when Adolphe Monet cut off his son remains obscure. Because Monet would have had no other income until that first fateful Salon, and showed no hardship during the period preceding it, the likelihood is that the break with his father came after the Salon.

Bazille's curious study of the kitchen door at the Cheval-Blanc, Chailly-en-Bière, is reproduced in Rewald (*The History of Impressionism*, 1961 edition, page

111) as *Farmyard at Saint-Siméon, Honfleur*.

That Courbet was twice present at Chailly is documented by his own pictures painted at Fontainebleau during the summer, and his sitting given Monet in the winter. A third visit indicated in the text is based on an assumption that he gave his advice on color when the picture was further advanced than at the period of his sitting. This, however, remains conjectural. The Jeu de Paume fragment also shows that Monet removed Bazille's beard from the figure at left, and reworked the head with himself as model. He also much reworked the two heads of Camille, finding even greater trouble with muddy surfaces and lost drawing.

That Courbet assisted Monet financially the younger man admitted many times (Geffroy, page 30). That Monet denied having employed the dark undertone suggested by Courbet made it difficult for him to explain why he abandoned the picture. He did, however, admit that Courbet had suggested alterations of color. Using the sketch as guide, one immediately sees that the only departures from plan (in portions of the canvas still extant—the far right section has disappeared entirely) are additions of red. The object of them then becomes clear, bearing in mind that over its somber base tone the picture was a disappointment. Boudin's "rigmarole" letter from Jean-Aubry.

It is worthy of note that Monet probably did more work at Chailly than has been realized. Surely a proportion of his pictures from this period was destroyed in the various incidents that befell his works shortly after. Others have remained unrecognized under an attribution to Bazille, whose own manner of working would appear to have been always thin and hesitant. Such qualities are as typical of him in the final family group (Jeu de Paume) as in the earliest Paris works. This is doubly true of his few forays into portraiture; where he uses more pigment, as in the self-portrait in the Chicago Art Institute, a clotted laboriousness soon asserts itself. Two heavily impasted works of about this period demonstrate a startlingly different and easier manner: the portrait of *Sisley* (11 by 12¼ inches—formerly with Wildenstein Galleries,

Paris, destroyed during World War II) and a presumed self-portrait (21¼ by 18⅛ inches, collection Frédéric Bazille, Montpellier). These are surely Monet canvases that happened to be mixed in with those of Bazille at the time of the latter's death in 1870.

Chapter Seven

FIRST FLIGHT

This period is one of those worst hit by the absence of essential papers and documents which only thirty years ago were still available. The account given here has been assembled from a residue of hints and mutilated quotations—all that can now be found. As in Chapter 4, a most grievous loss is the substantial correspondence that passed between Monet, Amand Gautier, and Mme. Lecadre, which probably told the entire story.

The seizure at Chailly is mentioned by Geffroy (*Claude Monet*, page 30), who evidently had it from Monet direct. Payment of Bazille's debts by his mother, secret in the sense that his father seems not to have known of it, from Poulain, *Bazille et ses amis* (where one finds Bazille's letter concerning Monet's working with him mornings and the unexpected visit of Adolphe Monet (page 59). Mme. Lecadre's inquiries concerning Camille are from Marthe de Fels, *La Vie de Claude Monet*, pages 82–83. The masked ball is from Poulain, page 59, as is the letter stating Monet had "been at work a long time," page 61. This, of course, contradicts the usual assertion that *Camille* was painted in four days, which derives from the critic W. Bürger, quoted here. Hurried the picture was, however, as Monet was surely aware they must vacate the studio. *Camille* is now in the Bremen Museum.

The frequent assertions that Monet's source for this figure (*Camille*) was a composition by Courbet I have felt it best to overlook. There is no evidence that Monet was familiar with the picture by Courbet that has been named, and one suspects the assertion has been made, and too often repeated, without reference to the far greater similarity between the finished *Camille* and Monet's own sketch. Alterations in the figure's outline, espe-

Notes

cially at right and against the floor, underline this contention by proving its contours were originally even more similar to the sketch.

A possibility exists that *Camille* may have been a second effort. In a letter written the following winter (December 1, 1866) Monet asks Bazille to send him an unfinished "canvas of a woman in white," on which he wishes to make an important marine (Poulain, pages 70–71). Presumably Bazille obliged, because this picture is unknown, and may have disappeared under the large harbor scene painted at Honfleur that winter. Bazille mentions having rented the gown of green satin (page 62, Poulain).

Letters to Gautier from Monet and his aunt Mme. Lecadre quoted here are the whole of severely truncated texts found in Fels. One hopes that this author arranged them in correct order, and that, for example, the letter from Monet—"She writes to tell me that she consents . . ." (page 96)—does in fact belong *after* his success at the Salon, and not to the earlier period when he took the house at Sèvres, when logically, because of the fact she *was* sending him money, she might also have written in this sense. Régamey (in "La Formation de Claude Monet" in *Gazettes des Beaux-Arts*, February, 1927) mentions that the house was actually at Sèvres, near the Ville d'Avray station.

Courbet's visit to Sèvres is mentioned by Geffroy (page 37), but the conversational exchange with Courbet was recounted by Monet to the Duc de Trévise and recorded in Trévise's "Le Pèlerinage de Giverny" in *Revue de l'Art ancien et moderne,* February 1927. This incident has been distorted by authors who deliberately chose to omit the fact that Courbet's rejoinder was spoken *"peut-être avec ironie"*—the quote is from Monet.

Bazille's letter concerning the "mad success" from Poulain; the manner of hanging *Camille* mentioned by Régamey and Edmond About, here quoted. Texts of criticisms published on *Camille* are from Geffroy. Monet himself was certainly aware of them at the epoch itself, as in my context; letters from Geffroy to Blanche Hoschedé-Monet (Jean-Pierre Hoschedé, Blanche Hoschedé-Monet)

show that Geffroy employed the clippings in Monet's own possession while writing his book. All translations of these criticisms are mine. The quotation from Monet—"My family at last . . ."—is from Thiébault-Sisson's interview in *Le Temps,* November 27, 1900.

Chapter Eight
FLIGHT AGAIN

Despite differences in appearance, all four costumes employed in the *Women in a Garden* are present in the sketch for the *Picnic.* That Monet undertook to paint the replica of *Camille* at Bazille's Paris studio is shown by the fact that it remained with Bazille after his flight; also his letter from Honfleur specifies that he had been unable to finish it *at Paris,* not Sèvres (Poulain's *Bazille et ses amis,* page 71). According to Gimpel ("At Giverny with Claude Monet" in *Art in America,* June 1927), Monet said that on departing Sèvres (called Ville d'Avray) he slit with a knife the canvases he could not take with him, estimated at two hundred. One suspects this was merely a good tale that Monet told late in life. However, it has been copied out by Rewald (*The History of Impressionism*) and all successive authors (for example: Germain Bazin, *Impressionist Paintings in the Louvre,* London, 1964, page 24) without consulting Monet's own letter to Bazille of December 1, 1866 (Poulain, page 71), which states, "I have not many things at Ville d'Avray." This letter also shows an awareness that the pictures were in salable, or unslashed, condition: "It would be terrible for me if she sold them."

The "conversation piece" is the well-known *Terrace near Le Havre,* or *Terrace at Ste-Adresse,* 38 by 50 inches, in the collection of the Rev. and Mrs. Theodore Pitcairn, Bryn Athyn, Pa. Poulain has advanced the interesting thesis that the *Women in a Garden* was based on family photos taken at Montpellier and in possession of Bazille. Because of the obvious relationship of this work with the *Picnic,* and the relationship of its poses with those in the former work (of which Poulain seems unaware), I have not stressed this thesis. But if Monet did see the Bazille photos, and had them in mind, this would lend support to the thesis here advanced after examination of the canvas itself: that the fourth figure, at right, has a later origin than the three at left.

When examining the "wagon" snow scene (*La Charrette*) in the Jeu de Paume, I noted at upper left that the trees of a previous picture painted on this canvas are discernible through the sky. Unfortunately I have not been able to examine the other pictures of this series with my own eyes; similar discoveries might possibly be made. The widest variation has appeared in dating this group of snow scenes. Monet's natural inclination, even at this early period, was to paint several studies of the same subject or effect; the *series* as it later developed was an unforced development of this habit. A second cause has been the carelessness with which letters are arranged in Poulain. A letter which from internal evidence must have been written in June, 1867, is said to date from the summer of 1866. In it Monet asks Bazille to send him a group of canvases, mentioning among them two snow scenes. The fact is that Monet had no opportunity to paint snow before the winter 1866–67, and corroboration that he did paint his snow scenes then is found in the letter of Alexander Dubourg, February 2, 1867: ". . . he has done some rather effective snow scenes. . . ." (Jean-Aubry's *Boudin*). Zacharie Astruc's letter to Bazille is from Poulain, pages 71–72. Germaine Bazin, *Impressionist Paintings in the Louvre*, mentions a letter belonging to the Louvre which "indicates that he painted it in 1865"; he is evidently unaware how wide of the mark were Monet's later recollections, especially of dates.

The small replica of *Camille* is on a canvas approximately 22 by 31 inches, or, allowing for alterations due to the keying and restretching of pictures, a standard French 25, such as had become his favorite size for landscape work. When exhibited at Edinburgh in 1957, an inscription was found on the stretcher: *Monsieur Monet, chez Madame Toutain, ferme de St.-Siméon, Honfleur*, evidently Bazille's own instructions for delivery (Catalogue *Claude Monet*, Edinburgh International Festival, 1957, page 40). Ba-

zille's purchase of the garden picture, and the altering sums, mentioned in Poulain, who confounds himself by suggesting that the picture may have been a commission: a logical non sequitur of the letters he quotes.

Zola's letter, written to Valabrègue, is dated April 4, 1867, and shows how soon the result of the jury's deliberations were known in Paris; Rewald, page 168. The reply of Jules Breton was recounted by Monet in later years to Marc Elder; see *À Giverny Chez Claude Monet*, page 39. That Bazille was painting a portrait of Monet (now unknown) is mentioned in a letter in Poulain, page 80. Adolphe Monet's extraordinary reply to Bazille from Poulain, pages 74–77.

Chapter Nine
CHILD OF CALAMITY

It should be pointed out that whether Monet and Camille stayed with Bazille in Paris is hypothetical; the sources as they are presently known remain silent. Here again, the Bazille letters, if they are eventually seen in complete form, may be more informative. However, Bazille's unusual absence from Paris at this season surely indicates that he was leaving his premises for their use. One regrets that except for two references in Bazille's letters, no details are known of the scheme for an exhibition. Internal evidence indicates that Adolphe Monet's letter to Bazille was written in April—thus only protracted hopes, and Monet's chaotic state, can explain his tarrying in Paris until June.

The picture of the church of St.-Germain l'Auxerrois is in fact dated "66" and most authors have assumed it was painted then. Examination of the three pictures as a group persuaded me they were done together in 1867. It is known that into the 1920's Paris dealers, among them Bernheim, brought Monet old canvases to sign and date. Monet recounted his day at the Louvre with Courbet to Marc Elder (*Chez Claude Monet*, pages 27–28). The letters to Bazille are from Gaston Poulain's *Bazille et ses amis*, where Bazille's letters concerning Courbet (page 66) and lack of money for an exhibition (page 83) are also found. Cabadi is mentioned in Monet's letters to

Bazille; his address is from the certificate of birth.

Incidents concerning the various artists said to have passed Latouche's window were recollected in later years by Monet, who recounted them in slightly varying versions and revolving about the *Women in a Garden.* Marthe de Fels, *La Vie de Claude Monet,* names Corot in place of Daumier, who appears in Elder, but such an act would seem untypical of Corot. That Manet had passed is mentioned in Thiébault-Sisson's interview in *Le Temps,* November 27, 1900. To avoid obvious pitfalls I have favored those versions naming a picture which a contemporary document verifies Latouche purchased. (The *Women in a Garden* was already at Montpellier.)

Manet's *Woman in Pink,* mentioned by Monet, is probably *La Femme au Perroquet,* exhibited at the Salon of 1868, and purchased by Durand-Ruel. After passing through the Hoschedé collection it was given by Erwin Davis to the Metropolitan Museum in New York.

Subjects Monet was painting at Ste.-Adresse were enumerated in his letter of June 25 to Bazille (Poulain, pages 92–93). The *Garden at Ste.-Adresse* is now at Leningrad, the Hermitage, catalogue No. 6505, and the woman in the picture was specifically identified as Mme. Paul Eugène Lecadre by her grandson, Maurice Thieullent, in his letter of April 13, 1965. The smaller study of this same garden is at the Jeu de Paume. Figures done from his father and aunt are recognizable in *The Beach at Ste.-Adresse,* the Metropolitan Museum, where Adolphe Monet's Panama hat is much in evidence.

Details of Camille's delivery from the official Minutes des Actes de Naissance, preserved in the Mairie of the seventeenth arrondissement, Paris. A more brief official transcript, given me for the fee of 65 francs, was dated April 8, 1957.

Chapter Ten
ANNALS OF THE POOR

The best assumption is that Monet employed Bazille's September remittance for his transit to Paris. If, as was Bazille's habit, the money was sent late, Monet would have arrived toward the tenth of the month. That Bazille's "exuberant and elegant" friend (description from F. Daulte, *Frédéric Bazille et son temps,* Geneva, 1952, who spells the name *Prat*—page 63) purchased the smaller of Monet's Ste.-Adresse garden scenes is shown by the catalogue of the Fourth Impressionist Exhibition (1879), where it is No. 157: *Jardin à Sainte-Adresse (1867): app. à M. Frat.*

The route by which Émile Zola obtained information concerning the personal relationship between Monet and Camille is easily traced. Bazille, who mixed far more widely in Paris than Monet himself, frequently during 1868 was taken by Cézanne to visit Zola (Daulte, page 66). Poulain, in *Bazille et ses amis,* page 99, mentions that Bazille agreed to be godfather; Monet's letter of January 1, 1868, and the draft of Bazille's reply, from the same source.

Boudin's letters, quoted in Jean-Aubry's *Eugène Boudin,* help to illumine this dark period. From him we discover Monet had settled at Bonnières. The free jury list of 1868, and manifesto, are from the Courbet documents gathered together by Étienne Moreau-Nelaton and given to the Cabinet d'Estampes, Bibliothèque Nationale, Paris.

Which picture Monet exhibited at the Salon of 1868 remains difficult to establish. All contemporary references are to a *Steamship,* and the previous summer Monet had written to Bazille that he was painting one for the Salon. But the title given in the Salon catalogue is *Ships Coming Out of the Havre Jetty,* demonstrating conclusively that the steamship was not alone. The only known picture which might suitably match descriptions of a *Steamship* is dated 1866 and surely represents Honfleur rather than Le Havre. A steamship present in its middle distance makes the matter more complicated, and Rewald *(The History of Impressionism,* page 155) suggests that this may have been the picture shown at the Salon. My reaction to Rewald's inference is entirely negative because (1) this is not the picture painted *at Le Havre* in 1867, mentioned in Monet's letter as being done specifically for the Salon, and (2) these ships are represented *in port* and not *coming out of the jetty* as specified in the Salon catalogue. Thus I have been forced to conclude that the picture shown at the Salon of 1868 is at present unknown.

Monet's address in the Salon catalogue this year is given as "8, Impasse St.-Louis, Batignolles," which would be a complete mystery were it not the place at which Camille had given birth the previous summer. Cabadi was thus enough a friend to permit the use of his address. In later years, a heavyset man with mutton chop whiskers, he visited Monet at Giverny: this is from my interview with James P. Butler, July 14, 1956.

The Count de Nieuwerkerke's intervention was recounted to Boudin by Daubigny himself the following winter, and recorded by Boudin in his letter of January 18, 1869, to Martin (in Jean-Aubry). Castagnary's mocking attack on Nieuwerkerke quoted from Poulain, page 113. It should be remembered that Castagnary was an intimate of Courbet, to whom a mass of Courbet's letters, preserved in the Moreau-Nelaton Collection (Bibliothèque Nationale), is addressed.

Chapter Eleven
THE KNIGHT OF THE WOEFUL COUNTENANCE

For this period too the order of the letters contained in Poulain's *Bazille et ses amis* is in error. The result has been wholesale confusion: Poulain places the Havre International Marine Exhibition in the spring of 1868, whereas it actually took place in the autumn. In their proper sequence the events surrounding this exhibition thus form an entirely new context.

Monet's letter, dated June 11 by Poulain (page 150), was therefore written at Fécamp, and must date from *1868*. That Houssaye paid 800 francs for *Camille* is mentioned in Geffroy's *Monet*, page 21. In later years Monet's surviving relatives made an effort to dispute his suicide attempt at Fécamp. The facts, however, are indisputable, and perfectly consistent emotionally and psychologically with events of that period. Unfortunately Mme. Blanche Hoschedé-Monet made herself ridiculous by writing to Poulain, May 21, 1928, "*Je voudrais bien savoir quel est l'imbécile qui a inventé cette histoire. . . .*" The *imbécile* was Monet

himself, in a document of the period: Monet's "suicide" letter to Bazille, dated June 29, 1868, from Poulain, pages 119–120.

Previous authors have noted Monet's deliberation in requesting that specific canvases be sent him at Le Havre. Because of the false context built by Poulain, it has universally been thought he was asking for canvases to paint over. In fact *all* these pictures, which Monet evidently considered the most advantageous to show, are still extant:

(1) *the two large avenues done at Fontainebleau, of the same dimensions:* Jeu de Paume, and Hansen Collection, Ordrupgard, Denmark. A third very similar study—possibly one of those requested, in fact—was exhibited at Durand-Ruel's Paris gallery, Exposition Claude Monet, 1959, No. 3.

(2) *the Chinese picture where there are flags:* collection of the Rev. & Mrs. Theodore Pitcairn, Bryn Athyn, Pennsylvania.

(3) *the rose bush at Guillemet's place:* identification is difficult from such a description. Evidently Monet had loaned it to Antoine Guillemet in Paris, and wished Bazille to retrieve it for him. Since presumably this is one of the pictures later seized at Le Havre, possibly it is one loaned the Fourth Impressionist Exhibition (1879), No. 155: *Un Jardin (1867): app. à M. Lecadre.* This work is now No. 6505 in the Hermitage Collection, Leningrad.

(4) *the very white snow scene:* presumably the *Road near Honfleur* reproduced by Rewald, page 115, present ownership unknown.

(5) *the road near Honfleur in the snow (in which a flock of crows fly over):* collection of Mr. & Mrs. Alex M. Lewyt, New York.

(6) *the marine with the little blue boats:* presumably the picture now in the Art Institute of Chicago, though the title could be stretched to fit others painted the summer of 1867.

(7) *the scene where one sees Le Havre from the distance with little cabins and much surf:* collection of Sir A. Chester Beatty, Dublin.

That Monet's family did take him in

when he appeared at Le Havre following the Fécamp suicide attempt is proved by the last paragraph of this same letter, in which he asked Bazille to send his canvases to the care of his father, "rue Fontenelle, 13, at Le Havre." The distribution of medals from Jean-Aubry's *Eugène Boudin*.

Technical analysis of the portrait of Mme. Gaudibert is from many examinations of the picture, in the Jeu de Paume. The quotation from Louis Gaudibert is in Geffroy, page 40; its wording supports evidence in the picture itself that Monet was much troubled by his task; of course his letter to Bazille also says it did not go easily. The meetings with Courbet and Dumas are from Geffroy; the letter to Courbet dated September 17 is in the Moreau-Nelaton Collection of Courbet papers: it addresses him *at Le Havre*.

That Monet painted Louis Gaudibert in addition to his wife is stated by Boudin in his letter to Martin dated January 18, 1869 (Jean-Aubry). Note the plurals: "*Il est regrettable que vous n'avez pas vu les portraits Gaudiberts, celui de madame surtout. . . .*" Of course it may have been children's portraits Monet painted, but Boudin's words strongly imply it was Louis Gaudibert himself. No further mention of this portrait, nor even a clue to its size, has ever appeared

Chapter Twelve
FRATERNITY OF VAGABONDS

Boudin's letters are remarkable for the quantity of hard facts he compressed into them. Thus on April 25, 1869, Jean-Aubry (*Eugène Boudin*) tells us, "It is to Gaudibert the large marines were knocked down at the derisory sum of eighty francs, I think." Boudin, who received this news only the following spring, after Monet returned to Paris, surely thought the sum was derisory. That Paul Eugène Lecadre purchased at least one picture at this same auction is proved by the loan he made to the Fourth Impressionist Exhibition (see notes to Chapter 11). It is more than remarkable that a picture already exhibited at the Salon, and a work of some size, should have been purchased at such a price. That some collusion took place becomes obvious even before one

learns that following the auction Gaudibert made up the prices in payments to Monet.

The little ritual of life into which Monet and Camille launched at Étretat is well recorded by three interiors Monet painted there. *The Luncheon* is now in the Städelsches Kunstinstitut, Frankfurt; the "maid of all work" appears in its background and in that of a nighttime sketch, at present unlocated, but reproduced in Elder, *À Giverny Chez Claude Monet*, plate 13. The third version is in the Burhle Collection. The two smaller interiors, painted by night, have long been erroneously called *Sisley's Dining Room*, and given dates as far removed as Geffroy's 1874. However, the age of the little Jean, who appears in the first sketch, is consistent with *The Luncheon*. Were that not sufficient, the oval table and chairs are the same in each case.

The "tough, violent piece," created on the beach front at Étretat, is in the Jeu de Paume, and strangely like the works of Winslow Homer, both as regards the figures and the mood and manner of painting the whole. The long letter to Bazille is from Poulain's *Bazille et ses amis*. Daulte, in *Frédéric Bazille et son temps*, dates this September 23 (page 69), which is impossible because (1) Monet could not have got himself free at Le Havre by that date, and (2) in September he would not describe Étretat as being in winter: ". . . or I even go into the country, which is so beautiful here that I find it perhaps more agreeable in winter than summer."

Boudin's letter of January 18, 1869, from Jean-Aubry. From that same source is ". . . Monet has returned from Étretat starving . . . ," part of the letter of April 25, 1869, quoted previously. Bazille's letter to his father concerning the electioneering from Poulain, page 111; Daulte, page 75, supplies the date of March 23, 1869. Alfred Stevens' letter, of the sort regularly written by jury members to their supporters, from Poulain, page 146. Daulte, page 75, gives a date of "May 1869," but as jury deliberations surely preceded the opening of the Salon, one sees this to be a guess and incorrect. Bazille's "animosity" letter from Poulain, page 147; for this too Daulte (page 75) guesses at a date, and is probably no closer because this letter also appears to have preceded the opening of the exhibition.

Boudin's letter of April 25, 1869, again supplies the facts concerning Monet's picture shown in Latouche's window. Notable is that after this Salon rejection Cadart appears to have done no further business with Monet.

The meeting with Édouard Manet was recounted by Monet to Thiébault-Sisson in 1900 (interview in *Le Temps*, November 27, 1900), from whom quotations are drawn. In giving this interview Monet was determined to insist on his own importance. Various misstatements of fact have been eliminated from the text as quoted here, but even so, one doubts that Monet would have brought Bazille to the Guerbois. Bazille had already been an intimate friend.of Manet for several years, and this reintroduction of Monet to Manet was probably accomplished by him.

I was fortunate in being able to see the Café Guerbois, or Brasserie Muller, as it later became, in 1956 shortly after it finally closed its doors to business. The Avenue des Batignolles had become Avenue de Clichy. Only from the *substitution*, executed by Mme. Doncieux in 1865, did I learn that at the period of the first courtship between Monet and Camille the Doncieux family lived at 4 Rue Truffault, and not yet on the Boulevard des Batignolles.

Chapter Thirteen
AN UNLUCKY CHAPTER

The presence of Camille and little Jean at Octeville is recorded by a picture Monet painted of the Octeville church showing them in the foreground. This canvas, 23¼ by 31½ inches, formerly belonged to Knoedler's, and was called *Rue at Fécamp*. The complete text of Monet's letter to Houssaye is found in *Le Figaro Illustré*, December 16, 1926; a shortened text is found in Marthe de Fels, *La Vie de Claude Monet*.

Renoir's letter to Bazille (undated) from Poulain's *Bazille et ses amis*, page 155. The works Monet painted along the river at Bougival are well known: in the text's order of appearance they are (1) *The River*, 32 by 39 inches, Art Institute of Chicago; (2) *The Seine at Bougival*, 25 by 36 inches, Currier Gallery of Art,

Manchester, New Hampshire; (3) *La Grenouillère*, 29 by 39 inches, Metropolitan Museum, New York.

Parallels between Monet and Renoir at La Grenouillère are based on the picture by Monet in the Metropolitan Museum and the similar Renoir composition (26 by 32 inches) in the National Museum, Stockholm. Another pair of pictures was painted side by side: Renoir's, 25⅝ by 36¼ inches (collection of Mrs. M. S. Walzer, Oxford, England) is interesting for the fact that though his canvas was slightly larger than Renoir's, Monet worked on a smaller portion of the subject. The contraction of Monet's vision was already quite obvious. His earliest works were panoramic; as time passed, he concentrated on increasingly small areas.

Monet's renewed appeals to Bazille are from Poulain. The still life Monet mentioned having sold that September, 1869, was one of a group containing fruits and game associated with the autumn months. All represent their subjects on a white cloth of squared linen against dark backgrounds, and have the added psychological interest of showing how a man often deprived of food will dwell on it even in his work. Two that can be named are (1) a basket of pears, with a pear and a peach beside, and three bunches of dark and light grapes, private collection, Paris, and (2) a pheasant, 16 by 31 inches, private collection, Neuchâtel, Switzerland.

Another misarrangement of letters in Poulain (pages 162–163) has had the unfortunate effect of placing Monet alone at Étretat in October, 1869. This letter obviously dates from the previous year, when Monet was living at Étretat with his family. Rewald (*The History of Impressionism*, page 232) compounds this error by the statement that Courbet and Monet were there together! A letter from Courbet to Castagnary dated Étretat, September 6, 1869, in the Cabinet d'Estampes, Bibliothèque Nationale, Paris, shows that Monet was not present, and in fact that Courbet himself departed before the period of the (misdated) Monet letter.

Émile Zola's note to Bazille concerning the sitting for Fantin-Latour from Poulain (page 166, note). Monet was evidently aware of Fantin's embarrassment at painting him, and in later life gave vent to great scorn. Examination of Bazille's picture seems to support the tradition that Manet painted Bazille into the group; the touch is different and more flowing than elsewhere, and a failure of perspective, which made Bazille so atrociously tall, itself implies that the figure is Manet's work. Manet's exclamation is from Daulte's *Frédéric Bazille et son temps*, page 131, where Bazille's own letter is also found.

That "no record has survived of what work he was able to prepare for the Salon of 1870" is a literal statement, though one that can be enlarged on. In his letters to Bazille Monet had mentioned that both he and Renoir hoped to paint *La Grenouillère* for the Salon. This frequently quoted reference demanded more attention when recently the archives of Durand-Ruel yielded a notation that in March, 1873, Monet was paid 2,000 francs for a picture entitled *Grenouillère, Bougival*. Nearly three times the highest price Durand-Ruel had paid Monet, this was surely a very large picture and almost certainly the 1870 Salon piece. Unfortunately nothing but this notation seems to have endured—a large picture on this subject is now unknown.

Renoir's son, Jean Renoir, circulated various tales in the recent biography of his father, *Renoir, My Father*, Boston, 1958. That nothing from his book has been employed here reflects my opinion of the reliability of its materials. Most amusing is the tale of Monet ordering his clothes from the best tailors and pretending their work was unsatisfactory when asked for money. This was not Monet but Ray Milland, in a film called *Kitty*, also starring Paulette Goddard, made during the period when Jean Renoir was in Hollywood.

Election of the jury for the Salon of 1870 from Rewald; Millet's presence and role in proceedings from Netta Peacock, *Millet*, London, 1905, page 146. Ziem's participation in the battle from Geffroy's *Claude Monet*, page 43.

Chapter Fourteen

THE HEIRESS

Bazille's important letter reflecting on Monet's marriage and its motivations is from Poulain's *Bazille et ses amis*. I have noted elsewhere ("New Materials on Claude Monet" in *The Art Quarterly*, Winter 1962, page 328, note 16) how extraordinary it is that though the French text of this letter has been in print and available to scholars since 1932, no one made any effort to verify its inference that Camille was given a dowry. An extract from the will of Antoine Pritelly, debarring Camille's succession, is quoted in Chapter 9.

The infirmity of Charles Claude Doncieux at this period is merely logical inference. His signature and initials show a trembling hand which could not be attributed to age alone; born in 1808, he was only sixty-two. In view of his death three years later one assumes him to have been a man already in failing health. Whether or not Adolphe Monet was informed of these contract negotiations, indeed whether he refused to attend, to delegate his sister, or was merely left in ignorance, it is clear that relations between him and his younger son were at a low ebb. That he took no part in this very serious occasion is distinctly strange, and must have been unusual in remarkable degree to all those present.

My earlier article devoted to this contract of marriage (in *The Art Quarterly*, mentioned above) put a different interpretation on it. My request for permission to have it photographed had been refused, and except for my notes I was unable to consult it and related documents further. Finally, in March, 1965, I succeeded in bringing Michael O'Reilly, my worthy photographer, to Paris to photograph in entirety the documents I had discovered earlier. Once I was able to study these lengthy and execrably written old documents at leisure, the subtleties became clear.

Previous authors, (Geffroy in *Claude Monet*, Venturi in *Les archives de l'impressionisme*, 2 vols., Paris–New York, 1939, Rewald in *The History of Impressionism*) have employed the date of June 26, 1870, for the marriage, demonstrating how the pious proliferation of footnotes can lead back to an original error. The true date, June 28, appears in Mairie records, and was adjoined to Monet's birth certificate preserved in the Archives de la Seine, Paris.

I have recounted elsewhere (*The Art*

Quarterly) how the account of a wedding written by Émile Zola into his novel *L'Oeuvre* (page 278) supplied clues which led to the discovery of these documents concerning Monet's marriage. Zola laid his account "in the rue Drouot, on the Mairie steps," the Mairie of the ninth arrondissement. Monet's wedding took place at the Mairie of the eighth arrondissement, in 1870 located at 11 Rue d'Anjou (now a post office). Shifting the scene by one arrondissement is of course the transparent concealment to be expected in a nineteenth-century roman à clef. Because he so certainly was describing Monet's marriage, I have taken over from Zola his character's hesitation. Zola must have heard a great deal about this wedding from Bazille, if he was not present himself, for on page 270 he is also aware that "they had a long time to wait for some of the necessary papers."

Boudin's letter is from Jean-Aubry's *Eugène Boudin*, page 104. He was writing in response to an announcement received in 1897 of Jean Monet's marriage to Blanche Hoschedé. The "persisting influence" referred to is largely in figures. As at La Grenouillère, and later at Argenteuil, whenever Monet took the trouble to characterize small figures in his outdoor work he did so in Boudin's style and with textures acutely resembling those of Boudin.

Another reflection on Camille's personality is that she would appear to have been a willing model. At least one of the many Boudin Trouville sketches preserved at the Musée du Havre appears to show Camille and her little sister (No. 119, *Dame en blanc sur le plage de Trouville*). A year earlier she may also have posed for a head painted by Bazille (reproduced in Daulte, *Frédéric Bazille et son temps*, catalogue No. 40, page 182, *Jeune Femme aux yeux baissés*). Bazille's somewhat inept sense of form makes him unreliable in portraiture, but individually the features shown check well against those of Camille as seen in the Renoir portrait in Zahar's *Renoir*, and there is the added coincidence that this expression with downcast eyes is exactly that mentioned by Zola in his notes for *L'Oeuvre*: "When the eyes close an exquisite tenderness. But basically passionate, the jaw a little prominent,

very strong. . . ." Quoted in full in my Monet article in *The Art Quarterly*.

Outbreak of the Franco-Prussian War is mentioned in all sources on this period. Particular reliance has been placed on Alfred Cobban, *A History of Modern France*, Harmondsworth, England, 1961, and Robert Baldick, *The Siege of Paris*, London, 1964. Bazille's reflection on Monet's military tastes, dated August 2, is not mentioned in Poulain but is found in Daulte (page 81, note). One suspects the basic cause of Monet's behavior during this period was the loss of his discharge papers. Because a replacement had been bought for him, it is dubious whether he could have been called up, even in this emergency. Only because he could not prove his own status was he open to doubt, arrest, and a possible forceful incorporation in the service.

Boudin's departure for Brittany, and Monet's subsequent discouraged letter, are mentioned in Jean-Aubry. The date Monet left for England is unknown, though various authors have proffered their guesses as fact (William C. Seitz, *Monet*, New York, 1960, says "September," page 24. In later years Monet was loath to speak about this period: we are therefore without the usual references to it in his interviews. The whereabouts of Camille and little Jean until his return to France is equally unknown.

That he frequented a French café in London was mentioned by Monet to Marc Elder (*À Giverny Chez Claude Monet*, page 24). His poor circumstances in London were stressed in Thiébault-Sisson's interview in *Le Temps*, November 20, 1900. Bazille's tragic death is recounted in Poulain, pages 195–196, and on page 206 is the assertion that Monet learned of Bazille's death from a newspaper. It would appear to have been Maître, Bazille's closest friend, who sorted out his papers and pictures left in the Paris studio (Poulain, page 206), and it is therefore to him that we owe the preservation of Monet's many letters. But that Maître was not himself a painter must also account for the fact that a number of Monet's smaller studies, left in Bazille's studio, were sent to Montpellier, where they have always been considered Bazille's work. See notes to Chapter 6.

Daubigny "friend faithful and sure" quoted from Monet's conversation with Elder (page 24); Daubigny's own remarks to Durand-Ruel from Fels (*La Vie de Claude Monet*, page 130). That Durand-Ruel had earlier noted Monet's works at the Salon is from the "Memories de Paul Durand-Ruel," published in Vol. 2 of Venturi's *Les archives de l'impressionisme*, page 179. In this account Durand-Ruel claims that though he admired Monet's work he never dealt with him "because he was almost never at Paris." This seems somewhat transparent in view of Monet's persistent efforts to find dealers. The account of Durand-Ruel's transference to England on the eve of the Paris siege is also from *Les archives,* where on pages 247–248 is found Durand-Ruel's letter to Pissarro.

Pissarro recounted his experiences to Wynford Dewhurst in a letter dated November 6, 1902, which Dewhurst incorporated in his article "Impressionist Painting: Its Genesis and Development (Part II)" in *The Studio,* July 15, 1903, page 94. Monet later denied the interest he had in Turner and Constable at that period, but of course the former is visible in his famous view of *The Thames with the Houses of Parliament,* and one feels the presence of Constable in a glowing study of *Tewkesbury Road* (28¼ by 36 inches, collection of Mr. and Mrs. Ernest Kanzler, Grosse Pointe Farms, Michigan).

In later years Monet had a natural inclination to deny all influences, and especially those of the English landscapists whom he studied on this trip. The works he did shortly after in Holland, however, show a very strong debt to Crome's *Moonrise on the Yare* (Tate Gallery). The silhouetted windmill, of which, as well as the balance and pattern, are reflected in the majority of Monet's Dutch works from 1871. Pissarro's letter to Théodore Duret quoted from Fels (pages 102–103).

Chapter Fifteen
TILTING AT WINDMILLS

Monet's short period in Holland is probably the least known of his career. The invitation from D'Esternelles de Constant is mentioned by Fels, in *La Vie de Claude Monet,* page 103, and the presence of Daubigny by most other sources. Rewald, in *The History of Impressionism,* page 263, cagily qualifies Monet's presence together with the latter, but in this context mistakenly says Daubigny "even purchased one of Monet's views of the canal of Zaandam," whereas Daubigny's purchase was made later in Paris and from Durand-Ruel: See "Memoires de Paul Durand-Ruel" in Venturi's *Les archives de l'impressionisme,* Vol. II, page 195. Rewald further states (page 273): "Monet also returned to that country to paint more views of canals, boats, and windmills"; but of this no evidence is known.

"Painted at least one portrait reflective of Mme. Gaudibert" refers to a work the author has been unable to find or examine. In Georges Besson's *Monet,* plate 17 is this *Portrait de Mme. D.* The reproduction is altogether persuasive, and clearly signed and dated 1871; the picture is said to belong to the Amsterdam Municipal Museum. The museum itself disavows such a work; its director, Dr. S. H. Levie, stated in a letter dated July 9, 1965, "This picture is not in our collection and never has been."

Monet's Paris housewarming is from Jean-Aubry's *Eugène Boudin,* where Boudin's letters are given. Durand-Ruel himself stated that he purchased "everything" Monet painted at this period (his "Memoires" in *Les archives de l'impressionisme*). This too categoric statement is of course the dim recollection of a later period, and I am obliged to the present head of the firm, M. Charles Durand-Ruel, for permitting researches into his archives, which produced lists of purchases found in this chapter and the following. These lists do not include purchases made from Monet in England, and possibly they omit a first group purchased from Monet on his arrival in Paris from Holland, December, 1871. In his letter to me of June 17, 1965, M. Durand-Ruel said that sixty-eight works were purchased from Monet during the years 1872–1873, for a total of 32,250 francs. But only fifty-six canvases are on the purchase lists discovered in the firm's archives, for a total of 21,900 francs.

No documentation survives to prove at what exact period Monet retrieved the ruined *Picnic* from Chailly. In March,

1965, the present M. and Mme. Paillard, still proprietors of the Cheval-Blanc, categorically assured me that all records had been destroyed in the lifetime of their predecessors. Three pieces of circumstantial evidence have caused me to place the transaction immediately after Monet settled at Argenteuil: (1) This was the first moment after his expulsion from the inn of 1865 when he possessed sufficient funds to consider retrieving that canvas; (2) he did so at a period when Camille was still alive; (3) by March, 1873, he was able to sell two other (seized?) Fontaine-bleau works to Durand-Ruel.

The first point of evidence requires no explanation. The second is more interesting, for when Monet was visited at Giverny in 1920 by the Duc de Trévise, the two men were photographed before a large fragment of this canvas. A fresh print of that photo obtained from Roger-Viollet in Paris shows an extra over-scale head of Camille at the right margin of the canvas. Probably after Monet's death the canvas was reduced on this right side, to eliminate this head. Then the left section was "discovered" at Giverny by Georges Wildenstein, who presented it to the Jeu de Paume. The right section has disappeared entirely and was presumably destroyed by Monet because of its rotted state.

Gustave Courbet's short political career is touched on in each of many volumes, including *Courbet raconté par lui-même et par ses amis,* Geneva, 1948, Charles Léger's *Courbet et son temps,* and Marcel Zahar's *Gustave Courbet.* Amand Gautier's drawing of Courbet in prison is reproduced opposite page 177 of *Courbet et son temps,* and leads one to believe he was chained. Boudin's letter is from Benjamin's *Eugène Boudin,* page 82; Courbet's reply is from the same source.

That it was Édouard Manet who made the necessary contact with Mme. Aubry-Vitet at Argenteuil is among the interesting discoveries made by Étienne Moreau-Nelaton and published in *Manet raconté par lui-même,* Paris, 1926 (Vol. II, page 22). The name of Merceron, Monet's notary at Argenteuil, was already familiar to me from the estate papers of Charles Claude Doncieux. I was therefore able to

check his roster for papers executed, discovering mention of the *procuration* and *décharge.*

Chapter Sixteen
DEATH IN THE FAMILY

Boudin's letter mentioning Monet's new contentment is from Jean-Aubry's *Eugène Boudin.* Paul Durand-Ruel is very pointed concerning his failure to interest clients in Monet's works at this period. Among the pictures purchased in November, 1872, several are easily identifiable, including *Westminster,* sold to Hoschedé and now belonging to Lord Astor of Hever, and *Femme en Rose,* presumably a part of the lilac series painted just before the marriage in 1870 (Walters Art Gallery, Baltimore).

In the vague contexts previously available it had always been accepted that Durand-Ruel acted with extraordinary courage and foresight. The newly revealed deal for nineteen works, for many of which he paid advanced prices, shows just how courageous he was. Among them, *Le Bodenier* was surely the large canvas that had appeared at the Salon of 1866, and is presently at the Metropolitan Museum. The two works called *Effet de Brouillard* may be the studies painted at Le Havre in 1872 (one of which in 1874 became the famous *Impression*).

The "explicit account of the path which meandered along the riverfront near his home" is of course the famous *Basin d'Argenteuil* in the Jeu de Paume. However, it is also possible that this work was painted slightly earlier, and is the *Promenade au Bord de l'Eau* purchased by Durand-Ruel in September, 1872. Such a title could fit a number of works from the Argenteuil period. This context, however, would not be altered in any respect by moving it up a few months into the summer of 1872. The study containing "the little long-skirted figure of Jean, with a coquettish Camille peeking out the door" is *The Artist's Garden at Argenteuil,* Art Institute of Chicago.

Camille's costumes remain an essential means for dating pictures, and, at times, for recognizing her. Fortunately her new hat for the spring of 1873 appears in a dated picture, *Les Coquelicots,* in the Jeu de Paume, where Jean's new garb, seen more fully elsewhere, is also established to its date. That *Les Coquelicots* was painted in the autumn is predicated on the assumption it was done during Renoir's visit, when he painted a comparable work, also in the Jeu de Paume, *Chemin Montant dans les Hautes Herbes*. (Arbitrary alterations in the costumes of both figures are attributable to Renoir's desire to make them stand away from their background more strongly.)

It is possible that Renoir came to Argenteuil more than once that year. However, the poppies, which in France bloom wild in September, do not contradict the autumn date appropriate to both the duck pond and garden scenes which are dated 1873. The Caravaggiesque peaches, so strangely resembling the scumbled peaches in the *Boy with a Basket of Fruit* (Borghese Gallery), are found in *Le Déjeuner* (Jeu de Paume).

Documents surrounding the death of Charles Claude Doncieux were discovered in the archives of the successor to Maître Aumont-Thieville, September 14, 1956. These comprised (1) a sheet of *formalités* briefly mentioning the place and date of the death, (2) a *copy* of the will, (3) Monet's authorization to Camille to act in his behalf in the compiling of the inventory, (4) the controversial inventory itself, (5) its certification, (6) a lengthy account of the cross-questioning to which Mme. Doncieux was subjected by Postel-Dubois, and (7) an inventory of the Pritelly estate to which she had succeeded. A final document of this group was (8) the *acte* of November 24, 1873, under which Camille and Monet extracted 4,000 francs from Mme. Doncieux. My previous article referring to these papers, in *The Art Quarterly*, Winter 1962, again will show considerable differences in interpretation. The cause is the same mentioned regarding the marriage documents given in Chapter 14, the subtleties of which I was not able to appreciate until in March, 1965, my photographer, Michael O'Reilly, was permitted to make copies. Because of the character of his intervention Postel-Dubois kept no record of what he did for Monet (my interview with his successor, Paris, September, 1956).

The extent of Durand-Ruel's purchases was outlined to me by Charles Durand-Ruel in his letters of June 17 and June 30, 1965. The contemporary reaction—first indifference, then hostility—is specifically mentioned in the "Memoires de Paul Durand-Ruel" (in Venturi's *Les archives de l'impressionisme*), who lists also the private collectors whom he urged to buy direct. Nadar's studio was located at 35 Boulevard des Capucines, and had a private entrance with a stairway leading direct to the second floor.

The use of Monet's boat can be defined by the appearance of dated works painted from the water. Significant also is that in a sketch he made of the boat itself (Rijksmuseum Kröller-Müller, Otterlo, Holland) the hull is painted with black pigment, which he was shortly to cease using. Thus both the appearance of the boat and the technical advances of the period can be dated to this period immediately after the return of his economic problems. Durand-Ruel mentions that he showed Whistler's works in Paris, never selling one. The study of Old Battersea Bridge, called *Nocturne in Blue and Gold,* has been in the Tate Gallery since 1905.

Chapter Seventeen

A NEW TACTIC

Durand-Ruel's large purchases had ceased in 1873; however, Monet did receive an additional 1,300 francs from Durand-Ruel during the year 1874. The charter date is so important to the sequence of events at this period that I have employed it here despite certain hesitations. It is found on page 312 of the revised 1961 edition of Rewald (*The History of Impressionism*), who in his notes, page 339, credits it "Information courtesy Oscar Reuterswärd, Stockholm," without explaining where this source derives his information or where the charter itself may be found.

The problem of Monet's titles at the 1874 exhibition is a complicated one, not the least so because Rewald, pages 316 and 339, gives an account which he credits to "Unpublished recollections of Edmond Renoir"—where are these found for verification? As found in Rewald, Edmond Renoir was disturbed by similarity in titles such as *Entrance of a Village, Leaving the Village, Morning in a Village,* etc., none of which could possibly apply to the works Monet is known to have exhibited. Monet's own version therefore seems more likely (*La Revue Illustrée*, March 15, 1898): "I was asked to give a title for the catalogue. I could not very well call it a view of Le Havre. So I said, 'Mark it *Impression.*'" The word "impression" was used by Monet himself in 1868, writing to Bazille from Étretat: ". . . what I do here at least will have the merit of resembling no one, because it will be the simple impression of my own experiences." (See Chapter 12.) Doubtless it was in the same sense that the word was offered to Edmond Renoir.

Whether the sun in this canvas is rising, as Edmond Renoir thought, or setting has also caused considerable discussion. Since all arguments must ultimately be settled by geography at Le Havre, I took the problem there, discovering that Monet habitually worked either from the principal jetty, nearest to his youthful haunts at Ste.-Adresse, or from the quay adjacent to this jetty. From either position an east-west axis will extend over the sea. Thus, this sun over the sea is in the *west*, or setting position.

These arguments assume that the Musée Marmottan picture is the same *Impression* exhibited in 1874. Recently this too has been challenged by Daniel Wildenstein, who supplied information for the new edition of Rewald. Though ingenious, I fear these gentlemen are misinformed. The earliest inventories and certificates of insurance, preserved at the Musée Marmottan, all refer to its picture as *"L'Impression."* This would mean only that Georges de Bellio *believed* his picture was the same as that exhibited in 1874, until one verifies that he had every means of being *certain*. After the exhibition the *Impression* was purchased by Hoschedé, and at his sale, June 5 and 6, 1878, the picture (No. 55, *"L'Impression" Soleil Couchant*) passed to de Bellio for 210 francs. In his early documents and insurance policies de Bellio merely carried on the title, in quotation marks, as it had come to him.

Further, in an undated letter to Monet, de Bellio lists his principal holdings of Monet's pictures, the fourth of which was *L'Impression*. That no further title was necessary indicates how complete was this identification, not only on the part of de Bellio but also of Monet himself. Finally, in their argument, Wildenstein and Rewald cite the fact that a canvas entitled *Effet de Brouillard, Impression,* from the de Bellio collection, was present in the fourth exhibition of 1879. They fail to note that such a fog scene on snow, *painted at Vétheuil*, is still present in the de Bellio collection at the Musée Marmottan. In his undated letter already quoted from, de Bellio lists this as *Vétheuil, Coucher de Soleil*. The picture at the 1879 exhibition was therefore this more recent one.

That Camille was the model for Renoir's *La Loge*, now at the Courtauld Institute, London, is based on comparison of that picture with the portrait of Camille reproduced by Zahar in his *Renoir*, plate 13. As stated earlier in these notes, the likeness is far more convincing than seems possible in Renoir's structurally weak portraits. Because at this period Lise had left Renoir, and Camille was his frequent model, there is every reason to believe the obvious evidence of the picture itself. Probably Camille's black hair was made brown because the picture already had quantities of black in stripes on the gown and its matching cloak, and in the evening clothes of Edmond Renoir, who sits behind. Rewald (page 334) states that a new model named Nini posed for this work, but does not support his contention by evidence.

Exact parallels in the works painted by Manet and Monet at this period have never before been pointed out. Manet's initial study of the three sailboats, showing two with black hulls, was formerly in the possession of Bernheim Jeune, Paris. The fact that it represents three boats, closely spaced, the foremost of which has an oval cockpit, proves them to be the same boats seen in Monet's more famous *Le Pont d'Argenteuil* (Jeu de Paume). Comparisons of the perspective would indicate that Monet stood at Manet's left while they worked. A very similar composition by Monet was also formerly in the possession of Durand-Ruel, and is reproduced opposite page 45 of François Fosca's *Claude Monet*. Only one sailboat appears in the foreground of this version, its hull the natural dark color.

Examination of the Jeu de Paume canvas proves the white of the foremost hull lies over another tone. The staff of the Rhode Island School of Design, Providence, are aware of my feeling that their equally famous and very widely reproduced *Bassin d'Argenteuil*, showing the same three sailboats, is in fact a studio variant concocted from the Durand-Ruel and Jeu de Paume pictures. Another sketch of this group by Édouard Manet, for which Camille and little Jean posed figures, is *The River at Argenteuil*, collection of Lady Aberconway, London.

Volumes could be written concerning the extraordinary influence of this picture and its figures, for it is the source from which Sargent took inspiration for his small and large versions of *Fishing* (collections of Mrs. J. L. Hughes and Tate Gallery). Sargent was natural heir to this particular phase of Édouard Manet's work, and was the only important figure painter of that period who both employed the full synthetic palette of Claude Monet, with its idiosyncratic use of colored accents, and carried through this phase of working by the water with figures. Sargent thus brought to fruition what Manet had begun.

Manet's picture of Monet at work in his studio-boat is in the Neue Staats-gallerie, Munich. A second version is listed by Adolphe Tabarant, No. 322. (*Manet: histoire catalographique*, Paris 1931). The "matching canvases" by Monet and Renoir, not a new phenomenon, belong (Monet's) to a private collection, Paris, and (Renoir's) to the Portland Art Museum, Portland, Oregon.

The picture for which Manet's wife and brother-in-law posed is *Argenteuil* (Tournai, Belgium, Museum). The identification of Rudolph Leenhoff is traditional, that of Mme. Manet based on other likenesses and photos. Rudolph Leenhoff in his undershirt is of course *Sailing*, Metropolitan Museum, New York. Camille is identified more by her hat and dress, which appear in so many other works painted that summer, than her profile, which Manet has deliberately made vague to simulate her veil.

Renoir's garden canvas was given to Monet immediately, and according to James P. Butler always hung at Giverny (interview, May 26, 1956). It is now in the possession of Mrs. Mellon Bruce, New York. Manet's irritated remark to Monet concerning Renoir was recollected by Monet in the presence of Elder (*À Giverny Chez Claude Monet*, page 70). It has been called false by Tabarant, but surely is typical of Manet's ire.

Chapter Eighteen
A PEDDLER
AND HIS WIFE

Renoir's portrait, dated "75," is in the Jeu de Paume. Monet is seen indoors, heavily dressed, and before the same curtain and potted plants which appear in the picture on which he works: *A Corner of an Apartment* (Jeu de Paume). Monet did at least one other indoor study of Camille at work embroidering, surrounded by the same potted plants; present ownership unknown. Édouard Manet's letter to Wolff is from the copy preserved in the Moreau-Nelaton Collection, Bibliothèque Nationale; Wolff's subsequent mention is from Geffroy's *Claude Monet*, page 57. Other notices which appeared before and after the sale are quoted in Geffroy, who also mentions discord at the sale. That the police were called is from Durand-Ruel's "Memoires" in Venturi's *Les archives de l'impressionisme*. Durand-Ruel also gives the total sum produced by the sale (page 201), and Geffroy quotes the spread of Monet's prices, the total of which, however, is found only in Rewald (*The History of Impressionism*), again from undivulged sources.

When I first discovered the Monet-Doncieux documents in September, 1956, the folder of estate papers had on top Monet's letter of June 28, 1875. Faced with so many complicated documents, my attention was concentrated more on them than this letter, of which I noted only the date. In March, 1965, when once more I gained access to these papers, the letter was gone.

Monet's letters to Édouard Manet as employed here are my own translations from the texts in Adolph Tabarant, "Autour de Manet" in *L'Art Vivant*, April, 1928. Rewald states, incorrectly, that the originals of these are at the Bibliothèque Nationale, where my searches produced nothing. Subsequently the obliging director of the Cabinet d'Estampes, M. Jean Adhemar, sent me copies of the *copies* made by Moreau-

Nelaton, which are a part of his collection (Yb³2401). Communicated to Moreau-Nelaton by Manet's son-in-law, Léon Leenhoff, these have been the basis of all published texts.

Manet wrote to Eva Gonzalès from the Hoschedé home that there were too many distractions to permit finishing the portrait (Moreau-Nelaton, autour de Manet). Hoschedé purchases of Claude Monet's works have been reconstructed from the catalogue of his *Vente Judiciaire*. Twelve Monets were included, all of them acquired from Durand-Ruel and listed among his purchases from Monet except *Dahlias Beside Water* and *Young Woman in a Massif of Dahlias*, which appear to have been bought from the artist direct. (*Dahlias Beside Water* is published as Elder's plate 15 [in *À Giverny Chez Claude Monet*] under the title *Argenteuil*.) By the time of the sale Hoschedé had a number of other works by Monet which were not included; Hoschedé is not mentioned as owner of the *Impression* in the catalogue of the 1874 exhibition. This is the only *presumptive* evidence that he purchased it after the exhibition and direct from the artist. However, the fact that this *Impression* fits none of the titles recorded by Durand-Ruel on the lists of his purchase from the artist does not support the contention.

It has been asserted that Monet visited Montgeron for the first time in 1876, and in her memoir, published in Jean-Pierre Hoschedé's *Blanche Hoschedé-Monet*, (page 6), Madame Hoschedé's daughter Blanche gives this date. The earlier year, 1875, is insisted on here because of the dated picture, *In the Garden*, painted on that visit; formerly in possession of Knoedler's, New York (Nos. A1780 and CA4977). Photos of Mme. Hoschedé at different times in her life are published by her son, Jean-Pierre Hoschedé, in *Claude Monet, ce mal connu*, Geneva, 1960. Possibly on this visit an unusual and highly finished charcoal drawing was made of Mme. Hoschedé (collection Sydney M. Shoenberg, St. Louis). Both the appealing look of the eyes and Monet's efforts to hide the distortion of her mouth are evident. This drawing has often been published as Camille, though comparison with photos of Mme. Hoschedé make it certain she is the woman represented.

Despite Monet's statement concerning the "marvelous robe" with which he was tempted, doubts cannot be entirely suppressed concerning whether he did in fact work from such a garment. This lavish costume's arrangement on the canvas, including its curiously hard contour and the curved sweep at bottom, suggest that possibly it was painted direct from a Japanese print. The letter to Chocquet is from Jules Joëts, "Les impressionistes et Chocquet" in *L'Amour de l'Art*, April, 1935.

Monet's letters to Georges de Bellio are at the Musée Marmottan, Paris. I am most grateful to the former director, Mme. Edmée Laperrière, who permitted me to transcribe these in January, 1957, and also to my friend, the artist John Manship, for assisting me to decipher Monet's script. To M. Richebé, present director, go renewed thanks for permitting me to bring Michael O'Reilly, my photographer, who made copies of them all in March, 1965.

Always at moments when their fortunes reached nadir, Camille became pregnant. That she allowed herself to be employed as a form of natural opiate thus becomes obvious. The nature of Camille's malady as reported to de Bellio—*il s'agit d'ulceration de la matricë*—makes it clear that she had undergone an abortion. The ailment is one commonly associated with maladroit deliveries, but Camille had given birth only once, nine years before, in 1867.

It is only a supposition that Monet sent to Manet the portrait painted in his garden. But support derives from the fact that this picture was later in the possession of Mme. Manet: Ambroise Vollard, *Souvenirs d'un Marchand de Tableaux*, Paris, 1948, page 78.

Chapter Nineteen
FORBIDDEN LOVE

Monet's letter to Charpentier is quoted from Fels, *La Vie de Claude Monet*. His letter to Murer is from Paul Gachet, *Lettres impressionistes*, Paris, 1957 (pages 116–117), where it is given the date January 8, 1878. Internal evidence concerning Camille's illness and the difficulties at Argenteuil make it certain the proper date must be 1877. The lengthy letter to de Bellio is among those preserved at the

Musée Marmottan, Paris. That Mme. Aubry-Vitet retained the *Picnic* becomes clear later. From Bordighera, March 11, 1884, Monet wrote to Durand-Ruel: "I am in correspondence with a former proprietor at Argenteuil who has kept an enormous canvas of mine in payment. . . . It is a six-meter canvas, and very mediocre. . . ."

The interior of the Rue d'Edimbourg apartment is preserved in Monet's final live image of Camille, *Madame Monet on a Sofa* (Jeu de Paume). Since the period when Monet worked in it, the Gare St.-Lazare has been enlarged considerably. The original sheds Monet painted are still in place, but have been extended farther out onto the track to accommodate longer trains. The letter to Chocquet is from Joëts, "Les impressionistes et Chocquet" in *L'Amour de l'Art*, April, 1935; de Bellio's purchase is now at the Musée Marmottan. Other sales of this series are indicated from (the owners' names are indicated in) the catalogue of the Third Impressionist Exhibition (Venturi, *Les archives de l'impressionisme*, Vol. II), where the *Basket of Flowers* loaned by Charpentier is also listed.

The estimate of 2,000 francs for Monet's earnings in this first quarter of 1877 is a conservative one based on sales mentioned in the text. The catalogue of the Impressionist Exhibition that April reveals another work, possibly of recent origin, sold to *Fromenthal*. How many more such sales he made in this period is unknown, and to them must be added his fee, doubtless a large one, from Hoschedé for the *Turkeys* (Jeu de Paume).

The exact growth of the relationship between Alice Hoschedé and Monet is difficult to document because essential letters, if there were any, have never passed from the hands of the family. In addition to Monet's two known visits at Montgeron, there is an interesting passage in the memoir prepared before her death by Alice Hoschedé's daughter Blanche, and published in Jean-Pierre Hoschedé's *Blanche Hoschedé-Monet*: "In 1878 we were very close with the Monets who had two children and whom we encountered often in the Parc Monceau. . . . We saw them also very often in his studio." That it was actually 1876–7 when Monet worked in the Parc Monceau is not a very grave

error. A brilliant study of a flowering bush, painted in the Parc Monceau, is dated 1876 (Metropolitan Museum).

Monet's letter of Thursday, October 25, 1877, to Chocquet is from Joëts, and the one to de Bellio, "Saturday morning," is from the manuscript preserved at the Musée Marmottan. The letter to Émile Zola is from the Bibliothèque Nationale, Paris. At the time of his death in 1903 Zola did own one painting by Monet, sold at auction for 2,805 francs. The "I could not be more unfortunate" letter to de Bellio is from the collection of his daughter, Mme. Donop de Monchy, Paris.

The disagreement between Monet and Manet was minimized by Monet each time he recounted the incident, which became a favorite in his later years. Thus it has never been put into proper perspective as a part of the ill feeling created by the obvious relationship existing between Monet and the wife of an important patron of all the impressionists. The facts behind Manet's acquisition of the Monet canvas can be found in Poulain, *Bazille et ses amis*, page 103, note. One version of the re-exchange was given Elder (*À Giverny Chez Claude Monet*, page 71), and the dialogue, which ought not to be taken too literally, is found in the Duc de Trévise's "Le pèlerinage de Giverny" in *Revue de l'art ancien et moderne*, February, 1927.

The receipt Monet gave Eugène Murer for his four canvases is in *Lettres impressionistes*, where the letter of December 18, 1877, to Dr. Gachet is also found. It does credit to the character of Édouard Manet that he called on Monet. His letter to Théodore Duret is from Duret's *Manet*, translated by J. E. Crawford Flitch, New York, 1937. That Manet next turned to Hoschedé occasions considerable surprise in view of the circumstances. Hoschedé's bland reply is from Tabarant's "Autour de Manet" in *L'Art Vivant*, April, 1928, where the text of Manet's note is also found.

Chapter Twenty
THE LAST FAVOR

Since my researches were undertaken in 1956 a new thesis—created as a direct response to my inquiries—has been advanced by a member of the Monet-

Hoschedé family. He has suggested that Mme. Hoschedé and her six children moved to Vétheuil in 1878 together with Monet and Camille. This amusing tale first appeared in Jean-Pierre Hoschedé's *Claude Monet, ce mal connu* (Vol. I, page 12). Perhaps the impropriety inherent in even this was pointed out to him, for in the pious memorial to his sister published the following year, *Blanche Hoschedé-Monet* (pages 9–10), Hoschedé enlarged the story to include his father as well! "Because the affairs of Monsieur Hoschedé became worse and worse, because Claude Monet had always great difficulties in selling his pictures, and also because the health of his wife required country air, the two families Hoschedé and Monet decided to leave Paris and install themselves at Vétheuil where they rented a house together. They remained there three years, from 1878 to 1881."

The presence of any member of the Hoschedé family at Vétheuil during the lifetime of Camille is not only unthinkable, but is directly contradicted by contemporary letters. These harp on the fact that Monet was *alone* with his ailing wife and two children: ". . . for a very long time I have been in misery and found it impossible to work, and all my time is passed in taking care of my wife and our little baby" (to Charpentier, spring, 1879); and "What a sad situation is mine, alone in the world with two children, without resources, without a penny before me . . ." written the day of Camille's death (to de Bellio, September 4, 1879).

Discolored patches surrounding Camille's eyes are notable in all portraits of her painted by Monet and Renoir, and suggest that she had a chronic kidney ailment in addition to an ulcerated uterus. Facts surrounding the declaration of Michel Jacques's birth were discovered at Paris's 8e arrondissement. That Alexis Emmanuel Chabrier ("compositeur, agé de 36, 23 rue Monnier") was second witness on the report of birth was a surprise, though he had loaned a Monet painting to the Fourth Impressionist Exhibition, and was the central figure in one of Fantin-Latour's groups.

Monet's appeal to Zola is from the Zola papers in the Bibliothèque Nationale, Paris; the letter of May 16 to de Bellio is from the collection of Mme. Donop de Monchy. Because of the varying titles Murer gave the pictures in his collection (see Paul Gachet, *Deux Amis des impressionistes: Le Docteur Gachet et Murer*, page 172, where they are listed), it is not possible to determine with any certainty whether he made purchases from the Hoschedé sale. One can only feel that it was a likely move for him to have made.

I am obliged to Ernest Hoschedé's exacting and forthright grandson, Mr. James P. Butler (interview, May 26, 1956), for the information that he departed France for Brussels, where he began another department store, which also subsequently failed. Mr. Butler also thought that his grandmother, Alice Hoschedé, retained her dowry, and this is confirmed by Pissarro in his letter of April 13, 1891. (See *Camille Pissarro's Letters to His Son Lucien*, New York, 1943, page 162.) The notification of an intended visit to Murer is from Gachet's *Lettres impressionistes*, in the editing of which the sequel, dated "Sunday morning," has become a letter sent Dr. Gachet instead of Murer.

The exact sequence of moves toward Vétheuil is impossible to disentangle, especially because Monet himself wrote a confused letter January 21, 1922, stating that he lived at Argenteuil from 1871 to 1878, first in the house which had been inhabited by Ribot, then in another on the Voie des Bancs. (See *Beaux-Arts*, Jan. 31, 1941.) The archives of Mme. Aubry-Vitet's notary verify that Monet took up residence at Argenteuil in 1872 between June 14 (*procuration*) and July 9 (*décharge*). That it was Mme. Aubry-Vitet who was still demanding the rent in 1876 makes it certain Monet inhabited the one house only these four years. The Voie des Bancs house may therefore have been occupied during this summer of 1878, before the final move farther out to Vétheuil.

The reproachful letter to Murer is from *Lettres impressionistes;* the picture Gachet carried off on this visit, *Chrysanthemums*, is now in the Jeu de Paume. Monet's letter "I have come to an age. . . ," dated December 30, 1878, is in the collection of Mme. Donop de Monchy. Monet did in fact ship a number of canvases to Caillebotte for this Fourth Impressionist Exhibition, one of them slashed in a fit of depression. Caillebotte's letters are from Geffroy's *Claude Monet;* Monet's to de Bellio, dated March 10, 1879, is in the collection of Mme. Donop de Monchy. Letters to Charpentier are from Fels, *La Vie de Claude Monet.*

The declared date of Camille's death is September 5, 1879, according to *Minutes* preserved at Magny-en-Vexin where the declaration was made. However, I have adopted the earlier date, September 4, in the belief that Monet was in error when recording this event. His letter to de Bellio, dated September 4, "alone in the world with two children," surely was written after her death, and curiously, his actual declaration was not made until March 4, 1881, or a full year after expiration of the legal time limit. It seems likely that the clerk had written to Monet, for though he supplied information about the date of death, and stated (falsely) that her property was valued at 300 francs and she had married him without contract, Monet did not sign the entry made in the *Minutes.*

Chapter Twenty-one
JOINT MÉNAGE

That Mme. Hoschedé first cared for Monet's two boys was the impression of her grandson, James P. Butler. I have accepted at face value Monet's reiteration in letters of the period that he was unable to work while caring for his wife and child. If this premise is accurate, any work definitely from the year 1879 must have been done after her death. Two such canvases dated 1879 are known to me: *Paysage à Vétheuil* (Musée des Beaux-Arts, Rouen) and *Paysage de Vétheuil* (Jeu de Paume). These works and others obviously related by motif must be the group Monet brought to Paris that December. A third work, *La Seine à Vétheuil, Soleil,* may also be dated 1879, but in any case is an obvious variant on the Rouen picture and already one of the five or six canvases in the group. My premise has at least one exception: *Flowering Apple Trees,* signed and dated 79 (Budapest Museum of Fine Arts), which proves that Monet ventured out at least once in the springtime of the year as well.

What still lifes he brought with him to Paris is less certain. Only one of those presently known could possibly be from this period: a mixed group of autumn flowers, grapes, apples and pears, which, when reproduced by Elder (*À Giverny Chez Claude Monet,* plate 21), was marked "Vétheuil 1878." The present whereabouts of this work is unknown, and whether Elder's designation was correct is made dubious by a companion canvas, obviously representing the same bowl of flowers and fruits, painted by Renoir (Museum of Fine Arts, Boston). Because Renoir is not known to have visited Vétheuil, one inclines to move this picture down to 1873–4, when he was frequently at Argenteuil. If this earlier date is correct, the only likely candidate for the picture sold Georges Petit vanishes. Unlike Durand-Ruel, the Galerie Georges Petit no longer exists, nor have its records survived.

The letter to Chocquet is from Joëts ("Les impressionistes et Chocquet" in *L'Amour de l'Art,* April, 1935); the one to Charpentier from Fels, *La Vie de Claude Monet,* page 141, where it is given with a second paragraph which surely must be from another letter. The Rue de Vintimille address appearing in these letters and those of a slightly later period is a mystery. The building still stands, a block of flats nearly identical with that in which Monet's studio had been located in the Rue Moncey. Probably it was where Alice Hoschedé lived at this period, but there is no proof.

Monet was deeply hurt by his interview with Faure, and in later years recounted it, word for word as used here, to Georges Clemenceau (*Claude Monet: The Water Lilies,* translated by Georges Boas, New York, 1930, page 89 *et seq.*). A shortened version is in Fels, page 107. The picture offered Faure would seem to be *La Débâcle, Vétheuil,* of which a color print appears in Elder (plate 22). The picture was then still in Monet's studio. Its present whereabouts is unknown, but it must not be confused with a very similar work (inclining more toward blue) purchased from Monet by de Bellio the previous winter, exhibited at the Fourth Impressionist Exhibition, April, 1879 (No. 146), and now in the Musée Marmottan.

The letter proposing *Le Dégel* to de Bellio is in the possession of Mme. Donop de Monchy; the sequel, dated "Friday 1.30," is at the Musée Marmottan. Monet's reception at Arnold & Tripp was recounted to Gimpel. (See his "At Giverny with Claude Monet" in *Art in America*, June, 1927.) The letter of January 8, 1880, to de Bellio, is at the Musée Marmottan. The letter to the impatient client is from Fels, pages 139–140. No identification of the addressee is provided, but one suspects it is Dr. Gachet, who had previously shown impatience, and once before had visited Vétheuil unexpectedly. Details of the *La Vie Moderne* exhibition are from its catalogue; Mme. Charpentier's letter is from Geffroy's *Claude Monet*.

Much remains hidden concerning the exact circumstances of Mme. Hoschedé's parting from her husband. That he came out of his bankruptcy of 1878 with some capital is certain from the fact that he was able to open another store in Brussels; he surely retained a considerable art collection also, including Édouard Manet's portrait of Jacques Hoschedé and Monet's decorative panels *La Chasse* and *Turkeys*. As late as 1890 his portrait was painted again by Louis Picard and exhibited at the Salon. As suggested in this chapter, their parting seems *not* to have been on financial grounds, yet no information is now available which would lend any certainty to whether Ernest Hoschedé left his wife or she left him. One cannot help feeling that Alice Hoschedé's eagerness to pick up with Monet implies she had been rejected by her own husband.

The date at which she moved from Paris to Vétheuil is obvious from Monet's pictures; after the hiatus of a sojourn in Paris for the Salon and *La Vie Moderne* exhibition his pictures suddenly became populated with numerous children (both boys and girls), and in a view of *Vétheuil sur Seine*, National Gallery, Berlin, Alice Hoschedé herself appears with a parasol. She is absent from a second version of this same composition, in the Jeu de Paume.

Throughout this chapter mention is made that *five* of her children came to Vétheuil, and this would appear to be the case. The four daughters were present, and the infant Jean-Pierre, who, nearly the same age as Michel, formed with him a duo called *"les petites."* The older Hoschedé boy, Jacques, approximately the same age as Jean Monet, seems absent, and may have been with his father (?). A photo bearing the caption *All the Family* appears in Hoschedé's *Claude Monet, ce mal connu*, after page 80 of Vol. I, but from the ages of the children this surely represents a joining together of Mme. Hoschedé's children after the death of their father in 1891.

A collection of 411 Monet letters addressed to Durand-Ruel and members of his family has been preserved in the Durand-Ruel archives, and they are printed (with some abbreviation of text) in Venturi's *Les archives de l'impressionisme*, Vol. I. The astonishing compositions of *Sunflowers* and *Chrysanthemums* are both in the Metropolitan Museum.

Chapter Twenty-two
THE SALESMAN'S GAME

The reader may perhaps question why no greater analysis has been given such dramatic alteration in Monet's fortunes. A variety of theses might be advanced to explain it, yet none could be entirely conclusive nor explain why the outcast of 1879 became the sought-after hero of 1880. At bottom the best and greatest of artists are still the playthings of fashion; in Monet's case the world merely had come into step with him. "Times change and styles change, and fashion, that plaything of the winds, is an unreliable weathervane"; these words, which I penned twelve years ago to describe the vagaries of Sargent's posthumous fame have universal application in the arts.

The last record of Adolphe Monet is his appearance, August 13, 1877, before the Havre section of a commission to reconstitute Paris records. (See notes to Chapter 1.) The impression of Mr. James P. Butler was that he died about this time, but the partial records preserved and reconstituted at Le Havre (after destruction in the last war) show no trace of him. Nor is his death recorded at Ste.-Adresse or in Paris. The deaths of Sophie Lecadre and her husband are recorded at Le Havre's Hôtel de Ville.

Monet's own recollections of this first meeting with Sargent were given the Hon.

Evan Charteris, who visited Giverny in 1925. Charteris gives a verbatim report (in French!) on page 130 of his *John Sargent,* New York, 1927, and from this one discovers that Monet mistakenly stated the meeting was "about 1876." When writing my own biography of Sargent I followed this account, and subsequently corrected the error in "Carolus-Duran and the Development of Sargent" in *The Art Quarterly,* No. 4, 1964, page 396.

That Sargent was "bowled over" is quoted from his letter to Jameson: Charteris, pages 123–124. This reaction derived in large measure from the fact that Monet's pictures were in absolute contrast with the brown and gray gamma of all painting seen at the Salon; their effect has been weakened for us because we are fully accustomed to pictures painted without brown tonality. The watercolor given Sargent by Édouard Manet was shown me in 1954 by Mrs. Francis Ormond, Sargent's surviving sister, and presently belongs to her son, Conrad Ormond; it is reproduced on page 49 in Robert Rey, *Manet,* Milan (undated). As this watercolor is said to bear the mark of the Manet sale, Mrs. Ormond was possibly in error when describing it to me as a gift. Paul Helleu also purchased for Sargent an oil study for *The Balcony* at the sale of Manet's work in 1884.

The only canvas known to me that Monet surely painted at Poissy is the inscribed study of fishermen in their boats. That he painted little while there is remarked on in the notes in *Blanche Hoschedé-Monet,* page 159. In the same work Jean-Pierre Hoschedé gives copious descriptions of the changes at Giverny and recounts the village wedding (page 24). Monet himself recounted to Elder (*À Giverny Chez Claude Monet,* page 12) the labors he performed at this time, and James P. Butler outlined to me the domestic arrangements. My own visits to the house and village have filled out these sources.

The portrait painted at Vétheuil in exchange for a pair of boots is mentioned in *Blanche Hoschedé-Monet,* page 159. An estimated monthly expenditure of 1,500 francs is based on Monet's sales as recorded in letters to Durand-Ruel and a statement in the letter of October 2, 1884.

Chapter Twenty-three

A PUBLIC FIGURE

Zola's clue to the true names of his characters is found on page 31 of *The Masterpiece.* He adhered far more closely to actual events than previously could have been verified because of the paucity of information surrounding Monet's marriage. By employing his clues I located the record of this marriage, thus proving without doubt on whom his account is based. The detail of Zola's knowledge is surprising: for example he relates (page 270) "they had a long time to wait for some of the necessary papers." A trivial detail invented for atmosphere one might think; but discovery of the *Fiche de Recruitment* (see Chapter 14 and notes) executed the day of the marriage proves that Monet did have embarrassments over his papers and was unable to produce his army discharge.

Refusal of the Legion of Honor in July, 1888, is mentioned by Fels in *La Vie de Claude Monet.* That it was John Singer Sargent who suggested to Monet the Olympia subscription is stated by the French artist George Jeanniot. (See page 107, *Manet raconté par lui-même,* Paris, 1926.) When writing my biography of Sargent a decade ago I accepted the usual assertions that this idea was Monet's own. However, Jeanniot's explanation is persuasive, and confirmation is found in the early date of Sargent's letter (Charteris, *John Sargent,* page 102), established from internal evidence. Sargent tells Monet, "I have had a friend speak to Roll . . . ," and Roll's own subsequent letter to Monet (Geffroy, *Claude Monet,* page 142) is dated July 24, 1889. Written *before* July 24, 1889, Sargent's letter thus precedes the whole of the correspondence concerning *Olympia* published by Geffroy.

Chapter Twenty-four

THE FIERY ANGEL

Monet recounted the origin of his *Haystacks* several times, and it is the despair of historians that in such instances the printed versions will always show variations. Thus the words I have quoted are generic; that is, I have based them on the quotation given by Trévise ("Le Pèlerinage de Giverny" in *Revue de l'art ancien et moderne,* February, 1927, page 126), but eliminated the too flowery *"si vous voulez bien,"* which I assume Monet to have interpolated when telling the tale.

While accounting for the variety of hues Monet saw, I would not insist that every hue found in his canvases was actually seen. The impressionist technique had a variety of weaknesses, among them the necessity to put quantities of synthetic red (alizarin or rose madder) on the canvas mixed with blue or green as the only real darkening agent. Depending on the strength of this pigment, such reds often had a far greater influence on surrounding areas than intended, and they are responsible for the dominant pink-purple gamma of most impressionist painting. The presence of red in these paintings will thus often denote nothing more than areas of another color which require darkening. Despite its singular beauty, Monet's color therefore had an abstract existence, and the hallucinatory quality referred to in the text had its origin in this.

A variety of textural experiments are found in Monet's work after 1880 some of which were dealt with earlier in the text. The *Haystacks* gave final precedence to his most important experiment, painting without medium, and with little alteration this was the method Monet employed throughout the last years of his life. An outline first was roughly sketched on the canvas in pigments thinned by turpentine. But from the moment body color was laid on he ceased to dip into the turpentine. The pigments therefore grew thick and corallike. Some medium was employed during final studio retouches, and these often can be located as fluid areas overlying dense pigmentation. A rather unpleasant inclination to stroke his skies in backhand—that is, from upper left to lower right—probably was caused by the direction of the light in his first studio at Giverny. Only at this angle could a dense pigment be applied without catching light from the windows.

Pissarro's judgments were inclined to be somewhat critical of Monet's recent developments, but this was muffled during the *Haystacks* period because at the end of April he had written of his financial troubles to Monet, who "promptly" sent him a thousand francs. Monet's letter to Durand-Ruel demanding funds is dated October 19, 1891 (Venturi, *Les archives de l'impressionisme,* page 195). Jean-Pierre Hoschedé dwells on the development of the household, but naturally turns his head away from the curious nature of this unmarried family life. The details given here are those supplied in interviews by Mr. James P. Butler. The blacksmith incident is from Stephen Gwynn, *Claude Monet and His Garden,* New York, 1934, page 59; the blacksmith's name was given me by Mr. Butler, who knew him at a later period.

Monet told Elder (*À Giverny Chez Claude Monet,* page 12) the origins of the *Poplars.* His letters to Theodore Robinson are from *Claude Monet and the Giverny Artists,* catalogue of an exhibition held March 22 through April 23, 1960, Charles E. Slatkin Galleries, to which I am much obliged for a copy of this catalogue, as I am to Mr. and Mrs. Raymond Horowitz for bringing it to my attention.

Mr. Butler told me that his grandmother and Monet were married as soon as the statutory mourning period expired, but when pressed he gave the matter earnest thought and admitted he did not know what year the marriage took place. Mr. Butler had not seen Boudin's letter to Monet (dated July 28, 1892), which is in Benjamin's *Eugène Boudin.* However, the statutory mourning period of nine months expired in December, 1891, and no marriage took place until the following July. My dear friend Welles Bosworth from Marietta, Ohio, took a hand in finding information on Theodore Butler, in which he was associated with Carroll Beckwith.

The second Mme. Monet's weight was not without artistic ramifications, especially when it became clear that her daughters would follow the same bulging outlines. Before the *Haystacks* Monet had essayed various compositions for which pairs of girls posed in a boat on the little river before their door. The models' sheer bulk was an effective deterrent to Monet's efforts, for they were inclined to resemble pachyderms on a picnic. The unfinished canvases remained long in the studio and were Monet's last serious effort at figure painting. From this point on his land-scapes are unpeopled.

The excerpt from Robinson's diary is drawn from the catalogue *Claude Monet and the Giverny Artists*. That Robinson referred to Monet's wife as Mme. Hos-chedé was probably no more than a slip in a diary intended as a personal record. This diary is now at the Frick Art Reference Library in New York, and persons desiring to leave documents must be warned against permitting them to fall into these hands. My request to see the diary was refused by Mrs. Howell, head librarian, and when I sought to explain the importance of it to my work, I was sent back the rude reply she had no time.

The diaries of Carroll Beckwith are in the National Academy of Design, New York; the Frenchman's *"en plein Middle-Ouest"* remark is from *Claude Monet and the Giverny Artists*. Pissarro's report of Monet in London is dated December 9, 1891. That Monet worked from the sec-ond floor of a novelty shop run by Éd-ouard Mauquit, at 81 Rue Grand-Pont, is the often quoted intelligence derived from Fels, *La Vie de Claude Monet,* pages 180–181. The buildings then in place were destroyed during the recent war and have been replaced by renumbered concrete structures. On two visits to Rouen for this purpose, March 18, 1957, and March 28, 1965, I established that Monet's angle of vision leads to the position of what is now the second shop south of the cross street (Rue du Petit-Salut). He therefore worked from the site of what is now 47 Rue Grand-Pont.

Chapter Twenty-five
THE ENGULFED CATHEDRAL

Raffaëlli's astonishing quotation was re-corded by Pissarro July 3, 1896; it is in his *Letters to His Son Lucien,* page 292. That Pissarro felt *puny and mean* is from the same source, page 218 (October 4, 1893). Nothing could better express the effect Monet's advances had on old colleagues. The contract granted Pierre Lagarde by a vote of six to four (!) is from Geffroy, *Claude Monet,* pages 189–190.

Though one full-fronted view of the Rouen cathedral, painted from another location, does show the normal dark morning effect (Jeu de Paume), all other known canvases except the *Tour d'Albane* version in the Boston Museum represent the cathedral after noon. A constant proc-ess of renewal and rebuilding has made the cathedral of today somewhat different from when Monet saw it. Originally four small towers, or *tourelles,* stood over the central doorway. Three of these were destroyed by a storm in 1683, and to balance the fourth (on the extreme left) in 1828 a new *tourelle* was added to the right. These two *tourelles* were seen by Monet. After 1900 those destroyed in the center were rebuilt. (Information is from l'Abbé André Fouré, *Aumônier* d'Erne-mont.) In addition to this confusion some nineteenth-century photos would appear to show a small cross on the pinnacle of the central decorative terminal. No record exists of the presence of this cross, a feature not in keeping with the tradi-tional Gothic cathedral (Notre-Dame, Chartres, Reims, etc.), and doubtless it originated in the piety of a photo re-toucher.

The only means of tracing Monet's presence at Rouen is through his letters, especially those to Durand-Ruel in Ven-turi (*Les archives de l'impressionisme*) and Geffroy. The Hotel Angleterre, conven-iently located facing the river three streets from the cathedral, was destroyed by bombs during the last war and is replaced by a new concrete hotel of the same name. The letter to Geffroy (March 28, 1893) is from his book, page 194. The laconic comment "It's finished" is from Fels.

The extent to which Monet reworked canvases in the Giverny studio is always difficult to establish. Only when discarded and unretouched examples can be found is one really certain, but from parallel examples it would appear that he often repainted the entire surface. From their state it appears obvious that the *Cathe-drals* were subjected to even more thor-ough revision, but the oft-repeated idea that he attempted to emulate the texture of stone is pure nonsense: The same texture is shared by the *Haystacks* and *Poplars.*

The four *Cathedrals* purchased by Count de Camondo were bequeathed to the Louvre in 1908 and now appear at the Jeu de Paume. The price Camondo paid is from his notebooks, quoted in Bazin's *Impressionist Painters in the Louvre*, page 260. A mystery surrounds the uncompleted *Cathedrals*. No hint of their fate has ever appeared, and one suspects they were destroyed by Monet himself in his famous 1925 fire. (See Gimpel, "At Giverny with Claude Monet" in *Art in America*, June 1927.) A further mystery is that of twenty works exhibited in 1895 only fourteen are known today.

Cézanne's visit to Giverny is recounted by Geffroy; his attacks on the other painters are related by Pissarro, January 20, 1896, who realized that Cézanne was "unbalanced." Mr. James P. Butler mentioned further that various of Cézanne's works, abandoned at Giverny's inn, remained unclaimed into the 1930's. Monet's letters concerning Zola were written to Geffroy, who prints them; he also wrote to Zola himself. But since Geffroy, like Clemenceau, was actively engaged in the defense of Zola, he may have desired to show more active interest than was justified by Monet's real attitude. Renoir's letters are also from Geffroy.

Chapter Twenty-six
THE PATRIARCH

The death of Mme. Doncieux is registered at Paris' ninth arrondissement. According to a transcript obtained May 24, 1957, her body was discovered by the concierge, Henri Delay, forty-two, and his assistant, Eugène Metge, twenty-three. Her daughter Geneviève had predeceased her at another address, 15 Rue Rodier, in the same district.

Throughout this chapter I am obliged to Mr. James P. Butler for his carefully expressed recollections. That he knew Camille was Renoir's subject in the portrait that hung at Giverny is important evidence; he also told me of Monet's travels to Madrid, which otherwise seem undocumented, and recollected with humor the trips by motorcar to Lavacourt, where he sometimes accompanied Monet. The letter of condolence to Boudin, whose wife died March 23, 1889, is from Benjamin's *Eugène Boudin*, page 99. The French text also appears on page 293 in Geffroy's

Claude Monet. The origins and growth of the water garden are treated in Gwynn's *Claude Monet and His Garden* and Hoschedé's and other sources previously quoted. Many photos exist of the garden in its prime, and during my first visit in September, 1956, I took a group of my own. Then, and on later visits, my greatest impression was of how much smaller the garden is than it appears in photos and paintings. Probably it does not exceed two acres. Though I found a gardener in charge on a return visit in March, 1965, the garden's aspect was very bare and somber after the loss of its trees.

Michel Monet was eventually married, in his fifty-second year, to Aline Fernande Gabrielle Bonaventure, at Paris, July 4, 1930. Eventually all the Hoschedé girls married too.

Photos show Monet seated in various positions before his canvases in the garden; later photos show him seated in the studio retouching works. Sargent's sketch of him, done in 1887 (Tate Gallery), also shows Monet seated before his canvas. Yet it is the recollection of Mr. Butler that Monet stood, and that the house was littered with the small folding triangular seats he used at a former time. Possibly what Mr. Butler recollected was work on larger canvases, before which it would have been impossible to sit.

Wynford Dewhurst's interview was for his series of articles, "Impressionist Painting, Its Genesis and Development," which appeared in *The Studio* in 1903 and became a book in 1904. The manner suggesting Rasputin and Svengali was demonstrated before René Gimpel. (See his "At Giverny with Claude Monet" in *Art in America*, June, 1927.) It is well to remark that Mr. James P. Butler, to whom I recounted this episode, observed that whereas he himself had never seen his grandfather act in this fashion, he could "imagine" his doing so. It was again to Gimpel that Monet abused Corot, though he had also done so earlier to Louis Vauxelles, as he tells in "Un Après-Midi chez Claude Monet" in *L'Art et les artistes*, December, 1905.

Sargent's visit to Monet's London hotel room is recorded by Charteris, *John Sargent*, who also quotes the letters cited here. The exact date of the visit, however, is unknown, and some complexity enters into it, for various of Monet's London views are dated between 1899 and 1905, though he is not known to have worked in London after 1901.

The definition of impressionism Sargent evolved took tremendous hold, and to this day it confuses the issue abominably. But what Sargent himself did not realize was that by sacrificing his own earlier place in impressionism, and distracting attention from the fact that he too in his outdoor work employed the limited impressionist palette and dissonant creation of darks, he exposed himself to the appalling and ignorant condescension of posterity. So recently as 1964 I was disturbed to find Donelson F. Hoopes writing in his catalogue of the Corcoran Gallery Sargent exhibition: "Perhaps the need is past to repudiate and to ignore those artists who did not contribute to the artistic revolution." Except Monet himself, who contributed more than Sargent?

Chapter Twenty-seven

VALEDICTORY

Except those to Evan Charteris, which are in the Charteris *John Sargent*, the Monet letters quoted in this chapter were all addressed to Durand-Ruel, and are published in Venturi's *Les archives de l'impressionisme*. Mr. James P. Butler mentioned that his grandmother had received a Christian burial, for which he thought she must have asked. He remembered her as a definitely religious person. The portrait by Carolus-Duran still hangs in Monet's bedroom at Giverny; the Manet portrait is presently in the possession of Durand-Ruel, Paris.

Monet's *Venices* were shown not at Durand-Ruel's but in the Galerie Bernheim, 15 Rue Richepanse, where for some years his works had been much seen. Some of these Venetian works do suggest architectural errors and impossibilities of vision. The campanile of San Giorgio is inclined to become square like the Big Ben clock tower, and his view of the Doges' Palace (in the Brooklyn Museum) presents bizarre complications. The point of view is from the Dogana, or Custom House, yet even before eight o'clock in the morning (when the sun would strike the Palace direct as in Monet's picture) the reflection does not come directly across the bay in the manner he portrayed. Like Turner, Monet created his own Venice.

Where he traveled in 1913 is a minor mystery, but probably it was one of the several expeditions to Madrid mentioned to me by Mr. Butler. Jean Monet's trout farm is in *Blanche Hoschedé-Monet* (page 14). That Monet had been only fifteen days with Gleyre was the story told the Duc de Trévise, who called on him in 1920. (See "Le Pèlerinage de Giverny" in *Revue de l'art ancien et moderne*, February, 1927.) Monet's remarks to Roger Marx concerning a mural decoration based on the water lily theme are reprinted in Geffroy's *Claude Monet,* page 240. One wonders whether Monet was acquainted with the small panel by Albert Besnard painted for the École de Pharmacie in 1888, which so surely forecasts his *Nymphéas* composition.

Many intimate details of this later period of Monet's life, and long verbatim extracts from conversations, were recorded by Georges Clemenceau in *Claude Monet: the Water Lilies.*

The date of the *Nymphéas* donation is that given by Jean-Pierre Hoschedé (*Claude Monet, ce mal connu,* Vol. 2, page 25). I have, however, considered genuine the remark attributed to Monet by Fels (*La Vie de Claude Monet*), which Hoschedé condemns as apocryphal. Clemenceau's letters are from Georges Suarez, *La Vie orgueilleuse de Clemenceau,* Paris, 1930. The visit to Giverny of Evan Charteris is recounted in his own volume on Sargent; the letter he showed Monet in translation is the same from which quotation is made in Chapter 26. It must be remembered, however, that it was not by such letters, but by expressing the same ideas personally on many occasions, that Sargent accomplished so much in behalf of Monet.

Index